AF515496

Emerging Trends in Banking, Finance and Insurance Industry

Emerging Trends in Banking, Finance and Insurance Industry

Edited by

Anand M. Agrawal
Krishn A. Goyal

Published by
ATLANTIC
PUBLISHERS & DISTRIBUTORS (P) LTD
7/22, Ansari Road, Darya Ganj,
New Delhi-110002
Phones : +91-11-23273880, 23275880, 23280451
Fax : +91-11-23285873
Web : www.atlanticbooks.com
E-mail : info@atlanticbooks.com

Branch Office
5, Nallathambi Street, Wallajah Road,
Chennai-600002
Phones : +91-44-64611085, 32413319
E-mail : chennai@atlanticbooks.com

ISBN 978-81-269-1214-8

Printed in India at Nice Printing Press, A-33/3A, Site-IV,
Industrial Area, Sahibabad, Ghaziabad, U.P.

Preface

Banking and finance industry plays a dominant role in building the economy of an individual as well as a nation. It has control over a large part of the supply of money in circulation. Banks are the main stimulus of the economic progress of a country. A strong banking and finance sector is, therefore, necessary for a developing country to emerge as a developed one. It is vital for growth, creation of jobs, generation of wealth, eradication of poverty, entrepreneurial activity and increasing the gross domestic product.

The book *Emerging Trends in Banking, Finance and Insurance Industry* is an outcome of the International Conference on "Service Industry: Challenges & Opportunities" organized by The Birla Institute of Technology, International Center, Waljat Colleges of Applied Sciences, Muscat, Oman. It includes papers presented in the conference on various aspects of banking and finance. The papers offer a scholarly review related to the new wave in banking and finance industry. It covers different issues relating to banking, insurance, real estates, securities market, financial derivatives, etc. The conference was attended by over 150 delegates from all over the world and was concluded after eight technical sessions.

This book is a modest attempt to present the trends in current global financial scenario. It will be useful to the academicians, banking personnel, financial advisors, practitioners, and students, teachers and researchers of banking and commerce.

We want to record our sincere thanks to all the contributors for their scholarly papers. We are highly thankful to M/s Atlantic Publishers and Distributors (P) Ltd. for publishing the book in time.

Anand M. Agrawal
Krishn A. Goyal

Contents

Emerging Issues in Banking Industry

N.D. Mathur

PROLOGUE

Service industry is the name of the game in today's economy. Services represent about 80 per cent of the US GDP and between 60 per cent and 80 per cent of the GDPs of the rest of the world's advanced nations. Service Sector in India has grown by leaps and bounds over the last two decades. The share of service sector in India was only 44.26 per cent of the GDP at factor cost, while it has raised to the level of 57.55 per cent during the year 2005. On the similar lines, the share of the financing, insurance, real estate and business services have also increased from 18.08 per cent to 22.36 per cent (CMIE, 2006) during the same period. Rise in the service sector's share in GDP marks a structural shift in developing economies and hence getting better at services management must be accorded a high priority. Some economists caution that if the service sector bypasses the industrial sector, economic growth can be distorted. They argue that service sector growth must be supported by proportionate growth of the industrial sector; otherwise the growth of service sector will not be sustainable. Hence, growth in service sector must be compatible with the growth of industrial sector for sustainable economic development.

The financial services sector in India is about to enter an era of unprecedented growth. The five 'seed' that are likely to fuel such growth are the trembling of the number of middle and high income households over the next decade, the rise of the modern consumer, the strengthening of the banking sector, widespread use of technology and the emergence of small and medium enterprises (SMEs). However, there are some 'weeds' such as the high cost of intermediation, the growing stock of non-performing loans (NPLs) and the polarisation of the banking sector that could affect the growth.

One and a half decade of economic and financial reforms has strengthened the fundamentals of the Indian Economy very effectively and transformed the operating environment for banks and financial institutions in the country (Purwar, 2003). During this period, banking culture has emerged in every nook and corner of the country and the traditional face of banking has undergone change from one of the mere intermediator to that of the provider of cost effective and efficient services (Bhide, 2002).

Although, the empirical studies have shown that in the initial years, PSBs were having lower profitability and efficiency but lately all the negative impacts disappeared (Shirai, 2001). Increasing globalization under WTO regime has provided opportunity to the domestic financial sector to perform and learn from the private domestic banks and foreign banks. Mattoo et al. (2001) have shown that services liberalisation is different from trade in goods, as former necessarily involves factor mobility. Foreign banks enter or move with their clients abroad and hence there will be presence of foreign banks from countries with which the host country has strong trade and investment relations (Pemerleano et al., 2001). Sen 2005 drew attention to the possible pitfalls in the way of the implementation of the Basel Norms regarding financial standards in Indian banking industry. Moreover, there is one (Asian Development Outlook, 2004) important lesson that can be learnt from the financial restructuring experience in developing Asia is the need for strong legal and institutional support accompanied by government resolve to improve the financial system. In the present era, the banking sector is growing vertically as well as horizontally and is being considered as the backbone of the service sector in particular and the whole economy in general.

BANKING SECTOR REFORMS

Financial sector reforms were initiated as a part of overall reform in the country and wide ranging reforms covering industry, trade, taxation, external sector, banking and financial markets have been carried out since mid 1991. Reforms were initiated in the middle of a 'current account' crisis occurred in 1991. The crisis was caused by poor macro economic performance.

Fifteen years (1991-2006) of economic and financial sector reforms have strengthened the fundamentals of the Indian economy and transformed the operating environment for banks and financial institutions in the country.

The most significant achievement of the financial sector reforms have been the marked improvement in the financial health of commercial banks in terms of capital adequacy, profitability and asset quality as also greater attention to risk management. Further, deregulation has opened up new opportunities for banks to increase revenues by diversifying into investment banking, insurance, credit cards, depository services, mortgage financing securitization, etc. At the same time, liberalisation has brought greater competition among banks, both domestic and foreign, as well as competition from mutual funds, non-banking financial companies (NBFCs), post office, etc. During the post WTO regime competition will only get intensified, as large global players emerge on the scene. Increasing competition is squeezing profitability and forcing banks to work efficiently on shrinking spreads. Positive fallout of competition is the greater choice available to consumers and the increased level of sophistication and technology in banks. As banks benchmark themselves against global standards, there has been a marked increase in disclosures and transparency in bank balance sheets as also greater focus on corporate governance.

Policy Initiatives

Banking sector reforms essentially consisted of a two-pronged approach. While nudging the Indian banking system to better health through the introduction of international best practices in prudential regulation and supervision early in the reforms cycle, the idea was to gradually induce competition in the system. The implementation periods for such norms were, however, chosen to suit the Indian situation. Special emphasis was placed on building up the risk management capabilities of the Indian banks. Following noteworthy policy initiatives were exercised in Indian banking sector:

1. Interest rates have been deregulated. Interest rates of deposits and lending have been deregulated with banks enjoying greater freedom to determine their rates. Currently on the deposit side the interest rate on saving deposits is administered (4%), whereas on the lending side, while sub-PLR lending has been permitted, the maximum spread is restricted to 4 per cent over the PLR of each bank and there is a ceiling of PLR on small loans up to Rs. 2 lac.
2. Financial regulation through statutory pre-emption has been lowered, while setting up prudential regulations at the same time. Prudential norms have been in terms of capital adequacy, asset classification, income recognition, provisioning, exposure limits, investment fluctuation reserve, etc.
3. Reduction in reserve requirements by lowering SLR to 25 per cent, CRR to 5 per cent, Bank rate to 6 per cent in the phased manner, thus releasing more lendable funds which bank can display profitably.
4. Steps have been initiated to strengthen Public Sector Banks (PSBs) through increasing their autonomy, and recapitalization. It was recognized that the restoration of health of the banking system required 'stock' solution (i.e. restoration of net worth) and 'flow' solution (i.e. an improvement in future profitability.
5. Measures have also been taken to broaden the ownership base of PSBs; consequently, the private share holding in PSBs has gone up, ranging from 23 per cent (Bank of India) to 43.70 per cent (State Bank of India). Strong banks have been allowed access to the capital market for raising additional capital.

6. The banking system has also witnessed greater levels of transparency and standards of disclosure.
7. New functional areas have been opened up for bank financing, insurance, credit cards, infrastructure financing, leasing, gold banking, besides of course investment banking, asset management, factoring, etc.
8. New instruments have been introduced with greater flexibility and better risk management: e.g., interest rate swaps, forward rate agreements, cross currency forward contracts, forward cover to hedge inflows under FDI, liquidity adjustment facility for meeting day to day liquidity mismatch.
9. Limits for investment in overseas markets by banks, mutual funds and corporate have been liberalised. The overseas investment limit for corporate has been raised to 100 per cent of net worth and the ceiling of $100 million on prepayment of external commercial borrowings has been removed.
10. Universal banking has been introduced with banks permitted to diversify into long-term finance and Development Financial Institutions (DFIs) into working capital. Guidelines have been put in place for the evolution of universal banks in an orderly fashion.
11. Technology infrastructure for the payments and settlement system in the country has been strengthened with electronic fund transfer, centralised funds management system, structured financial messaging solution, negotiated dealing system and move towards real time gross settlement.
12. Credit delivery mechanism has been reinforced to increase the flow of credit to priority sectors through focus on micro credit and self-help group. Definition of priority sector has been widened to include food processing and cold storage, software up to Rs. 1 crore, housing above Rs 10. lakh, selected lending through NBFCs, etc.

13. RBI guidelines have been issued for putting in place risk management systems in banks. Risk management committees in banks address credit risk, market risk and operational risk.
14. The limit for FDI in private banks has been increased from 49 per cent to 74 per cent. In addition, the limit for FII in private banks is 49 per cent.

This set of policy initiatives did have then positive impact on the system. There has been considerable improvement in the profitability of the banking system measured in terms of operating and net profits. The profile of asset portfolio and also the extent of the net NPLs as percentage of total assets have shown improvement. A positive externality of the reform process has been the building up of the institutional architecture in terms of markets, enabling environment through technological and legal infrastructure and improving the managerial competence, etc.

VISIBLE TRENDS

Banking sector reforms has established a comprehensive system driven by market forces. The process, however, has not resulted in disregard of social objectives. At the same time, the reforms period experienced strong balance sheet growth of the banks in an environment of operational flexibility. A policy initiative taken has brought positive results. Trends that have been enjoyed in last fifteen years (1991-2006) are highly encouraging.

Drastic *versus* Gradual Privatisation Approach

While India's financial reforms have been comprehensive and in line with global trends, one unique feature is that, unlike with other former planned economies such as Hungary and Poland, the Indian Government did not engage in drastic privatisation of PSBs. Rather, it has chosen a gradual approach toward restructuring these banks. Public Sector Banks continue to be dominant, they find it difficult to reduce personnel expenditure and Government finds it difficult to accept genuine competition within PSBs. In response to these concerns, the Government decided to gradually expand private sector equity holdings in PSBs, but still avoid the transformation of their ownership. In fact, premature privatization may give rise to banking crisis as happened in Hungary and Poland. Argentina promoted privatization of PSBs in a reasonably developed regulatory and infrastructure environment and improved productivity.

Diversification of Banking Activities

Another unique feature of Indian banking sector is that the RBI has permitted commercial banks to engage in diverse activities such as securities-related transaction and leasing activities. The 1991 reforms lowered the CRR and SLR, enabling banks to diversify their activities.

Firstly, diversification of banking activity provides them an opportunity to gain non-interest income and thereby sustained profitability. Secondly, this enables banks to maintain their life cycles and gives them an incentive to process inside information and monitor their clients. Thirdly, banks can stabilize their income by engaging in activities whose returns are imperfectly correlated, thereby reducing the costs of funds and thus rendering and underwriting costs. Fourthly, diversification may improve performance by diluting the impact of direct lending. Direct lending reduces the bank's incentives to conduct information processing and monitoring functions. As a result, this not only lowers bank profitability but also results in deterioration of efficiency and soundness. Virtual banking, investment services (like asset management, hedge fund managers, custody services) insurance related services (like insurance brokerage, reinsurance, etc.) intermediation and advisory services are the new emerging trends after diversification of banking sector.

Impact of Foreign and Private Domestic Banks

Another noteworthy feature of India's banking sector is that some large PSBs appear to have been performing reasonably well in the post reform period. This could be attributed to, (a) the import of better risk management skills from foreign and private domestic banks, (b) intensified competition, (c) the diversification effect, (d) reorganization i.e. mergers and acquisitions, and (e) goodwill.

While the entry of foreign banks brings with it benefits, it also carries certain risks for the host countries. Benefits are in the form of better quality banking services that are offered by foreign banks themselves and also through spurring competition and efficiency in the domestic markets. Recent empirical studies across several countries have shown that the presence of foreign banks is associated with improvement in banking sector efficiency through lower overhead expenses and interest margins for domestic banks. Arrival of foreign banks with better accounting and disclosure standards has led to an improvement in prudential regulation in domestic markets. Recent empirical studies across several countries have shown that the presence of foreign banks is associated with the improvement in banking sector efficiency through lower overhead expenses and interest margins for domestic banks. Arrival of foreign banks with better accounting and disclosure standards has led to an improvement in prudential regulation in domestic markets. Entry of foreign banks also has potential risk associated with it. Foreign banks have home country bias, which may cause downside effect and may lead to risk of banking crisis as happened in Chile and Brazil. Rapid foreign entry could be destabilizing as it could lead to erosion of franchise value of domestic banks. There have been some concerns that foreign banks indulge in 'cherry-picking' and as a result, less finance would be available to the more disadvantaged segments of the economy including farmers and small firms. Consequently, local banks will be left with less creditworthy customers leading to increased risk of their portfolios and segmentation of credit markets.

Lazy Banking *versus* Crazy Banking

The most significant achievement of the financial sector reforms has been the increased profitability, productivity and efficiency of PSBs. There has been an improvement in overall capital adequacy of banks. As on March 31, 2002 around 92 out of 97 commercial banks operating in India had capital adequacy above the statutory minimum level of 9 per cent. Introduction of prudential norms relating to asset classification, income recognition and provisioning, along with legal and institutional reforms, has led to visible improvement in asset quality in banks.

Net NPAs (i.e. the portion of NPAs which is not provided for) have declined gradually from 10.7 per cent in 1994-95 to 5.8 per cent in 2001-02. Increase in the number of players has raised competition, which is reflected in the decline of bank concentration ratio. Despite intensification of competition and introduction of prudential norms, all major bank groups in India have remained profitable. According to data analysed by RBI, there has been a noticeable decline in the difference between real interest rates in India and international benchmark rates since the mid 1990's, suggesting increased integration of the Indian banking sector with the rest of the world.

Electronic Banking

Technology is another emerging trend in the banking sector and new issues have started cropping up which is going to pose certain problems in the near future. The new entrants in the banking are with computer background, however, over a period of time they would acquire banking experience. Where as the middle and senior level people have rich banking experience but their computer literacy is at a low level. Therefore, they feel handicap in this regard since technology has become an indispensable tool in banking. Computer literate employees, who are handful in number, have suddenly become more important for the banking organization. They have to be kept in good humour over other senior level experienced employees. PSBs have not been able to keep pace with the technological developments in the banking sector. Technology adaptation in PSBs is very low, whereas foreign banks and new private sector banks have embraced technology right from the inception of their operations.

Global Banking

Growing integration of economies and the markets around the world is making global banking a reality. The surge in globalisation of finance has also gained momentum with the technological advancements, which have effectively overcome the national borders in the financial services business. Widespread use of Internet banking has widened frontiers of global banking and it is now possible to market financial products and services on a global basis. In the coming years globalization will spread further on account of the likely opening up of financial services under WTO. India is one of the signatories of Financial Services Agreement of 1997. This gives India's financial sector including banks an opportunity to expand their business on a *quid-pro-quo* basis.

Consolidation and Move Toward Universal Banking

We are slowly but surely moving from a regime of "large number of small banks" to "small number of large banks". The new era is going to be one of the consolidations around identified core competencies. Mergers and acquisitions in the banking sector are going to be the order of the day. Successful merger of HDFC Bank and Times Bank earlier and Stanchart and ANZ Grindlays has demonstrated that trend towards consolidation. In India, one of the largest financial institutions ICICI took the lead towards universal banking with its reverse merger with ICICI bank. Another mega financial institution IDBI has also adopted the same strategy, and has already transformed itself into a universal bank. Consolidated accounting and supervisory techniques would have to evolve and appropriate firewall built to address the risks underlying such large organizations and banking conglomerates.

EMERGING ISSUES

The Indian banking sector has come a long way since the publication of the report of the first and second Narsimham Committee in 1991 and 1998. Incremental changes in the industry continue to occur, mostly in the form of liberalization of FDI regulation. Further financial deepening perhaps requires a context in which major structural changes are required not only at the margin among the private sector banks that account for about 15 per cent of the banking sector's assets but also among the PSBs that continue to control about 80 per cent of the deposits and assets of the industry. Competition has had an impact on the performance and behaviour of these banks, but it is perhaps time to bite the bullet, and strategies for change of their ownership. Efforts should be made to invigorate the market for corporate securities to reduce liquidity risk and thereby facilitate greater financial intermediation, and financial deepening.

Treatment of Insolvent Banks

India's approach towards treatment of insolvent banks is an interesting issue. Rather then closing them down, policymakers in India have shown a preference to merge such banks with healthy PSBs. It has been felt in certain circles that such an approach may give rise to a moral hazard problem. Probably interest of small depositors has been paramount in the minds of policymakers, while dealing with insolvent banks. As the weight of private banks increases further thinking will need to be done on the subject, both in terms of prevention of insolvency through advance regulatory supervision and action and post insolvency measures that discourage moral hazard and eventual fiscal cost.

Corporate Governance

Effective implementation of corporate governance practices in financial intermediaries has been a long-standing concern of the regulators and supervisors across the world. In India too, instances of inadequacies in the implementation of corporate governance norm and disregard to prudential practices on internal control have come to light. Such instances have seriously compromised the financial health of a few private sector commercial banks and cooperative banks prompt corrective action including criminal proceedings against the errant individuals have been initiated by the authorities in such cases. Continuation of multiple regulators has been identified as major challenging issue before the authorities in effective regulation and supervision including implementation of corporate governance and internal control norms.

Non-performing Loans

Despite decline, continuation of considerable stock of NPLs in the banking system continues to be a cause for concern. Improved institutional and legal arrangements and strengthening of risk management practices by banks is likely to keep incremental NPLs low. Initiatives such as setting up of Asset Reconstruction Companies (ARCs) and greater emphasis on compromise settlements are likely to deal with the stock problem for NPLs. Banks may need to adopt a more proactive approach in dealing with these issues.

Declines in Direct Bank Credit to Disadvantageous Society

Another area of concern relates to the decline in direct bank credit towards disadvantageous but socially important sectors such as agriculture and small-scale industries. It is felt that in the past inadequate risk management practices constrained banks to more vigorously pursue financing of such sectors. With improved risk management, it is likely that banks would deploy larger portions of their funds in these sectors. Banks now should be able to distinguish the risk quality of individual borrowers, rather than treating the borrowers of a particular class as equally risky.

Ill designed Interest Rate Structure

In the area of interest on deposit/savings, there does not appear any systematic architecture of the interest rate structure. To substantiate, no defined time path or defined preconditions have been identified in the area of deregulation of saving bank rates. Probably there is a potential of instability in the form of shifts in saving bank deposits between banks, depending on the interest rate that emerge, thus it is essentially a structural issue and conditional on improvements in operational efficiency of PSBs rather than an overall interest rate issue in the macro economic sense.

Complex Resolution of Universal Banking

As in other parts of the world, changing income profiles and customer preferences have promoted the spread of universal banking in India. SBI, ICICI, HDFC Bank, LIC, PNB, etc. have successfully launched themselves towards universal banking. It is felt that universal banks are more complex to supervise given their heterogeneous character. In universal banks, the probability of conflicts of interest that arise from serving various clients increases substantially, given the breadth of their activities. Furthermore, universal banks by holding large blocks of stocks in industrial companies may be able to influence the structure of the national economy in ways that run counter to national interest. Also, such concentration of economic power in their hands may give them an additional ability to influence political decisions and shift the balance of risks and returns in their favour. Luckily in India, the regulatory framework is coorditioned among the RBI, SEBI and IRDA.

WTO and Banking Issues

India is a signatory of WTO Financial Services Agreement, 1997. There are broadly following major WTO related banking issues:

(a) Permission to foreign banks to enter India through the subsidiary route.

(b) Restrictions on foreign share of banking assets.

(c) Restriction on the number of branch licences per year.

(d) Cap on investment limit of foreign banks in finance companies.

(e) Issue of national treatment.

(f) Trading in banking services through modes of supply other than commercial presence.

Prudential Regulation—Prisoner's Dilemma

The procyclicity of bank behaviour raises an important issue about adequacy of capital in India. In other words what could be the appropriate cyclically adjusted ratio that might mitigate moral hazard behaviour? When there is a boom, banks tend to increase their lending in pursuit of higher profits, making themselves vulnerable to adverse selection. During period of slump, it is the same loans that turn bad and require larger provisioning, which impact already sagging balance sheet. A choice before regulator is to tighten the prudential norms during the boom and to impose tighter provisioning requirements, thereby dampening the profits. This may also lead to constraints on genuine credit growth.

Consolidation—Life Boat Operation

In India, the Narsimham Committee-II highlighted the need for restructuring of PSBs. The structural issues could pose a major stumbling block. A degree of merger/acquisitions moves among the new private sector banks is being witnessed in the banking sector. It is evident that new private sector banks with institutional parentage are making tremendous strides. They are also performing well in terms of enhancing shareholder value. It is the PSBs that need to evaluate the opportunities to consolidate as bigger players. SBI seems to be in a uniplayer market situation looking to its presence in the market.

The merger of Indian banking in the past has been more in the nature of 'life-boat' operations. It must be reckoned that what is required is not merger of a weak bank with a strong one, but of two strong banks. In this case we need Arcelor-Mittal type mergers.

Hazards of Electronic Banking

Internet banking screens for online payments commonly require the name, and account number. In practice an electronic transfer is processed solely on the basis of the account number. This has the effect that, if the payer keys in the wrong account number the payment will be made but to the holder of the account number that has been keyed in. The mistake may only come into light when the intended recipient tells the payer that the payment has not been received. When the payer tries to find out where the payment has actually gone, he or she may be told that the recipients name cannot be released for reasons of confidentially. This bank may claim that it acted as per instructions of the payer i.e. the account number.

The recipients' bank may claim that it has no liability because it acted on the instructions it received from the payer's bank. It may also seek to rely on the Bulk Electronic Clearing System Rules (The BECs). By the time the payer realises that the payment has gone astray, the recipients may have withdrawn and used the funds, with or without realising that there was a mistake. Hence, such may be the hazards of electronic banking.

CHALLENGES AHEAD

The various issues mentioned above help to bring into sharp focus the emerging challenges ahead.

Augmenting Profitability

The most direct result of the above changes is increasing competition and narrowing of spreads and its impact on the profitability of banks. The challenge for banks is how to manage with running margins while at the same time working to improve productivity, which remains low in relation to global standards. This is particularly important because with dilution in banks equity, analysts and shareholders now closely track their performance. Thus, with falling spreads rising provisions for NPAs and falling interest rates, greater attention will need to be paid to reducing transactions costs. This will require tremendous efforts in the area of technology and for banks to build capabilities to handle much bigger volumes.

Technology is the Key Now

Technology has now become a strategic and integral part of banking, driving banks to acquire and implement world-class systems that enable them to provide products and services in large volumes at a competitive cost with better risk management practices. The pressure to undertake extensive computerization is very real as banks that adopt the latest in technology have an edge over others. Customers have become highly demanding and banks have to deliver customised products through multiple channels, allowing customers access to the bank on 24 × 7 basis.

Risk Management

The deregulation environment brings in its wake risks along with profitable opportunities and technology plays a crucial role in managing these risks. In addition being exposed to credit risk, market risk and operational risk, the business of banks would be susceptible to country risk which will be heightened as controls on the movement of capital are eased. In this context, banks are upgrading their credit assessment and risk management skills and retaining staff, developing a cadre of specialists and introducing technology driven management information systems.

HR-IT Mix

The far-reaching changes in the banking and financial sector entail a fundamental shift in the set of skills required in banking. To meet increased competition and manage risks, the demand for specialized banking functions, using IT as a competitive tool is set to go up. Special skills in retail banking, treasury, risk management, foreign exchange, development banking, etc. will need to be carefully nurtured and built. Thus, the twin pillars of banking sector i.e. human recourses and IT will have to be strengthened.

Innovation and Greater Customer Orientation

In today's competitive environment, banks will have to strive to attract and retain customers by introducing innovative products, enhancing the quality of customer service and marketing a variety of products through diverse channels targeted at specific customer groups.

Responsibilities Towards Corporate Governance

Besides using their strengths and strategic initiatives for creating shareholder value, banks have to be conscious of their responsibilities towards corporate governance. Following financial liberalization, as the ownership of banks gets broad-based, the importance of institutional and individual shareholders will increase. In such a scenario, banks will need to put in code for corporate governance for benefiting all shareholders of a corporate entity.

Maintaining Internationally Followed Best Practices

Introducing internationally followed best practices and observing universally acceptable standards and codes is necessary for strengthening the domestic financial architecture. This includes best practices in the area of corporate governance along with full transparency in disclosures. In today's globalised world, focusing on the observance of standards will help smooth integration with world financial markets.

EPILOGUE

The structural adjustment process during banking reforms has not been completly painless. While there are achievements, there are pitfalls as well. What is important is to strike a balance: move on a careful middle path between the ex-cathera over zeal for intervention and a complacent belief in the ability of the banking system to self-rectify its problems. The real world is far divorced from idealism. A constant challenge, therefore, remains for the authorities in identifying new risks, eschewing harmful incentives and strengthening the banking sector to keep pace with the changes in technology.

Competition in banking sector is going to be tough with WTO agreement. Banks in India have to benchmark themselves against the best in the world. Competition in banks should be such that it is growth enchancing, cost effective and customer friendly. Presently, competition is largely in urban areas and metropolitan area that too is limited to few functional areas, viz. setting up of ATMs, issuance of credit/debit cards, retail/personal banking, and business on account of mutual funds, besides this there is no competition in rural areas.

In addition to this, PSBs in India have scale as well as goodwill advantage. A thorough restructuring of PSBs is required. Fifteen years of reforms have passed but PSBs have not shown loudable improvement in their performance. They have already been exposed to new regulatory environment and competition. Government should take further steps by promoting mergers and acquisitions of sound banks and close unviable banks rather than merging them with sound banks. It is high time for appropriate consolidation of Indian PSBs. It is the time of clarion call for Indian banking. Vigil is the eternal price of freedom, which includes economic freedom as well.

REFERENCES

Centre for Monitoring Indian Economy (2006). *Economic Intelligence Service*, New Delhi.

Asian Development Bank (2004). *Asian Development Outlook 2004*, Oxford University Press, New York.

Bhide M.G., Parsad A. and Ghosh S. (2002). "Banking Sector Reforms: A Critical Overview", *EPW*, February 2.

Ibrahim, Anwar (1992). "Challenges of the Banking Industry in an Emerging Newly Industrialised Country", *Association of Development Institution of Malaysia*, Kuala Lumpur, Hilton, April 21.

Joshi, P.N. (1999). "Banking Sector Reforms the Other Side of the Coin", *EPW* Commentary, April 3.

Leeladhar, V. (2005). "Contemporary and Future Issues in Indian Banking", Lecture Delivered to Kanara Chamber of Commerce and Industry, Mangalore, 11 March.

Mattoo, A., Rathindran, and Subramanian A. (2001). "Measuring Services Trade Liberalization and its Impact on Economic growth: An illustration", *Policy Research Working Paper No. 2655,* World Bank, August.

Mohan, Rakesh (2005). "Financial Sector Reforms in India: Policies and Performance Analysis", *EPW*, March 19.

Pomerleamo, M. and Vojta, G. (2001). "What do Foreign Banks do in Emerging Markets: An Institutional Study", Paper Presented at 3rd Annual World Bank, IMF and Banking Financial Markets and Development Conference, New York, April.

Purwar, A.K. (2003). "Banking Sector", *Annual Capital Market Review*, BSE, Mumbai.

Raje, Pradeep (2000). "Where did India Missed a turn in Banking Reform, Is there a Comeback", *Centre for the Advance Study of India*, Occasional Paper # 14, December.

Sen, S. and Ghosh, S.K. (2005). "Basel Norms Indian Banking Sector and Impact of Credit to SMEs and the Poor", *EPW*, March 19.

Sharai, S. (2001). "Assessment of India's Banking Sector Reforms from the Perspective of the Governance of the Banking System", Paper Presented at the ESCAP-ADB Joint Workshop, Bangkok, 22-23 November 2001.

Comparison of UAE Banking Sector with Other GCC Countries

2

M.A. Hashmi

ABSTRACT

The purpose of this study is to analyze the banking sector of the UAE and study its competitive strengths *vis-à-vis* financial system of neighboring GCC countries. This is an analytical and cross-sectional study of UAE banks that analyzes and compares the domestic and foreign banks' micro and macro characteristics. This study also compares UAE banks with other GCC banks. Secondary data sources are used for all six countries.

As of 2005, the small UAE banking sector was served by 21 domestic and 25 foreign banks, thus the UAE banking sector is quite fragmented. Banks incorporated in Abu Dhabi and Dubai hold more than 90 per cent of the total domestic assets, with this total being divided almost equally between Abu Dhabi and Dubai banks. A detailed analysis of these banks, particularly domestic banks, reveals a high growth rate, a healthy spread over the deposit rate, and an absence of major banking frauds. Central Bank of the UAE has played an important role in streamlining the banking operation and increasing consumer confidence. Furthermore, the DIFC has been a catalyst in attracting internationally reputed commercial banks and financial institutions.

The UAE banking sector is somewhat comparable with other five GCC counties. UAE equity to gross loans ratio (18.1 %) is the lowest among all countries which put UAE banks to at higher risk should there be dramatic increase in non-performing loans. Qatar and Bahrain based banks have much higher equity to gross loans ratio. Due to competitive and fragmented banking industry, UAE banks are generally less profitable compared to other five countries, as UAE ranked forth based on return on average equity and return on average assets rations. The efficiency ratios of the UAE banks are better than most of the GCC member countries. UAE banks' cost to operating income ratio is only 35.6 per cent which suggest a lower cost operation in UAE banks. Liquidity ratios of the UAE banks are in the middle of the all GCC members' ratios. The UAE banks have maintained good quality assets, which are evident by very low non-performing loans/gross loans ratio (2.7%). Only Saudi Arabia has slightly low ratio, while other four country's ratios are much higher so their assets quality is poor compared to UAE banks. This is an evidence of efficient and professional management of UAE banks and it had made UAE banks financially sound compared with the banks in other GCC countries.

INTRODUCTION

The United Arab Emirates (UAE) is a federation of seven small American Gulf emirates: Abu Dhabi, Dubai, Sharjah, Ajman, Umm Al Qaiwain, Ras Al Khaimah and Fujairah. UAE is a member of the Gulf Cooperation Council (GCC), and the country is traditionally an oil and gas exporting nation. Currenlty, each of the emirates has a relatively stable economic and political system, and the country has an ambition to emerge as a financial and service sector leader in the Middle East.

UAE has proven crude oil reserves of around 98 billion barrels (or 10% of the world's reserves). The oil wealth is concentrated in Abu Dhabi, which contributes approximately 90 per cent of the total oil production of the country. UAE also boasts substantial reserves of natural gas, accounting for 4 per cent of the world's reserves. The bulk of gas reserves (over 90%) are located in Abu Dhabi as well. The emirate of Dubai has also become an important financial center in the UAE because of its significant financial and services industries. Abu Dhabi and Dubai have emerged as the two most important emirates of the UAE.

UAE Banking Sector

The purpose of this study is to analyze the banking sector of the UAE and study its readiness to be a part of the global financial system. As of 2005, the small UAE banking sector was served by 21 domestic and 25 foreign banks, thus the UAE banking sector is quite fragmented. Banks incorporated in Abu Dhabi and Dubai hold more than 90 per cent of the total domestic assets, with this total being divided almost equally between Abu Dhabi and Dubai banks.

Market access for foreign banks was somewhat limited because they were not allowed to open more than eight branches throughout the modern banking operation (1980-2003). In 2003, however, laws were changed, and today banks are allowed to open more than eight branches but special permission is required. Foreign banks confronted no obstacles, however, when they wanted to open a representative office. At the end of 2004, there were thirty-six representative offices throughout the emirates. Thus, UAE has been well represented by a cross-section of foreign banks. A list of all domestic and foreign banks operating in the UAE is provided in Table 1 and a list of representative offices of foreign banks is provided in Table 2. (Central Bank of the UAE, 2006)

Federal Law 10, enacted in 1980, is the backbone of the conventional banking sector (excluding Islamic banks), and Federal Law 6 was promulgated in 1985 to legalize Islamic banking in the UAE. Islamic banking is still a small component of the UAE banking sector. According to Islamic banking laws, banks cannot charge a fixed interest rate on deposits or loans. Variable interest rates based on a profit/loss sharing model is the foundation of Islamic banking.

Under the Federal Law 10, the Central Bank of the UAE was also established, and it took over the responsibilities of the Currency Board. The bank's duties include advising the government on monetary and financial issues, issuing currency, maintaining gold and foreign currency reserves, and formulating a credit policy. All regulation and supervisory duties are under the direction of the Central Bank.

The UAE currency is pegged to the US dollar, which is why the central bank has a limited role to play in setting monetary policy and controlling interest rates; however, some monetary and credit controls are exercised through its sale and purchase of certificates of deposits. The central bank plays a role in formulating and monitoring credit policy, and in supervising the financial sector as well. All commercial banks incorporated in the UAE are licensed by the central bank, and therefore are subject to the central bank's requirements and regulations. In 1998, the central bank made it mandatory for all banks to use International Accounting Standards (IAS), and in early 1999, local banks were instructed to establish clear corporate structures. Furthermore, the UAE central bank requires banks to maintain a capital to risk-weighted assets ratio of at least 10 per cent at all times. According to the Central Bank of UAE regulations, all banks must be majority owned by UAE nationals. They also have to be registered as "Shareholding Company" under the UAE Companies Law and must be registered with the Federal Ministry of Economy and Trade. (Central Bank of the UAE, 2005)

Literature Review

Rao (2002) studied 35 domestic and foreign banks operating in UAE for 1998 and 2000. He examined cost efficiency, scale and scope measure, and cost productivity growth rate. As a result of his research, Rao (2002) concluded that substantial cost inefficiencies and scope economies existed in UAE banks. In addition, he found that only small banks improved their scale economies while large banks maintained *status quo*. This finding reveals that the management teams of small banks were capable of managing their portfolio more efficiently than larger banks.

Duncan and Elliott (2002) empirically examined the relationship between service quality and financial performance among a representative cross-section of Australian banks and credit unions. They found that all financial performance measures are positively correlated with service quality scores. Al-Tamimi and Al-Amiri (2003) studied two major Islamic banks in UAE (Dubai Islamic Bank and Abu Dhabi Islamic Bank). These two banks dominate the Islamic banking sector, operating 21 branches throughout UAE (only five per cent of conventional banks). They compared the service quality of these banks with well-established SERVQUAL standards. The study found that these two major banks have statistically significant perceived service quality. This finding is contrary to the belief that most of the domestic conventional and Islamic banks may have a service quality issue with customers. In order to compete with foreign banks, particularly when the banking sector opens up, UAE banks must focus on service quality. Most of the studies have indicated the existence of a positive relationship between service quality and profitability.

Prior studies have suggested that an efficient and growing banking sector is a predictor of the future economic conditions of a country. El-Kuwaiz (1995) and De Gregorio and Guidotti (1995) showed that measures of banking development are strongly correlated with economic growth in broad cross-section countries. Countries with efficient and growing banking sectors tend to grow rapidly. Similarly, King and Levine (1993) have established a strong link between the financial progress of a country and banking industry's growth. Prior to these two studies, Goldsmith (1969) concluded, on the basis of data from 35 countries between 1860 and 1963, that "a rough parallelism can be observed between economics and financial development if periods of several decades are considered." According to these studies, a well-functioning financial system is critical for sustained economic growth.

Research Methodology

This is an analytical and cross-sectional study of UAE banks that analyzes and compares the domestic and foreign banks' micro and macro characteristics. This study also discusses the readiness of domestic banks to meet global challenges. Secondary data sources are utilized for comparing individual banks and comparing the domestic/foreign banking sector in the UAE. The banks' financial reports, the website of the Central Bank of UAE, EFG Hermes's website, and other published sources are heavily used during the course of this study. All the data is either in millions of UAE dirham (AED) or millions of U.S. dollar ($).

For an in depth analysis, eight large conventional domestic banks, two large domestic Islamic banks, and the top ten domestic banks are included in this study. The top banks are selected according to the 2004 shareholder's equity (first tier capital) as defined by the Bank of International Settlements (BIS). At times, two comparable conventional foreign banks' data is also included for comparison purposes. In addition, aggregate data for all domestic and foreign banks is used, whenever available. However, comparable data was not always available before 2001 and after 2004, which is why the selected time period of this study is 2001-04.

Analyses of UAE Banking Sector

UAE banks, along with Saudi Arabian and Kuwaiti banks, have dominated the GCC and Middle Eastern Banking Sector. Because of the number of banks in the UAE, the country's banks are rated ninth, tenth, fourteenth, fifteenth, eighteenth, twenty-eighth, fortieth, forty-first, forty-eighth, and fifty-fifth among the top Middle East banks. This ranking is based on the tier-one shareholders equity as defined by Bank of International Settlement (BIS). A list of top ten conventional and Islamic banks with their rank among the top hundred Middle Eastern banks, capital, assets, profits, ROE and ROA are presented in Table 2.1. The most noticing observation is that all banks were profitable in 2004. The UAE Central Bank required banks to maintain a

Table 2.1: Financial Profile of Top Ten Domestic Banks (2004)

UAE Banks	Mid-East Rank	Capital ($ mil.)	Assets ($ mil.)	Capital/ Asset (%)	Profits ($ mil.)	ROE (%)	ROA (%)
Emirates Bank International (EBI)	9	1,585	10,371	15.3	281	17.7	2.7
National Bank of Dubai (NBD)	10	1,482	10,972	13.5	253	17.1	2.3
National Bank of Abu Dhabi (NBAD)	14	1,413	15,349	9.2	310	22	2.0
Abu Dhabi Commercial Bank (ADCB)	15	1,352	10,461	13.0	218	16.1	2.1
Mashreq Bank (MASHREQ)	18	1,244	8,699	14.3	226	18.1	2.6
Dubai Islamic Bank (DIB)	28	814	8,342	9.7	126	15.4	1.5
Union National Bank (UNB)	40	604	6,570	9.2	123	20.3	1.8
Commercial Bank of Dubai (CBD)	41	564	2,880	19.5	96	17.0	3.3
First Gulf Bank (FGB)	48	484	3,484	13.9	67	13.8	1.9
Abu Dhabi Islamic Bank (ADIB)	55	410	3,457	11.8	33	8.0	0.9

Source: Siddiqi (2005)

10 per cent capital/assets ratio and most of the banks exceeded the requirement. In fact, only three banks (NBAD, UNB, and CBD) had slightly lower capital/assets ratios, and even these banks were very close to the 10 per cent mark. The research also reveals that ROE and ROA were much higher in conventional banks than Islamic banks. The highest ROE in 2004 was reported by the Union National Bank (20.3%), while the highest ROA was reported by the Commercial Bank of Dubai (3.3%). The top UAE bank based on capital was the Emirates Bank International, and the top UAE bank based on assets was the National Bank of Abu Dhabi.

The involvement of UAE banks (domestic and foreign) in the local deposit and loan market is summarized in Table 2.2. The National Bank of Abu Dhabi (NBAD) has by far the most deposit and loan market share (about 13%). The National Bank of Dubai (NBD) has the second most deposits and Emirates Bank International (EBI) has the second most loan issues. It is observed that only two foreign banks are included among the top ten banks based on deposit and loan market share. The two foreign banks (HSBC and Standard Chartered) have a much smaller share of the deposit and loan market. Among all the 46 banks operating in UAE, domestic banks dominated the

Table 2.2: Deposit and Loan Market Share of Top Ten Domestic/ Foreign Banks (2003)

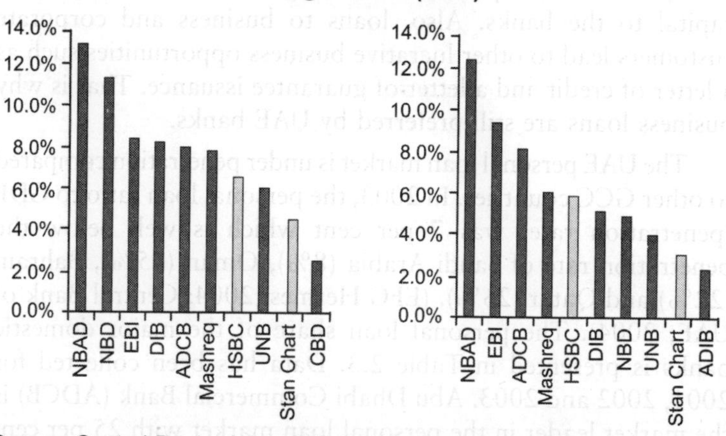

Source: Central Bank of the UAE, bank's financial statements.

deposit market share (74%) and the loan market share (79%) at the end of 2003. Most of the banks operating in UAE are very small, as the top five out of forty-six banks controlled 48 per cent of the deposits and 48 per cent of the loan market in 2003. (Central Bank of UAE, 2005)

The banks in the UAE are not separated from non-banking commercial activities. Banks are allowed to participate in stock brokerage, real estate brokerage, securities market and other non-banking activities. Because stock and real estate brokerage incomes are volatile, banks cannot completely rely on them. Other sources of non-interest income (also called core non-interest income) are foreign exchange related incomes and commissions/fees. Foreign exchange transaction income has been less volatile over the years so banks have tried to increase the share of foreign exchange income.

Retail Banking

The UAE has a rapidly growing retail banking sector because of the country's increasing expatriate population. Domestic and foreign banks have made a large investment in low cost distribution channels such as internet banking and ATM networks. UAE banks are still focused on corporate customers because they are considered low risk and lucrative. As a result, business loans have been increasing at the expense of personal loans, but retail deposits are still significant as they provide capital to the banks. Also, loans to business and corporate customers lead to other lucrative business opportunities such as a letter of credit and a letter of guarantee issuance. That is why business loans are still preferred by UAE banks.

The UAE personal loan market is under penetration compared to other GCC countries. In 2003, the personal loan ratio to GDP (penetration rate) was 7 per cent which is well below the penetration rate of Saudi Arabia (8%), Oman (15%), Bahrain (22%) and Qatar (26%). (EFG Hermes, 2004; Central Bank of UAE, 2004). The personal loan share of the major domestic banks is presented in Table 2.3. Data has been collected for 2001, 2002 and 2003. Abu Dhabi Commercial Bank (ADCB) is the market leader in the personal loan market with 25 per cent of the market share in 2001 and about 18 per cent of the market share in 2003. The other three banks each have a market share of between 10-12 per cent in 2003, thus the four banks control more than half the personal loan market. The reluctance by most of UAE banks to become heavily involved in the personal loan market can be explained by the absence of consumer credit reports and the lack of trust toward an expatriate workforce that has not had a long-term residency status. Expatriates cannot open a bank account or apply for any service without a guarantee letter from an employer and other personal guarantees.

Table 2.3: Personal Loan Share of the Domestic Banks

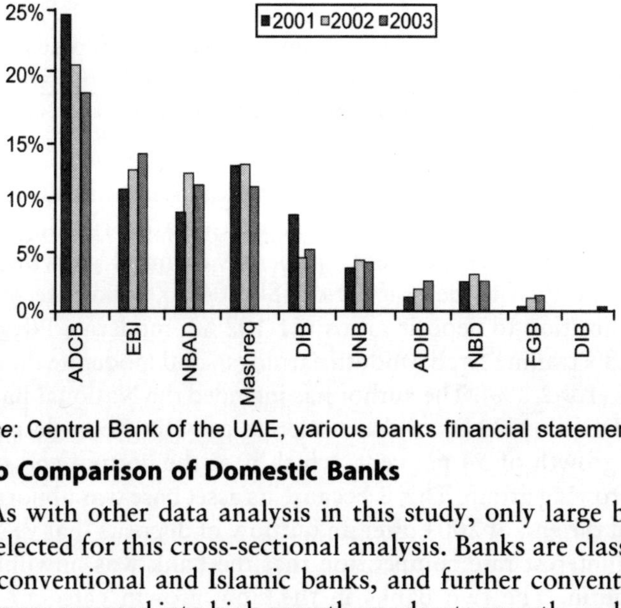

Source: Central Bank of the UAE, various banks financial statements.

Micro Comparison of Domestic Banks

As with other data analysis in this study, only large banks are selected for this cross-sectional analysis. Banks are classified into conventional and Islamic banks, and further conventional banks are grouped into high growth, moderate growth, and slow growth categories. The growth criterion is based on the asset growth during the 33 months period (from the end of 2001 to September 2004). Computed data is summarized in Table 2.4.

The banks characterized by fast growth (57-140% balance sheet growth) are also characterized by high earnings growth rates, high loan to deposit ratios (90-137%), high market capitalization to deposit ratios (100-165%), high historic earnings multiples (30-33 × trailing twelve months earnings) and low

Table 2.4: Domestic Bank's Growth Comparison

	Mkt. Cap* (AED mil)	Trade Val. (AED mil)	Asset Growth	Loan Growth	Deposit Growth	Loan/ Deposit
Fast Growth						
First Gulf Bank	6,133	113	140%	256%	119%	100%
Emirates Bank	26,749	47	57%	91%	46.3%	137%
Moderate Growth						
National Bank of Abu Dhabi	18,258	44	54%	70%	67.1%	96%
Union National Bank	11,557	61	39%	81%	26.9%	104%
Mashreq Bank	11,390	4	39%	62%	31.9%	80%
Commercial Bank of Dubai	7,312	9	28%	52%	41.4%	96%
Slow Growth						
Abu Dhabi Commercial Bank	15,638	51	23%	39%	30.2%	99%
National Bank of Dubai	15,648	95	13%	117%	11%	56%
Islamic						
Dubai Islamic Bank	9,520	238	83%	84%	85.0%	63%
Abu Dhabi Islamic Bank	4,075	146	77%	209%	96.3%	81%

Sources: Central Bank of UAE, 2005; Financial Statements of Respective Banks, and EFG-Hermes.

dividend yields (0.6-0.9%). The banks in the moderate growth category have balance sheet growth rates ranging from 28 per cent to 54 per cent, moderate earnings growth rates, moderate loan to deposit ratios (80-104%), moderate market capitalization to deposit ratios (51-102%), moderate P/E ratios (16-28 × trailing twelve month earnings), and moderate dividend yields (1.8-2.2%). The author has included the National Bank of Abu Dhabi (NBAD) in the moderate growth group despite an asset growth of 54 per cent, which is at the bottom end of the fast growing group. This is because its asset base was abnormally low at the end of 2001 after an outflow of deposits that year due to an interest rate competition that the bank was unwilling to engage in. The two banks in the slow growth category were going through structural changes during the selected period of the study.

Islamic banks as a group exhibit a mixture of the characteristics of both fast and moderate growth conventional banks: The two largest by market capitalization, Dubai Islamic Bank (DIB) and Abu Dhabi Islamic Bank (ADIB), are also the two most heavily traded among all domestic banks. Therefore, these two banks fit clearly into the fast growth group (growth of 77-83%). Despite fast asset growth, these banks have very low loan to deposit ratios (63-81%), indicating an easy ability to attract deposits and extremely conservative loan approval criteria. Financial valuations of domestic banks are mixed with the lowest market capitalization to deposit ratios in the universe (39-48%) and reasonable dividend yields (1.6-1.7).

UAE banks have witnessed a gradual increase in their total asset/liability figures which increased from AED 192,532 million in 1996 to AED 334,743 million in mid 2003. Foreign assets to total assets were roughly one-third throughout the selected period. At the same time, foreign liability to total liability ratios reduced to 8.7% in June 2003 from 22.7% in 1998. Selected macro data of the UAE banking industry is summarized in Table 2.5.

Table 2.5: Macro Data for Domestic & Foreign Banks in UAE

	2000	2001	2002	2003 (June)
Banks[1*]				
Total Assets/Liabilities	277,101	299,669	333,235	334,743
Foreign Assets	91,457	99,409	112,417	102,416
Foreign Assets to Total Assets (%)	33.0	33.2	33.7	30.6
Foreign Liabilities	26,584	30,677	29,932	29,050
Foreign Liabilities to Total Liabilities (%)	9.6	10.2	9.0	8.7
Deposits[2*]	170,034	182,893	209,647	213,268
- Residents[2]	161,805	172,848	198,244	202,261
- Non-Residents	8,229	10,045	11,403	11,007
Bank Credit(Net)[3*]	124,915	132,484	157,881	169,548
- Residents	109,156	115,416	133,723	145,030
- Non-Residents	15,759	17,068	24,088	24,518
Total Number of Domestic Banks & Branches[4]	311	324	345	355
- Head Offices	20	20	21	21
- Branches	291	304	324	344
Total Number of Foreign Banks & Branches[5]	109	109	112	112
- Head Offices	26	26	26	25
- Branches	83	83	86	87
Number of Workers in Banks (U.A.E.)[6]	14,621	15,191	16,080	16,408

Source: Central Bank of UAE, 2004

* Including deposits of UAE residents booked in overseas branches (including offshore)

1 Including the restricted license bank until March 2003.

2 Not including inter-bank deposits.

3 Not including loans to banks, also provisions from 1999.

4 Including pay offices.

5 Including a pay office.

6 Excluding non-banking staff.

Another interesting observation is that UAE residents have dominated the bank deposit and credit market. At the same time, the non-residents share of the deposits and credit market is increasing at a higher rate than the residents' market share. The fragmentation of the banking market is evident by the fact that the total number of domestic banks and branches had increased from 250 (in 1996) to 355 (in June 2003). In some UAE emirates, domestic banks are limited in their number of branches. Only Meshreq Bank has branches in all seven emirates. Foreign banks and their branches have increased from 110 (in 1996) to 112 (in June 2003). The modest increase of foreign banks branches is due to the fact that no foreign banking license has been issued for over a decade, and foreign banks were limited to only eight branches in the country, until 2003.

The banking sector is a major employer in the UAE, although most of the employees are expatriates. Emiritization laws have forced domestic and foreign banks to increase their employment of UAE nationals. In 1996, total number of banking employees was only 11,688, but this number increased to 16,408 by June 2003. Primarily, this increase is due to the new branches of the domestic banks. Expatriate still dominate the banking sector employment numbers. (Table 2.5)

Comparison of UAE Banking Sector with GCC Banking Sector

Utilizing the Gulf Cooperation Council (GCC) banking data, the UAE banking sector is compared with the other five GCC members' banks (Siddiqi, 2005). The results are summarized in Table 2.6. The UAE banking sector is somewhat comparable with other five counties. UAE equity to gross loans ratio (18.1%) is the lowest among all countries which put UAE banks at higher risk should there be dramatic increase in non-performing loans. Qatar and Bahrain based banks have much higher equity to gross loans ratio. Due to competitive and fragmented banking industry, UAE banks are generally less profitable compared to other five countries, as UAE ranked forth based on return on average equity and return on average assets ratios. The efficiency ratios of the UAE banks are batter than most of the GCC member countries. UAE banks' cost to operating income ratio is only 35.6 per cent which suggest a lower cost operation in UAE banks. Liquidity ratios of the UAE banks are in the middle of the all GCC members' ratios. The UAE banks have maintained good quality assets, which are evident by very low non-performing loans/gross loans ratio (2.7%). Only Saudi Arabia has slightly low ratio, while other four country's ratios are much higher so their assets quality is poor compared to UAE banks. This is an evidence of efficient and professional management of UAE banks and it had made UAE banks financially sound compared with the banks in other GCC countries.

Table 2.6: Aggregate Data for GCC Banking Sector (2004)

	Kuwait	Saudi Arabia	Oman	Qatar	UAE	Bahrain
Capitalization (%)						
Capital Adequacy Ratio	16.5	16.2	25.2	25.9	16.4	24.8
Equity to Total Assets	13.0	10.5	15.0	16.5	12.0	13.7
Equity to Gross Loans	22.9	19.5	18.2	31.5	18.1	24.9
Profitability (%)						
Return on Average Equity	20.6	26.4	9.3	20.4	17.4	13.6
Return on Average Assets	2.4	2.7	1.2	2.9	2.4	1.7
Net Spread	2.6	3.5	3.9	3.4	2.7	2.0
Dividend Payout Ratio	62.3	55.8	57.0	52.1	41.1	70.3
Efficiency (%)						
Cost to Operating Income	29.3	38.6	59.4	34.7	35.6	50.2
Staff Expenses/ Operating Income	17.2	21.7	24.2	16.2	20.8	27.9
Liquidity (%)						
Net Loans/Customer Deposits	83.4	63.0	105.0	65.0	90.1	92.7
Customer Deposit/ Total Deposit	95.4	87.2	89.2	74.6	88.4	79.8
Asset Quality						
Non-performing Loans ($ mil)	1,342	1,709	1,234	675	1,443	539
NPLs/Gross Loans (%)	4.5	2.2	14.7	5.0	2.7	7.0
Provisions/NPLs (%)	121	177	90.0	83.7	107.7	82.4

Source: Siddiqi (2005)

Summary and Future Directions

A total of 21 domestic and 25 foreign banks are operating in UAE, while another 36 foreign banks have opened representative offices. Despite these numbers, the UAE banking sector is dominated by the top five domestic banks that control about half of the loan and deposit share. As a result, most of the domestic and foreign banks are clinging to a very small market share. Only two foreign banks (HSBC, Standard Chartered) made it to the top-ten list of the banks operating in UAE, based on deposits and loans.

A detailed analysis of these banks, particularly domestic banks, reveals a high growth rate, a healthy spread over the deposit rate, and an absence of banking fraud during the 2001-04 period. Central Bank of the UAE has played an important role in streamlining the banking operation and increasing consumer confidence. Furthermore, the DIFC has been a catalyst in attracting internationally reputed commercial banks and financial institutions. In comparison to the GCC banks, UAE banks have performed better than other country's banks. Only Kuwati banks have generally better performed than UAE banks.

The banking sector, however, is not free from problems. Major domestic banks have received low Moody's financial strength ratings. One problem facing the banking sector which contributed to these low scores is the lack of supervision in multiple ownership situations. For example, commercial banks do maintain the majority share in insurance and equity firms, and there is no formal mechanism to monitor possible anti-trust violations. The contradictions among the banking laws of all six emirates and the inconsistencies between the federal and each emirate's banking laws pose more problems for the country. Because of these contradictions, the country's courts can make conflicting judgments in some instances.

International Monetary Fund (IMF) has positive comments about the readiness of the UAE financial and banking sectors to be part of a global system. UAE banking industry is profitable and well-guided by the Central Bank. In addition, the banking sector of the UAE is going to play a major role in further globalization of UAE economy.

REFERENCES

Al-Tamimi, Hussain and Abdulla, Al-Ameri (2003). "Analyzing Service Quality in UAE Islamic Banks," *Journal of Financial Services Marketing*, Vol. 8, 2, pp. 119-32.

Central Bank of the United Arab Emirates, January 2006, http://www.cbuae.gov.ae/

DeGregorio, Jose and Gudotti, Pablo E. "Financial Development and Economic Growth," *World Development,* March 1995, 23(3), pp. 433-48.

Dubai International Financial Centre (2006), www.DIFC.ae

Duncan, E. and Elliott, G. (2002). "Customer Service Quality and Financial Performance Among Australian Retail Financial Institutions," *Journal of Financial Services Marketing*, Vol. 7, 1, pp. 25-41.

Editors (2005). "Basel III Standards," *Khaleej Times*, January 3, 2005.

EFG Hermes. http://www.efg-hermes.com/

El-Kuwaiz, Abdullah (1995). "Banking in GCC: Challenges and Opportunities," *Arab Bank and Finance Directory*, 1994-95, pp. 372-74.

Financial Reports of the Sixteen Commercial Banks, 2003-04.

Goldsmith, Raymond W. (1969). *Financial Structure and Development.* New Haven, CT, Yale University Press, 1969.

King, Robert G. and Levine, Ross (1993). "Finance and Growth: Schumpeter Might Be Right," *Quarterly Journal of Economics*, August 1993a, 108(3), pp. 717-38.

Mahasneh, Quhafah (2004). "Strategic Orientation of Banking and Finance Managers in United Arab Emirates," *Journal of American Academy of Business*, March 2004, Vol. 4, 1/2, pp. 136-42.

Mazhar M. Islam (2003). "Development and Performance of Domestic and Foreign Banks in GCC Countries," *Managerial Finance*, Vol. 29, 2/3, pp. 42-73.

Rao, Ananth (2002). "Estimation of Efficiency, Scale & Scope and Productivity Measures of UAE Banks," *European Conference of Financial Management Association*, Copenhagen, June 2002.

Siddiqi, Moin (2005). "Banking Report: Strong Regional Economy Sees Banking Profits Soar," *The Middle East,* October 2005, pp. 34-43.

"United Arab Emirates: Financial System Stability assessment, including Reports on the Observance of Standards and Codes on the following topics: Monetary and Financial Policy Transparency, Banking Supervision and Payment Systems,"*IMF Country Report No. 03/20*, January 2003, International Monetary Fund, Washington, D.C.

Innovative Service Quality in the Banking Sector: An Assessment Based on SERVQUAL Measures

Prasanta Kumar Padhy, P. Balaram Babu* and *Satyabrat Dash

ABSTRACT

The global marketplace has virtually forced the service sector to transform itself into a truly customer-oriented, service-focused enterprise. Service quality innovation results when a firm is able to focus its entire energies to think on behalf of the customer—for an outcome that surpasses customers' expectation of superior value. However, such initiatives to innovate the service quality of service firms have often lead to increasing expectations among customers as well, and hence, constitutes a self-created challenge (Kandampully, 2002).

In the present study, the focus is on the critical factors determining service quality in the banking sector by using both traditional and modified SERVQUAL measures (Parasuraman et al., 1983, 1994). In the first study, responses of customers (N = 305) in a premier nationalized bank in India with regards to "expected" and "perceived" service quality were analyzed by using traditional SERVQUAL measures that comprised of five dimensions of service quality. Later, in another study, responses of customers (N = 200) were analyzed by using the modified SERVQUAL measures that comprised ten dimensions of service quality. A comparison among various service quality factors revealed that "Actual" service experiences perceived by the customer in the bank was lower than the "Expected" service quality, as evidenced through the corresponding scores obtained by the respondents. Both the studies revealed various critical dimensions of service quality, which could help bankers and researchers in differentiating the good and poor quality of services offered by the bank. Responses of customers with regards to service quality have also been crosschecked in the second study, by taking into account the responses of the Bank's staff (N = 55). Finally, the study focused on how appropriate innovations in banking services could yield benefits in the new organizational arrangements. A number of innovation forms that are of special relevance in the banking industry are also discussed. The present study is thus an attempt to identify the significant role of organizational and technological innovations in the banking sector. Among other findings, the study revealed service quality indices based on the suggestions of the customers, which are responsible for enhancing service efficiency in the bank. The findings of these studies offer interesting information on the level of service quality in the banking sector of a developing economy, i.e. India.

INTRODUCTION

Banking service in India has made remarkable progress since independence. It has undergone a major transformation class banking to mass banking. It is also emerging as ideal institution providing information to customers on effective financial transactions through tailor-made product development. The banking endeavors, to provide effective customer service at lower costs, have been further facilitated through innovation and communication aided by information technology. IT-based services such as automated teller machines (ATM), electronic fund transfer, anywhere-anytime banking, smart cards; net banking, 'swift', etc. are no longer alien concepts to Indian banking customers (Das Gupta, 2005).

Although public sector banks in India have slowly adopted new technology, their "diffusion" has been somewhat slow as compared with the newer, private sector banks. As India continues to move toward greater economic liberalization, there are moves to allow the public sector banks even greater freedom with regards to their monetary and credit policies (Kaushik, 1997; Thacker, 1997). It would, therefore, be safe to speculate that it all boils down to just a question of time and the availability of adequate resources for enhancing the service quality, for the banking system in India begins to closely resemble with other countries like US or Europe.

Meeting the expectations of the customers in all areas relating to customer service have been of prime importance for the banking sector in India. Global competition has forced Indian bankers to enter the trade-off between winning new customers and retaining old ones. Though Indian public sector banks are often criticized for contributing to high amount of bad debts and lower profits, the crucial roles played by them in development and diversification of the Indian economy during the last three decades are noteworthy (Prasad, 2006). Issues concerning service-quality in Indian public sector have to be studied extensively, so that they could sustain and grow on the face of stiff competition, by learning from their counterparts in developed economies like the USA and Europe (Kassem, 1998; Firoz and Maghrabi, 1994; Yavas et al., 1997).

A successful banker must have the ability to anticipate and satisfy customer needs (George, 1977). To provide faster and more efficient services, the Indian public sector banks have to realize the importance of customer care and satisfaction. However, customer needs are normally hidden deep inside the psyche of the customer and are hardly ever spelt out to the banker (Davido and Uttal, 1989). There has been growing concern among the customers availing public sector banking services in India. A study (Kumar, 2005) revealed that big public sector banks have poor record on customer service such as: delays in attending to and indifference towards customers. Research findings also revealed that there is a need to change the Indian bankers' attention, attitude and commitment, in order to improve the service quality (Mathur, 1999). However, the public sector banks in India have not yet geared up to take up these gigantic tasks concerning the intensity and quality of services delivered to customers.

Objectives of the Paper

Though improving the quality of service is one factor in business survival, cost and speed of service are also vital. Most of the service quality researches in the past have emphasized encounters only from the perspective of the service receiver. In addition, these approaches were concerned with unidirectional service quality. In this way, one of the main objectives of the present paper is to describe a conceptual framework of service quality involving both service provider and service receiver. Since present paper is an attempt to investigate the service quality issues from the perspective of the customers as well as staff in the banking industry of a developing economy like India, it has following objectives:

1. To present a detailed usage of various service quality dimensions in the banking sector in India;
2. To give a brief account of the critical factors of service quality revealed through the two studies carried out in a premier Indian public sector bank, and;
3. To analyze the service gaps and to draw inferences thereof, concerning the importance of different dimensions of service quality in these studies.

Research Literature on Service Quality

There are a number of models described in the literature that conceptualized the construct of service quality (e.g. Garvin, 1988; Albrecht and Zemke, 1985; Parasuraman et al., 1988; Lehtinen and Lehtinen, 1991; Dabholkar et al., 1996). The construct of service quality is a multidimensional phenomenon that contains various dimensions that make up the construct (e.g. Parasuraman et al., 1988). Thus, service quality has been considered by researchers as an attitude formed through long-term and overall evaluation of a firm's performance (Hoffman & Bateson, 2001).

Service quality has been described as a form of attitude that results from the comparison of expected and perceived services (Cronin and Taylor, 1992). There are many research findings to the effect that service companies are benefited tremendously through their loyal customers (Anderson and Zeithaml, 1984). Gronroos (1982) argued that customers, while evaluating the quality of a service, compare the service they expect with perceptions of the services actually received by them. Contrary to satisfaction, quality does not necessarily imply the service experience. Zeithaml et al., (1994) revealed that there could be a transaction—specific quality judgment as well as a global judgment reflecting the level of service. Service quality is generally measured in two ways (Urbany et al., 1989): (i) as an overall evaluation of quality of service (i.e. an overall attitude towards the whole service experience); or (ii) as consisting of a range of opinions about different aspects of the service experience (e.g. perceptions of Tangibility, Reliability, Responsiveness, Assurance, Empathy). Service quality endeavors have initially attempted to confirm the requirements of customers, meet their expectations and satisfy them. Hence, service firms gradually started recognizing the vital role played by customers (Headley and Choi, 1992). Successful service firms also tried to know the customers' vocabulary, because it often carried important information about customers' needs and expectations.

Juran (1999) elaborated the customers' perception of service quality as: "the features of services which meet customers' needs and necessities and thereby provide customer satisfaction." Researches revealed that customer satisfaction is often influenced by service quality, object quality, price, and other situational and personal factors (Muthukrishnan and Kardes, 2001).

Customers' perceptions of services are based on specific dimensions of services (Folkes, 1988) and are partly shaped by how well they believe they are performing their own roles in service delivery systems (Zeithaml and Bitner, 2003). The customer often expects the service to be provided in a specific way or by a specific individual when delivering the service (Sureshchander et al., 2001). Some customers are more demanding than others, having greater sensitivity to, and higher expectations of service. Perceptions are created after experiencing the service. However, dissatisfaction may occur if expectations are higher than the actual service experienced by the customer. The perception of actual service is low when the service providers misinterpret customers' expectations. Rises in customers' expectations are often difficult to control service quality and could cause communication breakdowns and faults in the service delivery system (Cristina Sousa, 2002).

Customer opinions and ideas, beliefs and thoughts about a product or service benefit a firm significantly (Urbany et al., 1989). The customer always attempts to bridge the gap between his/her imagination and experiences about the product or service availed (Hoch and Ha, 1986). This process is called by De Bono (1977) as "pattern-making system", in which a customer always tries to make new images and information about the products or services just to fit into what is already known. Hence, researches have suggested that there is a need for greater interaction between individual customers and the service providers (Martin and Pranter, 1989). Accordingly, an attempt has been made to highlight such interactions by using traditional (5-dimensional) and modified (10-dimensional) models of service quality, to justify our present work on innovative service quality in the banking sector.

Innovative Service Quality

Innovation is the generation, development, and adaptation of novel ideas on the part of the firm (Damanpour, 1991). Nohria and Gulati, (1996) defined innovation as "any idea, practice, or material artefact perceived to be new by the relevant unit of adoption". Since 'innovation' has a compounding strength, it is capable of creating the new and distorting the old. It nurtures a culture in which there are fewer hindrances to the creation of a synergy of thoughts and actions on behalf of the customer. As Peters (1997) suggests, it is essential to destroy the old so as to give way to new thoughts and subsequent new action.

Researches in the past revealed that customers often use existing knowledge to perceive about innovative services (Yamauchi and Markman, 2000; Roehm and Sternthal, 2001). Innovations are, therefore, the results of new learning by an organization that could lead to the creation of previously unknown services. Moreau et al. (2001) discovered that customers with extensive knowledge of services usually favour innovations. Comprehension of innovation, thus, involves the introduction of entirely new knowledge structures, which are based on customers' perceptions (Paxton and Roedder, 1997). Dimensions of Service quality relate the actual provision of services offered by an organization to its customers. They could result from the issue of service delivery and perceptible indication of business relationship between the organization and its customers.

Methodology

Both these studies incorporated into this paper have hypothesized that there will not be any significant gaps in the perceived and expected service quality as responded by the customers of public sector banks in India. The null hypothesis has been tested against the personal and demographic profile of customers, and the results thereof have been presented accordingly. Study-I of this paper has adopted one-tailed t-test, while study-II takes into account 2-tailed t-test, where the hypothesis shows that the expectation of service quality exceeds the perception of bank customers. The null hypothesis can be written as:

H0: $\mu 1 - \mu 2 = 0$, where $\mu 1$ refers to Perceived Service Quality and $\mu 2$ refers to Expected Service Quality;

H1a: $\mu 1 < \mu 2$ (our assumption that the expected service quality is more than his/her perceived service quality in the bank);

H1b: $\mu 2 < \mu 1$ (our assumption that perceived service quality is more than his/her expected service quality in the bank).

Samples of Study-I & II

Two different samples have been gathered from a premier public sector Indian bank in the southern region of Orissa State in India, and are utilized for preparing the present paper. For study-I we gathered a sample of 305 customers from the above bank administered by the traditional SERVQUAL instrument, which comprised of statements concerning 5 dimensions of service quality. The sample for study-II included employees and customers of the same bank. A total of 200 customers and 55 bank managers and staffs of the aforesaid bank were administered with modified SERVQUAL instrument, which comprised of statements concerning 10-dimensions of service quality. Since validity and reliability of these instruments have already been established through earlier researches, it supported the investigators to retain the responses of all the respondents for analyzing primary data. Stratified disproportionate random sampling method has been adopted in these studies. Study-I was completed in 2003, which followed study-II till May, 2006.

The SERVQUAL Instrument: Measurement of Service Quality

The SERVQUAL scale is the principal instrument widely utilized to assess service quality for a variety of services (including banks, credit card companies, etc.). The results of the initial published application of the SERVQUAL instrument indicated that five dimensions of service quality have emerged across a variety of services (Parasuraman et al., 1988). These dimensions include tangibles, reliability, responsiveness, assurance, and empathy (Carman, 1990; Parasuraman et al., 1985, 1988; Woodside et al., 1989).

According to Hemmasi et al. (1994), SERVQUAL is based on the "gap model", which is aimed at the assessment of the "gap" between customers' expected and perceived service quality. The "gap model" identifies five opportunities for quality failure, or what are called "Gaps", which can be perceived as a process for the design of a service.

Present paper takes into account two studies based on SERVQUAL approach to measure service quality, developed by Parasuraman et al. (1988, 1994). It takes into account, findings of two studies based on assessment of service quality for measuring (a) customer expectations from an 'Ideal' bank with regards to various aspects of service quality, and (b) customer perceptions of the 'Actual' services received from the bank on a 7-point Likert-type scale (Parasuraman et al., 1988, 1994). The approach starts from the assumption that the level of service quality experienced by customers is critically determined by analyzing the gap between their expectations from an "ideal bank", and their perceptions about the services actually experienced in the "own bank", i.e. the bank with which they transact. The basic assumptions underlying the use of SERVQUAL scales in the two studies, therefore have been: (i) performance of a firm below the level of expectation of its customers and staff results in poor service quality; (ii) a higher level of perception about a firm's performance indicates superior quality of service offered by it.

Parasuraman et al. (1988) have conceptualized a five dimensional model of service quality such as: reliability, responsiveness, empathy, assurance and tangibility. Their measurement instrument is known as SERVQUAL, which has become almost the standard way of measuring service quality, essentially captures the functional quality. The original SERVQUAL instrument comprising of 22 pairs of statements has been used in our first study to assess service quality across the aforesaid 5 dimensions. Further, each item of SERVQUAL has been used twice: to measure expectations and perceptions of service quality.

Models of service quality described in the literature (e.g. SERVQUAL) have been used in various contexts, but they seldom provided a method of managerial evaluation of service quality. Parasuraman et al. (1994) have developed a 10-dimensional model of SERVQUAL, based on which our second study was carried out. Further, because of an extension in the dimensions of service quality from original 5-dimensional model to that of 10-dimensional model, we have used the terms 'Innovative Service Quality'. The 10-dimensional model comprised of: reliability, responsiveness, competence, access, courtesy, communication, credibility, security, understanding the customer, and tangibles. We have used 47 pairs of statements to cover these 10 dimensions of service quality in banks. Our study-II is more vital since it takes into account both the customers' as well as the managers'/staff's perceptions of service quality in the respective branch of the bank. Outcomes of our studies are based upon the interpretations of both the actors (viz: customer and service provider) in the service encounter of banks.

Statistical Tools

Statistical tools used for computing data and analyzing them through the two studies carried out by us include: mean, percentage and t-tests are used for all the dimensions of service quality. Further, an attempt has been made in these studies to carry out gap analysis using the perceived and expected service quality scores. The difference between perceived scores and the expected scores is the gap in the quality of services.

In study-I, responses of customers on 22-pairs of items of SERVQUAL on a 7-point Likert-type scale have been computed. Based on the responses of customers, statistical means, percentages and significant t-values (p>0.05) were derived by using one-tailed t-test, on each of the 5-dimensions of customers' expected and perceived service quality.

In study-II, an attempt has been made to analyze the service quality based on customer's response concerning his/her personal profile; awareness of bank's innovative services, and deposits and loans availed from the transacting bank. An assessment of perceived service quality by the respective bank's staff has also been made. Significant positive and negative t-values by using 2-tailed t-test indicated the service quality in banks as superior and poor respectively, based on the respondent's rating on each of the 10 dimensions of SERVQUAL (Parasuraman, 1988).

Analysis and Interpretation of Data

Analysis of Data: Study-I

Service Quality and Degree of Customer Satisfaction and Awareness:

Analyses of customers' perceptions of service quality have been made in study-I, based on 5-dimensional model of SERVQUAL. The statistical values (including percentage and t-value using one-tailed t-test) are presented in Table 3.1 below.

Table 3.1: Degree of Customer Satisfaction and Awareness; and Assessment of Service Quality on 5-Dimensional SERVQUAL Model*

Service Quality Dimension		Physical Facility	Reliability	Responsiveness	Assurance	Empathy
Satisfied Customer	Expected Service Response (%age)	77.71	80.72	80.24	77.34	77.34
	Actual Service Response (%age)	39.75	48.19	46.26	51.32	44.81
	t-value = 3.98 (sig. P>0.05)					
Dissatisfied Customer	Expected Service Response (%age)	80.06	84.23	88.37	85.4	84.05
	Actual Service Response (%age)	54.5	63.66	61.8	64.05	59.81
	t-value = 4.01 (sig. P>0.05)					

Service Quality Dimension		Physical Facility	Reliability	Responsiveness	Assurance	Empathy
Customer Complaining Procedural Delays in Bank	Expected Service Response (%age)	76.13	81.81	84.54	85.45	81.81
	Actual Service Response (%age)	45.45	60.6	57.27	59.09	63.63
	t-value = 3.95 (sig. P>0.05)					
Customer Aware of Bank's New Schemes	Expected Service Response (%age)	77.28	82.39	84.36	83.52	82.25
	Actual Service Response (%age)	48.94	55.16	52.11	55.63	49.85
	t-value = 4.00 (sig. P>0.05)					
Customer Not Aware of Bank's New Schemes	Expected Service Response (%age)	81.53	86.92	91.69	86.15	86.15
	Actual Service Response (%age)	40.19	56.92	57.38	62.3	55.53
	t-value = 3.95 (sig. P>0.05)					

* t-values derived by using one-tailed t-test

The above table reveals that most of the satisfied customers (80.72%) rated 'reliability' as the most important dimension of their expected service quality from banks. However, the corresponding response towards their perceived service quality in the dimension of 'reliability' was very low (48.19%). The t-test (t-value = 3.98), based on these customers' responses across all the 5 dimensions indicated significant difference between the expected and perceived service quality in banks.

Analysis of responses of dissatisfied customers revealed that most of the customers (i.e. 88.37%) dissatisfied with bank's services rated 'responsiveness' as the most important dimension of their expected service quality. However, their corresponding response towards perceived service quality in the dimension of 'responsiveness' was low (61.80%). The t-test (t-value = 4.01), based on customers' responses across all the 5 dimensions indicated significant difference between the expected and perceived service quality in banks.

Table 3.1 indicates that most of the customers who encountered problem of procedural delays in banks (85.45%) rated 'assurance' as the most important dimension of expected service quality. However, their rating of the 'assurance' dimension was much lower (59.09%) towards perceived service quality in banks. The t-test (t-value = 3.95), based on customers' responses across all the 5 dimensions indicated significant difference between the expected and perceived service quality in banks.

Above table also reveals the relationship between customer awareness and service quality. Most of the respondents (i.e. 84.36%) aware of the new schemes launched by the bank, rated 'responsiveness' as the most important dimension towards their expected service quality in banks. However, the corresponding response towards customers' perceived service quality was much lower (52.11%). The t-test (t-value = 4.00), based on customers' responses across all the five dimensions indicated significant difference between the expected and perceived service quality in banks.

As shown in Table 3.1, the expected service quality in the dimension of 'responsiveness' was rated very important by most of the respondents (91.69%) not aware of the new schemes launched by the bank. However, the corresponding response towards these customers' perceived service quality in the dimension of 'responsiveness' was much lower (i.e. 57.38%). The t-test (t-value = 3.95), based on these customers' responses across all the five dimensions indicated significant difference between the expected and perceived service quality in banks.

Analysis of Data: Study-II

Service Quality and Personal Profile of Customers

Using the 10-dimensional SERVQUAL model on a 7-point Likert-type scale the analysis customers' responses were made, based on customer's personal profile (i.e. age, income, education, gender, rural/semi-urban/urban inhabitation, marital status, and occupation), study-II revealed superior and poor service quality in the bank as positive and negative t-values (derived by using 2-tailed t-test) respectively, which are presented in Table 3.2 below:

The Table 3.2 reveals that customers in the age group of 45-54 perceived 'competence' as the poor and 'communication' as the superior dimension (t-values = –46.80 and 12.08 respectively) of service quality. However, the old customers (65 years or older) perceived 'responsiveness' as poor (t-value =

Table 3.2: Customer's Personal Profile and Assessment of Service Quality on 10-Dimensional SERVQUAL Model*

	Personal Profile of Customer	Service Quality Dimension									
		Accessibility	Communication	Competence	Courtesy	Credibility	Feel Secure	Reliability	Responsiveness	Tangibles	Understanding
Age Group	**Under 25**	3.03	7.18	–0.33	1.36	2.19	1.34	1.98	–4.36	–1.36	0
	25-34	–1.08	3.17	–1.39	2.25	3.22	0.35	1.59	0.49	–1.69	3.21
	35-44	4.10	–2.68	3.01	–8.45	–3.96	–5.11	–1.13	–2.08	6.16	2.42
	45-54	–1.30	**12.08**	**–46.80**	–3.88	0.75	–12.50	–5.17	–1.41	–4.86	–0.08
	55-64	–0.83	1.57	2.09	–2.01	1.82	–1.09	–1.13	9.85	–1.98	–1.10
	65 or over	2.18	2.40	1.31	1.65	5.09	10.70	4.79	–31.40	0.54	–3.31
Income Group	**Below Rs. 10000**	–1.26	–2.47	–5.07	–5.07	–5.10	–7.06	–1.12	–6.53	1.16	–1.37
	Rs. 10000-50000	0.14	–3.01	3.15	3.31	7.81	1.80	–0.44	–6.96	2.61	1.24
	Rs. 50000-100000	–0.38	7.17	–0.07	**–46.96**	7.71	3.27	1.74	–4.38	–0.60	3.21
	Rs. 100000-200000	–2.59	–2.68	1.82	1.20	2.49	–8.32	–1.72	–3.06	–1.80	0.78
	Rs. 200000 above	0.82	0	–19.60	**12.80**	11.45	8.02	1.05	0.64	3.18	–17.20
Education	**Graduate**	–0.03	2.96	0.72	**–32.20**	3.22	0.56	–0.60	–1.25	2.41	1.04
	Postgraduate	3.15	–2.95	2.96	–1.06	–4.83	–18.60	–11.25	–7.08	–1.51	0
	Professional	–0.59	–4.5	0.705	2.66	5.41	1.76	4.61	–5.30	0.22	**6.92**
	Below SSC	–3.01	–3.57	–8.03	–0.40	–3.14	–0.10	–1.73	–1.56	2.38	–5.28
	Illiterate	–3.97	0.11	–2.01	–24.5	0.27	–3.64	–1.73	–24.55	3.12	–1.01
Gender	**Male**	–0.35	–3.09	–0.43	**–7.65**	6.90	1.89	–0.34	–4.16	**9.54**	1.76
	Female	–0.40	7.90	0.31	0.94	0.38	1.05	0.11	–0.44	0.49	–0.27

(Contd...)

	Personal Profile of Customer	Service Quality Dimension									
		Accessibility	Communication	Competence	Courtesy	Credibility	Feel Secure	Reliability	Responsiveness	Tangibles	Understanding
	Urban	–0.81	–1.67	–0.71	**–3.42**	1.724	1.687	–2.02	–0.96	**7.213**	0.729
Inhabitation	**Rural**	–2.12	**–3.60**	–2.395	4.39	**6.94**	1.05	1.57	2.94	–1.41	0.65
	Semi Urban	0.13	5.20	0.58	3.33	–1.72	1.69	**5.36**	**–5.94**	–0.81	1.83
Marital	**Married**	–0.49	–3.37	1.03	2.78	**6.39**	4.61	–1.70	–2.88	4.75	0.41
Status	**Unmarried**	–0.57	3.33	–0.81	1.40	1.26	0.48	2.00	–2.57	**–3.50**	1.24
	Dependents	–0.74	–8.89	–3.00	0.26	–3.60	–4.57	0.51	–4.21	0.51	–2.2
	Professionals	**13.72**	–1.92	4.07	9.35	4.41	4.79	–0.37	–3.47	–8.03	0.74
Occupation	**Employees**	–0.84	–7.74	–1.67	–2.82	11.54	1.50	1.02	–5.44	0.59	–12.43
	Managerial	2.13	–12.89	3.54	–17.13	10.58	6.56	**–19.13**	–13.17	2.62	2.18
	Business class	1.01	–5.01	5.54	–3.98	8.06	–1.53	–2.41	1.61	2.02	0.97

*Highest positive/negative significant t-values (p>0.05) using 2-tailed t-Tests have been underlined.

–31.40), and 'feeling secure' as superior (t-value = 10.70) dimension of service quality in the bank.

Customers in the income group of Rs. 50, 000 to 1 lakh per annum perceived 'courtesy' as poor (t-value = –46.96) dimension of service quality, while those in the income group of Rs. 2 lakh or above per annum perceived 'courtesy' as the superior dimension (t-value = 12.80) of service quality in the bank.

Among the customers with different educational background, graduates perceived poor service quality in bank in the dimension of 'courtesy' (t-value = –32.20). Those with professional qualification (viz: medical, engineering, law, etc.), however, perceived superior service quality in bank in the dimension of 'Understanding' (t-value = 6.92).

Male customers perceived poor service quality in the dimension of 'courtesy' (t-value = –7.65), and superior service quality in the dimension of 'tangibles' (t-value = 9.54) in their transacting banks. Strangely, the female customers were mostly neutral in their responses.

Semi-urban, rural and urban customers perceived poor service quality in the dimensions of 'responsiveness' (t-value = –5.94), 'communication' (t-value = –3.60), and 'courtesy' (t-value = –3.42) respectively. Similarly, these customers perceived superior service quality in the dimensions of 'reliability' (t-value = 5.36), 'credibility' (t-value = 6.94), and 'tangibles' (t-value = 7.21), respectively.

While unmarried customers perceived poor service quality in the dimension of 'tangibles' (t-value = –3.50), married customers perceived superior service quality in the dimension of 'credibility' (t-value = 6.39).

Among the respondents with varied occupational background, managers perceived poor service quality in the dimension of 'reliability' (t-value = –19.13), while other professionals (including doctors, lawyers etc.) perceived superior service quality in the dimension of 'accessibility' (t-value = 13.72), as experienced in their respective transacting banks.

Service Quality and Customer's Knowledge, Deposit & Loan Pattern

Results concerning superior and poor service quality in different dimensions (on 10-dimensional model) based on the customer profile (including his/her overall assessment, knowledge of innovative banking services, type of deposits and loans availed), and overall perception of service quality by bank's staff were also obtained. Finally, superior and poor service quality assessed by bank's staff and customers have been indicated through positive and negative t-values (derived by using 2-tailed t-test) respectively, as presented in Table 3.3.

With regards to overall assessment of service quality in the transacting bank, Table 3.2 reveals that customers' perceived service quality in the dimension of 'communication' was poor (t-value = –5.05). However, their perceived service quality in bank was superior in 'courtesy' dimension (t-value = 3.98).

While customers with adequate knowledge of bank's innovative services perceived poor service quality in the dimension of 'communication' (t-value = –2.53), those not having adequate knowledge about bank's innovative services perceived superior service quality in the said dimension (t-value = 12.20).

Among the depositors, those availing current deposit facilities from the bank perceived poor service quality in the dimension of 'credibility' (t-value = –20.40). However, their perceived service quality in bank was superior in the dimension of 'feeling secure' (t-value = 20.50).

Among the customers who did not avail any loan from the bank, service quality perceptions in the dimension of 'communication' were poor (t-value = –9.24). However, customers who availed loan(s) from the bank perceived superior quality of service in the bank in the dimension of 'tangibles' (t-value = 14.97).

Among the customers availing different loans from the bank, those who availed personal loan from the bank perceived poor service quality in the dimension of 'Understanding' (t-value = –48.40). At the same time, those who availed personal loan from

Table 3.3: Service Quality Assessment Based on Customer Profile and Perception of Overall Services by Bank's Staff on 10-Dimensional SERVQUAL Model*

Customer/Staff Profile		Service Quality Dimension									
		Accessibility	Communication	Competence	Courtesy	Credibility	Feeling Secure	Reliability	Responsiveness	Tangibles	Understanding
Overall Service Quality Assessed by Customers		–0.55	**–5.05**	–0.11	**3.98**	2.98	1.45	–0.07	–2.66	2.01	0.71
Customer's Knowledge of Innovative Service	**Adequate knowledge**	0.13	**–2.53**	0.08	–0.9	2.74	3.67	–0.49	–1.94	2.1	0.96
	No adequate knowledge	–1.71	**12.2**	–0.7	9.42	3.29	1.2	0.84	4.13	1.93	0.27
Customer's Deposit Profile	**Saving Deposit**	–0.78	–12.9	–0.92	–0.25	0.34	0.39	–0.03	–2.04	0.83	–0.16
	Fixed Deposit	–2.9	0.12	–2.97	–6.06	–6.32	–11.3	–1.15	–0.61	2.53	–2.69
	Current Deposit	0.77	–17.4	16.4	15.5	**–20.4**	**20.5**	6.95	–8.32	12.7	4.58
Loan(s) Availed by the Customer	**Loan(s) Availed**	1.8	0	4.33	0	5.34	–4.62	2.1	–1.79	**14.97**	1.09
	No Loan Availed	–0.86	**–9.24**	–1.42	3.21	2.55	0.6	0.13	–4.46	0.86	0.81
Type of Loan(s) Availed by the Customer	**Term Loan**	–0.33	–3.6	–1.95	–9.72	–2.8	9.09	–3.53	0.82	–2.43	–2.51
	Personal Loan	1.62	–1.33	3.48	–6.06	–8.96	–6.52	–0.3	**44.96**	–19.9	**–48.4**
	Home Loan	1.47	0.48	19.5	–4.6	–6.57	9.24	18.4	0.1	17.9	–0.2
Overall Service Quality Perceived by Banks' Staff		**–2.48**	**–2.6**	0.58	1.02	–0.88	**3.73**	–0.81	0.87	0.56	0.9

*Highest positive/negative significant t-values (p>0.05) using 2-tailed t-Tests have been underlined.

the bank also perceived superior service quality in the bank, in the dimension of 'responsiveness' (t-value = 44.96).

Service Quality Perceptions by Bank's Staff

Perceptions of service quality by bank's staff have been revealed through study-II, by administering similar measures of 10-dimensional SERVQUAL Model. It was found that the bank's staff perceived poor service quality in the bank in the dimension of 'communication' (t-value = –2.60), and accessibility (t-value = –2.48), respectively. Similarly, the perception of service quality by the bank's staff was rated as superior in the dimension of 'feeling secure' (t-value = 3.73).

Findings of Study-I & II

In study-I, by adopting 5-dimensional SERVQUAL model, we found that most of the satisfied customers of public sector banks perceived poor 'reliability' in the services offered by the bank. However, the dissatisfied customers perceived of poor 'responsiveness' in the bank.

Most of the customers complaining about procedural delays in banks experienced poor 'assurance' from the bank with regards to service quality. While analyzing the responses of customers based on their degree of awareness towards new services offered by the bank, study-I revealed that customers perceived poor service quality in the dimension of 'responsiveness'.

In study-II, we found that most of the customers in the age group of 45-54 years perceived poor 'competence' and superior 'communication' in the bank. However, customers above 65 years of age perceived poor 'responsiveness' and were 'feeling secure' with the bank's transactions. While graduate customers perceived poor 'courtesy', those with professional qualification perceived superior 'understanding' in the bank. Male customers perceived poor 'courtesy', while perceiving superior physical facilities available in the bank. Perceptions of female customers were not significant across most of the dimensions of service quality in the bank.

In sharp contrast to the findings of study-I, our study-II revealed poor perceived 'responsiveness' and superior 'reliability' in bank's services only among the semi-urban customers. Rural customers, however, perceived poor 'courtesy' and superior 'credibility' in the bank. Urban customers perceived poor 'courtesy', and superior 'tangibles' in the bank. The unmarried/ bachelor customers perceived poor 'tangibles', while married customers perceived poor 'communication' in the bank. Customers in the category of managers perceived poor 'reliability', while professionals (viz: doctors, lawyers, chartered accountants, etc.) perceived superior 'accessibility' towards the bank's services.

Overall assessment of service quality by customers in the above study revealed poor perceived 'communication', and superior 'courtesy' in the bank. Customers with adequate knowledge of innovative services offered by the bank perceived poor 'communication', while those without adequate knowledge perceived superior 'communication' in the bank. Customers who were depositors perceived poor 'credibility', while feeling secure to transact with the bank. Though the customers not availing loan from the bank perceived well about the 'tangibles', they had poor perceptions about 'communication' in the bank. Most of the customers who availed personal loans from the bank perceived poor 'understanding' and superior 'responsiveness' in the bank.

Analysis of service quality perceptions by banks staffs revealed poor 'communication' and 'accessibility' in the bank. However, the service quality perceptions by bank's staffs were rated as superior in the dimension of 'feeling secure'.

DISCUSSION

It could be inferred that in this era of competition, for retaining their satisfied customers, banks should maintain error-free customer orders and records, provide services as promised, and try to gain the first impression of the customer. The public sector banks should also learn how to provide prompt service to customers at once. We also inferred from study-I that public sector banks have failed to keep the customers informed about the new schemes launched by them, and are yet to develop willingness to help the customers. If such issues are not addressed soon, customers of the public sector banks might defect to competitors.

Findings of our study-I seemed to be aligned with the works of Parasuraman et al. (1985, 1988), since among the five dimensions of service quality, responsiveness was the most important dimension of customer's perceived service quality in bank, followed by reliability. Although all the five-dimensions of service quality assessed by customers did not entirely hold true in study-I, results of this study reinforced earlier research findings that the five dimensions of service quality are of varying importance, with reliability and responsiveness dimensions being most important (Angur et al., 1999).

It could be inferred from our study-II that the bank should provide innovative services (i.e. diversity and wide range of services including 24×7 service, core banking and tele-banking facilities at low service charges) for its customers. Another area of concern in the public sector bank studied is that of bank's poor 'responsiveness' shown towards its old customers. It is noteworthy to mention here that since most of the old customers and pensioners hold their account and feel secure to transact with the public sector bank, their service problems should be attended on a priority basis. We also found that the bank was not courteous towards customers in the lower income group, while customers in the higher income group perceived superior 'courtesy' in services offered by the bank. It is not a healthy sign for banking services in a developing economy like India, in which the vast majority of customers belong to the lower income group.

There is a growth in mass awakening of the customers towards public sector banking services in India, as evidenced through customers' perceptions towards courtesy, credibility and tangibility in both rural and urban areas. Since, we also found that there are some lapses in communication towards the married customers, the bank should evolve appropriate mechanism for open communication in the bank. Moreover, in our study-II customers in the occupation of 'manager' perceived poor reliability in bank's services. Keeping in view the needs of growing middle class in India with a large number of managers serving various sectors of economy, bankers have no choice than to offer reliable service to such customers.

We found while assessing overall service quality that most of the customers, including those who were aware of the innovative services offered by the bank, perceived poor 'communication' in the bank. We found that the customers who did not avail any loan from the bank, also perceived poor 'communication' in the bank. Customers who availed personal loans from the bank perceived poor 'understanding', while the depositors' perceived poor 'credibility' in the bank.

The aforesaid findings based on customer's perception of service quality were crosschecked in our study-II, by analyzing the corresponding perception by bank's staff. Our findings appeared to bear fruit since the bank's staff in the respective bank also perceived poor 'communication'. Bank's staff also perceived poor 'accessibility' in the bank. The only dimension in which the staff perceived superior quality of service in the bank was that of 'feeling secure', which could have resulted from the structural component of the state-owned bank.

It is, therefore, inferred that the communication dimension of service quality in the public sector bank is poor, and detrimental to its growth and prosperity. Hence, we suggest that the bank should communicate well with the customers with regards to the exact outcome of service provided (viz., time, interest rates, etc.), recognize customers on a regular basis, and ensure availability of most services in the respective bank.

CONCLUSION

There is a paucity of knowledge concerning the banking service in developing economies. It is difficult to conclude that both the nature of service and the constituents of service quality measurement are changing. The purpose of this paper was to assess the applicability of alternative measures of service quality in the banking sector of a developing economy. Based on the findings of the two studies undertaken by us, the present paper reaffirms that service quality assessment of banks in a developing economy should rely on a multidimensional construct including customers, bank's employees and the environment.

Two studies carried out on banking services in India have been incorporated into this paper. Moreover, as the banking industry is a major infrastructure component of a developing economy like India, findings of these studies could be useful for other countries as well. India has recently liberalized its economy, allowing the entry of numerous domestic and multinational firms to compete with the old public sector banks. Thus, service quality has become the key-differentiating factor for banks attempting to improve their market and profit positions.

The two studies taken into account for this paper are from the "service-quality perspective", and as such, were aimed at identifying some key aspects of customer relationship management. This paper was an attempt to explore the subtle, intricate details concerning dimensions of service quality, which might be helpful for bankers in gaining competitive advantage. India, being a huge developing economy, and its banking sector with a wide geographical reach catering to the needs of a huge clientele, offers an excellent scope for research on the issue of quality in banking (as perceived by the customers), and can provide the beacon for the evaluation of effectiveness of banking services in developing economies.

Challenges that lie ahead for banks is to satisfy customer needs, the need to face up to increased competition, the disruption of traditional supply chains and the need to be innovative (Jayawardhena and Foley, 2000). Banks pursuing a long-term perspective in terms of innovation and thinking are more likely to attain higher levels of business performance. The ability to produce novel services that satisfy the latent needs of customers is paramount. The high performing banks have to utilize the benefits from the latest technology. A strategic challenge facing banking organization today is the growing and changing needs and expectations of customers in tandem with increased education levels and growing economic conditions.

Indian customers have not only become technology savvy today, but also have started demanding more and more of quality and personalized services. With more of innovative or "high-tech" banking services provided to customers there has been growing concern for "high-touch" banking services, seeking involvement and interaction among various stakeholders. It is, therefore, imperative that more cross-country analyses with regards to service quality assessments in the banking sector would be of immense use for such service providers.

In this changing business environment, the customer focus and service provided by the bank is gaining importance, and as such, banks should innovate their deposit and loan schemes with modified rates of interest. Unless a customer is aware of the new schemes launched by the bank, it would be virtually impossible for the bank to implement these schemes.

REFERENCES

Albrecht, K. and Zemke, R. (1985). "Service America: Doing Business in the New Economy", Dow Jones Irwin, Homewood, IL.

Anderson, C. and Zeithaml, C.P. (1984). "Stage of the Product Life Cycle, Business Strategy, and Business Performance", *Academy of Management Journal*, Vol. 27, March, pp. 5-24.

Angur, Madhukar G., Nataraajan Rajan, Jahera Jr, John S. (1999). "Service Quality in the Banking Industry: An Assessment in a Developing Economy", *International Journal of Bank Marketing*, Vol. 17, No. 3, pp. 116-123.

Carman, J.M. (1990). "Consumer Perceptions of Service Quality: An Assessment of the SERVQUAL Dimensions", *Journal of Retailing*, Vol. 66, No. 1, pp. 33-55.

Cristina, Sousa (2002). "Customer Expectations and Perceptions of Service Quality in Retail Banking: A Comparative Study of Macau and Guangzhou Banking Consumers", University of Macau.

Cronin, J.J. Jr., and Taylor, S.A. (1992). "Measuring Service Quality: A Re-examination and Extension", *Journal of Marketing*, July, Vol. 56, pp. 55-68.

Dabholkar, P.A., Thorpe, D.I., and Rentz, J.O. (1996). "A Measure of Service Quality for Retail Stores: Scale Development and Validation", *Journal of the Academy of Marketing Science*, Vol. 24, No. 1, pp. 3-16.

Damanpour, F. (1991). "Organizational Innovation: A Meta-analysis of Effects of Determinants and Moderators", *Academy of Management Journal*, Vol. 34, No. 3, pp. 555-590.

Das Gupta, Soutiman (2005). "A Matter of Strategy", *Indian Express - Business Publications Division*, Issue of March.

Davido, W.H. and Uttal B. (1989). "Service Companies: Focus or Falter", *Harvard Business Review*, July-August, pp. 77-85.

De Bono, E. (1977). *Lateral Thinking*, Penguin, Harmondsworth.

Firoz, N.M. and Maghrabi, A.S. (1994). "The Role of Service Marketing in Economic Development: An Analysis", *International Journal of Management*, Vol. 2, pp. 641-747.

Folkes, V.S. "Recent Attribution Research in Consumer Behaviour: A Review and New Directions", *Journal of Consumer Research*, 14 (March 1988), pp. 548-65.

Garvin, D.A. (1988). *Managing Quality: The Strategic and Competitive Edge*, The Free Press, New York.

George, W. (1977). *The Retailing of Service—A Challenging Future, Journal of Retailing*, Vol. 53, No. 3, Fall, pp. 85-98.

Gregan-Paxton, J. and Roedder John, D. (1997). "Consumer Learning by Analogy: A Model of Internal Knowledge Transfer", *Journal of Consumer Research*, Vol. 24, pp. 266-84.

Gronroos, C. (1982). "Strategic Management and Marketing in the Service Sector", Helsingrors: Swedish School of Economics and Business Administration.

Headley, D.E. and Choi, B. (1992). "Achieving Service Quality Through Gap Analysis and a Basic Statistical Approach", *The Journal of Services Marketing*, Vol. 6, No. 1, pp. 5-14.

Hemmasi, M., Strong, K.C. and Taylor, S.A. (1994). "Measuring Service Quality for Strategic Planning and Analysis in Service Firms", *Journal of Applied Business Research*, Vol. 10, pp. 24-34.

Hoch, S.J. and Ha, Y.W. (1986). "Consumer Learning: Advertising and the Ambiguity of Product Experience", *Journal of Consumer Research*, Vol. 13, September, pp. 221-33.

Hoffman, K.D. and Bateson, J.E. (2001). *Essentials of Service Marketing: Concepts, Strategies, and Cases*, pp. 324 (2nd. Ed.), Australia: South Western Thompson Learning.

Jayawardhena, C. and Foley, P. (2000). "Changes in the Banking Sector—The Case of Internet Banking in the UK", *Internet Research: Electronic Networking Applications and Policy*, Vol. 10, No. 1, pp. 19-30.

Juran, J.M. (1999). "How to Think About Quality". In Juran, J.M., and Godfrey, A.B. (Eds.) *Juran's Quality Handbook*, 5th Edition, New York, McGraw-Hill, pp. 2.1-2.3.

Kandampully, Jay (2002). "Innovation as the Core Competency of a Service Organization: The Role of Technology, Knowledge and Networks", *European Journal of Innovation Management*, Vol. 5, No. 1, pp. 18-26.

Kassem, S. (1998). "Services Marketing: The Arabian Gulf Experience", *Journal of Services Marketing*, Vol. 3, pp. 61-71.

Kaushik, S. (1997). "India's Evolving Economic Model: A Perspective on Economic and Financial Reforms", *American Journal of Economics and Sociology*, January, pp. 69-84.

Kumar, Sharad (2005). "Innovation in Customer Service in Banks", *Professional Bankers*, The ICFAI University Press, pp. 32-35.

Lehtinen, U. and Lehtinen, J.R. (1991). "Two Approaches to Service Quality Dimensions", *The Service Industries Journal*, Vol. 11, July, pp. 287-303.

Martin, C.L. and Pranter, C.A. (1989). "Compatibility Management: Customer-to-Customer Relationships in Service Environments", *Journal of Services Marketing*, Vol. 3, No. 1, pp. 5-15.

Mathur, H.P. (1999). *TQM in Banking, Indian Management*, Vol. 38, No. 5, 1999.

Moreau, C.P., Lehmann, D.R. and Markman, A.B. (2001). "Entrenched Knowledge Structures and Consumer Response to New Products", *Journal of Marketing Research*, Vol. 38, pp. 14-29.

Muthukrishnan, A.V. and Kardes, Frank R. (2001). "Persistent Performance for Attributes: The Effect of Initial Choice Context and Uninformative Experience", *Journal of Consumer Research*, June, Vol. 28, No. 1.

Nohria, N. and Gulati, R. (1996). "Is Slack Good or Bad for Innovation?" *Academy of Management Journal*, Vol. 39, No. 5, pp. 1245-64.

Parasuraman, A., Berry, L. and Zeithaml, V. (1988). "SERVQUAL: A Multiple Item Scale for Measuring Customer Perception of Service Quality", *Journal of Retailing*, Vol. 64, pp. 12-40.

Parasuraman, A., Zeithaml, V.A., and Berry, L.L. (1985). "A Conceptual Model of Service Quality and its Implications for Future Research", *Journal of Marketing*, 49, fall, 41-50.

Parasuraman, A., Zeithaml, V.A. and Berry, L.L. (1994), "Alternative Scale for Measuring Service Quality: A Comparative Assessment Based on Psychometric and Diagnostic Criteria", *Journal of Retailing*, Vol. 70, No. 3, pp. 201-30.

Peters, T. (1997). *The Circle of Innovation*, Hodder & Stoughton, London.

Prasad, V.V.S. Siva. "Strategic Branding Trends in Banking Industry in India", *The Indian Banker*, February, 2006, Vol. 1, No. 2, pp. 1-3.

Roehm, M.L. and Sternthal, B. (2001). "The Moderating Effect of Knowledge and Resources on the Persuasive Impact of Analogies", *Journal of Consumer Research*, Vol. 28, No. 2, pp. 257-72.

Sureshchander, G.S., Rajendran, C., & Kamalanabhan, T.J. (2001). "Customer Perceptions of Service Quality: A Critique". *Total Quality Management*, Vol. 12, No. 1, pp. 111-125.

Thacker, S. (1997). "India", *International Financial Law Review*, July, pp. 29-30.

Urbany, J., Dickinson, P.R. and Wilkie, W.L. (1989). "Buyer Uncertainty and Information Search". *Journal of Consumer Research*, Vol. 16, pp. 208-215.

Woodside, A.G., Frey, L.L. and Daly, R.T. (1989). "Linking Service Quality, Customer Satisfaction, and Behavioural Intentions", *Journal of Health Care Marketing*, Vol. 9, pp. 5-17.

Yamauchi, T. and Markman, A.B. (2000). "Inference Using Categories", *Journal of Experimental Psychology: Learning, Memory, and Cognition*, Vol. 26, pp. 776-95.

Yavas, Ugur, Zeynep, Bilgin and Donald, J. Shemwell (1997). "Service Quality in the Banking Sector in an Emerging Economy: A Consumer Survey", *International Journal of Bank Marketing*, Vol. 15, No. 6, pp. 217–223.

Zeithaml, V.A. and Bitner, M.J. *Service Marketing* (2003), 3rd edition, pp. 70-75.

Zeithaml, V.A., Parasuraman, A. and Berry, L.L. (1994). "The Behavioural Consequences of Service Quality", *Journal of Marketing*, Vol. 60, April, pp. 31-46.

Role of Commercial Banks in Manufacturing Sector Development

(With Special Reference to Commercial Bank of Ethiopia)

R. Dhanuskodi

ABSTRACT

Banks play a pre-dominant role in building the economy of an individual as well as nation. They have control over a large part of the supply of money in circulation. Banks are the main stimulus of the economic progress of a country. A strong banking sector is, therefore, vital for growth, creation of jobs, generation of wealth, eradication of poverty, entrepreneurial activity and increasing the gross domestic profit, all necessary factors for a country to emerge as a developed one.

CBE is the leading public sector commercial bank in Ethiopia. This bank single handedly is having the branch share of 50 per cent in the country. It remained the predominant bank in the country in terms of branch network, public image and market share with no incredible indulgence from private banks.

Giving advances and accepting deposits are the most important aspects of banking business operation. The bank takes more care about lending because it deals with others money. CBE has several financing schemes to suit the various needs of the public. It adopts different financing schemes for different purposes.

This Paper highlights the CBE's role in the manufacturing sector development in Ethiopia. The bank lends money to the manufacturing sectors in the name of term loans and overdraft facilities. It has own terms and conditions for lending to this sector.

The present research work titled as "**Role of Commercial Banks in Manufacturing Sector Development with special reference to CBE**", it has been divided in to five chapters. The **first chapter** gives a bird's eye view of the historical development of Ethiopian Industry, the role of industrial sector to Ethiopian Economy, manufacturing industries in Ethiopia and Banks in Ethiopia. It also includes a brief description about the statement of the problem, objectives of the study and data analysis. The **second chapter** deals with review of related studies. The **third chapter** is devoted for the discussion of area profile and brief history of CBE. The **fourth chapter** gives the role of CBE in manufacturing sector development; the **fifth chapter** contains the summary, conclusion and suggestions for further study.

INTRODUCTION

Banks play a very important role in the economic development of every nation. They have control over a large part of the supply of money in circulation. Banks are the main stimulus of the economic progress of a country. A strong banking sector is, therefore, vital for growth, creation of jobs, generation of wealth, eradication of poverty, entrepreneurial activity and increasing the gross domestic profit, all necessary factors for a country to emerge as a developed one. Especially the commercial banks contribution in manufacturing sector is inevitable.

Historical Development of Ethiopian Industry

Industrial development has become the catchword of the twentieth century. From a historical perspective of the contemporary world, underdevelopment is manifested by the low level of industrial activities and predominance of agriculture over other occupations. But agricultural and industrial development have becomes closely interdependent that it is unrealistic to think of agricultural development and industrialization separately.

Ethiopia is characterized by low pattern of industrialization. Ethiopians industrial sector is backward in structure and technology of artisan manufacturing activity. Despite lack of recorded information about when and how modern industry was introduced in Ethiopia, many scholars agree that modern manufacturing industrial activities began in the late 19th century. It is also widely accepted that the major enabling conditions of the emergence and development of modern industries in Ethiopia were the establishment of central government in the second half of the 19th century, the Ethiopia-Djibouti railway construction, and the Italian invasion.

However, it was only since early 1950s that the industrial development was guided by deliberate government policy and strategy, and manufacturing began to play significant role in the economy.

Various studies reveals that the post-World War II, Ethiopian industrial development can be classified into three phases. The phases lasted from 1952 until 1974. In this phase, industrialization was characterized by promotion of foreign owned enterprises active in import substitution. The second phase was from 1974-1991; the phase was characterized by domination of nationalization of industry, promotion of state owned enterprise. The third phase is from 1991 to date. The characteristics of this phase are liberalization of the economy and promotion of the development of small and medium enterprise in the local resource based industries.

The Role of Industrial Sector to the Ethiopian Economy

The industrial sector plays an important role in the Ethiopian Economy. The sector's contribution to the economy can be seen from three angles, namely GDP contribution, Employment contribution and Foreign exchange contribution.

GDP Contribution

The industrial sector produces food and non-food items for the society. These items are necessary for the urban and rural population to satisfy their needs. The details of the sector's contribution to the Gross Domestic Product (GDP) in Ethiopia are given in the Table 4.1.

Table 4.1: Sectoral Contribution to GDP

(In Million Birr)

Sl. No.	Year	Agricultural and Allied Activities	Industry	Services	Total	Industry Share in Total
1.	1999-2000	7024.7	1731.3	7356.3	16112.3	1.74
2.	2000-01	7831.1	1818.1	7705.2	17354.4	10.47
3.	2001-02	7651.0	1923.4	8057.8	17632.2	10.90
4.	2002-03	6687.0	2012.2	8242.3	16941.5	11.87
5.	2003-04	7952.0	2150.8	8798.1	18900.9	11.37

Source: NBE Annual Report (2004-05) and computed.

As per the above table, the sectoral breakdown of total value of goods and services produced by the industrial sector are increasing trend (amount wise). In the view of industry share in total are fluctuating. In the year 2002-03, the contribution percentage is high i.e. 11.87.

Employment Contribution

The industrial sector is also an important source of employment for the growing population. The details about the employment are given in the Table 4.2.

Table 4.2: Employment Contribution

Sl. No.	Year	Public Sector	Private Sector	Total
1.	1999-2000	56,882	38,133	95,015
2.	2000-01	54,837	38,678	93,515
3.	2001-02	56,585	41,551	98,136
4.	2002-03	59,516	42,183	101,699
5.	2003-04	59,446	45,935	105,381

Source: Central Statistical Authority.

The Table 4.2 clearly indicates the employment opportunity provided by the industrial sector. In general the total employees are increasing except the year 2000-01.

Foreign Exchange Contribution

Ethiopia is essentially leading market oriented economy and its foreign trade has the major importance. It is well known fact that country is characterized by an agrarian economy where 90% of its total foreign exchange is generated from the agricultural sector; the exportable items of the industrial sector are few in numbers. The details about the major export commodities is given in the Table 4.3.

Table 4.3: Value of Major Exports

(In Million of US Dollars)

Sl. No.	Particulars	2001-2002	2002-2003	2003-2004
1.	Coffee	163.2	165.3	223.6
2.	Oilseeds	32.6	46.1	82.7
3.	Leather and Leather Products	55.5	52.2	43.6
4.	Pulses	32.9	19.9	22.6
5.	Fruits and Vegetables	9.4	9.6	12.7
6.	Sugar and Molasses	10.0	17.9	10.3
7.	Meat, Canned and Frozen	1.1	2.4	7.7
8.	Live Animals	0.8	0.5	1.9
9.	Chat	49.0	58.0	88.1
10.	Gold	35.2	42.1	48.7
11.	Others	62.6	68.8	58.8
	Total	452.4	482.7	600.7

Source: NBE Annual Report 2003-04.

The Leather and Leather products earned very attractive foreign exchange, for the years 2001-02, 2002-03 and 2003-04. The foreign exchange income from the Leather and Leather products were US $ 55.5, 52.2 and 43.6 million respectively.

Types of Industrial Activities

The industrial sector of Ethiopia is divided in to five namely, Mining and Quarrying, Manufacturing, Handcraft and small scale industries, Building and construction and Electricity and water.

Manufacturing Industries: Meaning and Definition

Manufacturing is a process, which converts raw materials into finished to products using labor and equipment. On the other hand, industry is the place where manufacturing takes place or conducted. In 1983, International Conference on Production Research defined manufacturing as "a series of interrelated activities and operations involving the design, material's selection, planning, manufacturing production, quality assurance, management and marketing of the products of the manufacturing industries".

Manufacturing Industries in Ethiopia

Ethiopia has had long history of handcrafts production, modern industry is a recent phenomenon. It began at the end of the 19th century, since then, it has undergone significant changes. The reasons for such changes include the establishment of strong central government, Italian occupation and increased demand for imported goods.

Pattern of Manufacturing Industry

The Manufacturing industry in Ethiopia is mainly classified into 15 different patterns. The patterns of manufacturing industries are as follows:

- Manufacture of food products and Beverages.
- Manufacture of Tobacco Products.
- Manufacture of Textiles.
- Manufacture of wearing Apparel, except Fur Apparel.
- Tanning and Dressing of Leather, manufacture of luggage and Hand bag, manufacture of Footwear.
- Manufacture of Wood and products of wood and Cork except furniture.
- Manufacture of Paper and paper products, printing and services related to printing.
- Manufacture of chemical and chemical products.
- Manufacture of Rubber and Plastic products.
- Manufacture of other non-metallic mineral products.
- Manufacture of basic Iron and Steel.
- Manufacture of Fabricated metal products except machinery and equipment.
- Manufacture of machinery and equipment.
- Assembly of Motor vehicles, Trailers and Semi-trailers.
- Manufacture of Furniture.

Number of Manufacturing Establishments

In Ethiopia, the manufacturing sector establishments are increasing every year. According to Central Statistical Authority (CSA), the year wise and ownership wise classification of manufacturing industries are given in the Table 4.4.

Table 4.4: Year-wise and Ownership-wise Classification of Manufacturing Industries in Ethiopia

Sl. No.	Manufacturing Sector	2000-01			2001-02			2002-03			2003-04		
		Pu	Pvt	To	Pu	Pvt	To	Pu	Pvt	To	Pu	Pvt	To
1.	Food and Beverage	43	208	251	43	239	282	43	245	288	43	279	322
2.	Tobacco	1	—	1	1	—	1	1	—	1	1	—	1
3.	Textiles	19	16	35	19	17	36	20	18	38	19	19	38
4.	Wearing Apparel	4	20	24	4	25	29	4	28	32	4	33	37
5.	Leather and Footwear	7	47	54	7	45	52	7	49	56	8	57	65
6.	Wood Products	8	6	14	8	13	21	7	10	17	7	13	20
7.	Paper and Printing	9	50	59	9	64	73	10	63	73	14	84	98
8.	Chemical and Chemical Products	11	27	38	11	30	41	11	34	45	13	33	46
9.	Rubber and Plastic	4	28	32	5	34	39	6	35	41	4	38	42
10.	Non-Metallic	18	69	87	21	79	100	21	94	115	18	106	124
11.	Iron and Steel	2	8	10	3	8	11	3	7	10	3	10	13
12.	Fabricated Metal	5	48	53	5	56	61	5	68	73	6	72	78
13.	Machinery and Equip	—	8	8	—	8	8	—	10	10	—	11	11
14.	Assem. Motor Vehi.	1	8	9	2	5	7	3	5	8	2	6	8
15.	Furniture	7	114	121	5	143	148	6	152	158	10	162	172
	Total	139	657	769	143	766	909	147	818	965	151	923	1074

Source: Central Statistical Authority (Pu. = Public sector; Pvt. = Private; To = Total)

The Table 4.4 shows that the food and Beverage sub-sector has maintained its dominance in terms of number of establishments i.e. 251, 258, 288 and 322 for the years 2000-01, 2001-02, 2002-03 and 2003-04 respectively.

Number of Employees

In general, manufacturing sector is one of the important contributors to job creation in the Ethiopia. The details about sector wise employees are given in the Table 4.5.

Table 4.5: Number of Employees in Manufacturing Sector

Sl. No.	Manufacturing Sector	2000-01	2001-02	2002-03	2003-04
1.	Food and Beverage	27260	28860	30570	31359
2.	Tobacco	822	792	792	785
3.	Textiles	24284	—	21938	22900
4.	Wearing Apparel	3720	—	4278	3806
5.	Leather and Footwear	7040	6740	7232	7665
6.	Wood Products	1033	1313	1669	1616
7.	Paper and Printing	5519	6142	6405	6940
8.	Chemical and Chem. Products	4069	—	4949	5017
9.	Rubber and Plastic	3401	4326	4429	4410
10.	Non-metallic	7328	8232	7967	9138
11.	Iron and Steel	1100	1448	1466	1699
12.	Fabricated Metal Prod.	2477	2740	3488	3453
13.	Machinery and Equip.	172	190	260	256
14.	Assem. Motor Vehi.	1060	1082	1021	1130
15.	Furniture	4230	5145	5235	5153
	Total	93515	98136	101699	105381

Source: Central Statistical Authority.

Banks in Ethiopia

The banking sector is not a new one in Ethiopia as in most other countries in the world. The Ethiopian banking system currently comprises a Central Bank, nine Commercial Banks (state owned and recently established private Banks).

The NBE as a Central Bank performs the usual Central Bank functions, services as issuer of the Bank notes and coins, Bankers to the banking sector and the government, controller of the money supply, supervisory of banking operations and administrator of foreign capital. The central bank's monetary board, which supervises the Bank's operation, management and administration, formulates major monetary and banking policies. It is responsible for the supervision and regulation of all commercial Banks.

The state owned Commercial Bank of Ethiopia (CBE) dominates the market in terms of per cent of assets, deposits, bank branches, total banking force although all other private banks are playing an active role in the nations financial market.

There are two government owned specialized banks in Ethiopia, The Development Bank of Ethiopia (DBE) and the Construction and Business Bank (CBB). DBE extents short, medium and long-term loans for viable development projects including industrial and agricultural projects. It also provides other banking services such as checking and saving accounts to its clients. The CBB provides long-term loans for construction, acquisition or maintenance of dwellings, community facility and real estate development. In addition, it offers all other commercial banking services to business.

After the implementation of licensing and Supervising Banking Business proclamation No. 88/1994, the private people are allowed to start new private banks in Ethiopia. At present there are 6 local private banks operating in the economy. The details of Ethiopia Banks are given in the Chart 4.1.

Chart 4.1.

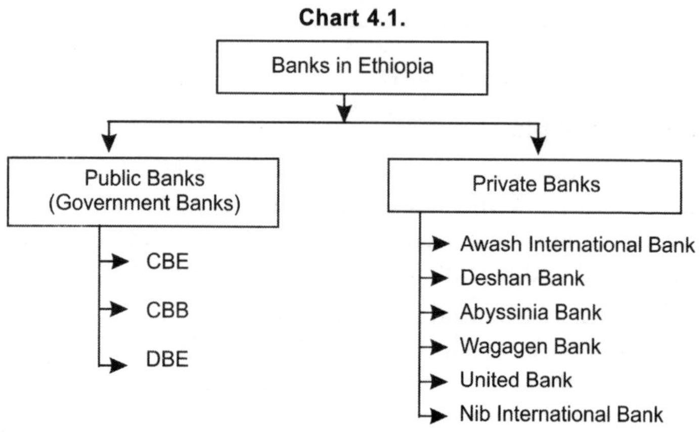

Branch Network of the Banking System

Ethiopia remains as one of the under banked countries even at sub Saharan African Countries standard. The bank branches to population ratio was 1: 98,050 the details about the branch network are given in the Table 4.6.

Table 4.6: Branch Network of the Banking System

Sl. No.	Banks	2002-03		2003-04			
		Total	% share	Region	Addis Ababa	Total	% share
1.	Public Banks						
	CBE	172	50.7	136	36	172	47.9
	CBB	20	5.9	15	6	21	5.8
	DBE	32	9.4	32	1	33	9.2
	Total (A)	224	66.1	183	43	226	63.0
2.	Private Banks						
	Awash Int. Bank	26	7.7	14	17	31	8.6
	Deshan Bank	28	8.3	15	16	31	8.6
	Abyssinia Bank	14	4.1	10	9	19	5.3
	Wagagen Bank	23	6.8	17	8	25	7.0
	United Bank	13	3.8	3	11	14	3.9
	Nib Int. Bank	11	3.2	1	12	13	3.6
	Total (B)	115	33.9	60	73	133	37.0
	Total (A) + (B)	339	100.0	243	116	359	100.0

Source: NBE Annual Report 2003-04.

Sector Break-down of Bank Credit

The Banks provide help to various sectors. Sectoral break down of bank credit are given in the Table 4.7.

Table 4.7: Sector Break-down of Bank Credit

(In Million Birr)

Sl. No.	Economic Sector	2002-03	2003-04
1.	Agriculture	445.2	583.0
2.	Industry	508.1	729.0
3.	Domestic Trade	1213.2	1463.6
4.	Export	541.5	795.7
5.	Import	434.1	867.2

(Contd...)

Sl. No.	Economic Sector	2002-03	2003-04
6.	Housing Construction	392.3	32.9
7.	Transport and Communication	151.1	490.6
8.	Hotel and Tourism	40.9	372.5
9.	Manpower	0.0	0.0
10.	Personal	45.1	70.1
11.	Others	326.4	807.0
	Total	4097.9	6211.6

Source: NBE Annual Report 2003-04.

The Total fresh loans disbursed by the banking system during 2003-04 reached birr 6211.6 million.

Statement of the Problem

Manufacturing sector have been facing number of problems like lack of sufficient capital to invest in industry, lack of modern industrial technology such as machine, equipment and factory goods, lack of skilled labor and industrial expertise. Inadequacy of capital leads to inefficiency of operation, only very few operators have own capital and majority of the operators depend mainly on private finance. CBE occupies a primary position in the matter of financing manufacturing sector in Ethiopia.

The Entrepreneur of the manufacturing sector should have to know the CBE's norms in lending, especially collateral, rate of interest, documents, repayment procedure, etc. Therefore, it is essential that the norms of CBE and its role in the manufacturing sectors development should be identified and analyzed.

Objectives of the Study

The objectives of the study are

1. To study the Development of Manufacturing Sector in Ethiopia.
2. To study the lending terms and conditions of CBE financé to manufacturing sector.
3. To highlight the extent of CBE's involvement in financing manufacturing sector.

Data and Sources of Data

The present study is based on the secondary sources of information. Secondary data were collected from NBE's annual reports, NBE's quarterly bulletins, CBE's annual reports, NBE's supervision of banks business directives, the house journals of CBE, newspaper and textbooks.

Period Covered for the Study

The study covered a period of ten years from 1994-95 to 2003-04.

Data Analysis

After the relevant data were collected, descriptive analysis was carried out which was preferred for assessment purposes. Hence for all data interpretations were made by tabulation, percentage, diagram, graphs and trend percentage have been used to support discussions related to findings, finally conclusion and recommendations were made accordingly.

Chapter Arrangements

The present study work is divided into five chapters; the first chapter gives a bird's eye view of the historical development of Ethiopian industry, the role of industrial sector to Ethiopian economy, manufacturing industries in Ethiopia and Banks in Ethiopia. It also includes a brief description about the statement of problem, objectives of the study and data analysis. The second chapter deals with review of related studies. The third chapter is devoted for the discussion of area profile and brief history of CBE. The fourth chapter gives role of CBE in manufacturing sector development. The fifth chapter contains the summary, conclusion and suggestions for further study.

REVIEW OF LITERATURE

Industrialization is the key to economic development and cultural change in an economy (Haile Hagos, 1995, p. 1) According to the United Nations Industrial Development Organization (UNIDO), quoted in Eshetu Chole (1986), industrialization is defined as, "the process of economic development in which a growing part of the natural resources are mobilized to develop a technically up-to-date, and diversified domestic economic structure characterized by dynamic manufacturing and consumer goods and capable of assuring a high rate of growth for the economy as a whole and of achieving economic and social progress".

According to the Central Statistical Authority (CSA) industrial sector can be classified into three, namely, large and medium scale manufacturing, small scale and cottage and handicrafts. This categorization is mainly based on the number of people employed and use of power driven machinery. Accordingly, large and medium scale manufacturing refers to these establishments that use power driven machinery and employing 10 persons and above. Similarly, small scale industries are those establishments that employ less than ten persons and use power driven machinery. Cottage and handicrafts are those establishments producing goods and services machinery in performing their main activities regardless of the number of people employed.

Master Book team work (2006, p. 961) has insisted the importance of industry in Ethiopia, "industry as a sector plays an important role in the Ethiopian Economy. The sector contributes to the economy by diversifying output, opening up employment opportunities and enhancing foreign exchange, Ethiopia exports certain industrial products of the world matter".

Manufacturing is the conversion of a design into a finished product, and 'production' has a narrow sense, namely the physical act making the product (Young and Mayer, 1984). In 1983 CIRP (International Conference on Production Research defined manufacturing as 'a series of interrelated activities and operations involving the design, materials selection, planning, manufacturing, production, quality assurance, management and marketing of the projects of the manufacturing industries' (Katsundo Hi, 1996, p. 4).

Dr. M.C. Vasih (1984, p. 379) pointed out that in modern times bank credit is required for many purposes and is employed by almost every sector of the economy. Indeed the demand for the credit is ubiquitous in the economy in every sector, the importance of credit is increasing from consumption to production sector. Dr. M.C. Vaish (1984, p. 664), finance is the life blood of industry, because the industrial development of a country is dependent upon the amount of capital available for investment.

AREA PROFILE AND BRIEF HISTORY OF CBE

Ethiopia has the longest history in the world and with thousands of years of sovereign statehood of an uninterrupted continuity.

Geography

Ethiopia is strategically located in the Horn of Africa. Its proximity to the Middle East and Europe, together with its easy access to the major ports of the region, enhances its international trade. Covering an area of approximately 1.14 million square kilometers (444000 squire miles), Ethiopia is bordered by the Sudan on the West, Somalia and Djibouti on the East, Eritrea on the north and Kenya on the south.

Climate

Ethiopia lies within 15 degrees north of the equators owing the moderating influence of high attitude, the country enjoys temperate and pleasant climate, with average temperatures rarely exceeding 20°C (68°F). The sparsely populated low lands, typically have sub-tropical and tropical climates. At approximately 850 mm (34 inches), the average annual rainfall for the whole country is considered to be moderate by global standards. In most of the highlands, rainfall occurs in two distinct seasons; the "small rains" during February and March and the "big rains" from June to September.

Population

The population of Ethiopia (2004 estimate) is 73 million. Approximately 85% of the population lives in the rural areas. The annual population growth rate is about 3 per cent, and the economically active segment, between ages 14 and 60, is about 50 per cent of the total population.

Language

Amharic, Oromigna and Tigrigna are the major languages used by two-third of the population. Amharic is the official language of the Federal government. English is the medium of instruction, and is widely used in business transactions, particularly in banking and insurance.

The Government

Ethiopia adopted a new constitution that establishes the Federal government is responsible for national defense, foreign relations and general policy of common interest and benefits. The Federal states comprise nine autonomous states vested with power for self-administration. The FDRE is structured along the lines of bicameral parliament, with the council of peoples' representatives being the highest authority of the Federal government while the Federal council represents the common interest if the nations, nationalities and people of the states. Members of both councils are elected by universal suffrage for a five year term. The Federal state is headed by a constitutional President and the Federal government by an executive Prime Minister who is accountable to the council of peoples' representatives. Each autonomous state is headed by a state president elected by the State Council. The judiciary is constitutionally independent.

Cities and Towns

Addis Ababa, the largest city, is the seat of the Federal Government of Ethiopia, and lies in the Central plateau at an altitude of 2400 meteres, 9° north of the Equator. Its average temperature is 16°C. Ethiopia's other important centers of trade and industries are: Awassa, DireDawa, Gondar, Dessie, Nazareth, Jimma, Harar, Bahir Dar, Mekele, Debre Markos and Nekemte.

Brief History of CBE

As per the proclamation No. 207/1995 of October 1963, CBE took over the Commercial banking activities from State Bank of Ethiopia. It started operations on January 1, 1964 with a capital of 20 million birr in the new CBE, in contrast with the former State Bank of Ethiopia.

As part of the economic reform, different financial liberalization measures and restructuring of financial institution have been undertaken. All the measures have the aim of promoting a competitive environment and efficient banking services to the public. The CBE was re-established in 1994 by Proclamation No. 202 taking over the rights and obligations of the CBE which was established under proclamation No. 184/1980. The bank's capital has been raised and is entrusted with engaging in all banking activities as customarily carried out by commercial banks.

The Bank was wholly owned by the State and operated as an out of risk institution under the commercial code of Ethiopia.

The main objectives of the Commercial Bank of Ethiopia are:

- To extend commercial banking services throughout the country.
- To encourage the mobilization of saving by making the people aware of the use of banking operations.
- To extend loans, credits and other banking facilities to anyone person for specific purpose and periods; and
- To spread widely banking habits among the people.

Vision: World class Commercial Bank. **Mission:** We are committed to maximizing shareholder value through enhanced financial intermediation and unparallel customer satisfaction. We deploy highly motivated, skilled and disciplined employees capable of providing banking products and services that meet international practices and standards. We strongly believe that reliability and public confidence are the bases of our success.

The CBE has continued to retain its leadership position with in the banking industry of the country despite the stiff competition; it has been increasingly facing from the other banks. Its overall volume of business has also continued to grow. The CBE today has 174 branches located in many parts of the country and accounts for about fifty per cent of all the banks operating throughout the country.

ROLE OF CBE IN MANUFACTURING SECTOR DEVELOPMENT

CBE gives two different services to the customers i.e., domestic and international banking services. The domestic banking service includes deposit service, loans and advances, local transfer, safe deposit locker and other activities. The international banking services covers Deposit accounts, Foreign credit services for import and export, Letter of guarantee, Western Union agent, Documentary collections (cash against Document) (CAD) and Foreign Exchange (FOREX) services.

Loans and Advances

The CBE extends various types of loans and advances to the following business sectors.

- Domestic Trade • Import and Export trade • Agriculture • Hotels and Tourism • Manufacturing • Construction • Transport • Services (education, health, etc).

Financing Procedure of CBE—An Overview

Giving advances and accepting deposits are the most important aspects of banking business operation. The bank takes more care about lending because as it deals with others money. Bank has several financing schemes to suit the various needs of the public. It adopts different financing scheme for different purposes. The financing scheme adopted by the CBE for financing manufacturing sector is in the name of term loans and overdraft facilities.

Term loans

A term loans is a loan granted to customers to be repaid with interest in a specified period of time. The loan can be repaid in periodic installments or in a lump sum on the due date of the loan, it depends upon the case. This term loan is granted to manufacturing sector in three forms i.e. short term, medium term and long term loan.

Rate of Interest: The rate of interest charged on term loan is 7.5 per cent. Penal interest is charged for delayed payments of installments. Penal interest at rate of 3 per cent is collectable.

Short Term Loan

A short tem loan is a loan that has a maturity period of one year or 12 months from the date of loan contract signed. The loan is extended to finance the working capital needs and /or to meet other short term financial constraints of customers.

Eligibility: Applicants can be individuals and business entities engaged in any type of business that can meet the following conditions. The client must have been in the business for which the loan is requested or in a related business for at least one year with a permanent address. The applicant needs to have opened an account at the branch where the loan is required. The applicant has to present the necessary documents required by the bank. The applicant must not have any record of default and misuse of his checking account in the banking system.

Collateral: The security offered must be able to cover both the principal and the interest of the loan.

Repayment of the Loan: The loan can be repaid monthly, quarterly, semi-annually or annually in a lump sum upon maturity depending on the nature of the business and cash flow statement. The periodic repayment amount incorporates both principal and interest.

Medium and Long Term Loan (Project Loans)

A medium term loan is a loan which has a maturity period exceeding one year, but less than or equal to five years from the date of loan contract is signed. A long term loan is a loan that has a maturity period if 5 to 15 years.

Purpose of the Loan: The purpose of the loan is to finance new projects, support the expansion of the existing projects, investment to meet the working capital needs.

Eligibility: Applicants can be either new or existing customers. To be eligible for the loan, customers must present the following.

For New Projects

A feasibility study, Lease agreement and certificate, Land holding certificate and Bill of quantity and specification. (If the project involves construction), Business license from authorized government bodies, Memorandum and Articles of association, Proforma invoice (not exceeding two months), Equity contribution by the customer and Curriculum vitae of the management group.

For Existing Projects: A feasibility study, audited financial statement, list of fixed assets which include their book value and market value, the list of the market value of fixed assets to be purchased, projected financial statements.

For Enterprises to be Purchased from the Privatization Agency

Bid document, Sales contract, Bill of quantity and specification (If the Project involves construction) and the Curriculum vitae of the management group.

Collateral: In addition to the acceptable securities, customers have to offer the entire asset of the project as additional collateral.

Repayment of the Loan: Based on the nature of the project and projected cash flow statement, the loan will be repaid quarterly, semi-annually and annually.

The bank may provide a grace period for the commencement of repayments.

Overdraft

An overdraft (O/D) is a credit facility by which a customer can withdraw in excess of her/his/its current account balance up to the limit approved by the bank.

Purpose of the Loan: The loan is intended to finance the day to day operational needs of a viable business.

Eligibility: Overdrafts can be considered for manufacturing, trading and service giving enterprises. To be eligible for the facility, customer should meet the following conditions.

The business must be in operation for at least two years, applicants should have a record of satisfactory utilization of current accounts for at least the year preceding their application for overdraft facility, O/D requests will not be considered for business with no-performing credit status and/or currently blacklisted by the CBE or any other bank, applicants must have settled at least one term loan with a good repayment record, customers' seasonable or temporary financial needs will not be entertained by an overdraft, customers O/D accounts may be cancelled or converted to learn loan (partially or fully) if they fail to properly utilize the facility.

Collateral: An O/D facility can be approved against any collateral acceptable to the bank, except motor vehicles and machinery.

Loan Repayment: In the case O/D facility, interest is calculated on the amount used by the customers. Customers have to pay the accrued interest regulatory so that the facility will not be overdrawn. By the time of the request for renewal, the outstanding overdraft balances have to be fully settled. The bank can claim the outstanding balance of the O/D facility at anytime.

Distribution of Bank Finance

Total Advances and Manufacturing Sector Advances

The CBE lends money to all sectors developments. The total advances are on the basis of requirement of the concerned sector. The following table gives a complete detail about the total advances and manufacturing sector advances for the period of ten years.

Table 4.8: Total Advances and Manufacturing Sector Advances of CBE

(In Million Birr)

Sl. No.	Year	Total Loans and Advances	Total Manufacturing Sector Advances	Share of Manufacturing Sector Advances in Total (%)
1.	1995	5033.96	444.27	8.82
2.	1996	6977.71	568.63	8.14
3.	1997	8121.08	695.40	8.56
4.	1998	9066.89	760.90	8.72
5.	1999	9784.71	864.32	8.83
6.	2000	10345.05	856.47	8.28
7.	2001	10482.10	1056.20	10.08
8.	2002	9181.77	1074.85	11.71
9.	2003	8097.53	1092.72	13.49
10.	2004	7911.33	1103.79	13.95

Source: CBE Annual Report.

As per the Table 4.8, the total loans and advances are continuously increased up to the year 2001, after that it decreases. For the years 2002, 2003 and 2004, the amount of total loans and advances are Br. 9187.77, 8097.53 and 7911.53 millions respectively. The weakened domestic and international economic environment and continued tightened regulatory situation made gross outstanding loan and advances almost stagnate. The share of manufacturing sector advances in total are increasing except the years 1996 and 2000, the same information is given in the Chart 4.2.

Chart 4.2: Total Advances and Manufacturing Sector Advances of CBE

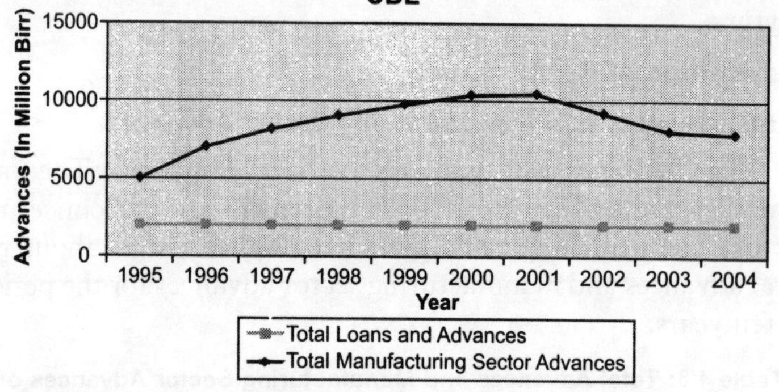

Comparison of Manufacturing Sector Advances with Agricultural and Domestic Trade Advances

The comparative details are given in the Table 4.9.

Table 4.9: Comparison of Manufacturing, Agriculture and Domestic Trade Advances

(In Million Birr)

Sl. No.	Year	Total agri. advances	Share of agri. advances in total %	Total manuf. sector advances	Share of manuf. advances in total %	Total dom. tr. advances	Share of dom. tr. advances in total %
1.	1995	147.42	2.92	444.27	8.82	2154.79	44.81
2.	1996	200.46	2.87	568.63	8.14	2956.97	42.38
3.	1997	318.11	3.92	695.40	8.56	3250.63	40.03
4.	1998	325.60	3.59	760.90	8.72	3129.86	34.52
5.	1999	404.61	4.13	864.32	8.83	2759.77	28.20
6.	2000	422.46	4.08	856.47	8.28	2643.59	19.75
7.	2001	454.72	4.34	1056.20	10.08	3460.62	33.01
8.	2002	557.38	6.07	1074.85	11.71	2768.25	30.15
9.	2003	489.61	6.05	1092.72	13.49	2795.44	34.52
10.	2004	481.69	6.09	1103.79	13.95	3251.14	41.09

Source: CBE Annual reports and computed.

As per the Table 4.9, Domestic trade advances occupies a dominant percentage in the total advances. Next to the Domestic trade, the manufacturing sector plays an important role. When we compare the manufacturing sector with agriculture and domestic trade, this sector advances are continuously increased except 1996 and 2000. The comparative information are given in the Chart 4.3.

Chart 4.3: Comparison of Agri., Manufacturing and Domestic Trade Advances

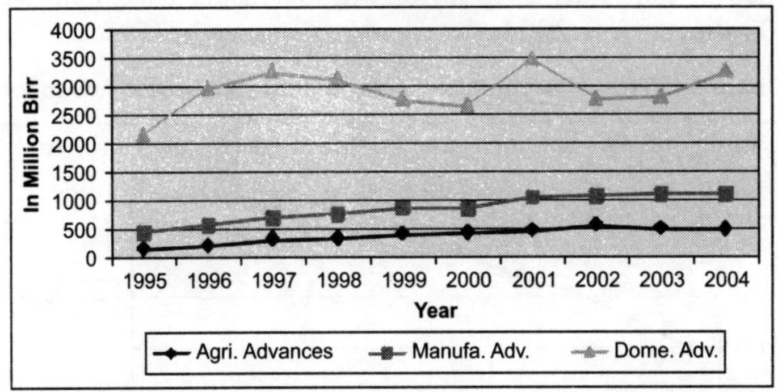

Trend Analysis

Ten years advances of CBE to the manufacturing sector are taken for the purpose of calculation of trend percentage, the years 1995 to 2004 are taken for this purpose. The year 1995 is taken as a base year, the trend percentage details are given in the Table 4.10.

Table 4.10: Trend Percentage of Manufacturing Sector Advances

(Base Year 1995) (In Million Birr)

Sl. No.	Year	Manufacturing Sector Advances	Trend Percentage
1.	1995	444.27	100
2.	1996	568.63	128
3.	1997	695.40	156
4.	1998	760.90	171
5.	1999	864.32	195
6.	2000	856.47	193
7.	2001	1056.20	238

(Contd...)

Sl. No.	Year	Manufacturing Sector Advances	Trend Percentage
8.	2002	1074.85	242
9.	2003	1092.72	246
10.	2004	1103.79	250

Source: CBE Annual Reports and computed.

The Table 4.10 clearly indicates the trend percentage of manufacturing sector advances by CBE. It is very clear that the trends of manufacturing sector are increasing except the year 2000. In the year 2004, the trend percentage is 250.

Chart 4.4: Trend Percentage of Manufacturing Sector Advances

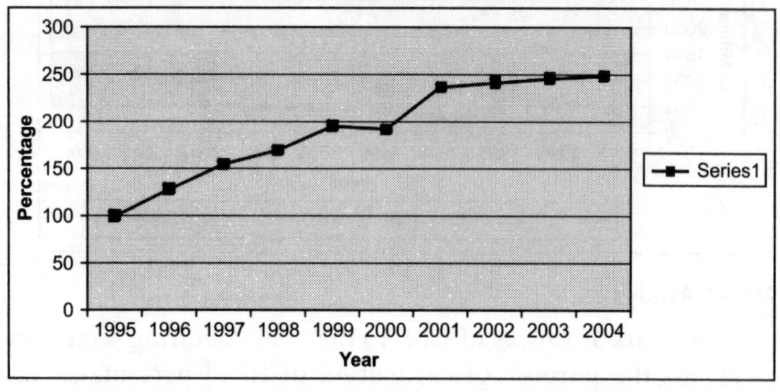

SUMMARY, CONCLUSION AND SUGGESTIONS

Summary of Findings

With the help of the analysis, the researcher has observed the following findings. The findings are as follows:

1. The loans and advances have increased from the year 1994-95 to 2000-01.
2. The loans and advances have started to decrease from the fiscal year 2001-02.
3. The main reasons for slight decrease in the total loans and advances in the year 2002-03 and 2004 are weakened domestic and international economic environment and continued tightened regulatory situation.

4. The share of manufacturing sector adavances in total (percentage) advances is increasing except the years 1996 and 2000.
5. The amount-wise advances of the CBE to the manufacturing sectors are increasing except the year 2000.
6. When comparing with other sectors advances, the manufacturing sector advances are continuously increasing.
7. The trend of manufacturing sector advances by the CBE has increased.
8. In the year 2004, the trend of manufacturing sector advances are 250 per cent.
9. Within 10 years, the manufacturing sector advances are increased by 150 per cent.

Suggestions

Gross loans and advances for the year 2004 amounted to Birr 7911.33 million which is lower than that of the proceeding year by 2.3 per cent. This could be attributed to the decrease in fresh loans disbursement; hence, the bank should take necessary steps to increase the loans and advances to all sectors and in specific manufacturing sector.

At present, the share of manufacturing sector advances in total is increasing trend, therefore the bank should maintain the similar policy on the manufacturing sector lending.

Conclusion

The primary function of CBE is the extension of credit to worthy borrowers. Through the extension of credit, CBE render a great deal of social services through their actions, production is increased, investments are expanded, and a higher standard of living is realized. Through the realization of this function, CBE participates in the financing of manufacturing sector. In simple, CBE plays a very important role in the effort to attain the economic growth in the country as a whole.

REFERENCES

Books

1. Katsundo Hitomi. *Manufacturing Systems Engineering*, II Edition, Taylor and Francis Publishers, 1996.
2. Haile Hagos. *Sectoral Analysis of the Ethiopian Economy*, I Edition, HHB Publishers, Addis Ababa, 1995.
3. Solomon Ayele. *A New Guide to Secondary School Geography Grades 9-12*, I Edition, Aster Publishing Private Limited Company, 1991 EC.
4. Mesfin Wolde Mariam. *An Introductory Geography of Ethiopia*, I Edition, Berhanena Selam H.S.I. Printing Press, Addis Ababa, 1972.
5. Philip F. Ostwald, Jiro Munoz. *Manufacturing Processes and Systems*, IX Edition, John Wiley and Sons, 2002.
6. P.N. Rao. *Manufacturing Technology, Foundry Forming and Welding*, 12th Revised Edition, Tata McGraw Hill Publishing Company Limited, 1998.
7. Shekhar and Shekhar. *Banking and Practice*, 18th Revised Edition, Vikas Publishing House, Private Limited, New Delhi.
8. *Master Books Team Work For Grades 9 and 10*, Kuraz International Publishing Enterprises, Addis Ababa, 2006.

Reports

1. "Addis Ababa Business Directory" 2000-01 and 2001-02 Editions, Addis Ababa Chamber of Commerce.
2. "Second Annual Report on the Ethiopian Economy", Addis Ababa.
3. Central Statistical Authorities, "Statistical Abstract 2001, 2002 and 2003", Addis Ababa.
4. CSA. "Repot on Large and Medium Scale Manufacturing and Electricity Industries" Survey Addis Ababa.
5. "Ethiopian Trade Directory 1990," Chamber of Commerce, Addis Ababa.
6. Commercial Bank of Ethiopia: Annual Reports
CBE Forum
CBE News Letters
7. National Bank of Ethiopia: Annual Reports
Quarterly Bulletins

Working Papers

1. Seifr Dendir, "Prudential Performance of the Ethiopian Banking Sector" (1991-92—1997-98).

2. Hassan Ghaziri, "Information Technology in the Banking Sector: Opportunities and Strategies" 1998.
3. Charles Harrey: "Banking Reform in Ethiopia."
4. NBE : Supervision of Banking Business Directories.
5. Monetary and Banking Proclamation No. 83/1994.
6. Licensing and Supervision of Banking Business No. 84/1994.

Measuring Service Quality: A Re-Examination and Extension in the Banking Sector of an Islamic Country

Kambiz Heidarzadeh Hanzaee

ABSTRACT

During the past few decades service quality has become a major area of attention to practitioners, managers and researchers owing to its strong impact on business performance, lower costs, customer satisfaction, customer loyalty and profitability.

The operation of Islamic bank derives from the Islamic Law and thus differs in spirit, cultural background and practice from conventional bank operations. Because of the strong competition, customer expectation to receive high quality services and quick changes of technology, Islamic banks must, therefore think strategically by providing high quality products and services to satisfy their customers. This study indicates that it is important for Islamic banks to put cultural differences at the front when adopting SQ, and suggests using an Asian model to measure SQ which is presented by SRK (2002).

It focuses on investigating the critical factors of customer perceived service quality in banks of a developing economy—Iran. Compares and contrasts the three groups of bank in Iran with respect to the service quality factors from the perspective of the customers. There seems to be a great amount of variation with respect to the level of service quality offered by the three groups of banks. Identifies the factors that discriminate the three groups of banks. Customer in developing economies seem to keep the "technological factors" of service such as core service and systematization of the service delivery as the yardstick in differentiating good and bad service while the "human factors" seem to play a lesser role in discriminating the three groups of banks. The service quality indices with respect to the three groups and the Iranian banking industry as whole, offer interesting information on the level of service quality delivered by banks in Iran.

The Selected Conference Theme

Banking, Finance and Accounting Services

INTRODUCTION

The banking industry in Iran has witnessed for the last decade several regulatory changes that have resulted in a heightened level of competition among the banks.

The historical lack of interest in services can be partly explained by the fact that there was little understanding of the differences between the management of services and the management of manufacturing organization (Bitran and Lojo, 1993: 271-82). However, it is true that basic management principles are similar for both types of companies; services have some characteristics that require a different emphasis from management on some of these principles. The characteristics that differentiate services from manufacturing in terms of quality have been described by many writers (Bitran and Lojo, 1993: 271-82, Parasuraman et al., 1993: 140-47) as follows:

- Nature of products which are basically intangible in services including a tangible action, so customer satisfaction in services is not only influenced by objective measures of performance but also influenced by intangible aspects during the service performance.
- Heterogeneity, that creates another challenge for quality management in services, because quality in service is not just ensuring conformity to standards, but taking into account service diversity of customers while the service delivery is taking place, the behaviour and expectation of the customer being served and to customise the service delivery accordingly.

- Simultaneity which means most services are produced and consumed in the same time. That represents a difficulty in quality management of services because it is not usually feasible to actively monitor all service deliveries that are taking place and the service cannot be inspected before its consumption.
- The human contact, because services are often characterised by the existence of human contact between employee and the customer.

As a result of the above differences and in addition to the vague of quality concept, many attempts to define quality, total quality management (TQM), and finally SQ found in the literature.

The majority of researches on SQ support the following definition; quality is "What the customer says it is", thus, how could Islamic banks know whether they give services which are judged 100 per cent satisfactory by 100 per cent of their customers? They would have to ask, observe, find out from the customers themselves, see whether they recommended the bank to others or not, and so on. Therefore, a focus on the customers is the key to adopt and deliver SQ or total SQ management, TSQM as John Peters (1999) named it. The Islamic bank must think about quality this way, because if it figures out what its customers like and delivers it the same in everytime, they will come back and tell others about bank services and successes.

In contrast to this, Parasuraman, working with Zeithaml and Berry (1985), concentrated from the outset on SQ. their so-called "Gap" school defined SQ as the "degree and direction of discrepancy between customer's perceptions of service expectation".

The other way to think about quality is operations' efficiency, that means if the bank can discover the most efficient ways to produce products and services, stop wasting time and materials, and replace unsatisfactory services, it will also become more successful.

Therefore, SQ tends to play an important role in many service industries, such as banking services, because excellent SQ is not an optional competitive strategy which may, or may not, be adopted to differentiate one bank from another, but it becomes an essential to corporate profitability and survival. as banks become more "high-tech," their technical services are becoming standardized, reducing the importance of such services as a differentiating factor; thus, consumers will evaluate banks based more on their "high-tech" factors than on their "high-tech" factors (Angur et al., 1999: 116-23). However, for instance, many banks have provided financial incentive for consumers to utilize automatic teller machines (ATMs), such as teller fees, etc. the "unique selling proposition" (Kotler, 1997) of a bankstill appears to be personal banking services. Furthermore they could use only personal banking services to promote effectively to their target market as referred by (Urban & Hauser, 1993) "core benefit proposition". In view of this, SQ has become a key contrast in the banking industry.

The main objective for this paper is to examine the performance of alternative measures of SQ proposed by different authors, such as Parasuraman, Berry and Ziethaml (1985, 1988, 1993 & 1994), and Cronin and Taylor (1992 & 1994), in an Islamic banking industry and also to suggest unique measures that might be used by Islamic banks and to test whether they are valid or not.

DETERMINANTS OF CUSTOMER-PERCEIVED SERVICE QUALITY

Instrument for Measuring Service Quality

The research literature on service quality contains numerous models by different researchers across the world. However, the SERVQUAL instrument (Parasuraman et al., 1988: 12-40) a 22 item scale that measures service quality along five factors, namely: reliability; responsiveness; assurance; empathy; and tangibles, forms the foundation on which all other works have been built. Interestingly, the conceptualization, dimensionality, operationalization, measurement and applications of SERVQUAL have been subjected to some severe criticisms as well (Buttle, 1996: 8-32). In spite of such reprehension on the efficacy of SERVQUAL across different service setting, there is a general agreement that the 22 items are reasonably good predictors of service quality in its wholeness. But a careful scrutiny of the 22 items implies that the item at large deal with the element of human interaction/intervention in the service delivery and the rest on the tangible facets of service such as the effect of atmospherics, design and décor elements, appearance, etc.

Therefore, the SERVQUAL instrument seems to have overlooked some other important factors of service quality namely:

- The service product or the core service;
- Systematization/standardization of service delivery (the non-human elements);
- The social responsibility of the service organization (Sureshchandar et al., 2003: 234).

In an effort to conceptualize service quality by taking into account all the aspects of customer-perceived service quality, including those already addressed in the existing instruments and those that are left out in the empirical service quality literature, (Sureshchandar et al., 2001: 111-24) identified five factors of service quality as critical from the customers' point of view (SRK model). These factors are:

1. Core service or service product;
2. Human element of service delivery;
3. Systematization of service delivery: non-human element;
4. Tangibles of service-service capes; and
5. Social responsibility.

Numerous other research studies have discussed in detail the importance of the aforementioned factors of service quality. Table 5.1 depicts the literature evidence on the criticality of these service-quality factors from the customers' point of view. Table 5.2 briefly summarizes the different factors of service quality. In another research work (Sureshchandar et al., 2002: 9-34) empirically validated the proposed service-quality factors, by developing a survey instrument consisting of 41 items.

Table 5.1: Topology of the Quality Management Literature Accentuating the Criticality of the Various Factors of Service Quality from the Perspective of the Customers

Critical Factors	Literature Evidence
Core service or service product	Neslin (1983); Chapman and Jackson (1987); Hauser and Clausing (1988); Rust and Oliver (1994); Schneider and Bowen (1995);
Human element of service	Parasuraman et al. (1985, 1988, 1991, 1994a,b); Schneider and Bowen (1985, 1992, 1993, 1995); Mills and Morris (1986); Norman (1991); Harber et al. (1993a, b); Stebbing (1993); Schneider et al. (1994, 1996a, b)
Systematization of service delivery: non-human element	Sasser and Fulmer (1990); Zemke and Schaaf (1990); Spenley (1994); Ahire et al., (1995); Milakovich (1995); Smith (1995)
Tangibles of service-service capes	Shostack (1977a, b); Booms and Bitner (1982); Rapport (1982); Parasuraman et al. (1985, 1988, 1991, 1994a, b); Upah and Fulton (1985); Zeithmal et al. (1985); Bitner (1986); Berry and Clark (1986); Baker (1987); Schneider and Bown (1995)
Social responsibility	Zemke and Schaaf (1990)

Source: Sureshchandar et al., 2003: 235.

This instrument has been developed on the basis of an exhaustive review of the literature (prescriptive, conceptual, empirical and practitioner) and also based on a pilot survey among customers of banks in Iran. Feedback has also been collected from experts (i.e. academicians and researchers) in the field. The instrument has been refined several times based on the pilot study findings and on the comments and suggestions of the experts. Also, the instrument has been developed in order to maximally capture all the aspects of service quality, and to specifically address the issues of the banking industry. The different operating elements of service quality with respect to the five factors are presented in the appendix.

Methodology and Instrument Standardization

The items with respect to the various dimensions have been jumbled and arranged in a random order in the instrument. The sampling procedure used for the study was stratified random sampling. The stratification has been done based on the type of bank (e.g. public sector, private sector and specialized bank). Table 5.2 shows the name of some of the Iranian banks in each sector.

Table 5.2: The Name of Banks in Each Sector

Category of Banks		
Public Sector	Private Sector	Specialized Sector
Bank Melli Iran	Saman Bank	Bank of Industry and Mine
Bank Sepah	Eghtesade Novin Bank	Export Development Bank
Bank Saderat Iran	Karafarin Bank	...
Bank Tejarat	Parsian Bank	
Bank Mellat	...	
Bank Saderat		
Bank Refah Kargaran		
Bank Keshavarzi		
Bank Maskan	...	

From each group of banks, about 300 customers (retail banking) have been randomly selected. Data have been collected using the "personal-contact" approach, i.e. the respondents have been approached personally and given a detailed explanation about the survey (including its purpose, the meaning of the items and what is expected of the respondents).

Questionnaires have been distributed to the customers and they have been asked to give their perception of the level of service quality delivered by the banks on a Seven point Likert scale (ranging from 1 – indicating very poor to 7 – indicating very good). The respondents have been asked to contact the researchers, whenever they encounter any difficulty in responding to the questionnaire.

A total of 904 customers from 101 different banks have been approached, from whom 554 correctly completed questionnaires from 86 banks have been obtained, thereby yielding a response rate of about 60 per cent. Table 5.3 shows the number of banks in each sector and the corresponding number of respondents (customers) who have participated in the study. The high response rate is due to the personal-contact approach used followed by periodic follow-ups over the telephone and personal visits.

Table 5.3: Distribution of Respondents (Customers) Among the Three Groups of Banks

	Category of Banks			
	Public sector	Private sector	Specialized sector	Total
Number of banks	30	28	28	86
Number of respondents	196	172	186	554

The standardization of the instrument has been carried out by test of unidimensionality, reliability, convergent validity, discriminant validity and criterion-related validities using a confirmatory factor analysis approach. The service-quality factors thus arrived at from the basis for the analysis reported in the present study.

ANALYSES, RESULTS AND DISCUSSION

An attempt is being made here to study the level of service quality (from the viewpoint of the customers) in the Iranian banking sector. The difference between the three groups of banks with respect to service quality delivered to the customers have been found by using ANOVA, along with the *post hoc* test of Bonferroni (Darlington, 1990) and multiple discriminant analysis. Service quality indices (SQI) have also been calculated for the three sectors of banks.

Discrimination in the Three Groups of Banks with Respect to Customer-perceived Service Quality—ANOVA and Bonferroni

The three groups of banks have been compared from the customers' view of service quality in order to accomplish comparison; the following hypotheses have been tested:

H1. There is no significant difference between the three groups of banks in terms of service quality with respect to core service.

H2. There is no significant difference between the three groups of banks in terms of service quality with respect to human element of service delivery.

H3. There is no significant difference between the three groups of banks in terms of service quality with respect to the standardization of service delivery.

H4. There is no significant difference between the three groups of banks in terms of service quality with respect to tangible of service.

H5. There is no significant difference between the three groups of banks in terms of service quality with respect to social responsibility.

The results of ANOVA and the post hoc test of Bonferroni for the five factors are summarized in Table 5.4. It can be inferred from the F values that there are significant differences between the three groups of banks with respect to all the five factors of service quality. Therefore H1 to H5 have been rejected implying significant relationships between the three groups of banks with respect to all the five factors of service quality.

Table 5.4: Results of ANOVA and Benferroni to Test for Significant Differences Between the Three Groups of Banks in Terms of Service Quality with Respect to the Five Factors (H1-H5)

Sl. No.	Critical dimensions	ANOVA (F) Benferroni comparisons
1.	Core service or service product	66.45** PSB – PtSB*, PSB – FB*, PTsb – FB*
2.	Human element of service delivery	46.64** PSB – PtSB*, PSB – FB*, PTsb – FB*
3.	Systematization of service delivery: non-human element	51.34** PSB – PtSB*, PSB – FB*, PTsb – FB*
4.	Tangibles of service-service capes	37.66** PSB – PtSB*, PSB – FB*, PTsb – FB*
5.	Social responsibility	39.77** PSB – PtSB*, PSB – FB*, PTsb – FB^{NS}

Notes: (*): Significant at the 0.05 level; (**): Significant at the 0.01 level; (NS): not significant

Further, the Bonferroni comparisons have related significant differences between public sector banks and private sector banks, public sector banks and specialized sector banks, private sector banks and specialized sector banks with respect to four out of the five factors of service quality, namely:

1. Core service;
2. Human element of service delivery;
3. Standardization of service delivery; and
4. The tangible facet of service.

With respect to social responsibility there are significant differences between public sector banks and private sector banks and public sector banks and specialized sector banks. But there are no significant differences between private sector banks and specialized banks in the case of social responsibility.

Discrimination in the Three Groups of Bank with Respect to Customer-perceived Service Quality—Multiple Discriminant Analysis

In order to ascertain the factors that discriminate the three groups of banks most, the following hypothesis has been formulated:

H6. There is no significant difference between the three groups of banks with respect to all the service-quality factors taken together.

In order to test the above hypothesis, multiple discriminant analysis has been performed on the five factors of service quality. The results of the discriminant analysis showing the significance of the discriminant functions are shown in Table 5.5.

Table 5.5: Results of the Discriminant Analysis—Significance of the Discriminant Functions

Function	Eigen value	% of variance	Canonical correlation	Wilk's lamda	dof	x^2
1.	2.12	98.53	0.82	0.31	10	317.78*
2.	0.03	1.47	0.18	0.97	4	8.46^{NS}

Notes: (*): Significant at the 0.01 level; (NS): not significant

It can be observed that the first function turned out to be highly significant, while the second function is not. The first function contribution to 98.53 per cent of the variance and the second function contributes to just 1.47 per cent of the variance.

The Wilk's Iamda transformed as the x^2 for function 1 has found a significant difference between the three groups with both the functions taken together. The Wilk's Iamda for the second function has turned out to be insignificant in differentiating the three groups.

Therefore, H6 is rejected indicating significant differences among the three groups of banks with respect to all the factors of service quality across the first function only.

The results of the structure matrix, i.e. structural correlations between the dimensions and the canonical discriminant function are shown in Table 5.6. These values indicate the relative contributions of the service-quality factors in discriminating the three groups of banks.

Table 5.6: Results of the Discriminant Analysis—Structure Matrix

Factor	Function 1	Function 2
Systematization of service quality	0.41	0.60[a]
Core service	0.47	0.56[a]
Social responsibility	0.36	0.53[a]
Tangibles	0.35	0.47[a]
Human element of service delivery	0.40	0.29

Note: [a] Denotes largest absolute correlation between each variable and any discriminant function

The results of discriminant analysis have indicated that the technological factors (viz. systematization of service delivery and core service) seem to be contributing more to the discrimination than the people-oriented factors (namely, the human element of service delivery). This may be because of the fact that in developing countries like Iran, the standardization of the technological aspects of service production and delivery is yet to take place resulting in high variation among these factors across the different groups of banks. This finding is in contrast to the developed countries, where there is a good level of standardization of the technological factors, and hence customers view the human aspects of service delivery for differentiating services (Angur, 1999: 116-123). This observation also shows that the human element of service delivery appears to be almost equally prevalent among the three groups of banks as far as developing countries are concerned

SQI for the Different Factors of Service Quality Among the Three Groups of Banks

The SQI values for the different factors of service quality with respect to the three sectors are summarized in the Table 5.7.

Table 5.7: SQI for the Three Groups of Banks

Sl. No.	Factor	Public Sector	Private Sector	Specialized Sector	Overall
1.	Core service	4.44	5.53	6.24	5.38
2.	Human element of service delivery	4.55	5.5	5.99	5.41
3.	Systematization of service quality	4.49	5.37	6.02	5.26
4.	Tangibles of service	4.35	5.25	5.87	5.14
5.	Social responsibility	6.46	4.56	4.41	5.18

The SQI for a particular sector (public sector, privet sector and specialized banks) with respect to a particular factor is the average value (mean of the customers' scores) of that factor score per item. For instance, the SQI for core service with respect to public sector banks has been computed to be 4.44. This is calculated by taking the average of the 196 responses (number of respondents in the public sector category) and normalizing it by dividing by five (number of items with respect to this dimension).

The SQI for the three groups have shown that the specialized banks perform well with respect to four of the five factors of service quality (with the exception of social responsibility). Having competed with world class banks in other countries, the specialized banks, no wonder, are able to deliver top class service, especially in terms of developing and delivering service products (e.g. ATM, room service facility, telephonic banking, round the clock banking, and other innovative service products) more effectively and by streamlining their operations (evident from the high SQI they got for the factors core service and systematization of service delivery). Banking being a high contact service, in addition to what is delivered and how it is delivered (both human and non-human aspects), the physical environment also has a great impact on the service perceptions by customers.

The specialized banks seem to be doing well in this aspect as well. Close to the heels of the specialized banks are private sector banks which also do fairly well with respect to these four factors. But, the lack of responsibility to society by both specialized banks and private sector banks is evident from their poor SQI for social responsibility.

The public sector banks with their wide network of branches, serving as a guiding mechanism for the socioeconomic metamorphosis of the country, are naturally perceived to have high social responsibility by the customers. But their SQI for the other four factors are not encouraging. The public sector banks have been taking the customers for granted as there were not many alternatives available to the customers. But with the entry of the private sector banks and specialized banks, Iranian customers have now more options to choose from. In addition, the customers tend to compare the services offered by public sector banks with their counterparts in the private sector and specialized categories, thereby giving a poor rating to public sector banks on these factors. Customer service is such an important aspect of the banking industry that if organizations tend to overlook it, it may prove disastrous for them. Only if public sector banks take immediate action on focussing more on the service quality issue immediately, will they be able to keep pace with specialized banks and private sector banks, in terms of delivering quality service in the foreseeable future.

The SQI for all the banks taken together here indicates a reasonably good performance with all the indices exceeding "7" on a seven-point scale. This is again because of the presence of specialized banks and private sector banks, which have done very well with respect to these dimensions. But a lot seems to be desired in terms of delivering quality service when compared to the excellent services that are provided by world class banks.

CONCLUSION

The present study has critically examined the service-quality issues (from the perspective of customers) with respect to a developing economy—Iran. The three groups of banks in Iran (public sector, private sector and specialized sector) have been compared with respect to each of the five factors of service quality. The three groups of banks in Iran seem to vary significantly in terms of the delivery of the five service-quality, factors. From the customer perceptions of service quality, the technological factors (core service and systematization of the service delivery) appear to contribute more in differentiating the three sectors while the people-oriented factor (human element of service delivery) appears to contribute less to the discrimination. The results have also indicated that specialized banks seem to be performing well followed by private sector banks and public sector banks. The overall SQI for the different service-quality factors have revealed that there is considerable scope for improvement as regards the Iranian scenario.

This research work has been carried out in Iran (which is a developing economy), and hence there is a possibility of cultural bias playing a role in the outcome of the study as quality management practices in developing economies may vary significantly from those of developed economies. For example, the study has established that the technological factors seem to be the differentiating factor among the three groups of banks as far as customer perceptions of service quality are concerned. This finding highlights the unstable nature of these facets in developing economies, which may not be true in developed economies. Therefore, there is a need to duplicate this study in developed economies as well.

Such transnational studies across different nations and economies are indispensable for a clear understanding of the criticality of the various factors of customer-perceived service quality across different cultures. This is even truer given the fact that the research issues with respect to service quality have been extensively researched in developed economies, while there is a scarcity of such research works (especially empirical) in developing economies, the present study, therefore attempts to add value to the topic of bank service quality, especially in a developing economy, from the perspective of the customers.

APPENDIX I: INSTRUMENTS FOR MEASURING CUSTOMER PERCEPTIONS OF SERVICE QUALITY

The service quality instrument has asked for the respondents' perception of the actual level of service quality delivered by the bank with respect to the 41 items on a seven-point Likert scale as shown below:

Very poor;
Poor;
Slightly poor;
Average;
Slightly good;
Good; and
Very good.

The items have been jumbled and arranged in a random order in the original instrument. The items corresponding to the five factors of service quality and customer satisfaction are given below.

(a) Core service or service product

1. Diversity and range of services (having a wider range of financial services from the bank, e.g. deposits, retirement accounts, loans for purchases of cars, houses, foreign exchange, traveler's cheques, safe deposit lockers, etc.).
2. Intensity and depth of service (having a higher number of options in every service/transaction, e.g. various fixed deposit or recurring deposit schemes with different interest rates, quick cheque clearing facility with a higher service charge, etc.).
3. Service innovation (providing information/details on a regular basis through post; telephonic banking; ATM; room service facility; cards to defence personnel, etc.).
4. Availability of most service operations in every branch/ department of the bank.
5. Convenient operating hours and days (e.g. working on Saturdays and Sundays, extended service hours during evenings, weekdays, etc.).

(b) Human element of service delivery

1. Providing services as promised.
2. Effectiveness of the employees' skills and ability for actions, whenever a critical incident takes place (i.e. when a problem arises).
3. Whenever a critical incident takes place (i.e. when a problem arises), the degree to which the organization succeeds in bringing the condition back to normality by satisfying the customer.
4. Providing services right the first time.
5. Providing services as per the promised schedule.
6. Apprising the customers of the nature and schedule of services available in the bank.
7. Prompt service to customers.
8. Willingness to help customers and the readiness to respond to customers' requests.
9. Extent to which the feedback from customers is used to improve service standards.
10. Regularly apprising the customers about information on service quality and actual service performance *versus* targets in the organization.
11. Employees who instill confidence in customers by proper behaviour.
12. Making customers feel safe and secure in their transactions.
13. Employees who are consistently pleasing and courteous.
14. Employees who have the knowledge and competence to answer customers' specific queries and requests.
15. Effectiveness of customer grievance procedures and processes.
16. Giving caring and individual attention to customers by having the customers' best interests at heart.
17. Employees who understand the needs of their customers.

(c) Systematization of service delivery: non-human element

1. Having a highly standardized and simplified delivery process so that services are delivered without any hassles or excessive bureaucracy.
2. Having highly simplified and structured delivery processes so that the service delivery times are minimal.
3. Enhancement of technological capability (e.g. computerization, networking of operations, etc.) to serve customers more effectively.
4. Degree to which the procedures and processes are perfectly fool-proof.
5. Adequate and necessary personnel for good customer service.
6. Adequate and necessary facilities for good customer service.

(d) Tangibles of service (services capes)

1. The ambient conditions such as temperature, ventilation, noise and odour prevailing in the bank's premises.
2. Extent of the physical layout of equipment and other furnishings being comfortable for customers to interact with employees.
3. Having house keeping as a priority and of the highest order in the organization.
4. Visually appealing signs, symbols, advertisement boards, pamphlets and other artifacts in the bank.
5. Employees who have a neat and professional appearance.
6. Visually appealing materials and facilities associated with the service.

(e) Social responsibility

1. Equal treatment stemming from the belief that every one, big or small, should be treated alike.
2. "Service transcendence"—making customers realize their unexpressed needs by giving more than what they expect.

3. Giving good service at a reasonable cost, but not at the expense of quality.
4. Having branch locations in most places convenient to all sections of the society (e.g. villages, down town areas, etc.)
5. A social responsibility characterized by "deserving service" to people belonging to all strata of the society (e.g. giving loans to economically and socially downtrodden people, needy ones, entrepreneurs, etc. with less rigid loan conditions associated with security, flexible repayment modality, and easy credit terms).
6. A sense of public responsibility among employees (in terms of being punctual, regular, sincere and without going on strikes).
7. Extent to which the organization leads as a corporate citizen and the level to which it promotes ethical conduct in everything it does.

REFERENCES

Ahire, L.S., Landeros, R. and Golhar, D.Y. (1995). "Total Quality Management: A Literature Review and an Agenda for Future Research", *Production and Operations Management*, Vol. 4, No. 3, pp. 277-306.

Angur, M.G., Nataraajan, R. and Jahera, J.S. (1999). "Service Quality in the Banking Industry: An Assessment in a Developing Economy", *International Journal of Bank Marketing*, Vol. 17, No. 3, pp. 116-23.

Baker, J. (1987), "The Role of the Environment in Marketing Services: The Consumer Perspective", in Czepiel, J.A., Congram, C.A., Shanahan, J. (Eds). *The Service Challenge: Integrating for Competitive Advantage*, American Marketing Association, Chicago, IL, pp. 79-84.

Berry, L.L. and Clark, T. (1986). "Four Ways to make Services more Tangible", *Business*, October-December, pp. 53-4.

Bitner, M.J. (1986). "Consumer Responses to the Physical Environment in Service Settings", in Venkatesan, M., Schmalensee, D.M. and Marshall, C. (Eds), *Creativity in Services Marketing*. American Marketing Association, Chicago, IL, pp. 89-93.

Bitran, G. and Lojo, H. (1993). "A Framework for Analysing Service Operations", *European Management Journal*, Vol. 11, No. 3, pp. 271-82.

Booms, B.H. and Bitner, M.J. (1982). "Marketing Services by Managing the Environment", *Cornell Hotel and Restaurant Administration Quarterly*, Vol. 23, No. 5, pp. 35-39.

Buttle, F. (1996). "SERVQUAL: Review, Critique, Research Agenda", *European Journal of Marketing*, Vol. 30, No. 1, pp. 8-32.

Cornin, J. and Taylor, S. (1992). "Measuring SQ: A Re-examination and Extension", *Journal of Marketing*, Vol. 56, July, pp. 55-68.

Cornin, J. and Taylor, S. (1994). "SERVPERF versus SERVQUAL: Reconciling Performance-based and Perceptions-minus-expectations Measurement of SQ", *Journal of Marketing*, Vol. 58, January, pp. 55-68.

Darlington, R.B. (1990). *Regression and Linear Models*, McGraw-Hill, Singapore.

Harber, D., Burgess, K. and Barclay, D. (1993). "Total Quality Management as a Cultural Intervention: An Integrative Review", *International Journal of Quality and Reliability Management*, Vol. 10, No. 6, pp. 17-27.

——. "Total Quality Management as a Cultural Intervention: An Empirical Study", *International Journal of Quality and Reliability Management*, Vol. 10, No. 6, pp. 28-46.

Hauser, J.R. and Clausing, G.I. (1988). "The House of Quality", *Harvard Business Review*, Vol. 66, No., pp. 63-73.

Kotler, P. (1997). *Marketing Management: Analysis, Planning, Implementation, and Control*, 9th ed., Prentice Hall, Inc., Englewood Cliffs, NJ.

Mills, P.K. and Morris, J.H. (1986). "Clients as Partial Employees of Service Organizations: Role Development in Client Farticipation", *Academy of Management Review*, Vol. 11, No. 4, pp. 726-35.

Neslin, S.A. (1983). "Designing New Outpatient Health Services: Linking Service Features to Subjective Consumer Perceptions", *Journal of Health Care Marketing*, Vol. 3, pp. 8-21.

Norman, R. (1991). *Service Management*, John Wiley & Sons, Chichester.

Parasuraman, A., Zeithaml, V.A. and Berry, L.L. (1985). "A Conceptual Model of Service Quality and its Implications for Future Research", *Journal of Marketing*, Vol. 49, No. 4, pp. 41-50.

—— (1988). "SERVQUAL: A Multiple-item Scale for Measuring Consumer Perceptions of Service Quality", *Journal of Retailing*, No. Spring, pp. 12-40.

—— (1991). "Refinement and Reassessment of the SERVQUAL Scale", *Journal of Retailing*, Vol. 67, No. 4, pp. 420-50.

—— (1993). "Research Note: More on Improving SQ Measurement", *Journal of Retailing*, Vol. 69, No. Spring, pp. 140-147.

—— (1994). "Alternative Scales for Measuring Service Quality: A Comparative Assessment Based on Psychometric and Diagnostic Criteria", *Journal of Retailing*, Vol. 70, No. Fall, pp. 201-30.

—— (1994). "Reassessment of Expectations as a Comparison Standard in Measuring Service Quality: Implications for Further Research", *Journal of Marketing*, Vol. 58, No. January, pp. 111-24.

Peters, J. (1999). "Total SQ Management", *Managing SQ*, Vol. 29, No. 1, pp. 6-12.

Rapoport, A. (1982). *The Meaning of the Built Environment*, Sage Publications, Beverly Hills, CA.

Sasser, E.W., et al. (1990). "Creating Personalized Service Delivery Systems", in Bowen, D.E. (Eds), *Service Management Effectiveness*, Jossey-Bass, San Francisco, CA, pp. 213-33.

Schneider, B. and Bowen, D.E. (1985). "Employee and Customer Perceptions of Service in Banks: Replication and Extension", *Journal of Applied Psychology*, Vol. 70, No. 3, pp. 423-33.

—— (1992). "Personnel/human Resources Management in the Service Sector", *Research in Personnel and Human Resource Management*, Vol. 10, pp. 1-30.

—— (1993). "The Service Organization: Human Resources Management is Crucial", *Organizational Dynamics*, Vol. 21, No. 3, pp. 39-52.

—— (1995). *Winning the Service Game*, Business School Press, Boston, MA.

Schneider, B., Brief, A.P. and Guzzo, R.A. (1996). "Creating a Climate and Culture for Sustainable Organizational Change", *Organizational Dynamics*, Vol. 24, pp. 7-19.

Schneider, B., Gunnarson, S.K. and Niles-Jolly, K. (1994). "Creating the Climate and Culture of Success", *Organizational Dynamics*, Vol. 23, pp. 17-29.

Schneider, B., et al. (1996). "Design, Validity, and Use of Strategically Focused Employee Attitude Surveys", *Personnel Psychology*, Vol. 49, pp. 695-705.

Shostack, G.L. (1977). "Breaking Free from Product Marketing", *Journal of Marketing*, Vol. 41, No. April, pp. 73-80.

Shostack, G.L. (1977). "Banks Sell Services—Not Things", *Bankers Magazine*, Vol. 32, No. Winter, pp. 40-5.

Smith, S. (1995). *The Quality Revolution*, Jaico Publishing House, Bombay.

Spenley, P. (Ed.) (1994). *Total Quality Management—A Peratec Executive Briefing*, Chapman & Hall, London.

Stebbing, L. (1993). *Quality Management in the Service Industry*, Ellis Horwood, Chichester.

Sureshchandar, G.S., Rajendran, C. and Kamalanabhan, T.J. (2001). "Customer Perceptions of Service Quality—A Critique", *Total Quality Management*, Vol. 12, No. 1, pp. 111-24.

Sureshchandar, G.S., Rajendran, C., Anantharaman, R.N. (2002). "Determinants of Customer Perceived Service Quality: A Confirmatory Factor Analysis Approach", *Journal of Services Marketing*, Vol. 16, No. 1, pp. 9-34.

Sureshchandar, G.S., Chandrasekharan, Rajendran and Anantharaman R.N. (2003). "Customer Perceptions of Service Quality in the Banking Sector of a Developing Economy: A Critical Analysis", *International Journal of Bank Marketing*, Vol. 21, No. 5, pp. 233-42.

Upah, G.D. and Fulton, J.M. (1985). "Situation Creation in Services Marketing", in Czepiel, J., Solomon, M. and Suprenant, C. (Eds), *The Service Encounter*, Lexington Books, Lexington, MA, pp. 255-64.

Zeithaml, V.A., Parasuraman, A. and Berry, L.L. (1985). "Problems and Strategies in Services Marketing", *Journal of Marketing*, Vol. 49, No. 2, pp. 33-46.

Zemke, R. and Schaaf, D. (1990). *The Service Edge*, Penguin Books, New York, NY.

Effect of Globalization on Efficiency & Quality of Services of Commercial Banks

Umara Noreen and *Pareesa Raza Khan*

ABSTRACT

Commercial banks—assaulted by the pressures of globalization, competition from non-banking financial institutions, and volatile market dynamics—are constantly seeking new ways to add value to their services. The question "What drives performance?" is at the top of the minds of managers and policymakers alike, as the first step in understanding superior performance and, hence, striving for it. Substantial research efforts have gone into addressing this question, starting from the strategic level and going down to operational details.

Innovation in technology has been the main force behind innovations in the banking sector. Technology has brought about many new media, and methods of transacting. In this era of tough competition, superior performance of a service firm is contingent with the customer services.

Efficiency measurements, of course, imply a prior knowledge of the inputs and outputs of a bank. For example, research on operational efficiency—the most widely studied efficiency issue—assumes as inputs there sources of a bank (e.g., personnel, technology, space, etc.) and as output some measurable form of the services provided (e.g., number of accounts serviced, or loans and other transactions processed, etc.)

This research paper gives a comparison of privatized and nationalized commercial banks for providing their quality services and efficiency. The paper segregates the two groups of banks on the basis of the services being offered, communication of the bank, and efficiency of customer representatives. This study reveals that there was found a significant difference between the two groups of banks for quality and efficiency. Privatized banks were found to be more responsive towards any new innovation in the market and their customer representatives were more knowledgeable, quick for their provisions of services and had high levels of interactions with their customers.

How can nationalized banks improve themselves in terms of services to meet the challenges of globalization more effectively? This is the question which will help to build a model for future researchers.

INTRODUCTION

Globalization, a word that evokes images of power-hungry multinationals, greedy elites, "New World Orders" and the wrenching pain of the Developing World, as well as the continuing abuse of our environment, also offers, to those inclined to consider it, the promise of tremendous potential, the prospect for transformational progress, and the seeds for a more unified level of human existence. The solution, it appears, is in the "problem" (Alexander R. Malaket) and if we don't significantly change our way of doing business, we will be out of business or outsourced. (Circa 1993)

The historical lack of interest in services can be partly explained by the fact that there was little understanding of the differences between the management of services and the management of manufacturing organisations (Bitran & Lojo, 1993). However, it is true that basic management principles are similar for both types of companies, services have some characteristics that require a different emphasis from management on some of these principles. The characteristics that differentiate services from manufacturing in terms of quality have been described by many writers (e.g. Bitran and Lojo, 1993; Parasuraman, et al., 1993 and Zeithaml, et al., 1996) as follows:

- Nature of products which are basically intangible in services including a tangible action, so customer satisfaction in services is not only influenced by objective measures of performance but also influenced by intangible aspects during the service performance.

- Heterogeneity, that creates another challenge for quality management in services, because quality in service is not just ensuring conformity to standards, but taking into account service diversity of customers while the service delivery is taking place, the behavior and expectations of the customer being served and to customise the service delivery accordingly.
- Simultaneity which means most services are produced and consumed in the same time. That represents a difficulty in quality management of services because it is not usually feasible to actively monitor all service deliveries that are taking place and the service cannot be inspected before its consumption.
- The human contact, because services are often characterized by the existence of human contact between employee and the customer.

Commercial banks—assaulted by the pressures of globalization, competition from non-banking financial institutions, and volatile market dynamics—are constantly seeking new ways to add value to their services. The question "What drives performance?" is at the top of the minds of managers and policymakers alike, as the first step in understanding superior performance. And, hence, striving for it. Substantial research efforts have gone into addressing this question, starting from the strategic level and going down to Operational details. Innovations are the transformation of knowledge into new products, processes, and services involves more than just science and technology. It involves discerning and meeting the needs of customers (Porter & Stern, 1999). Innovations do not look at one aspect, but focus on several factors. Some of the major of these factors are a focus on customer satisfaction, technology, and high quality product and services. The banking sector, too, has been busy in innovating to meet the needs of its customers. Many new products and services have come up. Technology has been incorporated into many a function of banking. Newer technologies have helped banks to grow and make profit despite the pressures of competition.

Innovation in technology has been the main force behind innovations in the banking sector. Technology has brought about many new media, and methods of transacting for example, many banks have started to develop their own websites. These websites give the consumer information about the services offered by the bank.

Interestingly, innovating to newer techniques not only helps the consumers, but also helps banks by cutting costs. For instance, not only have ATMs helped to facilitate the customers, but also they have reduced the cost per transaction for a bank. If a customer were to withdraw money from a teller, or an ATM machine, the cost difference would be huge. The teller costs about $ 1.4 per transaction, where as the ATM machine is much cheaper and cost $ 0.40 per transaction. This is $ 1.00 cheaper than the human teller (Frei, Harker and Hunter, 1998). Efficiency measurements, of course, imply a priori knowledge of the inputs and outputs of a bank. For example, research on operational efficiency—the most widely studied efficiency issue—assumes as inputs there sources of a bank (e.g., personnel, technology, space, etc.) and as output some measurable form of the services provided (e.g., number of accounts serviced, or loans and other transactions processed, etc.). More recent innovative studies benchmark the effects of human resource management practices (Harker and Hunter, 1997), look into the efficiency of alternative delivery processes (Frei, 1995), and investigate the effects of the environment (Athanassopoulos et al., 1997). These efficiency benchmarks are constructive: not only they identify the most efficient unit—bank, branch or delivery process—but they also aid in explaining efficiency differences, see, e.g. Berger and Mester (1997). A senior executive involved in trade in New York was once heard to say words to the following effect:

"I don't care if we have a bunch of hamsters moving the paperwork in a back room, as long as the transaction is successful and our service delivery looks good to the client."

Client relationships are everybody's business in many trade finance groups, there is a conspicuous lack of coordination between operations, sales and structured trade, in managing client relationships and business development. A key study benchmarking the strategies of leading retail banks was carried out by the Bank Administration Institute; see Roth and van der Velde (1992). This study—based on the opinions of heads of retail banking at all US commercial banks—established the linkage between marketing, operations, organizational structure, and human resource management in achieving excellence. Trade services operations are often an untapped source of current and practical insights into the business and transactional challenges faced by clients. With basic coaching, even the most transaction-oriented operations unit can become a valuable source of information, insight and opportunity. Integrated trade finance teams require frequent, organized and active communication across all levels, about client relationships, client needs and expectations. Client management must involve all members of the trade finance team, in an ongoing process guided by shared ownership of the relationships.

Rationale of the Study

The rationale behind this research study is to improve researchers understanding of the key variables involved and to get an insight into the topic. The aim of this research is to analyze that what is the impact of the role of information technology, privatization and competition on the quality of services of commercial banks. Researchers have taken three different groups of banks to identify the difference in terms of services being provided.

Problem Statement

A problem does not necessarily mean that something is seriously wrong with a current situation that needs to be rectified immediately. A problem could simply indicate an interest in an issue where finding the right answers might help to improve an existing situation. It is the intention of a researcher to do something. There is always a gap between desired and current state which the researcher is trying to cover up.

Financial globalization is not harmful but it increases risk. However, the problem with financial globalization is not that it is harmful itself but that increased risk comes with its opportunities. This paper stresses on the realization of benefits of globalization by Nigerian banking services sector *vis-à-vis* minimization of incidence of risk associated with it.

Literature Review

Whatever, assessment one makes of globalization, whether it is viewed overall as a positive force or not, the acceptance of globalization, to varying degrees and in some form, will assist in better directing the energy and enhancing the quality of the creative outcomes of this phase of human development (Alexander R. Malaket, 1998).

The findings indicate that consumers have well-conceived ideas about service quality, and that certain quality attributes are considered important for most types of services which were examined including banking (Mersha, et al., 1992).

Another study explains the problems associated with the measurements of quality of services and presents a set of indices to provide measures of expectations, perceptions, and overall satisfaction. A quality of the UK banks' services which provided to small firms has been measured (Ennew, et al., 1993).

This research examines six-dimension model for SQ in banking industry (Responsiveness, Empathy, Staff conduct, Access, Communication and Reliability) with 27 items.

The six dimensions with 27 items were empirically reduced to 17 items across four factors. The dimensions to emerge are staff conduct, credibility, communication, and access to teller services. The instrument's reliability, dimensionality and validity have been empirically tested; the results are encouraging both in their own right and when compared with other studies. Avkiran (1994) represents a list of characteristics of bank quality as perceived by customers, identifies the underlying dimensions of bank quality and assesses the importance of the characteristics as also perceived by them. Seven factors were found in determining bank quality. They include: employees and employee/customer interactions, the number of accessible and working ATMs, company structure, and four available services. Over 82 per cent of the respondents felt that banks provided quality service (Stafford, 1996).

The findings indicate that the ultimate success of any service quality program implemented by a bank can only be gauged by creation and retention of satisfied customers. (Yavas, et al., 1997).

The findings indicate that credit unions rate significantly higher than banks on 11 of the 14 SQ questions: access; courtesy; communication; credibility; security; empathy; tangibles; basic service; fairness; fixing mistakes; and guarantees. Also they indicate that neither banks nor credit unions do a good job of surveying customer needs or retaining customers (Anthony, et al., 2000).

Methodology

This is a form of *hypothesis testing study* because it explains the nature of certain relationships or establishes the difference among groups or the independence of two or more factors in a situation. Since we are interested to find out the impact of globalization on quality and efficiency of services in different banks so it is the measure of difference. For the sake of convenience and simplicity in analysis and interpretations, we have grouped commercial banks in to three categories.

- Nationalized banks
- Privatized banks
- Foreign banks

The extent of scientific rigor in a research study depends on how carefully researcher chooses the appropriate design alternatives taking into consideration its specific purpose.

Data collection methods are an integral part of research design. Both primary and secondary data are used in this research. The following three methods are generally popular in a management oriented research work:

- Surveys
- Case Studies
- Articles

This research opted for questionnaires, articles and related research papers reason being, research requirement involves in-depth contextual analysis.

Sample/Participants

The type of sampling procedure used in this research project is "Non-Probability Sampling" Further in non-probability sampling, it is *judgmental and convenience sampling.* 160 respondents filled up the questionnaire. The respondents were from the age 18 and above which include both sexes. We tried to keep the sample equal, in three groups i.e. nationalized, privatized and foreign banks in order to obtain a clear and unbiased picture. Although we found that most of the people maintain their bank accounts in privatized commercial banks and many nationalized banks are on their way to privatization. Mostly the respondents were government or, private employees. Some of the students also participated in this survey.

Instrument and Measures

The purpose of this questionnaire is to collect information about the quality and efficiency of services of commercial banks. The questionnaire is designed to collect information on following dimensions of services.

- Tangibility
- Reliability
- Assurance

Questionnaire consisted of four parts

Part I is about the demographic information i.e. sex, income, age, and education. This section also asks about the name of banks in which respondents have their accounts.

Part II is about the level of customer satisfaction, physical facilities (tangibility) range of services by the bank (reliability).

Part III asks about the communication of the bank staff.

Part IV is about the customer services representative knowledge, ability, courtesy and responsiveness (assurance).

Results and Findings

Question 1

What is the level of satisfaction with this bank's customer services?

It was found that customers were highly satisfied with the foreign banks, as compared to the other groups; however majority of the customers were satisfied with privatized and nationalized banks.

Bar Chart

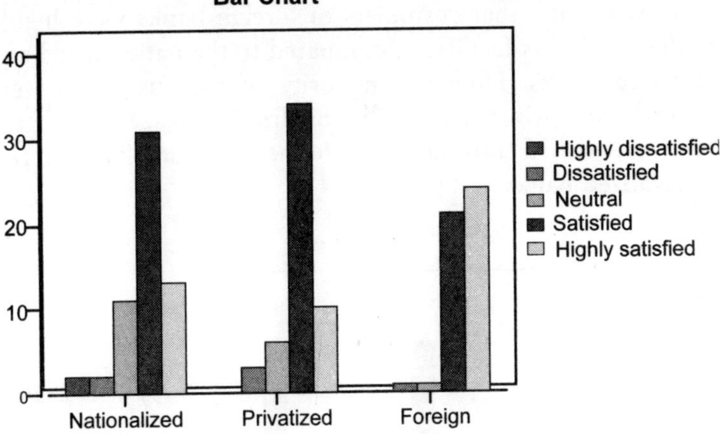

Question 2

How far you are satisfied with the process of getting your complaints honored?

Generally speaking, respondents were satisfied, as far as their complaints were concerned. But in nationalized banks, segment was highly dissatisfied, as compared to the other two banks category. In foreign banking system, the complaints honored process was excellent. Also the level of dissatisfaction is the lowest.

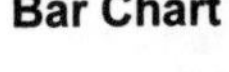

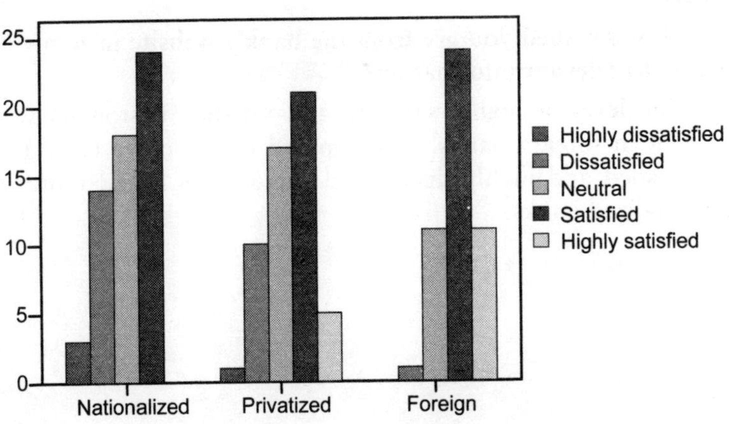

Question 3

How satisfied are you from the appearance of physical facilities such as waiting areas, ATM machines, etc.?

It was found that customers of foreign banks were highly satisfied with this facility, as compared to the nationalized and privatized banks. However, majority of the customers were satisfied with privatized and nationalized banks. Over all the highly dissatisfied customers were found in nationalized and few in privatized banks.

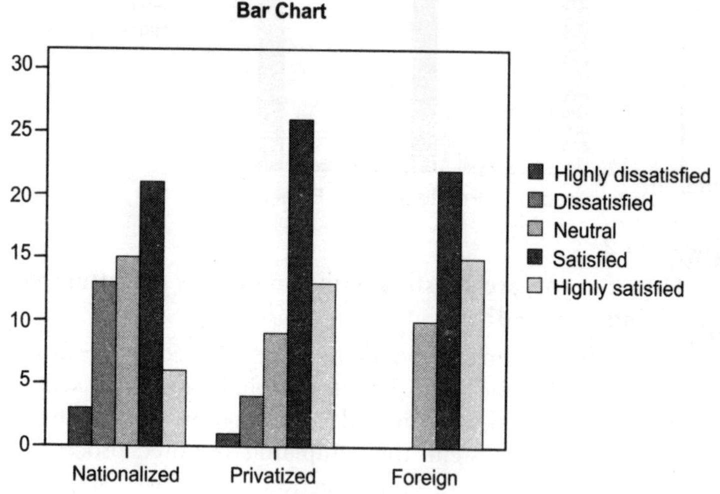

Question 4

How satisfied you are from the bank's website in terms of access to relevant information?

The level of highly satisfied and satisfied customers was present in foreign banks, as compared to the other two. The dissatisfied and highly dissatisfied option was found more in nationalized banks.

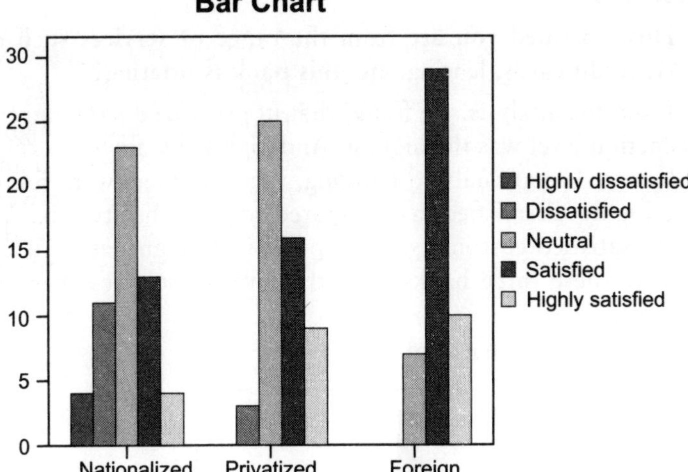

Question 5

How satisfied you are from the bank's website in terms of usefulness of information?

From graphical representation, we can see that the highly satisfied customers were found in private banking system. The satisfaction level was the highest in foreign banking in this regard. The dis-satisfaction level was the highest in nationalized banks.

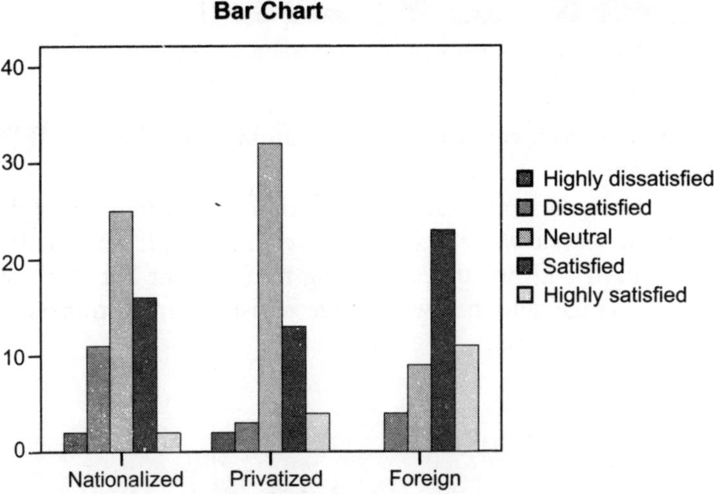

Question 6

How satisfied you are from the range of services such as ATM, credit cards, leasing, etc. this bank is offering?

From the analysis, we found that in privatized banking, the satisfaction level was the highest. And highly dissatisfied level is the lowest. In nationalized banking, the customers were found more highly dissatisfied, as compared to the other two banks. Highly satisfied customers were found in foreign banks, if we compare these three banks with the level of services they are providing.

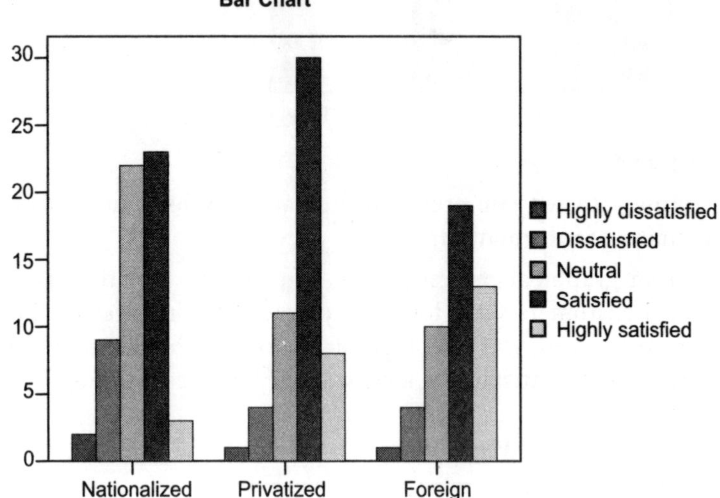

Question 7

How do you rate the communication of the bank staff by telephone?

As from the graphical representation, it was found that the telephone service was excellent in foreign banks. It was good in nationalized and privatized banking to an extent but was also found average and below average satisfaction customers in nationalized banks.

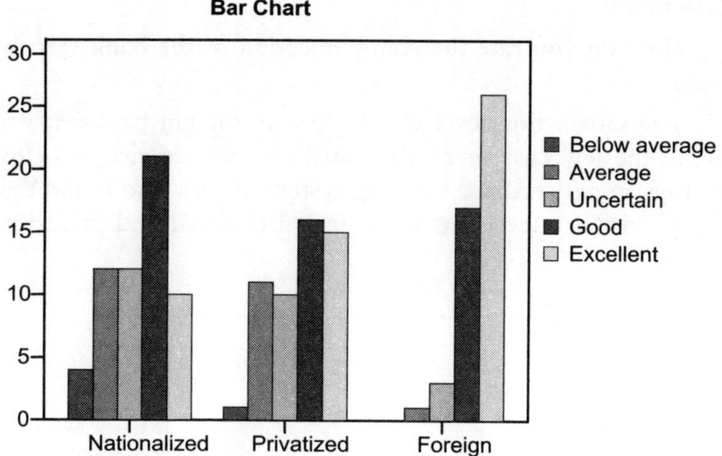

Question 8

How do you rate the communication of the bank staff by e-mail?

Generally speaking, respondents treated the e-mail facility as good in private banks. The uncertain and below average level was the highest in nationalized banking. The level of e-mail facility was also found satisfactory in private banks.

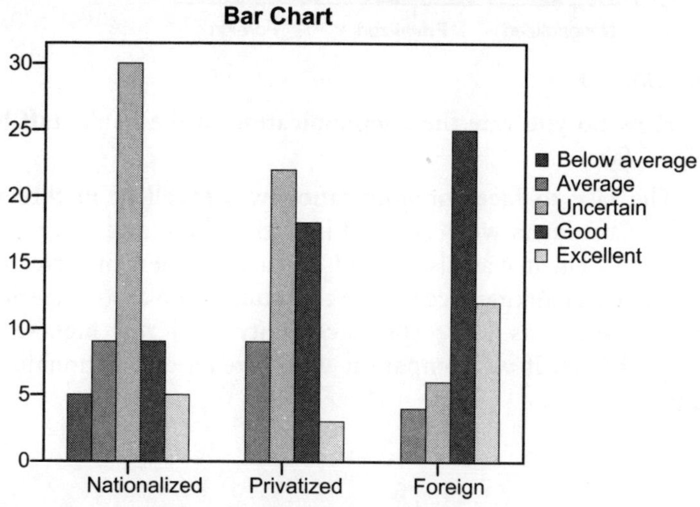

Question 9

How do you rate the communication of the bank staff by post?

The satisfaction level was highest in foreign banks. It was found the few customers also rated the post service as below average in nationalized banking system. It was also found that the uncertainty level was more in nationalized and privatized banks.

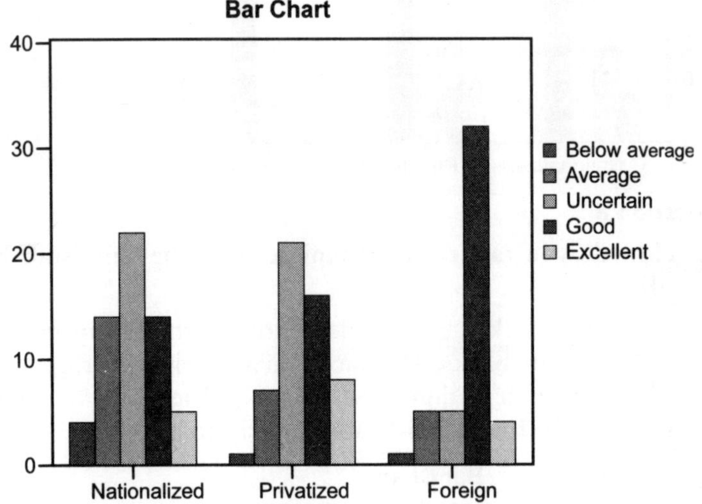

Question 10

How do you rate the communication of the bank staff by face to face?

The face to face communication was excellent in foreign banks. Customers were satisfied in nationalized and privatized banks as well. It was also found some customers also treated nationalized banking face to face communication as average and below average as well. The uncertainty level was highest in private banks, if we compare it with foreign and nationalized banks.

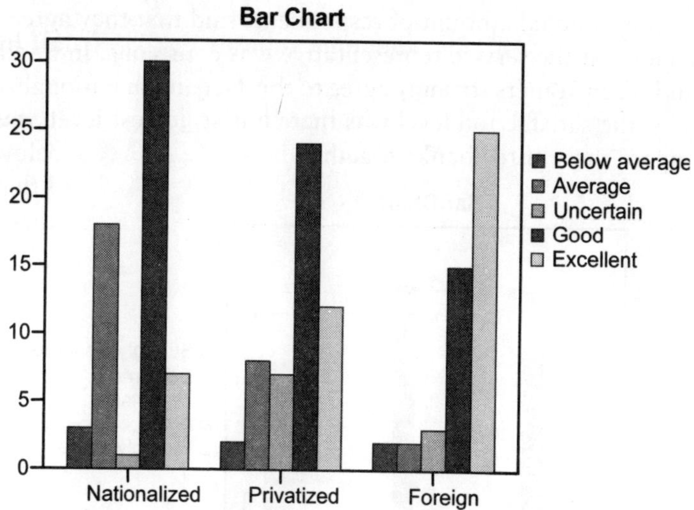

Question 11

The customer service representative is very courteous.

All most equal amount of respondents said that they agree to the fact that the service representative was courteous.

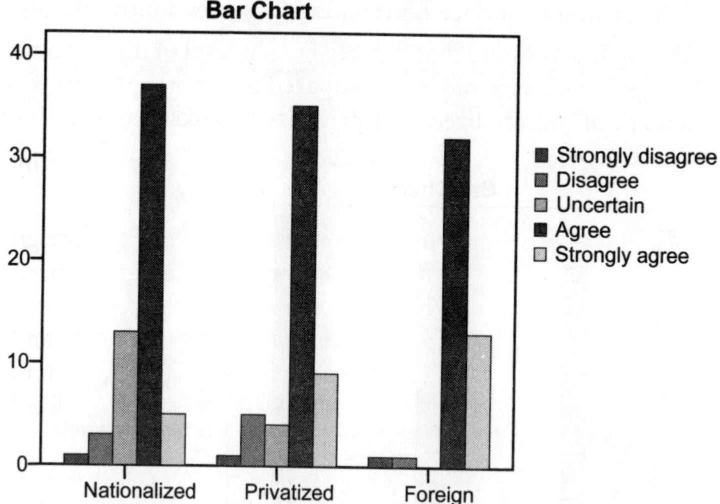

Question 12

The customer service representative handles my calls quickly.

Almost equal amount of respondents said that they agree to the fact that the service representative was courteous. In foreign banking, customers strongly agree to this fact and in nationalized banks, the satisfaction level was there but at lowest level, if we compare these three banks together.

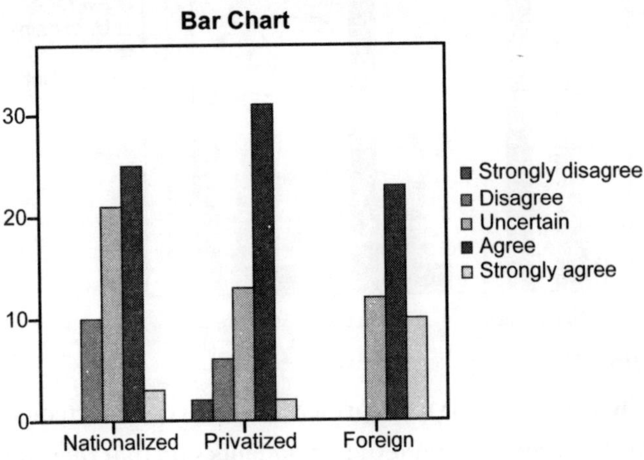

Question 13

The customer service representative is very knowledgeable.

Again, it was found that the satisfaction level of the customers of foreign banks were more as compared to the other banks. Few customers of nationalized and privatized banks dis-agree with this statement.

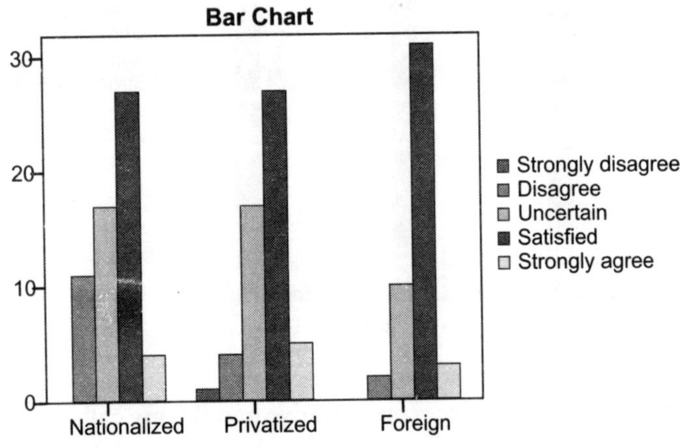

Question 14

The waiting time for having my questions addressed was satisfactory.

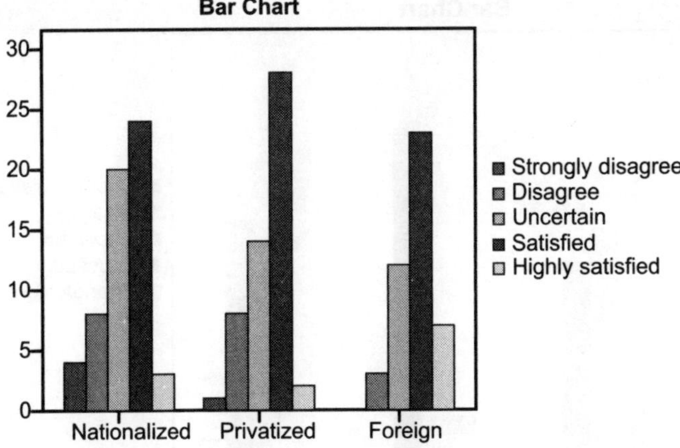

Question 15

The customer representative has performed waiting time for having my questions addressed was satisfactory.

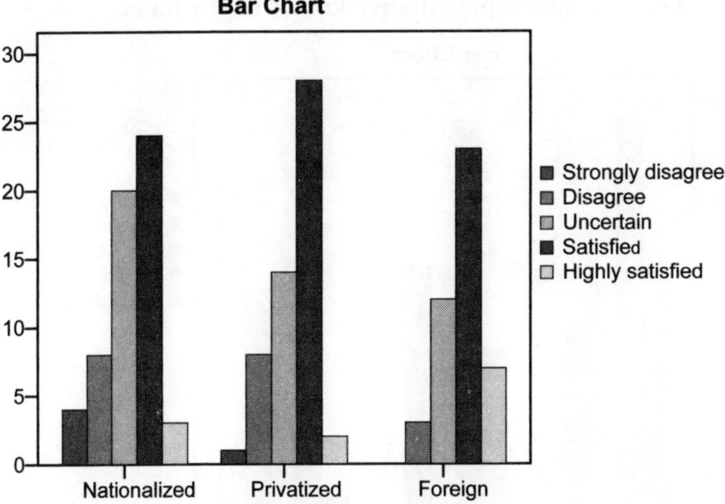

Question 16

The customer representative has performed the promised services accurately.

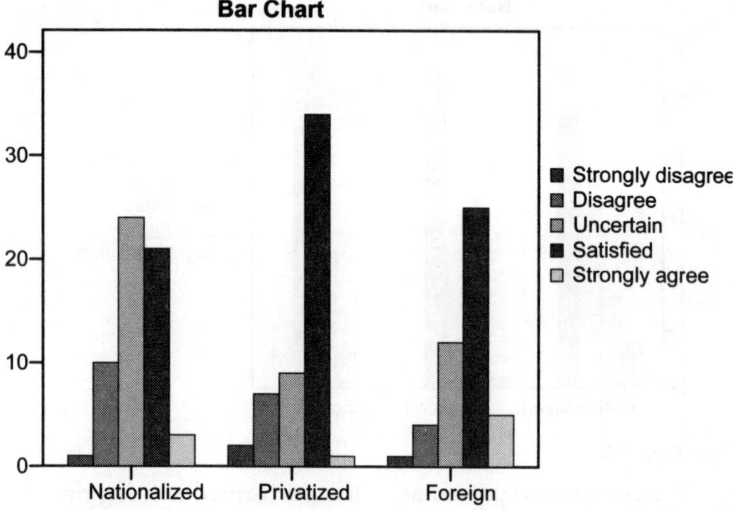

Question 17

The customer representative knows me by name.

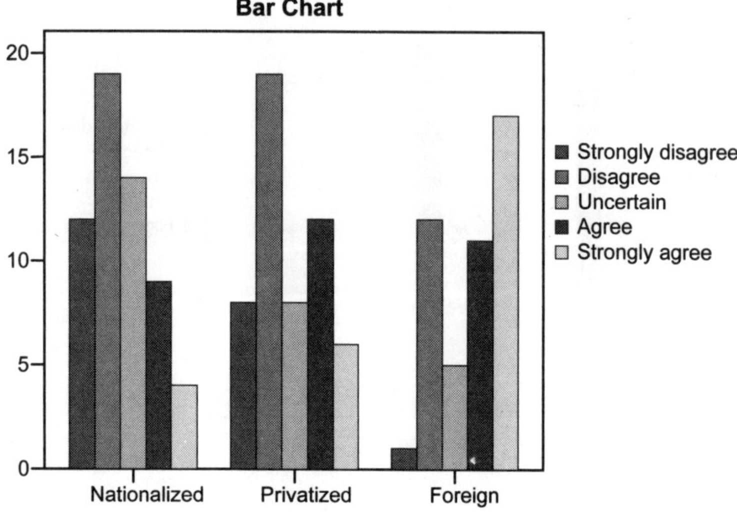

Question 18

The bank updates itself for any new innovation.

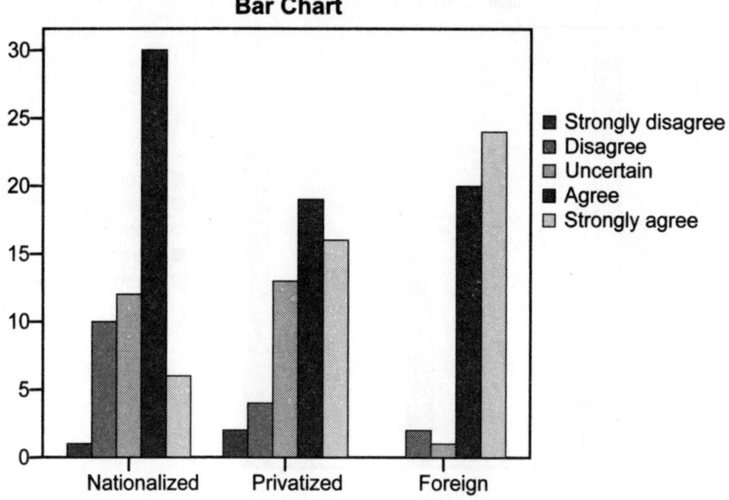

Question 19

The bank gives me reminder calls for payments.

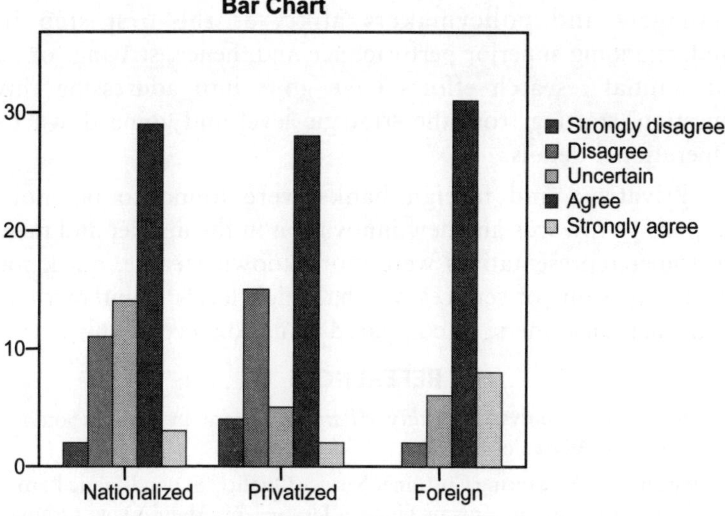

Question 20

The bank offers me new product at a discount rate.

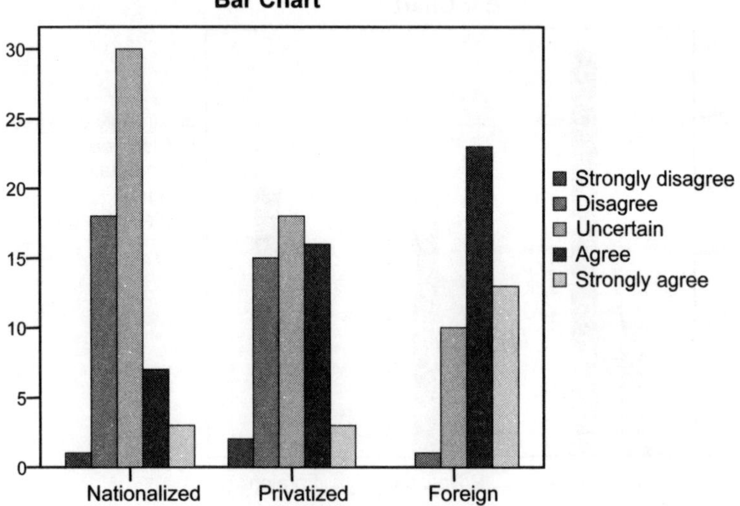

CONCLUSION

"What drives performance?" is at the top of the minds of managers and policymakers alike, as the first step in understanding superior performance and, hence, striving for it. Substantial research efforts have gone into addressing this question, starting from the strategic level and going down to Operational details.

Privatized and foreign banks were found to be more responsive towards any new innovation in the market and their customer representatives were more knowledgeable, quick for their provisions of services and had high levels of interactions with their customers, as compared to nationalized banks.

REFERENCES

Efficiency, Profitability and Quality of Banking Services by Andreas Soteriou Stavros A. Zenios 97-28.

"Adopting and Measuring Customer Service Quality (SQ) in Islamic Banks: A Case Study in Kuwait Finance House" by Abdul Qawi Othman and Lynn Owen, *International Journal of Islamic Financial Services* Vol. 3, No. 1.

Globalization as a Harmonizing Force by Alexander R. Malaket, Principal OPUS Advisory Services International.

Is There Time to Evolve, or Is It Time to Reinvent by Alexander R. Malaket *Learning to Work Together* by Alexander R. Malaket

http://www.cas.bris.ac.uk/quality/QoS-Employers.doc

http://www.questionspro.com

http://www.bris.ac.uk/cas

http://www.tradefinance.com

Books

Practice and Law of Banking in Pakistan 7th Edition by Dr. Asrar H. Siddique

Research Methode for Business

Marketing of Banking Services

Anil Mehta

7

ABTRACT

Traditionally, Indian banks have not really paid adequate attention to marketing. Today, Banking Sector is an integral part of national economy and an important tool for development. It has contributed significantly in collection of small savings, capital formation, channeling the funds in productive plans and in the socio-economic development of our country. Indian banking sector has undergone substantial changes over the last five decades. These changes have passed through five stages: pre-independence, post-independence, pre-nationalization, nationalization and post-liberation period.

Reasons for Growing Importance of Bank Marketing

Competition: Phenomenal growth of banking sector and establishment of new banks in private sector has increased competition in India. The intensity of competition has further moved upward after coming of foreign banks. The term-lending institutions such as IDBI, UTI, ICICI have also opened their own commercial banks.

Increased Expectations of Customers: Customer expectations have increased. They want quality services. There is no customer loyalty. They may close their accounts and switch over to other banks if their exceptions are not met.

Dual Role of Public Sector Bank: Public sector banks are expected to play dual role. On one hand, they are expected to meet the requirements of priority sector, on the other hand they also bear the responsibility of generating profits and maintaining commercial viability which is not possible unless business is increased through efficient marketing.

Introduction of New Services: Development of sophisticated Information Technology has opened new vista for banking industry. It has enabled banks to introduce new services, such as 24 hours Automatic Teller Machine (ATM) services, Electronic Clearing Services (ECS), Direct Deposit of Payroll, Internet banking, Debit and Credit Cards, etc.

Launching of New Services: Keeping in view the requirements of various categories of customers, banks are launching innovative financial products.

Bank Marketing—The Concept

The evolution of marketing concept in banking profession is traced in the west. Deryak Weyer of Barleys Bank has given a very comprehensive definition of Bank Marketing. According to him, Bank Marketing consists of identifying the most profitable markets, now and in future, assessment of present and future needs of customers, setting business development goals, making plans to meet them, managing various services and promoting them to achieve the plans—all in the context of changing environment in the market.

Features of Bank Marketing

1. Marketing Mix: Similar to other service generating organizations, marketing of banking services is concerned with product promotion, pricing, place, people, process and physical appearance.

2. Responding to the Changing Needs: Bank marketing aims at responding to the changing needs of the customers. It matches services with the market requirements.

3. Customer Satisfaction Approach: It identifies the customer's needs, fulfils the identified needs by providing the required services in the best possible way. It gives due weightage to the customer satisfaction.

4. Marinating Balance: Bank marketing is an integration of social interests, profitability and professional excellence. It has to maintain balance between organization and social interests.

5. Maintaining Printability and Commercial Viability: It is a managerial approach to market the services profitably and maintaining commercial viability by excelling in a competitive environment.

The User of Banking Services

The banking organizations have to transact with different types of customers. Their classification is significant from the point of view of bank because the kind of services, the planning and development of services, the pricing or the interest charged for the services and the promotional strategies depends substantially upon the nature and types of services customers using the services of the bank.

Two types of customers are using the services of the banks as shown in the chart given below:

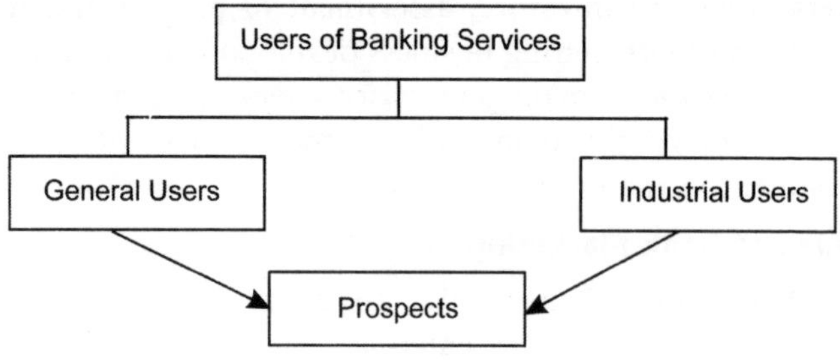

1. General Users: General users are small sized customers who have an account with the bank and who avail limited services of the bank such as deposit and withdrawal of amount, collection and issue of cheques/drafts, etc., borrowings for domestic requirements.

2. Industrial Users: Industrial users are those who are having bank account with the bank and use credit facilities and other services for the establishment and expansion of business.

Prospects: Prospects are those who are not presently the customers of the bank and not availing the services but they have potentials to become the customers if motivated in proper manner. They may be either general user or industrial user prospects.

Behavioral Profile of Users

It is very essential from the point of view of marketer to study the behavioral profile of prospects/customers as it affects the marketing mix substantially. Strategic marketing decisions and business planning also depend upon the changing behavioral profile of the customers. Although study of behavioral profile is a challenging task since customers may not alike, number of persons can be clubbed in a segment and the behavioral profile of the entire customers related to that segment is found by and large the same. In the 21st century, the behavioral profile of the customers is fast changing. Increasing rate of literacy, the changing level of income, significant development in transportation and communication, increasing role of corporate sector, changing life style, etc. are some of the factors that a banking professional cannot afford to ignore as they affect the expectations of customers and strategic marketing decisions.

Factors Influencing the Behavioral Profile of the Users

There are number of factors that may influence the behavioral profile of the users. Broadly, they can be classified into three parts:

1. Social Factor: The social factors influence the behavioral profile of the customers significantly. Savings potentials will depend upon the marital status of the family member, size of the family, age group and the status of the head of the family, life-style, working couples, social status, etc.

2. Economic Factors: Economic factors play decisive role since it is ultimately the income that influences the life style. There is a positive relationship between income and savings. The state of national economy, optimistic or dismal business environment, international economic environment influence the behavior profile.

3. Psychological Factors: Attitude, learning and motivation are the key factors influencing the behavior of the customers. Study of these three factors helps bankers to make the services more useful and innovative.

The aforesaid factors may not remain static, hence, it becomes essential for the banking professionals to keep themselves aware about the changes through intensive study about the changing trends.

Marketing Information System

In today's highly competitive environment, organizations cannot afford to commit mistakes by taking a wrong decision. In order to minimize risk in decision-making, marketing professionals have to base their decisions on information rather than intuition. According to Philip Kotler, "Marketing Information System consists of people, equipment and procedures, to gather, sort, analyze, and distribute, needed, timely and accurate information to marketing decision-makers".[1]

In the banking organizations, MIS is very helpful in taking various decisions at branch, regional and corporate level. At the branch level, it can be used for market development plans. At the regional level, MIS can be used for regional planning, implementation and reviewing the situation and at the corporate level, it can be used for objectives and goal setting, and formulation of marketing strategies. MIS is helpful for the banking organizations in the following way:

1. Marketing information system is very helpful in making innovative decisions.
2. It is helpful in exploring the profitable opportunities of business.
3. It helps in identifying the intensity of competition.
4. It is helpful in expansion and diversification program.
5. It is helpful in building favorable image of the bank.

Market Segmentation

Banking organizations have to satisfy the needs of various types of customers. The classification of these customers in different segments enable banking professionals to identify their needs, designing the products according to their requirements and satisfy them more effectively. Following may be the criteria for segmenting the market for banking organization:

1. Economic System: An important criteria for market segmentation is the economic system, in which we can include agriculture sector, industrial sector, services sector, household sector and rural sector.

2. Household Sector: This sector can be further classified into different professions, income groups and gender. For example, higher income group, middle-income group, low-income group, man, woman, etc.

3. Institutional Sector: This segment can be further classified into different such as: cultural organizations, charitable organizations, service organizations, industrial organizations, etc.

Marketing Mix for Banking Organizations

In order to provide competitive edge and to run banking organization profitably, proper formulation of marketing mix is very essential. Besides the four traditional mix, such as product mix, promotion mix, price mix, and place mix; the people, physical appearance, and process are important for banks. The formulation of marketing mix is just like the combination of ingredients, spices in the marketing process.

The Product Mix: Banks primarily deal with the services. The changing life style, increased level of income, increased dominance of foreign banks and the changing need of the customers at large make it essential to develop or modify their service mix. In the formulation of services, the banks can follow two approaches. First, the proactive approaches in which the needs of the target market is visualized and accordingly, new services are innovated. Second, the reactive approach, in which bank provides services as per the expressed needs.

Product Portfolio: A wide variety of services may be included in the bank product portfolio under deposit schemes, international banking operations, consultancy, loans and advances and miscellaneous services. All the services included in the product portfolio may not be equally profitable because of the different stages of the product life cycle of different products. The bank professionals are supposed to develop a balanced service mix in which those services are included which are profitable at present as well as those new services likely to be profitable. Services, which are at their declining stage or not performing well, may be dropped.

Designing an Attractive Package: Designing of packaging in the banking involves combining different services and schemes in such a way, which offers to the customers' benefits and conveniences. Banking professional must have an in-depth knowledge about the requirements and preferences of the target market. It is also important that a bank manager is familiar with the package developed by the leading competitive bank since it would help them in innovating the package. The purpose is to make it profitable, convenient and useful to the customers so that they prefer to transact with the bank. It is a persuasive effort that helps the bank in increasing the business.

Product Development: Product development is an ongoing process. Banks also need to develop new products and services so that they offer something new much earlier than their competitors. Though it is difficult to develop new products and services in the banking sector since they have to operate under Reserve Bank of India's regulations, they can do it in a very limited way by adding some additional or different features.

Promotion Mix

Promotion deals with informing and persuading the customers regarding the banking services. It involves decisions regarding advertising, publicity, sales promotion, personal selling, word-of mouth publicity and telemarketing. The different components of marketing mix help the bank professionals in promoting the banking business.

Advertising: Advertising is dissemination of information concerning an idea; product or services to induce action in accordance with the intent of the advertiser. Banking organizations have to use advertising with the purpose of promoting the business. The key decision areas in advertising that help banking organizations are as under:

1. Defining Advertising Goals: Banking professionals have to define the goals that Advertising intends to achieve. Advertising can be undertaken to realize several goals such as informing public about the services, increase in the sale of existing services, build up atmosphere for future sale, build up goodwill, coping with the competition, etc.

2. Determine Advertising Budget: This is related with the formulation of advertising budget for the advertising. In this task, the top management of the bank has to play crucial role. Various approaches may be used for determination of budget such as affordable, percentage of business, objective-and-task, etc.

3. Media Decision: Various advertising media are available for advertising such as print media, out-door media, electronic media, direct mail, etc. Bank professional should select appropriate advertising media after careful consideration of their effectiveness.

4. Advertising Copy Decisions: Since advertising message and appeal to the target audience is conveyed through advertising copy, it should be prepared with utmost care. The advertising professionals have the responsibility of preparing an advertising copy, which could gain attention, create interest, arouse desire, and ensure action.

5. Testing the Effectiveness: For making the ad campaign effective, it is essential to pre-test the advertisement before releasing it commercially. A trial run of the advertisement may call for certain modifications in the advertisement copy.

6. Measuring the Advertising Effectiveness: A bank, which has spent a sizable amount of money, efforts and time on advertising, would be interested in knowing the results, i.e. in knowing how far advertising has been able to achieve its objectives. The banking professional needs to evaluate the advertising for at least three purposes: (1) to improve the effectiveness of advertising by making changes in the advertising, media, timing, etc. (2) to convince the bank management about the instrumentality of advertising in improving the profitability and (3) to determine the optimum level of advertising expenditure.

Public Relation: Public Relation is an intentional effort to establish, maintain and develop relationship with the masses. It is a planned and continuous effort to build a favorable image and goodwill of the institution. Public relations in banking organization bear a high importance. Bank professionals should release news, stories and features regularly through media of mass communication. The messages go to the customers as news rather than advertisement through prestigious media will influence prospects more effectively. Public relation activity should be targeted to (1) Employees of the bank, (2) Present and prospective depositors and borrowers, (3) Employees of local institutions, (4) Local Administration, (5) Public Representatives, and (6) Media (Radio, TV, Press). It is a misconception that the responsibility of public relations is confined to Public Relation Managers of the bank. In fact, every employee of the bank can play a positive and constructive role in public relation and building a favorable image of the bank. Needless to mention here that favorable image of the bank will bear ultimately upon the performance of the bank and the behavior of its employees.

Personal Selling: Personal selling is an important method of selling. It is the process of assisting and persuading the prospective buyers through direct and personal contact. It involves an oral presentation in a conversation with one or more prospective customers for the purpose of making the sale. This means that it is an individualized service requiring a two-way communication.

Personal selling is a friendly source of getting all the information about the services. It is one-to-one relationship where the customer can ask pertinent question and get answer. Marketer can observe customer interest and adjust his approach to the customer's mood, and capitalize it at the right moment.

In the personal selling, the feedback is instantaneous, if the customer doesn't understand what the salesman is saying, than the salesman can explain it in further detail.

The target market can be selected very carefully and the prospects with high priority can be attended, Presentations can be planned according to the specific need of the customer. There is also a high possibility of immediate sale. Many times prospects can be convinced in the very first meeting of the customer and the salesperson.

The banking organizations can use personal selling successfully with the help of efficient sales force. Intensive training programs would be helpful to develop them. If the bank staff has an in-depth knowledge of various schemes as well as selling techniques, the task of turning prospects into customer would be easier.

Sales Promotion: Sales promotion involves marketing activities other than personal selling, advertising and publicity, that stimulate customer's purchasing. As and when the banking organizations offer new services and schemes, they can use various tools of sales promotion. In order to boost the business, the banking organizations can offer promotional incentives to bankers as well as customers. Bank staff can be offered various incentive schemes like gifts, contests, commission on business, entertainment and other allowances, low interest financing, etc. However, these schemes should be linked with their performance. Similarly, offering gifts, discounts and commission can be to the new and existing customers using different package of services. Banking professionals should study the competitor's strategy of sales promotion and come out with innovative promotional schemes.

Word-of Mouth Promotion: Friends, relatives, well-wishers and opinion leaders may significantly influence buying decisions. The process of persuading the prospect will be more effective if these persons can strongly recommend the excellent services being offered by a particular bank by communicating their positive opinion. The existing satisfied customers of the bank can help in moving this process in the long run. Banks should use this source of promotion in an organized and planned manner. Branch managers should identify such persons and invite them on dinner or get together, may offer them small gifts and explain them new schemes. This tool of promotion can be used successfully only when the quality of services are excellent.

The Price Mix

Pricing assumes a significant role in a competitive economy. It is a major determinant of success. If prices are too low, the business is lost. If price is too low, the organization will be at loss. Price structure affects the competitive position and the share in the market. Price also affects the other components of marketing mix. A firm can improve the quality of services, can increase the number of accompanying services, and can spend more on promotional activities.

The pricing in banking sector is governed and regulated by Indian Bank Association and Resave Bank of India. Pricing decisions become complicated particularly in case of public sector banks because on one hand they have to fulfill the social objectives towards weaker sections of the society and priority areas and on the other hand they have to generate sufficient profits to remain commercially viable.

Liberalization process has provided banks bit autonomy in determining rate of interest on borrowings and deposits, fee and charges for various services. However, increasing number of domestic banks in private sector and foreign banks have made the pricing strategies more competitive.

The Place Mix

This component of marketing mix is concerned with selecting the appropriate locations for branches of the bank and providing the promised services to the customers. Branches have to be opened as per the guidelines of Reserve Bank of India. Branch location directly affects the volume of business. Certain parameters must be considered in selecting the location of the branch. It should be easily accessible to the existing and potential customers. It should fulfill safety and security norms. It must have sufficient space. It should be located in the area where it has sufficient potentials to generate new business, except those branches, which are to be established in rural and remote areas, it should have sound infrastructure facilities. It must have adequate parking facilities. The interior of the branch should be aesthetic Adequate attention should be paid on the sitting arrangements and comforts for the customers and staff.

The People

People constitute an important dimension in marketing of banking services. Time bound and efficient services, practical and profitable guidance to customers and accuracy in transactions are key factors in the building creditability of the bank. Better services cannot be provided to the customers unless the workforce in the bank is committed, competent and qualified. For the integrated marketing efforts every employee of the bank should become a sales person for its services. The courteous and polite behavior, a sense of responsibility and positive attitude become very important. Banking professionals should aim at developing total quality people. Selections purely based on merit, on-going training and developmental activities, direct linkage of reward and recognition with the performance and better quality of working life will go a long way in developing people in banks.

The Physical Attributions

A customer needs the service, but it is also important how the service is being offered. Good housekeeping and cleanliness, the peripheral services, chequebook, token, pay slips and withdrawal slips, and other forms carry the image of the bank. Secondly, every bank employee represents the bank. Attractive schemes and better services are important but the impressive personality of the employees would be helpful in transforming prospects into customers and promoting new business. The physique, impressive and attractive looks, well-dressed, proper hairstyle, aesthetic séance; decent and emphatic behavior is quite helpful in projecting professional image of the bank.

Note

1. Kotler Phillip, *Marketing Management*, 11th edition, Prentice Hall of India, New Delhi, 2005, p. 123.

Indian Banking: Global Benchmarks

Shalini Srivastava and *C.P. Mall*

8

ABSTRACT

With increase in global trade and finance, there is need for a level playing field and this gap is sought to be filled by the WTO, which has laid down common rules to facilitate smooth trade among member countries. Another fallout of globalisation is the increase in volatility and vulnerability of markets. In order to detect timely fault lines in global financial markets and put in place appropriate corrections, the adoption of international standards and global benchmarks becomes important.

To strengthen the banking system in an increasingly competitive environment and guard against financial fragility, financial sector reforms were initiated as part of the economic reforms launched in the country since 1991-92. Significant progress has been made in the past few years to strengthen the Indian banking system, make it more vibrant and bring it closer to international standards.

Even as Indian banks move closer to global benchmarks, there are some areas that will need greater attention and banks will have to prepare themselves to grapple with these challenges if they are to become strong and compete with global players.

This paper is an attempt to analyze the following issues relating to Indian Banking in the global context:

1. Need to check NPAs
2. Sharp increase in the volume of business and the explosion in information technology

3. Even as banks move closer to international standards, they cannot lose touch with the realities of the Indian economy. e.g. agriculture, small industries, small business and other service sectors.

OVERVIEW

The theme "Indian banking—global benchmarks" states a great change, i.e. from Indian banking to global banking—which clearly reflects today's reality; the increasing globalisation of the Indian economy.

Over the past decade, India has emerged as one of the fastest-growing economies on the globe. The rest of the world has been impressed to see that the reforms initiated in the early 1990s are bearing fruit. A decade of economic sector and financial sector reforms has strengthened the fundamentals of the Indian economy and transformed the operating environment for banks and financial institutions in the country. The sustained and gradual pace of reforms has helped avoid any crisis and has actually fuelled growth.

Today, our financial system is rapidly changing. Some of the features of this change are:

- Increasing sophistication of capital markets.
- Emergence of global investments.
- Industry consolidation.
- Heightened focus on customer relations.
- Proliferation of new players entering the market.

INDIAN BANKING: RANKING GLOBALLY

On a global scenario, let's, first take a look at the ranking of Indian Banks amongst the global banks. Twenty Indian Banks are in the list of top 1000 world banks according to the list prepared by "The Banker' (Financial Times, London) in July, 2004. India's entry in the top 25 Asian Banks (excluding Japan) is State Bank of India (SBI) at No. 10. An encouraging finding of "The Banker's" analysis is that the twenty Indian Banks in the list of 1000, continue to provide the highest average return on capital amongst the Asian banks, going up to 34.2 per cent compared to an already high 27.1 per cent in the year 2003.

CHANGING ENVIRONMENT

1. The most important factor shaping today's world is globalisation. Companies are moving in search of low-cost markets, technology is driving growth in production and productivity and competition is becoming more intense.
2. A second factor is the faster growth in private capital flows, notably short-term flows by banks and financial institutions, portfolio flows by mutual funds and pension funds and direct foreign investment.
3. A third factor is the increasing share of emerging market economies in world trade.

All this has been made possible by the explosion in communication technology, which has led to greater integration of financial markets across the world. But in this environment, crisis also spreads quickly and there is greater danger of contagion than ever before.

With increase in global trade and finance, there is need for a level playing field and this gap is sought to be filled by the WTO, which has laid down common rules to facilitate smooth trade among member countries. Another fallout of globalisation is the increase in volatility and vulnerability of markets. In order to detect timely fault lines in global financial markets and put in place appropriate corrections, the adoption of international standards and global benchmarks becomes important.

INDIAN BANKING SECTOR: ADOPTION OF GLOBAL STANDARDS

To strengthen the banking system in an increasingly competitive environment and guard against financial fragility, financial sector reforms were initiated as part of the economic reforms launched in the country since 1991-92. Significant progress has been made in the past few years to strengthen the Indian banking system, make it more vibrant and bring it closer to international standards.

Union budget 2005-06 has already begun the process of unshackling the potential of the Indian banking industry to make it more globally competitive.

To begin with, the Reserve Bank of India (RBI), the regulatory authority of banks, has been asked to come up with a comprehensive roadmap for banks aimed at improving competition. To facilitate this, Finance Minister Mr. Chidambaram has promised that the government will introduce a comprehensive amendment to the Banking Regulation Act, the law that governs banking in India.

India has adopted international prudential norms and practices with regard to capital adequacy, income recognition, provisioning requirement and supervision and these norms have been progressively tightened over the years. There has been a steady decline in the level of resource pre-emption from the banking system in the form of CRR[1] and SLR[2] Interest rates in various segments of financial markets have been deregulated in a phased manner. The mark to market practice for valuation of government securities has been gradually enhanced and further refinement, in line with international best practices, carried out in valuation and classification of investment by banks. Risk management in banks has been strengthened and measures put in place to mitigate credit risk and market risk and efforts are on to measure and control operational risk. Banks have been given greater freedom with regard to investing as also raising funds abroad and managing their external liability, subject to prudential guidelines.

In the area of supervision, the Basel core[3] principles for effective banking supervision are being followed. Along with off-site surveillance there is periodical on-site supervision for monitoring the risk profile of banks and their compliance with prudential guidelines and a "CAMELS" based rating system is being followed. The Reserve Bank's regulatory and supervisory responsibility has been widened to include financial institutions and non-banking financial companies.

The government has also led state-run Indian banks to raise funds without fearing about the government's holding falling below the 51 per cent marks. The Finance Minister Mr. P. Chidambaram has sought to do this by allowing banks to issue preference shares.

About 11 state-run banks have already lined up plans to raise about US $ 100.9 billion this year, essentially to shore up their capital adequacy ratio to comply with global requirements. Collectively, Indian banks have to raise their capital by US $ 3.6 billion by March 2007 when the Basel II[4] norms come into effect.

Mr. Chidambaram's budget 2004-05 also has diluted the importance of traditional monetary tools such as CRR, from then there has no minimum or maximum stipulations of CRR, which has given RBI flexibility in managing monetary policy.

In the words of Mr. A.K. Purwar, Chairman, SBI, Universal banking has been introduced. With this, banks are permitted to diversify into long-term finance and DFIs into working capital, guidelines have been put in place for the evolution of universal banking.

Prudential norms for capital adequacy, asset classification, income recognition and provisioning are now close to global standards. RBI has introduced Risk Based Supervision of banks (against the traditional transaction based approach). Best international practices in accounting system, corporate governance, payment and settlement systems, etc. are being adopted.

The end result of all these and other reforms is that the Indian banking sector has been considerably strengthened; there is greater transparency in the balance sheet and closer convergence of Indian financial system with practices prevailing in international financial markets. In line with international practice, there is special focus in banks on corporate governance and specialised board level committees including Executive Committee, Risk Management Committee, Audit Committee, Compensation Committee, Asset-Liability Management Committee, Shareholders'/Investors' Grievances Committee, etc. have been established.

India has complied with almost all the Core Principles of Effective Banking Supervision and is one of the early subscribers to it. The Reserve Bank's Standing Committee on International Financial Standards and Codes under the chairmanship of Dr. Y.V. Reddy has identified global standards and codes as part of the efforts to create a sound financial architecture and aligning India's standards and practices in the light of evolving international practices. RBI is examining preparation of roadmaps and time frame for convergence to such standards that are relevant, applicable and feasible.

CHALLENGES AND OPPORTUNITIES IN THE DAYS AHEAD

Even as Indian banks move closer to global benchmarks, there are some areas that will need greater attention and banks will have to prepare themselves to grapple with these challenges if they are to become strong and compete with global players.

This paper is an attempt to analyze the following issues relating to Indian Banking in the global context:

1. Need to Check NPAs

One of the major threats to the health of Indian banking comes from the high level of NPAs. Although the situation has improved overtime, this is largely in terms of net NPAs. The Banking industry in India has fortunately had a sufficiently long period of soft interest rate regime. With large investments in government securities, banks were able to make substantial profits without much effort. This helped them to make large provisions and show impressive figures in terms of NPAs. Another reason for lower NPAs has been the reluctance on the part of Public Sector Banks to recognize problem loans as NPAs. Instead, they have tended to resort to restructuring or even 'ever-greening'. Many non-performing loans continue as such on the books of banks. Managers have tried to avoid unpleasant decisions and consequent accountability for decisions which can be questioned later. In such cases, recovery will be an extremely difficult task due to a long lapse of time. Thus, the problem of NPAs is in fact more complex then it appears at first sight.

This problem has to be tackled on several fronts. First of all, the banks will need to improve credit quality. This calls for better skills, better risk management systems and improvements in monitoring and follow-up. There are reports of poor documentation and consequently, difficulties in enforcing loan contracts. On the whole, the system of supervision and accountability within Public Sector Banks and many old Private Sector Banks needs to be improved. These are issues that have to be tackled by bank's managements themselves. They need to compare their own systems to those of the global banks, in which the quality of credit appraisals is far superior, supervision is strict and penalties for serious mistakes instantaneous.

Government is keen to strengthen the hands of Bank Managements in tackling recoveries. The Securitisation and Reconstruction of Financial Assets and Enforcement of Security Interest Act, 2002 conferred powers upon banks and financial institutions to enforce Securities Interest against defaulters without intervention of courts and DRTs.[5] This was challenged before the Supreme court and while the constitutional validity of the Act itself has been upheld, sub-section (2) of Section 17 (Securitisation Act) was struck down. This has made certain amendments in the Act essential. These have been finalized and we hope to be able to effect the amendments speedily. The proposed amendments will aim at dissuading the borrowers from adopting dilatory tactics and enabling creditors to make speedy recovery by enforcement of securities.

Alongwith strengthening of the Securitisation Act, we propose to introduce Credit Information Companies (Regulation) Act, 2004, in the Winter Session of the Parliament. Information is vital for improving the quality of credit appraisals. Availability of required information on borrowers would in course of time, reduce the harassment of borrowers. It will help banks in making speedy appraisals and credit decisions. A well-established system of Credit Information should also minimize financial frauds, which can become problematic for certain categories of loans like housing loans. Given the importance of information for improving credit climate, we propose to bring about a law to provide legal sanction for collection, sharing and regulated dissemination of credit information and setting up of Credit Information Companies. This initiative should enable our banks to benefit from access to credit information, like banks in USA, UK, Australia, New Zealand, France, Germany and nearer home in Sri Lanka.

A related issue, however, is that of Lenders' liability. While developing the database of credit histories of individual borrowers, banks can intrude upon citizens' privacy. They have, therefore, an equal obligation to ensure proper customer service. They need to follow certain norms in considering, appraising and deciding proposals for credit. They also need to disclose all the information that the borrowers should have. When in genuine difficulty, the honest borrower needs to be given timely help. In many countries of the world, banks are mandated by law to respect the rights and interests of lenders, depositors and other customers. There is a demand for a similar law in India, which many consider justified. However, the Government of India has agreed to achieve this objective for which the RBI has come out with a fair practice code of conduct. Thus, if Indian banks aspire to be global players, they will have to display greater respect for this code.

2. Sharp Increase in the Volume of Business and the Explosion in Information Technology have also given Rise to Scope for Some Weakness

"Indian Banking Sector Analysis (2006-07)" report (which provides extensive research and objective analysis on the growing banking industry, their product quality, and their services in India) shows the following key findings:

Key Findings

- The banking sector witnessed strong growth in deposits and advances during the year 2004-05. As of March 2005, the number of commercial banks stood at 289.
- The aggregate deposits of scheduled commercial banks increased from US $ 331 billion in March 2004 to US $ 374 billion in March 2005.

- Credit of commercial banks in India saw an increase from US $ 185 billion in March 2004 to US $ 242 billion in March 2005.
- Investments of scheduled commercial banks (SCBs) also saw an increase from US $ 149 billion in March 2004 to US $ 162 billion in March 2005.
- India's retail-banking business is expected to grow at the rate of 16 per cent a year over the next four years.

But this sharp increase in the volume of business and the explosion in information technology have also given rise to scope for some weaknesses. The increase in frauds and scams in the financial sector is a cause for concern and calls for greater vigilance on the part of banks and financial institutions. It is, therefore, very vital that the internal controls including internal inspection and audit, submission of control returns, risk management systems, documentation procedures and internal communication channels are strengthened. The implementation of such control systems would necessitate revisions in operational manuals, audit procedures and closer follow up by controlling officials. The recent guidelines on 'Know Your Customer', being followed internationally, would also need to be implemented with spirit.

Changes in Information Technology

In introducing Information Technology, our banks are making impressive progress. The new generation banks are doing particularly well. An important area where the advantage of Information Technology is to be emphasized in the area of 'Payment and Settlement Systems', because they constitute the life-line of any economy. In order to provide an explicit legal basis for Payment and Settlement Systems and confer the necessary regulatory powers on the Reserve Bank of India, Government proposes to enact a law on Payment and Settlement Systems. The Government has introduced a bill on the proposed legislation in the Winter Session of the Parliament (2004-05) (Finance Minister Mr. P. Chidambaram speech to the Banker's Conference 2004).

3. Even as Banks Move Closer to International Standards, They cannot Lose Touch with the Realities of the Indian Economy, e.g. Agriculture, Small Industries, Small Business and Other Service Sectors

Even as banks move closer to international standards, they cannot lose touch with the realities of the Indian economy. In this context, agriculture, small industries, small business and service sectors, important constituents, with crucial backward and forward linkages in the economy. Over the last three decades, banks have done considerable amount of work with over 15 per cent of bank credit going to agriculture. However, the 18 per cent benchmark, achieved by several banks a few years ago, has fallen now. Banks should, therefore now try to increase the flow of credit to the rural sector especially lending to tap the potentialities in agriculture, small-scale industry, small business, etc.

With globalisation, the Indian public sector banks have to compete with new generation private banks and foreign banks. International trends suggest that consolidation has reduced the chances of credit risks. There is a near consensus on the issue that to attain global aspirations and provide greater banking services to rural and hitherto unbanked areas, banks have to consolidate. However, the consolidation has to be addressed not merely to create large behemoths but to benefit from the synergy created by mergers. Their footprints should cover the most interior rural areas and provide support to far flung sectors which at present face enormous difficulty as small banks find such remote branches unviable. Large banks would be in a position to set up branches in hitherto unknown areas even if these were not totally viable, as these banks would have the long-term financial sustainability to be able to cross subsidize.

Such large banks would also be able to meet Basel II norms providing comfort to the clients and the stakeholders. The strategy should thus be for public sector banks to analyze consolidation with entities, which maximize synergies and create larger banking entities, able to compete globally. State Bank of India, India's largest bank having an asset size of $ 127 bn, is ranked 83rd among the World's banks according to asset size.

This gives an indication of what our banks need to do to have a global presence and thereby maximizing client satisfaction within the country. While consolidating, special care will have to be taken to satisfactorily address HR issues in the overall context of technology introduction and rationalization of branches. The entire process should be market driven and based purely on commercial and economic considerations. It needs also to be emphasized that regional and ethnic considerations have to be built into any proposal for consolidation. Thus, the issues that need to be factored in while considering consolidation should be maximizing synergies in terms of regional balance, network of branches, HR cultures, asset commonality and ensuring that legacy issues are not overlooked.

CONCLUSION

Global banking is becoming a reality in more and more countries. Financial firms are operating in an increasingly open, global and competitive environment. Therefore, firstly, Banks have to adapt to an environment that makes effective risk management all the more important. Supervisory oversight also needs to continuously evolve to keep pace with market changes. Basel II is an important step in this direction.

Secondly, greater domestic and foreign competition can lift the efficiency of local banks and other financial institutions. This is a development to manage, but not to impede.

Finally, accounting standards need, as far as possible, to become more harmonised internationally. The work of the IASB[6] is therefore of major importance in helping market discipline to work effectively.

In an age where the world has become smaller and money moves as quickly as information, achieving global benchmarks is important for global players. But underlying this is the need to have sound fundamentals. There is no doubt that only banks and financial institutions that are focused on efficiency, productivity and profitability have a chance to survive in the highly competitive environment and, therefore need to equip themselves thoroughly.

Indian Banking has made a vital contribution to the nation's development. It has progressively matured. It is a measure of its robustness that it is now looking outwards to realize its global aspirations. In this process, it will need to meet many difficult challenges. Our Finance Minister proudly says that "I have, however, no doubt that Indian Banks will meet these challenges successfully and at least some of them be counted among global leaders in not too distant a future".

REFERENCES

Finance Minister Mr. P. Chidambaram speech to the Banker's Conference "Indian Banking: Realising Global Aspirations, 2004" (Ministry of Finance).

Theme presentation by Shri A.K. Purwar, Chairman, FICCI's Banking and FIs Committee and Chairman, SBI on Conference on "Indian Banking: Global Benchmarks".

Indian Banking Sector Analysis (2006-07).

C.P. Chandrasekhar. "What is Happening to Indian Banking" *Frontline*.

Balwinder Saini, 25 May 2005. "Banking Sector Reforms in India: An Overview".

Mitali Kalita, 16 Dec. 2004. "Basel II and Indian Banks".

A.K. Purwar, Chairman, SBI, "Banking Sector".

A Presentation on Changing Environment Conference on "Indian Banking: Global Benchmark".

Speech by Malcolm D. Knight, General Manager of the BIS at the 4th Conference of the Federation of Indian Chambers of Commerce and Industry (FICCI), Mumbai, 5 Oct. 2005, "Global Banking—Paradigm Shift".

"NPAs Improve but Need More attention," S. Lakshmi Narasimhan.

Gowri J, "Public Sector Banks will Lose Out to Competition."

Paper by Leeladhar—CMD, Union Bank of India, Conference on "Indian Banking: Global Benchmark".

Article "Going Global: Chidambaram Helps Banks Take First Step".

Kalpana Morparia, Ex- Director, ICICI Bank Ltd, "Financial Service Sector".

Speech by Dr. Dalbir Singh, CMD, Central Bank of India and Chairman IBA Conference on "Indian Banking: Global Benchmark."

NOTES

1. Cash Reserve Ratio.
2. Statutory Liquidity Ratio.
3. The Basel committee formulates broad supervisory standards and recommends guidelines for sound practices in the area of banking system supervision and regulation. This committee does not enforce compliance with the standards it issues. Rather, the expectation is that national authorities will take steps to put in place the necessary arrangements, statutory or otherwise, that are best suited to their own national systems.
4. Basel II represents a much more comprehensive approach to the greater complexity of present day banking. It covers,
   (a) Capital adequacy requirements.
   (b) Supervisors see not only on a bank's calculation of its need for capital, but also how the bank manages a wide array of risks.
   (c) To ensure that banks achieve the high standards of public disclosure that are needed for market discipline to be effective.
5. Debt Recovery Tribunal.
6. International Accounting Standards Board.

Mobilization and Promotion of Saving Habits among Rural-Based SCI Owners through "Cost Plus Deferred Sale" Mode of Interest-Free Banking Financing System

9

(A study based on rural-based small and cottage industry (SCI) finance in Bangladesh by Islamic banks on Bai-Mujjal mode of financing)

Mohammed Nurul Alam

ABSTRACT

The rural-based industrial sector in least developed and developing nations contribute greatly towards economic development by generating employment opportunities. This sector of economy suffers a great deal due to the lack of sufficient funds and a good entrepreneurship capabilities. The research based on the rural-based SCI (Alam, 2002) shows that the rural-based SCI sector plays a predominant role in mobilizing rural savings towards productive sectors. It is revealed from the study that the "Cost Plus Profit under deferred Sale (Bai-Muajjal) mode of financing used by Islamic banks is a unique means that not only promote the mobilization of rural savings towards productive sources but also develop the saving habits among rural entrepreneurs. The paper describes how and to what extent the lending process of the Bai-Muajjal mode of Islamic banking finance serves to institutionalize the saving habits of rural-based small industry owners and to what extent this lending technique successfully mobilize rural savings towards productive and profitable projects.

In order to study this phenomenon, I used a theoretical framework called the "Institutional-Network Approach" (Alam, 2002). The theoretical model are applied to study how Islamic banks lend funds to the rural-based SCI owners through Bai-Muajjal mode of financing and develop a lender-borrower network relationships, which ultimately contribute in developing saving habits among rural-based small and cottage industry owners. The empirical studies were conducted in Bangladesh and required data for the study were collected from both Islamic banks and the rural-based small industry owners in the counter. In order to understand the lender-borrower relationships in depth, a qualitative nature of research methodology was used in the study. Since case studies reveal various facts about a particular phenomenon and allow a researcher to get very close to his or her informants, I used a case study method while collecting data from the field. I interviewed numbers of rural-based small industry owners, clientele of various Islamic banks, from different areas of Bangladesh.

INTRODUCTION

The rural-based small and cottage industry (SCI) sector in developing nations contributes greatly towards economic development by generating employment opportunities and mobilizing rural savings towards productive sectors. It is revealed from many researches that this SCI sector is one of the most neglected sectors of economy in almost all least developed and developing nations of the world. Among others rural-based SCI owners suffers from lack in working capital, institutional credit facilities and poor management. Due to the shortage of capital they are compelled to borrow funds from local moneylenders at a high rate of interest. This practice brings endless miseries to the rural-based poor SCI owners. With regards to the burden of debts of the rural poor there is a proverb in developing nations, which says, 'The rural poor are born in debt, live on debts and die in debts'.

It is observed from the study that most of the rural people are savings minded and they try to save from, whatever little earnings they have. Unfortunately, the efforts of these people remain unattended. Formal as well as informal lending organizations seldom consider the issue of rural savings as an important factor for generating working capital for rural SCI owners. Institutionalization of saving habits through lending procedures might contribute to a greater extent in developing saving mentality among rural-based SCI owners and also to mobilize these savings towards productive sectors.

In recent years different Interest-free banks in Bangladesh started lending funds towards rural-based SCI projects. Some of the lending procedures of this financing system are designed in such a way that a client must show minimum personal savings in order to be qualified for a loan. The CPSDP mode of Interest-free banking finance is one of them. This lending mode of Interest-free banks is normally used while giving credit to the rural-based SCI owners. In this article, I tried to highlight on how the CPSDP mode of financing contributes towards developing and institutionalizing saving habits of their clients.

The study was carried out in Bangladesh and used a theoretical model; 'Institutional-Network Approach' (Alam, 2003). While conducting the empirical study, I interviewed 125 rural-based SCI owners who were clients to different Interest-free banks in the country. Among these respondents 40 clients were running grass-root type (poultry/dairy firms and handloom industries) of small and cottage industries. The Social Investment Bank Limited (SIBL); one of the Interest-free banks in the country gave loans to them on the CPSDP mode of financing. Based on the said theoretical perspective, I tried to analyze data in order to see as to what extent the CPSDP mode of financing of Interest-free bank contributes towards developing saving habits and the way the bank institutionalized this habit of the rural SCI owner. The article also highlights on the extent to which this particular lending procedure of the bank assists clients to make proper use of their borrowed funds and to develop lender-borrower network relationships. In order to understand the lender-borrower relationships in depth, a qualitative nature of research methodology was used in the study. Since case studies reveal various facts about a particular phenomenon and allow a researcher to get very close to his or her informants, I used a case study method while collecting data from the field. Besides rural-based SCI owners, I also interviewed number of Interest-free banks that give loans to different rural-based SCI sectors in Bangladesh.

The article is designed in a few major sections. Firstly, I tried to highlight on the theoretical and methodological approaches that I used in the study. The second section includes a brief description of Interest-free banks and different investment techniques followed by these banks. The third section includes a brief description of the CPSDP loan giving procedures followed by the Social Investment Bank Limited while lending funds to the grass-root level SCI owners. The final section of the article represents an analysis of the results obtained from the study.

THEORETICAL AND METHODOLOGICAL APPROACHES

As mentioned above, based on Whitley's (1992a) 'Business System' institutional approach, I developed an analytical frame of references to study the lender-borrower relationships between different financing organizations and rural-based small and cottage industries. The theoretical model is designed in such a way that different small and cottage industries as well as financing organizations of similar nature are grouped and institutionalized into different SCI systems and Financing Systems. The theoretical model is also used to carry out a comparative study as to how financing organizations under different financing system differ from each other while lending funds towards SCI owners under different SCI systems.

In order to achieve the said objectives, I developed the concept of four components of different SCI systems and financing systems. These components for example, are nature of organization, market organization, employment systems and authority and control systems. According to Whitley (1992b) a comparative analysis of the 'business system' is the systematic study of these configurations and as to how they become established in markets. Like Whitley's (1992b) 'business systems', the Islamic financing system is seen as a 'financing business system of its own, with a foundation based on religion, having its own rules governed by the Islamic laws'. These rules differ from those of other financial systems. Different financial systems (for example, market based financing system (MBFS) such as conventional banks, cooperative financing system (CFS), and (TMLS) traditional money lending system viewed as particular arrangements of hierarchy-market relations that become institutionalized and relatively successful in a particular context. A similar arrangement is also done to institutionalize different rural-based small and cottage industries. Different small and cottage industries of similar nature are thus, grouped into three different SCI systems, such as grass-root level (GL), season-based (SB) and semi-mechanized (SM) SCI systems. Different financing organizations and small and cottage industries under different financing systems and SCI systems are regarded as economic actors acting within these organizational fields.

Since the network relationship part of the hierarchy-market relationships is poorly developed in Whitley's (1992b) 'Business Systems' approach, concepts of Jansson's (2000) network institutional model was also taken into consideration for developing my theoretical frame of references. In his network institutional model, Jansson (2000) highlights network relationships between the multinational corporations (MNC) in India and major external parties in the product/services market like customers, intermediaries, competitors and suppliers. It also gives some examples of external institutional factors that affect the networks. Like the network relations between the MNC and major external parties financial organizations in the present study influence and are influenced by various commercial actors in the financial market and other markets in Bangladesh. Since one of the main objects of the study is to study network relations between financial organizations and other major external parties in the financial market, especially the SCIs, regarding the use of the network approach among many others (for example, Rasmussen, 1988; Kuklinski and Knoke, 1988; Anderson and Carlos, 1976; Easton and Araujo, 1991; Elg and Johansson, 1992; Easton, 1992; Håkansson, 1993; Aldrich and Whetten, 1981; Emerson and Cook, 1984), I found the concept of Janssons's (2000) model appropriate for the present study. Thus, based on the existing theoretical models as mentioned above, I developed 'Institutional-Network' model (Alam, 2001) for studying the lender-borrower relationships between economic actors in different financing systems and SCI systems, especially with regards to financing towards small and cottage industry (SCI) sector. The theoretical model also includes various background societal institutions like country culture, legal systems, religion, family/clan, government, etc. that have direct or indirect influences on lending and borrowing activities between different financing organizations and the rural-based SCI owners. The article is designed to highlight the empirical finding relating to lender-borrower relationships between small and cottage industries under the grass-root level (GL) SCI system and Interest-free banks under the interest-free financing

Methodological Approach

In order to develop a theoretical model my methodological approach used in the study was a combination of both **deductive** and **inductive** (Glaser, 1978; Strauss and Corbin, 1990; Jansson et al. 1995) approaches. In the deductive approach, one tests the hypothesis or the validity of a theory. It is a method by which one may study an individual case using a general law—that is, a logical analysis of what the general theory says about a specific event. Initially, the research design was based mainly on Whitley's institutional theory (1987, 1990, 1992 a, b), and the network institutional theory of Jansson (2000), and network theories of Kuklinski and Knoke (1988), Johansson et al. (1992). and Håkansson (1993). The inductive approach principle means a journey made by a researcher from the empirical point to the stage of a theory development. At one point in the work, based on the data collected from the field. I modified the originally defined theories and developed a theoretical frame of references based on which data collected from the field are analyzed.

The research methodology applied in the study is of a qualitative nature (Jick, 1979; Merriam, 1998; Sherman and Webb, 1988; Patton, 1985). A qualitative type of research is characterized by collection of data directly from respondents in the field. This is because the entire research program is based on facts acquired from the material world, that is, the practical field of study. The study of lender-borrower network relationships between rural-based SCI owners and Interest-free banks was conducted through 'in-depth' interviews with respondents under review.

A case study (Yin, 1994) method was adopted as a research strategy in order to focus on contemporary phenomenon within the real life context of different rural-based SCI owners under various SCI systems and their relationships with financing organizations within the Islamic financing systems.

THE LACK OF INSTITUTIONAL CREDIT FOR SCIs IN BANGLADESH

The SCI sector in Bangladesh suffers greatly due to the lack of an institutional credit facilities. There are many formal as well as informal financing organizations that are functioning in the money market of Bangladesh. Formal financing institutions like government and privately owned commercial banks normally give loans to large and medium scale industries. Cooperative banks in the country although gives loans to the rural-based small and cottage industry owners, they confine their credit giving activities mainly to the members of the bank. One of the specialized banks in Bangladesh called 'Grameen bank' (Yunus, 1993; Nabi, 1996) also gives loans to the rural-based poor people. But due to the limitation of amount of credit to customers, high risks and administrative costs, the bank has not initiated any loans to small and cottage industry owners in the country. Moneylenders in rural Bangladesh are also an important source of lending funds to the SCI owners. Since last two decades a few Interest-free banks started financing different industrial and business sectors. Some of these banks extended their loan giving activities towards rural-based SCI owners.

During my field studies I interviewed 125 different rural-based SCI owners who are customers of different Interest-free banks in the country. In my interview I tried to acquire knowledge from these respondents about different sources that they used to get funds before taking loans from the Interest-free banks. The result shows that 30 of 125 clients received loans from conventional banks of which twenty from government commercial banks and ten from private commercial banks. Among remaining clients 57 raised their funds from friends and personal savings, 4 from cooperative banks and 34 from moneylenders. The figures are demonstrated in percentage in figure 9.1.

It is noted from the above figure that more than 70 per cent SCI owners interviewed raised their funds from informal sources

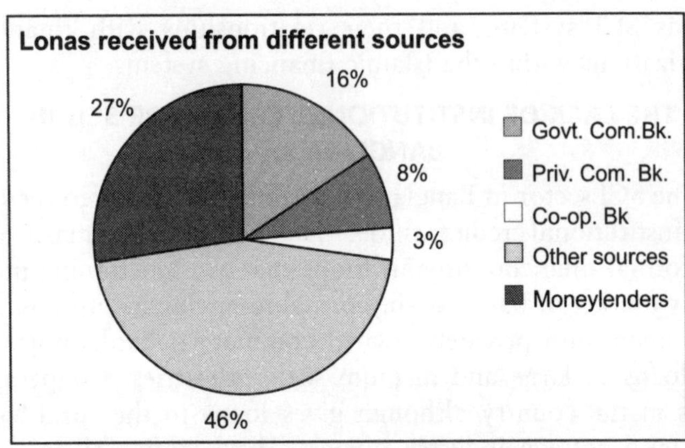

Source: Field study on SCI in Bangladesh 1997.

Figure 9.1: Sources of funds of rural-based SCI owners

of credit. Only 27 per cent SCI owners received loans from formal credit giving institutions.

It is mentioned in the earlier section that like other conventional banks financing organizations in the Interest-free banking system render financial services towards different industrial sectors in the money market of Bangladesh. For reader's knowledge, before introducing Interest-free banks and its relationships with lenders especially the grass-root level small and cottage industry owners, a brief description of an Interest-free bank and its investment modes is given in the following section.

AN INTEREST-FREE BANK: A BANK WITHOUT INTEREST

An Interest-free bank may be defined as a financial intermediary whose objectives and operations as well as principles and practices must conform to the principles of Islamic Law (Shariah); and, consequently, is conditioned to operate all its activities without interest (Alam, 2001). The aim of Islamic economics, as observed by Molla et.al. (1988), is not only the elimination of interest-based transactions but also the establishment of a just and balanced social order free from all kinds of exploitation. An Interest-free bank is not only a financier but also a partner in business. The system essentially involves sharing of risk between the owner of capital and the entrepreneurs, as well as sharing the result of the collective efforts. Thus, it differs from an interest-based system in which the risk is mainly borne by the entrepreneur or by the user of capital. In other way we can call Interest-free banking as participatory banking.

Nassief (1989), Ahsan (1989), and Kazarian (1991) observed that more than 70 Interest-free banks and Insurance houses are rendering interest-free services in Asia, the Middle East, the Far East, Africa and Europe and North American countries. The Islamic Society of North America Canada (ISNA, 2000), has initiated Interest-free banking activities in recent years and started lending interest-free funds to their customers especially for housing and other projects. The interest-free housing loans are given through the ISNA controlled organization called "Islamic Co-operative Housing Corporation Limited (ICHC). A few Western banks such as, the Kleinworte Benson, Citibank and ANZ Grindlays also started to adopt the pattern of Interest-free banking in cost-plus financing, leasing and equity financing for their clients in the Middle East, South-East Asia and a few international corporations in Europe and Latin America (Gathura, 1996; Roula, 1995; Ken, 1994; Parker, 1993; Heffernan, 1999).

INVESTMENT MODES USED BY INTEREST-FREE BANKS

An Interest-free bank renders similar services to their customers as other conventional banks but due to the differences in the principles of Interest-free banking systems the modes or techniques of accepting deposits and lending funds to customers differ from conventional banks. The investment modes that an Interest-free bank uses while investing funds are discussed below:

Mudaraba or Capital Financing

Under the Capital Trust Financing or Mudaraba mode of financing Interest-free banks supplies the entire capital of the business and the customer gives his time and expertise, which form a relationship between the supplier of capital and the user of capital. Thus, the bank and the customer work together and share profits and losses.

Musharaka or Partnership Financing

The word 'Musharaka' means a profit sharing joint venture, designed to limited production or commercial activities of long duration. In this case, the bank and the customer contribute capital jointly. They also contribute managerial expertise and other essential services at agreed proportions. Profit or losses are shared according to the contract agreed upon. An individual partner does not become liable for the losses caused by others. Due to this joint venture this technique is also known as Equity Participation mode of investment. Profit is distributed according to a predetermined ratio and loss, if any is also shared according to the capital ratio. Both the bank and the customer take part in the management and control of the entrepreneurial activities.

Murabaha (Mark-up or Costs-Plus Profit based financing)

Khoja and Ghuddah (1997, Chap. 1, p. 2), state that the mode of Murabaha sale connected to a promise is used by the Interest-free banks which undertake the purchaser of commodities according to the specification requested by the customer. The bank then resells them on Murabaha to the one who promised to buy for its cost price plus a margin of profit agreed upon previously by the two parties. Under the Murabaha mode of investment the bank agrees to purchase for a client who will then reimburse the bank in a stated time period at an agreed upon profit margin. The mark-up price that the bank and the buyer agree to is mainly based on the market price of the commodity. Thus, the bank earns a profit without bearing any risk.

CPSDP or Cost-Plus Sale Under Deferred Payment

The CPSDP mode of investment is as like as a Murabaha mode of investment with an exception that the sale under this cost-plus sale modes investment is made on a credit basis rather than cash. The main feature of this technique consists in procurement of goods at the request of the client and selling it to him on credit. This mode follows the same conditions as Murabaha mode of investment except the following:

The bank transfers the possession of goods to the client before payment.

In order to cover the sale price of the goods the bank obtains collateral securities from the client.

The bank normally takes property of Municipal area as mortgage. In case the client fails to repay the sale price the bank realizes the amount by selling the mortgage property.

Bai-Salam or Advance Purchase

Under Bai-Salam mode of investment the bank purchases industrial and agricultural products in advance from their customers. The main features of this mode are:

The price is normally paid with the execution of an agreement.

According to the terms of agreement the bank receives the goods in due time.

Hire-Purchase Investment Under Shirkatul Meelk

Interest-free banks in Bangladesh also invest funds under Hire-Purchase mode. Under this investment technique the bank sells building, transport and other valuable items to the client. The value of hire-purchase amount is payable in installments. When the client pays back the value of the goods including rent, the ownership is transferred to him.

Ijara or Leasing

The word 'Ijara' indicates leasing. The leasing purchase is another technique followed by Interest-free banks in financing customers. This system is almost similar to the leasing activity provided in traditional banking. Leasing is a contract between the bank and the customer to use particular assets. In this case the bank is called lessor and the customer is called lessee who wants to use the assets and pays rent. Zineldin (1990), in this regard argued that the leasing agreement is based on profit sharing in which the bank buys the movable or immovable property and lease it to one of its client for an agreed sum by installments and for a limited period of time into a saving account held with the same bank. These installments are invested in Mudaraba investment (Venture) for the customer's account. The accumulated profit generated from the payments, and the payments themselves are invested in the bank's investment ventures over the time period of lease, contributing to eventual purchase of the leased assets.

Ijara-wa-iqtina (Leasing Purchase)

According to the Western leasing system the lessee pays specific rentals and a fixed rate of interest over a given period for the use of specific assets. But in the Interest-free banking system of leasing the risk related to leasing has to be shared between the bank and the lessee, in case of any damage to the leased assets. The contract is called 'ijara-wa-iqtina' i.e. leasing purchase, when the ownership of the assets is transferred to the clients after the completion of the leasing contract.

Quard E Hasan

Quard E Hasan means an interest-free loan given by the Interest-free bank to the needy people in a society. The practice of dealing with this sort of investment differs from bank to bank. Quard E Hasan is normally given to needy students, small producers, farmers, entrepreneurs and economically weaker sections of the society, who are not in a position to obtain loan or any financial assistance from any other institutional sources. The main aim of this loan is to help needy people in a society in order to, make them self-sufficient and to raise their income and standards of living.

INTEREST FREE BANKING FINANCE TOWARDS SCI SECTOR

One of the major aims of this financial organization under Islamic financing system is to render financial services to the rural-based SCIs sector in a society. In many ways, Interest-free banks are similar to other privately-owned formal financial intermediaries. The main difference is that an Interest-free bank neither accepts deposits nor invests funds to its customers on interest. Instead, the bank shares profit or loss. As noted in figure 9.1 above, Nienhaus (1993) also observes that the rural based SCI owners are not being benefited much either by the state-owned or the privately-owned financial organizations. One might, therefore, find it interesting to observe how an Interest-free bank acts as 'bank for rural SCI owners'; for example, how far an Interest-free bank, with its motive of investing funds on a 'profit and loss sharing' basis, may contribute towards financing and promoting rural-based SCIs sector.

LENDING FUNDS THROUGH CPSDP MODE: AN EMPIRICAL REVIEW

As mentioned in my early discussion, I interviewed a number of rural-based small and cottage industries that are clients of different interest-free banks in Bangladesh. One of the interest-free banks called Social Investment Bank Limited (SIBL) gives loan to the SCI owners under the grass-root level SCI owners involved in poultry/diary firms, handloom industries, etc. These sorts of SCIs are grouped and institutionalized as grass-root level (GL) SCI system in my study. I conducted in-depth interviews with 40 GL, SCI owners in two rural villages who are clients of the Social Investment Bank Limited. Among these respondents twenty are poultry firm owners and twenty handloom industry owners. The bank gives loans to these SCI owners under the CPSDP mode of interest-free banking finance. The lending procedures under this financing mode initiate in a different way than the normal loan giving process followed by other conventional banks. A brief description of lending policy of the Social Investment Bank Limited towards the rural base grass-root level SCI owners is discussed in the following section.

The Formation of Groups and Teams Among Customers

This bank gives interest-free loans to its customers on the condition that they first create a group amongst themselves. Customers who intend to take loans are asked to form a group of five members before the request for a loan may be assessed. Each group requires a volunteer group leader to organize all aspects of the business and to assist the other group members in various activities. In such a group-wise loan, group members are jointly liable for the mistakes the other members might make. The bank then forms a **team**, which consists of five individual groups of poultry farmers. All the groups within a team are in turn also responsible for each other's activities and they relate every instance back to their designated team leader. The group leaders of five different groups work as members of a

team executive committee and this committee selects one president, one cashier, and one secretary.

The bank's staff is responsible for training the group leaders. The training consists of information sessions where everyone learns general ideas and techniques about their production activities. For example, in case of poultry firm, the team leaders of the poultry firms are taught how to care of chickens at every phase of the chickens life; this includes how one ought to administer medicine and other nursing aids when the need arises.

Organizing Group Activities and Group Members by the Bank

Under the supervision of the Social Investment Bank Limited staff, grass-root level SCI owners (respondents) organized the different groups comprised of five farmers in each group who were interested in borrowing funds from the bank. An officer is usually assigned by the bank to organize meetings with each group on different days of the week. Thus, each group has the opportunity to contact the bank directly, through the persons of either bank officer, if they feel the need to discuss any issues they are facing.

Opening of a Savings Account with the Bank

In order to obtain a loan from the bank, every member in a group is required to open a savings account with the bank and deposit an agreed-upon amount of money every week. The savings accumulate gradually and steadily using this method, for up to ten weeks. The respondents opened savings accounts with the bank under their own names. These types of accounts are called 'Mudaraba Savings Accounts' (also known as Profit & Loss Savings Accounts). After the account had been opened, each member of a group was expected to begin depositing both a minimum amount of TK. 25 and a maximum of TK. 50[1] every week.

Weekly Deposits to the Account by Clients in the Group

It is the group leader's duty to collect money during the week from the members of his or her group and to record how

1. 1,00 USD is equal to 57.4000 BDT, Live Rates as of 24.06.2001 (http://www.xe.net/ucc/convert.cgi)

much each person contributed in a ledger. At the end of every week, the leader submits the entire sum of cash, along with the record of names of the depositors, to the cashier of the team. The bank officer incharge of supervising the projects visits the project-site once in a week and collects these deposits from the cashier of team. The amount that is collected is then credited to the respondents' savings accounts.

Minimum Deposits Required to Obtain Loans

The staff of the bank responsible for collecting information about customers determines whether various project proposals the customers intended to initiate using the bank's money were feasible. The bank handles the weekly sum of savings quite carefully because a customer's deposit figure must exceed 5 per cent of the loan he/she applied for or he/she will not be entitled to receive any loans from the bank. For this reason, the bank officer regularly gives business advice that will be necessary if his clients are to succeed. He encourages them to be punctual with the deposits of their weekly savings so as to avoid hassles. Apart from this regular advisement and encouragement, the bank officers incharge of the project also give the respondents training in their respective fields of expertise.

Bank Officers' Direct Contacts

During the ten-week saving period, it is also the duty of the bank officer-in-charge to inquire about each borrower's working capability and the types of business they are interested in for the future. The bank officers meet every group at different times to educate them about the Interest-free banking systems, and particularly about its techniques and its aims. At the same time, he also gives them information about how their new banks have developed.

Initiation of Loan Process After the Saving Period Ends

When the ten weeks of the term of the savings with the bank came to an end, the group leaders arrange a meeting with all the individual members of each group. In this general meeting, a resolution is drafted and passed regarding the amount of loan each member intended to borrow from the bank. A copy of this resolution is then prepared for the bank officer when he came to visit the site. After considering this resolution, the visiting bank officer fixes a date with each individual member of the various groups to come to the bank with their group leaders to sign the contract for the loan.

Payment of Loans

When the above-mentioned processes ended the bank sanctioned loans to the clients on a CPSDP mode of financing. As mentioned earlier, under this mode of financing, the bank does not issue the agreed-upon loan amount to the customer in cash, as is the custom of most conventional banks. When they signed their loan agreement with the bank, the respondents under review were asked by the bank to select a raw material supplier and to bring invoices for the price of the raw materials that they required for their industry. The respondents promptly complied and immediately sought suppliers and collected invoices from them. Another bank officer was incharge of supervising this aspect of the project and giving any professional assistance that was required of him. Once the bank authorities were satisfied with the invoice prices, the quantity of materials, etc., he made necessary arrangement to pay the money directly to the suppliers. They then debit the same amount from each customer's account, in accordance to the amount each had stated was necessary for his/her specific needs. In this way, the bank ensures that the fund borrowed by SCI owners will be directed efficiently and that the customer will be successful in achieving his or her goal.

The Supervision of Borrowed Funds

The SIBL allows its customers free access to their entire borrowed fund, with an important stipulation; before one is able to get unlimited access, one must prove to the bank that the amount being lent will only be spent to buy raw materials or other accessories for the development of the farm. In order to do this; the customer must produce new invoices from the vendors of the raw materials each time he visits the bank. They may then utilize the whole amount all at once, or however, else they may see fit. This is allowed to take place only after the loan has been sanctioned and credited to the individual's Profit and Loss Savings Account.

Profits Charged by the Bank

A further condition within the SIBL's lending policies under CPSDP mode that deal with the clients in the grass-root level SCI system is that the bank officials who deal with them calculate a percentage of profit on top of the invoice price after the customers present their invoices for the materials they intend to buy. The principle of the CPSDP mode of financing is that the bank first buys goods for customers and then sells these goods back to them at a profit. The bank realizes the principal amount of loans plus the profits from customers in separate, equal installments. In this particular case, the SIBL charged the SCI owners 14 per cent of their net profits made on the goods bought by the bank for the customer. Soon after the purchase was made, the respondents became the owners of the goods and were responsible for its proper use.

Security

As a security measure, the bank asks the respondents to produce their land property title documents as well as a letter of recommendation either from a person notarized by the bank or from an influential customer of the bank in the locality.

Repayment of Loans

The repayment of loans, including profits, was divided into a number of equal installments. The SIBL fixed the installment rate of repayment of the loan. This repayment time starts two weeks after the customer receives the loan or soon after the product is ready for sale in the market.

CPSDP MODE OF FINANCING AND ITS EFFECTS ON SCI OWNERS: A CRITICAL ANALYSIS

The study reveals that the mobilization of the rural savings is one of the prime aims of the organizations in the interest-free financing, where their lending techniques develop the saving mentalities among the customers, especially the rural-based SCI units. It is noted from the above discussions that the financing organizations in the Islamic financing system while lending funds to firms in the grass-root level SCI system demands deposits from their customers. The clients in this SCI system accumulate these deposits through individual savings. Financing organizations in the interest-free financing supervise and monitor the customers' savings activities through certain established rules. In this section a detailed analysis is done to see how changed saving habits are regulated and savings are mobilized towards productive projects by the financing organizations in the Islamic financing system through CPSDP lending mode of financing.

It is noted from the empirical record that the Social Investment Bank Limited through its CPSDP lending technique develops new ways to save i.e. how saving is institutionalized to become new or behavioral rule of these organizations. It is also found that the development of new saving habits among the SCI owners promotes network ties with different actors within and outside the SCI units. Since the interest-free financing introduced its special lending policy in the grass-root level SCI system, the saving of the SCI owners is governed by the new rules creating another saving habit. In order to borrow funds, the grass-root level SCI owners are required to abide by these saving rules. Thus, through the lending process new saving habits of the rural people have been institutionalized.

Habits Viewed as an Institution

Habits originate as serial repetition of behavior within the complex interaction of human beings. Habits are either hereditary in nature or grows through imitation, but in both cases based on replication of a precedent. Every society considers social habit to be a significant factor in determining social law and customs, and *vice versa*. According to Veblen (1919, p. 239), institutions themselves are comprised of 'settled habits of thought common to generality of men'. Man is socialized by societal agents and forces, thus habits are an outcome of social behavior, customs, traditions and law. Habits influence economic as well as non-economic activities of human beings in their everyday life.

Habits play out in human life in various ways. Some habits are natural, essential for living such as physical necessities of eating and sleeping, whilst other habits are acquired from the social environment. Habit, as mentioned, is also established in human life through imitation of others. Regardless of the mode of entrenchment, habits have a great impact on the economic and social activities of a society. Good habits reduce the social burden and, arguably, *vice versa.* Hodgson (1988, p. 127), observes as "We acquire habit in various ways. Sometime it is through the imitation of others. This does not always result from full conscious choice, as all animal species are born with some capacity to imitate. The development of the intellectual and political skills of young children is based largely on imitation, and we retain this faculty in later life, other without conscious thought about what we are doing".

While discussing on the subject rural savings and saving habit of grass-root level SCI owners, I think it is needed to highlight on traditional saving habits that play an important role in rural economy of Bangladesh. In order to that the first part of the discussion in this section includes an overall position of the traditional saving habit and sources of savings. Then it discusses the extent to which the organizations in the Islamic financing system contribute to mobilizing the rural savings towards the productive sectors.

Traditional Habits of Savings

Veblen (1919) views habits as either hereditary in nature or that they grow through imitation. The author further argues that institutions themselves are comprised of settled habits of thought common to the general public. Saving habits influence economic as well as non-economic activities in almost all societies. Ashe and Cosslett (1989, p. 94), reports that household savings in the informal sector is an essential element in the growth of developing economies. Partly, because informal sector is larger than formal sector.

It is observed from the study that the rural-based SCI owners are usually habituated to save funds. Saving tendencies are a hereditary part of these people's nature. The majority of respondents in the SCI units in rural areas informed that, although they used to save money on their own initiative, they could hardly use these funds in a profitable way. It was also known from the study that the rural-based SCI owners are used to saving money for different purposes. Some of these are discussed below.

Motives Behind the Traditional Savings

Saving is found to be a very common habit among the majority of the SCI owners. But the motive behind creating saving differs from person to person and from family to family. While interviewing grass-root level SCI owners it was found that almost all grass-root level SCI owners were trying to save a little from what they had. But the motive behind the savings was different. 21 respondents among 40 grass-root level SCI owners interviewed expressed the motive of savings was to accumulate funds for the matrimonial ceremonies of their children. Ten clients intended to use savings for buying gold or land. Three of them intended to spend for religious and cultural functions and seven invest in business. These figures are demonstrated in percentage by the following figure.

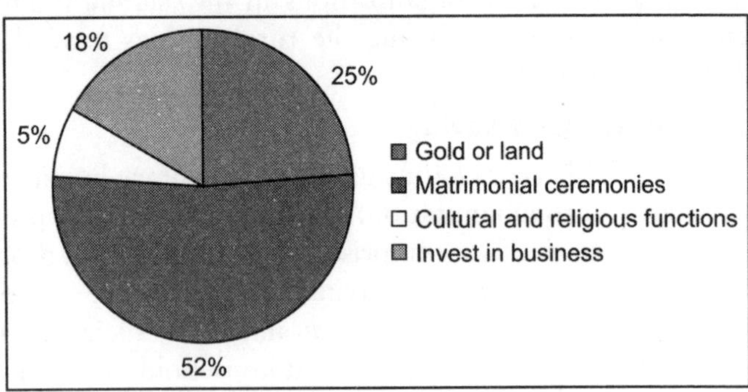

Source: Field studies on SCI in Bangladesh 1997

Figure 9.2: Utilization of Savings

The above figure shows that more than 50 per cent respondent having children were worried for the marriage of their daughter and they start saving a little of what they have for their matrimonial ceremonies. Only 18 per cent showed their interest in utilizing their savings for the business or productive purposes. They were afraid of using their savings funds for business purposes because of their lack of entrepreneurial mentality, the risk involved, and the lack of experience in business. Therefore, large amounts of rural savings are not being utilized in any productive activities, instead being locked in unproductive sources.

CHANGING SAVING HABITS: THE ROLE OF THE INTEREST-FREE FINANCING SYSTEM

The lending policy of the financing organizations in the Interest-Free Financing gives prime priority to the saving habits of people. As one of their lending principles, owners of the grass-root level SCI owners deposit a certain percentage of the borrowed funds. They are required to make these deposits from their weekly savings. The following section includes a discussion about various reasons as to why the Social Investment Bank Limited give preference to their clients accumulate weekly deposit, thereby creating new habits of saving for these organizations and in that way institutionalizing new ways of saving.

Developing a Saving Mentality Among Rural Poors

The SCI owners in the grass-root level SCI system are poor rural people, who have very little educational qualifications and professional skills. They are therefore unable to understand how to save in a proper way for example using savings in productive ways. In order to develop the saving mentality among rural SCI owners the financing organizations within the Islamic financing system arrange their lending activities in such a way that the borrowers initiate group savings before they apply for loans. It takes a few weeks for the SCI owner in the grass-root level SCI system to obtain a loan. During this period, the Interest-free banks contact their customers from time to time, to discuss various issues concerning their projects, and to monitor the progress of the group savings in order to develop the proper savings mentality. Thus, the organizations within the Islamic financing system establish close contacts with the SCI owners in the grass-root level SCI system and encourage them to save and plan how and in which way to spend their savings. In developing the saving mentality of the SCI owners they assist them to accumulate their idle funds and to use the same for productive purposes.

Educating About Saving Habits

As noted above, although the SCI owners in the grass-root level SCI system are poor, many of them spend, whatever they have saved in unproductive ways, for example, on dowries at marriage ceremonies. Since the organizations within Islamic financing system do not start lending before the groups savings are initiated, the lending rules themselves educate the clients about the advantage of savings. Moreover, bank officials, through personal contact, discuss various issues regarding the drawbacks of the old saving habits. Thus, it is concluded that the rural SCI owners are educated about how to make proper utilization of their savings in productive ways. New saving habits are thereby being institutionalized. By giving them a proper understanding of the value of their savings, the lending organizations within the interest-free financing encourage poor SCI units to start saving from the little they have in their hands.

Uniting Customers' Efforts

The bank also had the idea of developing the saving habits to establish unity among people from different walks of social life. The lending activities initiated through the group savings established unity among rural people of different social categories, since it encourages different individual SCI owners to work together in harmony. Thus, new saving habits not only unite the rural SCI owners but also their skills and efforts. This ultimately results in the investment of funds towards productive activities. The rule to collect individual savings encourages customers to fulfill the group obligations. Thus, the savings of the individuals are mobilized from unproductive uses towards productive fields.

In his discussion of social life and group behavior, Hughes (1939) observed that anything socially established can be called an institution. It is mentioned in earlier sections that the rural people in Bangladesh try to save from, whatever income they have, but this habit is neither taken care of nor guided by any lending organization. Human habits do not change without a change in catalytic circumstances. For example, if one is inclined to believe that a change of habits or a development of a new habit in everyday life is likely to be of benefit, materially or financially, one may not hesitate to transform habits as a conscious act of volition. Within the societal domain, however, it may require an institutional process or policies adopted either by the government or the individual institution. By way of example, let us refer to the case of saving habits among people in a society. Needless to remind, that every spending that is incurred by people may not be productive. A proper motivation and guide for people to save money may end up with a good result if, in return, they are shown a profit oriented and productive project in which to invest their savings.

CPSDP mode of savings as observed in the earlier section, changes socially established saving habits of rural-based SCI owners. The traditional habit is changed to a newly developed saving habit. The entire lending process of the Interest-free bank consists of certain rules, procedures which in a way is used in organizing the behavior of the bank's clientele. Thus, it may rightly be said that, through the CPSDP lending process saving habits of the rural SCI clientele are institutionalized. Regarding institution Jansson (2000) observed that, an institution usually means rules, procedures, and conventions typical for a more specific way of organizing human behavior—a (legitimized) social grouping of some kind—for example family, clan organization, nation, market game or ceremony. Within these institutions are found rules and conventions typical of specific organization, which led to habitual and routinized behavior or action. Regarding the concept of institutionalization Berger & Luckmann (1966, p. 72) observes: "Institutionalization occurs, whenever, there is a reciprocal typification of habitualized actions by types of actors.... They cannot be created instantaneously. Institutions always have a history, of which they are the products. It is impossible to understand an institution adequately without an understanding of the historical process in which it was produced." Genell (1997) argued that the institutionalization is the process by which a constituted reality becomes "real", that is, apparently independent of its structures, and hence, taken for granted. The critical analysis of the CPSDP mode of Interest-free banking finance indicates that the entire process of savings and its uses contribute towards developing other new habits. For example, the people of the different SCI units start to think along the lines of productive activities. The savings activities are organized and arranged in such a way that they develop lender-borrower relationships and establish close ties with co-workers within the locality. Furthermore, the newly developed, saving habits direct them to think in advance regarding a particular project in which they might invest their savings. The traditional, saving habits of SCI owners discontinue with the gradual development of new habits. This mobilization of the savings takes place through institutionalization of new saving habits. Institutionalization of saving habits is a process of changing spending behavior of the rural poor and promoting a goal oriented saving habits among these people.

The saving habits of the clients are established through certain rules. The process used by the bank is a unique means of organizing human efforts and behavior. It is thus concluded that an important part of the lending policy of this bank is aimed at institutionalizing saving habits of the rural-based SCI owners and organizing savings towards productive activities.

The new institutionalized saving habits of the SCI owners in the grass-root level SCI system are characterized by the following factors:

- Savings are generated from self-earning.
- Savings are initiated and supervised by the financing organizations in the Islamic financing system.
- Savings are deposited with the financing organization.
- Customers knows about the purposes of their savings.
- Savings are returned back to customers as capital for production.
- Capital formation is done through depositing savings with the financing organizations.
- Savings are utilized in productive sectors.
- Savings are utilized in a proper way to create job facilities.
- Saving habits develop network relations within the co-workers and with financing organizations.

CONCLUSION

In conclusion it may be said that as seen above the spending habits of the people in rural Bangladesh are habits influenced by societal institutions (Alam, 2001) such as family/clan, religion, country culture, etc. Since a major portion of rural savings is not used in productive purposes, it brings economic miseries in a society and contributes towards intense poverty among rural people. A country like Bangladesh is in need of an organization-based guide to safeguard the rural savings and to make use of these idle funds. Since many rural poor are not aware of the proper utilization of their savings, the institutionalization of saving habits through the CPSDP mode of lending procedure, educate them to spend their savings towards productive venues. It is thus, apparent from the above discussions that the CPSDP mode of Interest-free banking finance is a unique means of institutionalizing and developing saving mentality among the rural-based SCI owners and mobilizing their savings towards productive purposes.

REFERENCES

Ahsan, A.S.M.F. (1989). "Interest-free Banking in Perspective." Proceedings and Papers of International Seminar, *Interest-free Banking and Insurance*, pp. 163-79, Dhaka, 1989.

Johanisson, B. and Nowicki, K. "Using Networks to Organize Support for Entrepreneurs.... A Graph Analysis of Swedish Contexts." Paper presented at the Babson College Entrepreneurship Research Conference, Fontainebleau, France, 1992.

Ken, B. "Interest-free Banking: Faith and Creativity", *New York Times* (Late New York Edition) D1 + Apr 8, 1994.

Anderson, B.O. and Carlos, M.L. "What is Social Network? Power and Control, Social Structures and Their Transformation." *SAGE studies in International Sociology*. 1976.

Hughes, E.C. "Institution". In Park R.E. (Ed), *An Outline of the Principle of Sociology*. New York, Barnes and Nobles, 1939.

Kazarian, E. "Finance and Economic Development, Interest-free Banking in Egypt", *Economic Studies*, No. 45, Lund University, Lund, 1991.

Khoja, E.M. and Gudah, A.S.A. "Instrument of Islamic Investment," Dallah Al-Baraka Group, Research & Development Department. Al-Baraka Investment & Development Co. Interest-free Banking Finance, 1997.

Easton, G. and Araujo, L. "Language, Metaphors and Networks", Paper presented at the 7th I.M.P. Conference, International Business Networks; Evaluation, Structure, and Management, 1991.

Gathura, G. "Banking on Islam (growth of Interest-free banking)", *World Press Review*, Vol. 43, No. 5, May 1996.

Aldrich, H. and Whetten, D.A. "Organisation Set, Action-Sets and Network; Making the Most of Simplicity" in P.C. Nystrom and W.H. Starbuk (eds) *Handbook of Organizational Design*, Volume 1, Oxford University Press, pp. 385-408, 1981.

Håkansson, H. "Industrial Network and Technological Innovation". Uppsala University, Anders Lundgren, Stockholm School of Economics, 1993.

Jansson, H. *International Strategic Management in Emerging Markets: Global Institutions and Networks*, Gotenborg University, Gotenborg (Unpublished), 2000.

Jansson, H. "Marketing to Projects in South East Asia: A Network" Working Paper 1985/3, Department of Business Administration, University of Uppsala, 1985.

ISNA, Islamic Society of North America Canada, Islamic Co-operative Housing Corporation Limited.

Ashe, J. and Cosselett, C.E. "Credit for the Poor" *Past Activities and Future Directions for The United Nations Development Programme*, UNDP Policy Discussion Paper, United Nations publications, New York, 1989.

Kuklinski, J.H. and Knoke, D. *Network Analysis Series, Qualitative Application in the Social Sciences*, SAGE University Press, 28, 1988.

Rasmussen, J. "Goodbye Theory—Hello Reality? Recent Trend in Social and Regional Theory; its Consequences for Network Studies in Africa". Center for Development Research (CDR) Working Paper 88.3. Jan-Mar. Vol. 8, No. 2, 1988.

Nabi, K.A. *Grameen Bank Model and Its Replication in The USA* Minar Offset Printer, Chittagong, 1990.

Roula, K. "Banking the Islamic Way" (Citibank position in Bahrain), *World Press Review*, 42:35, 1995.

Alam, M.N. "Financing of Small and Cottage Industries within the Context of Interest-free Banking Systems" Paper presented at the Final Ph.D. Final Thesis Seminar, Department of Business Administration, Lund University, Lund.

Alam, M.N. "Interest-free Banking Systems: A Challenge in the Modern Financial Market" *International Journal of Islamic Financial Services*. Vol. 1, No. 4, Jan-March, 2000. ISSN 0972-138X.

Yunus, M. "Grameen Bank Project in Bangladesh—A Poverty Four Seed Rural Development Programme," Grameen Bank, Dhaka, 1982.

——. "Dr. Mohammad Yunus and His Grameen Bank", Embassy of People's Republic of Bangladesh, Stockholm, 1993.

Zineldin, M. "The Economics of Money and Banking, A Theoretical and Empirical Study of Islamic Interest-Banking", Stockholm University, 1990.

Parker, M. "Getting the Message Across". (Interest-free banking gets recognized by the Western banks). *The Middle East*, Oct. 1993, 227.

Patton, M.Q. "Quality in Qualitative Research: Methodological Principles and Recent Development". Invited address to Division J of the American Educational Research Association, Chicago, 1985.

Nassief, N. "Interest-free Banking Around The World", Interest-free Banking and Insurance: Proceedings and Papers of International Seminar held in Dhaka, pp. 11-24, Dhaka, 1989.

Emerson, R.M. and Cook, K.S. "Exchange Network and the Analysis of Complex Organization", Research in the Sociology of Organization, Vol. 3, pp. 1-30, 1984.

Molla, R.I. et al. (1988). "Frontiers and Mechanics of Islamic Economics," University of Sokoto, Nigeria, 1988.

Sherman, R.R. and Webb, R.B. "Qualitative Research in Education: A focus", In Sherman, R.R. and Webb, R.B. (eds), *Qualitative Research in Education: Focus and Methods*. Bristol, Pa.: Falmer Press, 1988.

Whitley, R.D. "Taking Firms Seriously as Economic Actors: Towards Sociology of Firm Behavior", *Organisation Studies*, 8: 125-47, 1987.

——. "Eastern Asian Enterprise Structure and the Comparative Analysis Forms of Business Organization". *Organization Studies*, 11(1): 47-54, 1990.

——. "The Comparative Analysis of Business Systems," *European Business Systems*, Richard Whitley (Ed) London: Sage, 1992a.

——. "Business System in East Asia", *Firms, Markets and Societies*, London: Sage, 1992b.

Yin, R.K. *Case Study Research, Design and Methods*. Beverly Hills, Sage, 1994.

Merriam, S.B. *Qualitative Research and Case Study Applications in Education*, Revised and Expanded from Case Study Research, Jossey-Bass Publishers, San Francisco, 1998.

Heffernan, S. *Modern Banking in Theory and Practice*, John Wiley & Sons Ltd., 1999.

Jick, T.D. "Mixing Qualitative and Quantitative Methods: Triangulation in Action". *Administrative Science Quarterly*, 24, pp. 602-11, 1979.

Veblen, T.B. *The Place of Science in Modern Civilization and other Essays*. New York: Huebsch, 1919.

Elg, U. and Johansson, U. *Dagligföretags Strategiska Agerande -En Analysis or ett Interorganisatoriskt Nätverkperspective*, Lund University Press, Lund. 1992.

Nienhaus, V. "Conceptual and Economic Foundations of Interest-free Banking", Paper to be published, in Gian Maria Piccinelli (ed), *Banche Islamiche in Contesto Nonislamico* (Interest-free banks in a non-Islamic Framework), Rome(Instituto per I-Oriente), 1993.

Challenges and Opportunities of Integrating Nigeria's Banking Sector Services into Globalized Economy

I.A.O. Bakare

ABSTRACT

Extreme protagonists of globalization perceive it as a high speed elevator to universal peace and prosperity while its critiques charge it with impoverishing the world's poor, enriching the rich and devastating the environment (World Bank, 2000). Nevertheless, the opportunities of globalization are not automatic but depend on a number of fundamental requirements. In consequence, the paper undertakes the challenges and benefits of integrating Nigerian banking services sector into the globalized economy. The paper discovers that in the short-term period, it is unlikely that Nigerian Banking Services Sector amidst current reforms cannot satisfy most of the globalization requirements particularly in the areas of provision of favourable macroeconomic environment, sound state of infrastructure, effective corporate governance, transparency and accountability; as well as adequate and effective regulatory and supervisory framework of banking services.

However, the problem with financial globalization is not that it is harmful itself but that increase risk comes with its opportunities. The major challenge in this paper stresses the realization of benefits of globalization by Nigerian banking services sector *vis-à-vis* minimization of incidence of risk associated with it.

1. INTRODUCTION

Until the acceptability of financial globalization, financial liberalization was the key policy believed to accelerate efficiency in the financial sector. Infact, many less developed countries (LDCs) embarked on financial liberalization reforms as part of their recommended structural adjustment programmes (Soyibo, 1994 and Aryeetey, 2000).

The rapid growth of international transactions and capital flow is one of the single most profound outcomes of globalization. For instance, global gross capital flows in 2000 amounted to $ 7.5 trillion, a four fold increase over 1990. The growth in cross-border capital movement also resulted in larger net capital flows, rising from $ 500 billion in 1990 to $ 1.2 trillion in 2000. The causes of this growth has been attributed to the removal of statutory restrictions on capital account transactions, economic liberalization and financial deregulation in both industrial and developing countries, macroeconomic stabilization and policy reform in developing countries, enterprise privatization, multilateralization of trade and growth of financial instruments (IMF, 1998).

In corroboration of the argument above, Feldstein (2000) argues that free capital movement permits a more efficient global allocation of savings and direct resources toward its most productive uses because capital is allowed to seek the highest rate of return. Capital mobility strengthens portfolio diversification, risk sharing and intertemporal trade. Free capital flow allows the global economy to reap the efficiency gains created by specialization in the production of financial services. Similarly, capital mobility promotes the dynamic efficiency of the financial sector, arising from increased international competition.

On the contrary, large capital inflow has its inhibitions; it leads to greater risks, thereby raising the potential for systematic disturbances in the financial system as well as capital flow reversals (sudden outflows). Capital inflow may create difficulties for monetary policy management, inflation control and exchange stability and export competitiveness. Moreover, free capital mobility can also be associated with costly financial crisis and payment difficulties as the case of the Asian tigers. This is particularly true in countries with vulnerable financial sectors and inappropriate macroeconomic policies.

Therefore, the major thrust of this paper is to examine the challenges and opportunities involved in integrating banking services sector of Nigeria into globalized economic system. Apart from the general introduction, the structure of the paper is arranged as follows: section two presents trends in global capital flows. Section three captures previous studies while section four highlight benefits and challenges of globalization. Section five and six focuses on: Nigeria and globalization drive and globalized status of Nigerian financial services sector. The last section is devoted to conclusion and policy recommendations.

2. TRENDS IN GLOBAL CAPITAL FLOWS

Today, the principal constraints on national policies are created by the activities of multinational companies and banks (Streeton, 2001). The great depression of the 1930s made some countries, including the UK and US, to abandon the gold standard, devalue their currencies and pursue expansionary policies. Some European countries still stayed on gold but they raised tariffs and used exchange controls to create a series of bilateral trade agreements. The rejection of constraints, such as fixed exchange rate and limits on the discretion of monetary and fiscal policies, led to greater integration of national economies by encouraging full employment and creation of a welfare state. However, this also led to international disintegration among countries of the world, particularly as some were recording deficits and macroeconomic instability while others had surpluses were generated in the 1970s by a few oil-rich countries, later by Germany and Japan and more recently by Japan, including the Asian Tigers. On the other hand, many less developed countries were experiencing current account deficits.

In many respects, the financial markets of today are more closely integrated than those of the past. The range of financial instruments that are traded internationally is broader today.

Whereas, bonds were more important than equity claims before 1914, the two types of instruments contribute roughly equal proportion to international investment today. Similarly, FDI is now undertaken by multinational firms in various manufacturing and service sectors. The differences between 19th century finance market behaviour and the current behaviour underscore the importance of information asymmetries. When information is highly symmetric, investors will concentrate on projects and companies whose assets are tangible and whose operations are most transparent.

The deeper and broader financial integration today can be partly explained by the diminution of information asymmetries. The recent changes in information technology has played an important role in accessing and processing information at cheaper cost. Technology has also made it increasingly difficult for governments to control international capital flows. For example, computer trading complicates the task of monitoring or attempting to control or tax foreign exchange transactions. Although information asymmetry remains, it is easier to obtain information on finance markets, companies and transaction now than it was several years ago.

There was an explosive growth of capital flows, especially private capital flows, to developing countries during the 1990s. Advanced countries are the largest suppliers and also the largest recipients of foreign investment, both FDI and portfolio investment, in the global economy. The channels for private capital flow have also changed. For many years, commercial bank lending accounted for nearly two-third of private capital flowing to developing countries. It has now been overtaken not only by FDI but also portfolio capital flows (Table 10.1). Table 10.1 shows that both FDI and portfolio investment have increased sharply in both regions in recent years.

The composition and destinations of capital flows during the recent surge were different from the surge that preceded the 1982 debt crisis. In the 1970s, bank lending was the largest component of capital flows, the most important recipient of which was the public sector. In the 1990s, in contrast the surge was dominated by bonds, foreign direct investment and portfolio investment, and portfolio investment and the private sector did most of the external borrowing (Lopez-Meija, 1999). Today, bonds and equities account for more than a third of total private capital flows to developing countries, whereas bank lending accounts for less than a third (IMF, 1998). This development can be adduced to technological change, privatization, and deregulation of financial markets, growth of institutional investors like pension funds and mutual funds and macroeconomic and trade reforms in developing countries. Cross-border transactions in bonds and securities of the industrial countries have grown as well from about $ 50 billion in 1979-82 to nearly $ 550 billion in 1993-96.

Capital mobility is much more problematic in developing countries, because supply constraint and volatile international capital flows can take place. Net flows to developing countries have tripled from roughly $ 50 billion a tear in 1987-89 to more than $ 150 billion between 1994 and 1996 (IMF, 1998). Private flows now dominate official flows, private flows accounted for only 3 per cent of developing countries' domestic investment in 1990, but by 1996 they accounted for 20 per cent (World Bank 1997). Out of these flows, just 10 countries receive about 80 per cent or 14 countries account for 95 per cent of net private flows to developing countries. Table 10.2 shows that the surge of inflows has been widespread and especially strong in East Asia and Latin America and Caribbean, particularly after 1990. The factors driving foreign private investment to the region include investors' desire for portfolio diversification and higher profits, availability of guarantees from host government, export credit agencies, sound policies and macroeconomic and structural reforms in these countries (World Bank, 1997). Capital inflows have been sluggish and small in South Asia and sub-Saharan Africa throughout the review period. Table 10.2 shows that SSA enjoyed more than tenfold increase in net capital flow between 1990 and 1996, before it fell to single digits in 1997, 2000 and 2001.

Only few developing countries have benefited from growing private foreign investment and capital inflow. These countries are concentrated in East Asia and Latin America/Caribbean such as Brazil, Mexico, Indonesia, Taiwan, South Korea, China, etc. For example, five countries accounted for more than 50 per cent and twelve countries accounted for 75 per cent of total flows, while 140 of 166 developing countries accounted for less than 5 per cent of capital flows (Lopez-Mejia, 1999). The large, poor masses of the sub-Saharan African region have not benefited substantially from the growth of foreign investment and capital. For example, only about 4 per cent of FDI to developing economies during 1995-2000 went to Africa, and the region remains a marginal recipient of global FDI (Collins, 2002). Africa's share of FDI in total FDI to developing countries has remained as low as 3 per cent (Ajayi, 2001). The reasons for Africa's situation are the unconducive business environment, high production costs, inadequate legal framework, slow economic growth and small domestic market, capital control, slow progress on privatization, inward orientation, macroeconomic instability, civil strife, bureaucracy in business licensing, rigid tax and investment laws, poor infrastructural base, etc.

Table 10.3 shows that average foreign investment inflow between 1970 and 1979 and from 1986-90 increased in every region by three to seven times. Developing countries like advanced countries experienced large increases in FDI inflow in the 1990s. However, the growth in FDI inflows to industrialized countries slowed down in 1990 and fell in 1991 and 1992 from the 1990 level, mainly in response to slow economic growth in major home countries (United Nations, 1993). A feature of investment flows is that they are highly concentrated. For instance, four-fifths of inflows went to the advanced countries receiving 70 per cent of the share of all developing countries in total FDI flow. Another sign of concentration is that the European Community, Japan and United States are the major sources of outflows. The surge of FDI, particularly from Japan, the Netherlands and the United Kingdom, to the United States as a major host country has influenced the distribution of FDI to the developing countries. Particularly, it has helped to increase the position of South-East Asian Countries (a major destination of Japanese FDI).

The recent rapid increase of FDI flows has been accompanied by a transformation in the sectoral composition of both the flows and stocks of this investment. Service industries received about one quarter of total FDI stock in the early 1970s; by the late 1980s, the share of services in the world FDI stock was about half and services accounted for some 55-60 per cent of annual flows. The same trend continued in the early to mid 1990s. The growth of the services sector in the world economy has been partly due to technological advancement in the information and knowledge components of services industries to transnational services companies such as banking, financial services and hotels; and the structural and long-term factors responsible for sustaining the shift towards services industries, particularly in developed countries (United Nations, 1993).

3. LITERATURE REVIEW

There are several arguments surrounding the efficacy of flows of capital into global economy. Each argument tries to justify fundamental reasons for international capital flow. A few of these are presented below.

(Deepak et al., 2001) argues that the classic case for international capital mobility holds when capital flows from capital-abundant to capital-scarce countries raise welfare in the receiving countries. This is based on the assumption that the marginal product of capital is higher in the latter than the former. That is, the returns on new investment opportunities are higher where capital is limited. Relocation of capital from capital-abundant to capital-scarce countries will boost investment in the recipient country. However, in practice, this theory is not always true, as we find that new investment is more productive infrastructure. This explains why capital does not flow from rich to poor countries (Lucas, 1990). Thus, a consistent finding is that new capital flows tend to go to countries that have received large flows in the past and that investors also seek countries where there are favourable business environments (Mody and Scrinivasan, 1998). This explains why capital flows to low income countries are declining (Deepak et al., 2001).

In accordance with the submission of Montiel (1994), a country could be said to be fully integrated into external financial markets when its residents are free to trade in financial assets with residents of different countries. This analysis would allow residents of the country to pursue an optimal pattern of consumption and investment over-time. In the light of this, several methods exist to assess the extent to which countries are integrated into external financial market and four methods were identified by Montiel (1994). Existing evidence for developing countries suggests that few can be considered financially closed. For the majority of developing countries, however, either formal tests of financial integration have not been conducted or only very limited evidence is available. In the study conducted by Montiel (1994), the evidence suggests that a substantial number of developing countries can be considered financially open.

According to IMF (1998), of 136 IMF-member developing countries, 113 were classified as maintaining formal restrictions on capital account transactions. Empirical evidence suggests that during 1967-97, capital flows to industrial countries were strongly positively correlated with the share of industrial countries classified as open. But no such correlation exists for LDCs. However, there are periods when the series behaved unexpectedly, which imply that the indicator may reveal less about the degree to which a country is financially globalized. In support of this, Quinn (1997) indicator of capital accounts have become steadily more open since 1958, while on the other hand, capital account openness among developing countries are more complex. This suggests that one should not be surprised if the relationships between this measure of capital account openness and other variables of interest (e.g., net capital inflow, economic growth, productivity, etc.) are sensitive to time period and country sample (Collins, 2002).

Edison et al. (2002) provide evidence on the relationship between financial integration and economic growth using different indicators of financial integration, as well as quantitative measures such as gross capital flows and accumulated stocks of capital flows where they explore a wide range of interaction effects. They find that financial integration is not robustly linked with growth, although there were isolated exceptions. They conclude that "we do not reject the null hypothesis that international financial integration is unrelated to economic growth even when allowing for this relationship to vary with economic, financial, institutional and macroeconomic characteristics" (p. 26). Bennett (1996), attempts to ascertain the extent to which countries of the Caribbean Community (CARICOM) are integrated into external financial markets, using different tests of financial integration between 1972 and 1993. The findings indicate a relatively high degree of integration, which implies that CARICOM countries should be able to attract private capital in the current era of financial globalization; however, the underdeveloped state of capital markets in the region is a constraint to portfolio capital inflow.

There is abundant literature on why some countries or regions are able to attract capital inflow more than others. Mody and Murshid (2001) find that developments within an individual developing country such as financial market development, economic growth, exchange rate regime or stability, current/capital account openness, tax levels, business incentives, legal and other institutional factors (corruption and governance), political regime, security and peace, infrastructure, geographical location, size of market and factor price, availability of certain resources, transaction costs, etc. are important factors. Other factors external to the country include economic growth, interest rates and financial market conditions in industrial countries (Calvo et al., 1993). Gruber and McLeod (1998) tested the relationship between growth and capital inflows using Granger causality approach for 18 emerging market countries and find that higher capital inflows are associated with faster growth, as faster growth is also associated with higher capital inflows.

Mordy and Murshid (2001) find that FDI inflows seem less sensitive than other types of inflows to changes in indicators of macroeconomic policy and performance. This explains why a number of developing countries, such as those with natural resources, have been able to attract significant FDI inflows despite relatively poor policy indicators and low credit rating (country risk). Furthermore, Mode (2002) finds that FDI inflows are correlated with the existing stock of FDI. He associates this to a combination of agglomeration effects, information effects and a type of herding behaviour among foreign investors. Carlson and Hernandez (2002) find that faster GDP growth is associated with increased FDI inflows only in countries with persistently high real growth, such as in East Asia. They find no such correlation for countries where GDP growth is very volatile.

There is along-standing concern that capital inflows will boost consumption and reduce saving, with little effect on investment and growth. Bosworth and Collins (1999) study the effects of capital inflows on investment and saving for 58 developing countries 1978-95. They find that capital inflows have been directed to investment, and there is a small, not statistically significant negative impact on national saving. An increase of a dollar in capital inflows is associated with an increase in domestic investment of about 50 cents. Similar conclusions have been made by Gruben and McLeod (1998). Bosworth and Collins (1999) also find that FDI seems to increase investment one-for-one, while portfolio inflows have no discernable impact on investment and the effect of additional loan is between the two. In support of this, Collins (2002) concludes that FDI inflows do seem to be associated with increases in domestic investment. Mody and Murshid (2001) find a strong link between FDI and investment, but find that portfolio flows and loans have similar effect. They also find significant differences by region, with relatively strong effect for South Asia and Africa, but weaker effects of capital flows on investment in East Asia and the Pacific as well as in Latin America. They conclude that the differences may reflect different composition and volatility of flows to these different regions.

In majority of the cases, empirical evidence suggest that capital flows are more productive in countries with skilled workforce and well-developed physical infrastructure (Deepak et al., 2001). For example, Borenstzein et al. (1998) confirm that FDI is more productive (increase economic growth) in countries with better educated labour force. In the same vein, Eichengreen (2001) also finds that studies support the hypothesis that private capital flows are more efficient in higher-income countries. Collins (2002) finds that capital inflow in SSA could boost domestic productivity, which implies that rapid capital accumulation per worker is growth enhancing in Africa. Similarly, the evidence suggest that private flows, especially portfolio flows, have been associated with the development of domestic capital markets, which in turn, bolster growth. However, private capital flows can increase the vulnerability of a country with weak financial markets to banking and exchange rate crises (Deepak et al., 2001). This explains the importance of strengthening the domestic financial sector as a country integrates financially with the rest of the world.

The impact of international capital flow on an economy is less definitive and clear. Despite the ambiguities, private capital flows are generally found to have significant impact on domestic investment, with the relationship being strongest for foreign direct investment and foreign bank credits and weaker for portfolio flows (Bosworth and Collins, 1999). Private capital flow may increase either domestic consumption or investment, or increase a country's foreign exchange reserves. When a country is poor and saves little, additional capital from outside the country can help it realize higher investment. For example, a study by Deepak et al. (2001) has found that 1 per cent increase in capital inflows to Africa boosts investment by more than 1 per cent. However, very little private capital is directed to Africa and because of the low productivity of investment in many SSA countries, the long-term impact of foreign capital on growth may be small. They also found that over time, as a country becomes better integrated with the rest of the world, a dollar of foreign capital raises investment less than it did in the past, which is due mainly to the changing composition of capital flows to the region.

4. BENEFITS AND CHALLENGES OF GLOBALIZATION

Several benefits and challenges of financial globalization have been documented so far based on the views of (Clarke et al., 2001; Peek and Resengreen, 2000; Negro and Kay, 2002; Focarelli and Pozzolo, 2000).

4.1 Benefits

A. Efficiency

One of the main benefits related to globalized banking is the increased efficiency of the financial system. This view suggests that efficiency increases after foreign bank entry into developing countries. For one thing, banks that expand abroad are typically the "best of the crop" in the country of origin (Focarelli and Pozzolo, 2000). Hence, they are likely to export improved management and information technology practices to the host country. The literature finds also that foreign banks are generally more efficient than domestic competitors (Barajas, Steiner and Salazar, 2000). A number of other studies find that foreign bank entry has been associated with increased efficiency of domestic financial intermediaries. As Levine (2000) argues, there is substantial empirical evidence supporting the following causal chain; first, foreign bank entry enhances the efficiency of the banking sector; second, efficiency in the intermediation sector spurs growth by boosting productivity.

Generally, under the global advantage hypothesis, some efficiently managed foreign banks are able to overcome cross-border disadvantages and operate more efficiently than the domestic institutions in other nations. These institutions may have higher efficiency when operating in other nations by spreading their superior management skills or best practice policies and procedures over more resources, lowering costs (Berger et al., 1999). They may also raise revenues through superior investment or risk management skills by providing superior service quality, the variety that some customers prefer, or by obtaining diversification of risks that allow them to undertake higher risk-higher expected return investments.

B. Access to Diversified Source of Funds

Global banks are generally larger and have a more diversified portfolio of assets, than local banks. The international portfolio diversification of global banks is advantageous for the host country's financial system both *ex post*, in the event of a crisis, and *ex ante*. If a crisis occurs, global banks are likely to have less portfolio exposure to the domestic economy and greater access to liquidity than local banks. *Ex ante*, according to standard portfolio theory, the presence of international banks may imply that the interest rate paid on loans by domestic firms is lower, other things being equal, than when only local banks are present.

Since local banks have all their eggs in one basket, they are willing to add one more egg to that basket only if the price is high enough to compensate them for the additional risk they are undertaking. Global banks have all their eggs in many baskets. Hence, the additional risk undertaken by international banks of putting one more egg in the domestic basket is lower than that undertaken by a local bank, so the international banks might be willing to demand a lower return.

C. Improvement in Financial and Regulatory Reporting

Proponents of banking globalization refer to the multitude of banking crisis during the last two decades and point to the weaknesses of the regulatory and supervisory environment in many emerging markets. They thus argue that by allowing foreign bank entry, emerging markets indirectly benefit from the more advanced supervisory and disclosure environment in the country of origin. These improvements in financial reporting are likely to have positive spillover effects, as personnel switch to domestic competitors and as regulators, investors and depositors become aware of differences between the operators of domestic and foreign banks.

D. Reduction in Severity of Domestic Shocks

The presence of well-capitalized foreign banks may lessen the severity of domestic shocks by mitigating the extent to which the funds of worried domestic savers and investors flee the country when adverse shock is anticipated. Foreign banks provide a safe haven for depositors who might otherwise choose to remove their funds in a failing domestic bank. Such a "flight to quality" would, however, cause further pressures on foreign exchange rates and liquidity, draining the country of hard currency (Peek and Roseengren, 2000). In countries that allow foreign currency deposits, depositors may be more comfortable placing such deposits in foreign banks that have more ready access to foreign currency during a banking crisis, with the lender of last resort for the bank being the central bank in the banks home country rather than that of the host country.

4.2 Costs

While banking globalization confers considerable benefits to both the domestic economy and local banks, it also engenders considerable risks. Unless these risks are properly understood, managed and priced very efficiently, they may lead to banking instability. These include;

A. Lending Discrimination to Small Enterprises and Domestic Borrowers

One of the most cited arguments against foreign banks is that they are "niche" players often catering for foreign companies (usually the multinationals). They concentrate on international trade and business while neglecting small customers whose contributions to the process of economic growth have often been found to be very critical to the local economy. Berger, Klapper and Udell (2000) find that small businesses are indeed less likely than larger one to receive credit from foreign banks. The problem from the "cherrypicking" of customers by foreign banks is twofold; first, they leave domestic banks with a worse pool of potential creditors than before; second, indigenous firms (usually small) that are often relied upon as catalysts of economic development are frustrated.

B. Competition with Local Banks

Most time, domestically owned banks are unable to compete with international banks. This is because they operate with outdated technology and services in a protected environment that does not penalize efficiency. They were able to accept smaller profit margins than their domestic competitors because of their greater ability to use leverage. By squeezing the interest margins and profitability of domestic banks, the entry of foreign banks may push local banks out of market. This reasoning implies that entire sectors that were previously dependent on local banks (small firms for instance), may find themselves without access to credit, with detrimental consequences for the economy.

C. Instability

Opponents of globalized banking argue that the presence of foreign banks may mean that the host country may inherit global shocks. By permitting foreign banks to enter, host countries open themselves up to the possibility that economic fluctuations in the home countries of their entrants might have an impact on foreign lending and, thus, on their general level of economic activity. Although it is often mentioned that even in the absence of foreign banks, emerging markets are not isolated from global financial shocks, as shown in the Asian crisis, yet some argue that the presence of foreign banks exacerbates the host country's exposure to global shocks. In summary, a country that opens its banking system to foreign banks may become less sensitive to its own shocks but at the same time increase its exposure with respect to shocks generated elsewhere.

D. Domestic Capital Flight

The fact that international banks are perceived to be sounder than local banks in times of crisis has led some to argue that foreign bank presence opens the possibility of a capital flight at home. Before the appearance of foreign banks, investing abroad was the only safe haven for domestic depositors, given the lack of credible deposit insurance. Now, under the assumption that foreign banks are strong enough to withstand a crisis, all depositors need to do is transfer their savings from local to foreign banks. Kane (2000) reports some evidence of such a "flight of quality" during the Asian crisis and during the Tequila crisis in Argentina.

E. Lack of Domestic Regulatory Control

Another frequently raised issue is that regulatory and monetary authorities may have less control of the banking sector if there is sizable foreign bank presence (Peek and Rosengreen, 2000). In many countries, the banking system is an instrument for government credit allocation schemes, with lending directed to sectors viewed as major by the government. This can be done directly through government controlled lending agencies or mandates to domestic banks, or indirectly by encouraging lending to preferred sectors. Furthermore, the central bank's ability to engage in moral suasion may be lessened when dealing with an entity more focused on the expected financial returns than the domestic goals promulgated by government.

5. NIGERIA AND THE GLOBALIZED ECONOMY

There are several indices by which a country's level of integration into the global economy can be measured. One of such measure is the extent of participation of a country in international trade. This extent is measured by the ratio of the value of imports and exports of a given country to its gross domestic product: (Adegbite, 2003)

$$PIIT = \frac{M + X}{GDP} \quad \text{.......} (1)$$

Where M = value of imports

X = value of export

GDP = gross domestic product

Another measure is the extent to which a country has been a participant in international capital markets either as a source or a recipient of capital. When a country experiences a surplus in its current account, it implies that the country has been involved in capital outflow as its residents acquire financial assets outside the country. It implies that there has been an inflow of capital as the country's residents have sold assets to foreigners. Hence, the absolute value of a country's current account balance is a reflection. On the other hand, when a country experiences current account deficit, it of the extent of the country's participation in the international capital market, either as a source or a recipient of capital. The level of such capital inflow or outflow can be compared with the overall level of economic activity in that country, given both the cross-national and cross-temporal comparisons of the country's participation in international capital markets:

Absolute Value of PICM

$$= \frac{\text{Current Account Balance}}{\text{Gross Domestic Product}} = \frac{CUB}{GDP} \quad \text{......} (2)$$

A third measure of globalization of an economy is the extent of penetration of foreign capital into that economy. This is the ratio of foreign capital to the gross domestic product:

Absolute Value of PFCDE

$$= \frac{\text{Foreign Capital}}{\text{Gross Domestic Product}} = \frac{FC}{GDP} \text{ .... (3)}$$

The higher this ratio, the more globalized an economy is. A proxy for this measure is the ratio of foreign direct investment to gross domestic product:

$$PFCDE = \frac{FDI}{GDP}$$

Where FDI = Foreign Direct Investment

A fourth measure of globalization of an economy is the extent to which the country's real rate of interest equals the world's rate of interest. In fully integrated international capital markets, investors are different (at the margin) as to whether they invest in asset A in country 1 or in country 2, because real interest rate equality is supposed to hold when capital moves freely across borders (Obstfield and Taylor, 2001).

Hence, the extent to which domestic real interest rate equals the world's real interest rate is a measure of globalization of a country's capital market. The focus here is usually on the long-term bond yield.

Let

$$r_{td} = i - TI_{td} \text{ .... (4)}$$

where

r_{td} = real interest rate for the domestic economy at time t.

i_{td} = nominal interest rate for the domestic economy at time t.

TI_{td} = the inflation rate for the domestic economy at time t.

then

$$r_{tw} = i_{tw} - TI_{tw} \text{ .... (5)}$$

defines the world's real rate of interest at time t.

The extent to which r_{td} exactly equals r_{tw} is a measure of globalization.

$$RIP = r_{td} = r_{tw} \quad \text{......} \quad (6)$$

Equation Six stic rate of interest (r_{td}) must be identical with the world; real rate of interest (r_{tw}). Another way to measure equation 6 is to calculate the real interest differential. The closer to zero the differential, the more globalized the focus country's capital market:

$$r_{twd} = r_{tw} - r_{td} = 0 \quad \text{......} \quad (7)$$

where r_{twd} = real interest differential

Equation (6) maintains that for the identity required in equation (6) to hold then the differential between the domestic real rate of interest and the world real rate of interest must be exactly zero.

Table 10.4 measures Nigeria's level of globalization in terms of its degree of participation in international trade. The table covers a period of 35 years (1970-2004). It is evidenced from the table that Nigeria has a high degree of openness. From statistical perspective, the values of Nigeria's international trade hover from 32 to 47 per cent between 1970 and 1981 of its GDP. Relative to the industrially developed countries, even Nigeria's degree of openness in terms of international trade is really high. Regrettably, the degree of openness nosedived to as low as 20 per cent in 1986, in face of excruciating external-debt burden, Nigeria made tremendous efforts to reduce the level of its imports (Adegbite, 1998) but unfortunately was not successful in increasing the level of exports. This led to reduced participation in international trade. However, with the adoption of structural adjustment programme and the accompanying liberalization policies of the last trimester of the 1980s, came renewed and increased participation in world trade, which increased the index of openness to as high as 71 per cent and above in the 1990s. Between 1999 when Nigeria embraced democratic administration and 2004, the level of participation of the former declined from 61 per cent to 25 per cent owing largely to acute political turmoil as a result of structural reforms orchestrated by the government.

Employing the ratio of absolute value of its current account balance to its GDP to measure the degree of globalization of the Nigerian economy in terms being a recipient of capital or capital mobility, Nigeria's participation in, or integration into, the global economy is still very low. With reference to Table 10.5, Nigeria's level of integration with the global capital market is extremely low. Between 1970 and 1973, the ratio of international capital (flowing into or out of Nigeria) was less than 5 per cent of Nigeria's GDP. The 1980s on the other hand witnessed an improvement, even though the ratio of international capital flowing in and out of Nigerian in the 1980s was only about 10 to 26 per cent. Most of the increase probably reflects how much Nigeria was paying for international services, especially interest payments on loans. The situation in the 1990s was discouraging as international capital relative to GDP slashed from 11 per cent in 1990 to 9.8 per cent in 1999. The magnitude improved from 14 to 21 per cent between 2000 and 2004.

On account of flow of foreign direct investment as a measure of the penetration of foreign capital into the domestic economy, we found that as maintained by Ajayi (2001), Africa (which is inclusive of Nigeria) gives Foreign Direct Investment (FDI) pride of place because of the belief that FDI has the potential to stimulate economic growth. However, from the 1980s, there has been a gradual decline in the inflow. This seems to confirm the position of developing countries' economists that the flow of capital in general (foreign direct or otherwise) to developing countries has been skewed in favour of the middle-income developing countries and against the poor developing countries of which sub-Saharan Africa is key (Ojo, 1999). Table 10.6 reveals the extent of penetration of direct foreign investment into the Nigeria economy as a measure of globalization of investment in Nigeria. The extent of foreign capital penetration into the Nigerian economy seems to be noticeable. From a high level of 22 per cent in 1972, the level fell to as low as 4 per cent in 1996 and 1997 and 3 per cent in year 2000 and year 2001, rising marginally to 4 per cent in 2004.

In consideration of the globalized nature Nigeria's financial assets coupled with their perfect substitutability for those of the rest of the world, they consider two financial instruments at the short-end of the financial market, the bank deposit rate and the Treasury bill rate. A careful look at the configuration of real rates of interest on bank deposits for Nigeria and ten of her principal trading partners from Table 10.7 reveals that real rates of interest on bank deposit in Nigeria were negative most of the time given her high rates of inflation, while those of her trading partners were positive. This clearly removes any possibility of parity between the real rates of interest on deposit in Nigeria and that of the world, where we can use the US rates as a proxy for the world rate, or use the average of these principal partner's rates as a proxy for the world rate. The assessment of the real return on treasury bills produces similar results during the period of financial crises, by reference to table.

6. WHY WEAK GLOBALIZATION OF THE NIGERIA'S FINANCIAL SERVICES SECTOR

From Section 5, it is obvious that while Nigeria could be considered fairly global, in terms of international trade given the extent of the country's openness to trade, in terms of capital flow and investment the country cannot be termed global. The Nigerian capital market is not in any way integrated with the international market. In terms of participation in the international capital market, the level is still as low as 21 per cent in 2004. In terms of penetration of foreign capital into the domestic economy, the rate is as low as 4 per cent. This latter phenomenon is even of greater concern, given that the rate used to be as high as 19 per cent in the early 1970s.

$$\left(\frac{(1CAB1)}{GDP}\right) \qquad \left(\frac{FDE}{GDP}\right)$$

Two factors are fundamental to movement of capital both within and outside national boundaries, two factors are very important. The first is the return on assets and the second is the associated risk. For any investment, the investor must consider the return and the risk. The theory on return states that when returns on any assets are identical across countries (when expressed in a single currency), then capital moves freely. From Tables 10.7 and 10.8, it is obvious that returns on Nigeria's assets are not at par with those of her trading partners. First, the level of inflation in Nigeria is much higher than those of her principal trading partners (who all turn out to be developed, industrial countries and who are also the principal countries in the global capital market). Given this much higher level of inflation, the real rate of return in Nigeria is very low. In fact, from Tables 10.7 and 10.8, the real rates of return are more negative than positive. For instance, on bank deposits, the real rates of return were negative for Nine out of the fifteen considered. For treasury bills, the real rates were negative for five out of the nine years considered. Given this scenario, there is no way a rational foreign investor will put his money in the Nigerian asset market. Rather, he will prefer the principal trading partners.

Several factors affect the risk of an investment. Some of these factors are (see Odozi, 2002): inappropriate macroeconomic policy; inconsistent and unstable policy; policy infidelity; fiscal indiscipline; inadequate policy coordination; social political instability; flawed incentive regime inadequately and inappropriately targeted and inefficiently administered incentives; and high cost of doing business and multiple taxes and levies. All of these factors prevail in the Nigerian financial services sector and make the risk of investing in Nigeria high. This discourages the penetration of foreign direct investment into the Nigerian economy and discourages other capital flows. Three examples are sufficient to demonstrate the kind of risk foreign investors face, which discourages them from investing in Nigerian assets. First, the level of fiscal indiscipline in Nigeria is legendary. According to Egwakhide (2003), fiscal deficits in the year 2000 was N 103.8 billion and this rose to N 221 billion in 2001, an increase of over 100 per cent. What is more, most of this excess expenditure has been, in the words of Egwakhide, "wastefully substantial". This kind of fiscal indiscipline fuels inflation and makes real rates of return on assets negative. Second, in 1994, the federal government announced that the exchange rate in the IFEM had been pegged to N 22 per dollar. Exactly a year after, government announced that the rate had been let loose again. In 1997, the monetary authorities announced that interest rates had been capped as they used to be prior to 1986. However, within twelve months they changed their minds and uncapped the interest rates again. In June/July 2003, there was social crises as a result of increase in the price of petroleum products, which led to many deaths. The crises led to the closure of banks and other institutions in the country closed for almost seven days, leading to the loss of several millions of naira. No foreign investor would be willing to carry such heavy risks. Such policy reversals and social/political conflicts make investment in Nigeria a very dicey affair and discourage the flow of capital (either short or long-term) into the system. A third reason for the poor level of integration of Nigeria's financial services sector with the international capital market is the low level of Nigeria's participation in international services. In the current account section of the balance of payments, payments are made for insurance, banking, shipping and all such services (non-factor services). Payments are also made on interest, royalty (factor services), etc., but Nigeria hardly provides insurance, banking and shipping services for other countries that she would be paid for, nor does she provide any significant factor service that she would receive factor payments for. Hence, low level of Nigeria's participation in international services.

7. CONCLUSION AND POLICY RECOMMENDATIONS

Attempts have been made in this paper to examine the trends of global capital flows, several arguments surrounding the efficacy of capital flows into globalized economy, benefits and challenges of globalization, several indices by which a country's level of integration into global economy can be measured and factors responsible for weak globalization of Nigeria's financial services sector. With respect to the degree of financial globalization the paper finds that inappropriate macro economic policy, policy infidelity, fiscal indiscipline among others are responsible for poor level of integration of Nigeria's financial services sector into globalized economy.

The paper recommends that for Nigeria financial sector services to take substantial benefits of broad participation in globalization, the following conditions need to be fulfilled.

- Provision of sound macroeconomic policy framework with high degree of certainly the future of investment. This factor is premised on absence of sudden policy and lack of policy infidelity.
- The flow of FDI can be increased if there are some measures of stability (social and political) and some degree of willingness on both the past of government and the private sector to make the Nigerian economy especially the banking services sector.
- There is also need to reduce fiscal deficits and improve monetary management in order to prone down inflation rates and bring about a more competitive real returns on Nigeria's asset *vis-à-vis* Nigerian's trading partners.
- The private sector participation also needs to be strengthened to compliment government in its efforts in the liberalization process of banking sector. However, the more private operators take advantage of the liberal policies of government in the financial sector, the more there will flow in, fresh, foreign capital in form of equity and other portfolio investment.
- More fundamentals is the need on the part of multilateral institutions including IMF and World Bank to create a more supportive operating environment for private business and funding in support of long-term investors in infrastructure. In the face of increased capital transaction as a result of globalization, developing economy like Nigeria might be susceptible to balance of payment difficulties, in which case IMF should be supportive through provision of funds without strangulated conditionalties.
- The banking sector also needs to sack up by adequate supervision and regulation. The on going reforms in the banking sector will in no small measure.

REFERENCES

Adegbite, E.O. (2003). "Consolidation the Deregulation of the Nigerian Financial Services Sector for Beneficial Globalization." In *Globalization and African's Economic Development*, Selected Paper for 2003 Annual Conference of the Nigerian Economic Society.

——. (1994). "Exchange Rate Regimes and Economic Performance: A Comparative Analysis." An Unpublished Ph.D Thesis Submitted to the Department of Economics, University of Ibadan.

——. (1998). "An Aggregate Analysis of Manufactured Exports in Nigeria." *Nigerian Journal of Banking and Finance Issues* 1(1), April.

Ajayi, S. I. (2001). "What Africa Needs to do to Benefit from Globalization." *Finance and Development* 38(4): 6-8.

Aryeetey, E. (2000). "Recent Developments in African Financial Markets: Agenda for Further Research." Plenary Paper AERC Workshop, Nairobi, Kenya, 2-7 Dec 2000.

Barajas, A.R., Steiner and N. Salazar (2000). "Foreign Investment in Columbia's Financial Sector." In Claessens, S. and M. Jansen (eds) *The Internalization of the Financial Services*. Boston. Mass: Kluwer Academic Press.

Bennett, K.M. (1996). "International Capital Mobility and the CARICOM Economies." *Social and Economic Studies*, 45: 2&3.

Berger, A.N., L.F. Klapper and G.F. Udell (2000). "The Ability of Banks to Lend to Informationally Opaque Small Business." FRB Chicago Working Paper Series.

Berger, A.N., et al. (1999). "Globalization of Financial Institutions: Evidence from Cross-Border Banking Performance." Federal Reserve Bank (FRP Working Paper Series (WPS) WP-99-25, Chicago.

Bhattacharya, A.C., Aknox Lovell and P. Sahay (1997). "The Impact of Liberalization on the Productive Efficiency of Indian Commercial Bank." *European Journal of Operational Research* 98: 332-45.

Borenstzein et al. (1998). "How Does Foreign Direct Investment Affect Economic Growth?" *Journal of International Economics*. No. 45 June: 115-36.

Bosworth, B. and S.M. Collins (1999). "Capital Flows to Developing Countries: Implications for Saving and Investment." *Brookings Papers on Economic Activity* 1: 143-69.

Calvo, G. (1993). "Contagion in Emerging Markets: When Wall Street is a Carrier." University of Maryland, College Park, mimeo.

Carlson, M. and L. Hernandez (2002). "Determinants and Repercussions of Composition of Capital Inflows." IMF Working Paper No. WP/02/86.

Clarke, G.R. Cull; M. Soledad Martines Peria; and S. Sanchez. (2001). "Foreign Bank Entry-Experience, Implications for Developing Countries and Agenda for Further Research." World Bank (PRWP) 2698.

Collins, S.M. (2002). "Capital Flows, Investment and Growth in Developing Countries: Issues and Implications for Africa." Paper presented at the African Economic Research Consortium, Biannual Research Workshop, December, Durban, South Africa.

Deepak, M., A. Mody and A.P. Murshid (2001). "Private Capital Flows and Growth." *Finance and Development* 38(2), June.

Edison, H., R. Levine, L. Ricci and R. Slok (2002). "International Financial Integration and Economic Growth." IMF Working Paper WP/02/145.

Eichengreen, B. (2001). "Capital Account Liberalization: What Do Cross-Country Study Tell Us?" *World Bank Economic Review* (forthcoming).

Feldstein, M. (2000). "Aspects of Global Economic Integration: Outlook for the Future." NBER Working Paper No. 7879 Cambridge, Massachusetts.

Focarelli, D. and A. Pozzollo (2000). "The Determinants of Cross Border Shareholding: An Analysis with Bank Level Data from OECD Countries." Banca d'Italia Discussion Paper 381.

Gruben, W. and D. McLeod (1998). "Capital Flows, Savings and Growth in the 1990s." *The Quarterly Review of Economics and Finance* 38(3): 287-301.

IMF (1998). "Capital Account Liberalization: Theoretical and Practical Aspects." Occasional Paper 172. Washington, D.C: International Monetary Fund.

Kane, E.J. (2000). "Capital Movements, Bank Insolvency and Silent Runs in the Asian Financial Crises." *Pacific-Basin Finance Journal* 8: 157-75.

Levine, R. (2000). "International Financial Liberalization and Economic Growth." *Review of International Economics*, pp. 688-702.

Lopez-Meija, A. (1999). "Large Capital Flows: Causes, Consequences and Policy Responses." *Finance and Development* 39(3), September.

Lucas Jr, R.E. (1990). "Why Doesn't Capital Flow from Rich to Poor Countries?" *American Economic Review* 80: 92-96, May.

Mody, A. and K. Scrinivasan (1998). "Japanese and US Firms as Foreign Investors: Do They March to the Same Tune?" *Canadian Journal of Economics*, 31: 778-99.

Mody, A. and A. Murshid (2001). " Growing up with Capital Flows." IMF Research Working Paper WP/02/75, April.

Montiel, P.J. (1994). "Capital Mobility in Developing Countries: Some Measurement Issues and Empirical Estimates." *The World Bank Economic Review*, 311-50, 8 September.

Negro, M.D. and S.J. Kay (2002). "Global Banks, Local Crises: Bad News from Argentina." FRB Atlanta, *Economic Review* 87(3): 89-106.

Obstfield, M. and A.M. Taylor (2001). "Globalization and Capital Markets." Paper Presented at the NBER Conference on *Globalization in Historical Perspective* at Santa-Barbara, 4-5 May 2001.

Ojo, A.T. (1999). "Developing Countries Facing Globalization and Regionalization: Economic Prospects and Challenges." In Karl-Bsef Kuschel et al. (eds) *nEun Ethos Fur Eine Wettz Globalisierungals Ethische Neurausferdering*, Campus Verlag Frankfurt/New York.

Peek, J. and E.S. Rosengreen (2000). "Implications of Globalization of the Banking Sector: The Latin American Experience." FRB Boston, *New England Economic Review*, September, 45-62.

Soyibo, A. (1994). "Financial Liberalization and Bank Restructuring in Sub-Saharan Africa: Some Lessons for Sequencing and Policy Design." Plenary Paper, AERC Workshop 4-9 Dec., Nairobi, Kenya.

Streeton, P. (2001). "Integration, Interdependence and Globalization." *Finance and Development*, 38(2), June.

United Nations (1993). "Explaining and Forecasting Regional Flows of Foreign Direct Investment." New York, July, United Nations.

World Bank (1997). *Private Capital Flows to Developing Countries: The Road to Financial Integration.* New York: Oxford Press.

Table 10.1: Portfolio and Direct Investment Flows, 1973-2000 ($billion)

	Gross Outflow						Gross Inflow					
	1973-78	1979-82	1983-88	1989-92	1993-96	1997-2000	1973-78	1979-82	1983-88	1989-92	1993-96	1997-2000
Ind. C.		46.9	88.2	201.3	259.6	867.9	17.9	36.6	69.3	141.9	173	704.3
PI	28.6	35	126.5	272.6	436.4	Na	24.2	51	343	549.9	Na	
Dev. C	11.8								15.5			
DI		1.1	2.3	10.4	19.2	16.4	5	14.6	4	37.8	106.4	210.4
PI	0.4	17.8	-5.1	10.3	19.2	na	1.3	3.1		27.5	95.9	na
	5.5											

Note: Ind.C. – Industrial Countries, DI – Direct Investment, PI – Portfoilio Investment, Dev.C. – Developing Countries

Source: IMF, Balance of Payments Statistics 1998; IMF, World Investment Repot 2002.

Table 10.2: Annual Long-Term Private Net Capital Flows by Region (US $Billions), 1978-2001

Flow by Region	1978-81	1982-89	1990	1991	1992	1993	1994	1995	1996	1997	1998	1999	2000	2001
SSA	4.7	2.5	0.9	1.5	0.7	2.1	5.2	9.5	11.8	7.4	10.4	13.7	5.8	6
EA & P	7.9	9.6	20.5	25.6	42.5	62.8	71	74.3	108.7	79.8	73.2	68.6	65.7	Na
LA & C	28.9	10.3	10.7	22.8	27.9	57.7	53.6	55.5	74.3	5.7	69.5	79.3	97.3	Na
ME & NA	4.1	3.5	0.2	-0.1	1.6	1.6	5.8	4.5	6.9	4.9	10.4	-3.9	1.1	0.2
SA	0.7	2.8	2.6	3	1.8	5.6	8.5	7.8	10.7	8.2	2.4	6.3	9.3	15.5
E & CA	7.3	5.8	9.6	4.6	24.3	27.8	17.2	21.3	31.2	28.3	14.5	29.8	32.9	20.9

Note: SSA – Sub-Saharan Africa; EA&P – East Asia and the Pacific; LA&C – Latin America and the Caribbean; ME&NA – Middle East and North Africa; SA – South Asia: E&CA – Europe and Central Asia.

Source: World Bank, 1998; Eduardo and Monitel, 1996; and IMF/World Economic Outlook, 2003.

Table 10.3: Average/Annual Inflows of Foreign Direct Investment (FDI), by Host Region, 1970-2001 (US $ Billion)

Region	1970-79	1980-85	1986-90	1991	1992	1993	1994	1995	1996	1997	1998	1999	2000	2001
Ind. C.	17	38	130	113.3	118.4	143.2	138.2	216.6	193.9	267.9	484.2	837.7	1227	503.2
Dev. C.	5	13	26	41.8	63.4	74.4	98.8	101.6	119.3	191	187.6	225.1	237.9	204.8
L.A.&C.	3	6	9	12.8	14.4	13.4	27.5	28.8	40.2	56.7	62.1	69.2	75.1	77.5
E.S.& SEA	1	5	13	20.9	25.9	45.6	56.4	64.7	73.6	96.3	86.2	99.9	131.1	94
Africa	1	1	3	2.5	2.6	2.9	4.2	4.4	4.6	10.7	9	12.8	8.7	17.2
Others	0.5	0.7	0.9	0.4	0.6	1.8	2.5	3.4	1.2	na	na	na	na	na

Note: Others include West Asia, Oceanic, Malta, Yugoslavia and least developed countries, L.A.&C. – Latin America and the Caribbean, E.S.&SEA – East South and South East Asia.

Source: UNCTAD, IMF Balance of Payments Statistic and World Investment Directory, United Nations, 1992; IMF, World Investment Report, 2002.

Table 10.4: Extent of Nigeria's Participation in International Trade (1970-2004)

Years	Import (M) (N'million)	Export (X) (N'million)	(M + X) (N'million)	GDP at Current Mkt Price (N'million)	M + X GDP (N'million)
1970	756.4	885.4	1,641.8	5,203.7	0.32
1971	10,789	1,29.4	2,372.3	6,670.9	0.36
1972	990.1	1434.2	2424.3	7208.3	0.34
1973	1224.8	2278.4	3503.2	10990.7	0.32

(*Contd...*)

Years	Import (M) (N'million)	Export (X) (N'million)	(M + X) (N'million)	GDP at Current Mkt Price (N'million)	M + X GDP (N'million)
1974	1737.3	5764.8	7532.1	18298.3	0.41
1975	3721.5	4925.5	8647.6	21558.8	0.40
1976	5148.5	6751.1	11899.6	27297.5	0.44
1977	7093.7	7630.7	14724.4	32747.3	0.45
1978	8211.7	6064.4	14276.1	36083.6	0.40
1979	7472.5	10836.8	18329.3	43150.8	0.42
1980	9095.6	14186.7	23282.3	50848.6	0.46
1981	12839.6	11023.3	23862.9	50749.1	0.47
1982	10770.5	8206.4	18976.9	51709.2	0.37
1983	8903.7	7502.5	16406.2	57142.1	0.29
1984	7178.3	9088.0	16266.2	63608.1	0.26
1985	7062.6	11720.8	18783.4	72355.4	0.26
1986	5983.6	8920.6	14904.2	73061.9	0.20
1987	17861.7	30360.6	48222.3	108,885.1	0.44
1988	21445.7	31192.8	52638.5	145243.3	0.36
1989	30860.2	57971.2	88831.4	224796.7	0.40
1990	45717.9	109886.1	155604.0	260636.7	0.60
1991	87020.2	121535.4	208555.6	324010.0	0.64
1992	145911.4	207266.0	353177.4	54980.8	0.64
1993	166100.4	218770.1	384870.5	697090.5	0.55
1994	162.788.8	206,059.2	368,848.0	914940.5	0.40
1995	755127.7	950661.4	1705789.1	1977740.0	0.86
1996	562626.6	1309543.4	1872170.0	2823900.0	0.66
1997	845716.6	1241662.7	2087679.3	2939650.0	0.71
1998	837418.7	751856.7	1589275.4	2881310.0	0.55
1999	860523.3	1189006.5	2051531.8	3352650.0	0.61
2000	692232.8	2287433.0	2979633.1	4980943	0.60
2001	1240241.3	2006498.9	3346740.2	5639865	0.58
2002	–1,311,382.9	1882668.2	571285.3	6398907.7	0.09
2003	–1,356689.6	2924134.9	1,567,445.3	6255470	0.25
2004	–1,474518.2	3,143800.8	1,669,282.6	6665040	0.25

Source: CBN Statistical Bulletin, 2004.

Table 10.5: Participation as a Source or Recipient of International Capital (1970-2004) (Nm)

Years	CAB	GDP at Current Mkt Price	FDI/GDP
1970	–50.0	5,203.7	0.009609
1971	–229.4	6,670.9	0.034913
1972	–322.7	7208.3	0.44768
1973	52.7	10990.7	0.004795
1974	4671.5	18298.3	0.255297

(Contd...)

Years	CAB	GDP at Current Mkt Price	FDI/GDP
1975	42.6	21558.8	0.001976
1976	–2584	27297.5	0.009466
1977	–647.5	32747.3	0.010773
1978	–1157.4	36083.6	0.032076
1979	9427.3	43150.8	0.218473
1980	13057.9	50848.6	0.2568
1981	19970.3	50749.1	0.198433
1982	7980.9	51709.2	0.154342
1983	6752.3	57142.1	0.118167
1984	8234.3	63608.1	0.129454
1985	10738.9	72355.4	0.146419
1986	8006.6	73061.9	0.109587
1987	17138.2	108,885.1	0.157397
1988	31586.1	145243.3	0.21747
1989	59112.0	224796.9	0.262948
1990	79810.1	260636.7	0.114374
1991	51969.8	324010.0	0.160396
1992	93680.5	54980.8	0.170387
1993	–3414.7	697090.5	0.049369
1994	–52304.3	914940.0	0.057167
1995	–186084.6	1977740.0	0.940990
1996	240180.0	2823900.0	0.085053
1997	36033066	2939650.0	0.122576
1998	–330108.7	2881310.0	0.1145689
1999	–330108.7	3352650.0	0.098462
2000	706977.0	4980943.0	0.14
2001	269309.7	5639865.0	0.05
2002	69,838	6398907.7	0.01
2003	1054,635.1	6255470	0.17
2004	1374769.7	6665040	0.21

Source: CBN Statistical Bulletin, 2004.

Table 10.6: Extent of Penetration of Foreign Capital into the Nigerian Economy (1970-2004)

Years	FDI	GDP at Current Mkt Price	FDI/GDP
1970	1003.2	5,203.7	0.19
1971	1322.8	6,670.9	0.20
1972	1571.1	7208.3	0.22
1973	1763.7	10990.7	0.16
1974	1812.1	18298.3	0.10
1975	2287.5	21558.8	0.11

(Contd...)

Years	FDI	GDP at Current Mkt Price	FDI/GDP
1976	1339.0	27297.5	0.09
1977	2531.4	32747.3	0.08
1978	2863.2	36083.6	0.08
1979	3153.1	43150.8	0.07
1980	3620.1	50848.6	0.07
1981	3757.9	50749.1	0.07
1982	5382.8	51709.2	0.10
1983	5949.5	57142.1	0.10
1984	6418.3	63608.1	0.10
1985	6804.0	72355.4	0.09
1986	9313.6	73061.9	0.13
1987	9993.6	108,885.1	0.09
1988	11339.2	145243.3	0.08
1989	10899.6	224796.7	0.05
1990	10436.1	260636.7	0.04
1991	12243.5	324010.0	0.04
1992	20512.7	54980.8	0.04
1993	66787.0	697090.5	0.10
1994	70714.6	914940.5	0.08
1995	119391.6	1977740.0	0.06
1996	122600.9	2823900.0	0.04
1997	128331.9	2939650.0	0.04
1998	152409.0	2881310.0	0.05
1999	154188.1	3352650.0	0.05
2000	157535.0	4980943	0.03
2001	160882.2	5639865	0.03
2002	225972	6398907.7	0.04
2003	259250.4	6255470	0.04
2004	249.157.7	6665040	0.04

Source: CBN Statistical Bulletin, 2001.

Table 10.7: Real Rates of Interest on Bank Deposits (1986-2000)

Years	Nig.	USA	UK	Japan	Germany	France	Netherlands	Switzerland	Italy	Spain	Belgium
1986	–7.96	2.62	1.45	1.72	3.61	2.90	3.33	3.41	6.49	0.55	2.80
1987	2.59	3.16	4.47	1.66	3.00	1.20	4.25	1.68	2.30	3.77	3.40
1988	–41.55	3.71	3.65	1.06	1.99	1.80	2.78	2.60	1.59	4.26	3.34
1989	–35.82	4.29	3.71	–0.33	2.70	1.00	2.39	5.28	0.73	2.75	2.03
1990	11.88	2.75	3.04	0.46	4.37	1.10	0.81	2.58	0.30	3.96	2.63
1991	1.92	1.64	4.38	10.84	5.92	1.30	0.08	1.73	0.34	4.27	3.05
1992	–26.56	0.68	3.76	11.65	2.91	2.10	0.00	1.50	2.01	4.53	3.85

(Contd...)

Years	Nig.	USA	UK	Japan	Germany	France	Netherlands	Switzerland	Italy	Spain	Belgium
1993	–32.96	0.17	0.84	1.87	2.40	0.51	0.20	13.29	13.29	5.03	18.31
1994	–43.91	2.03	1.16	1.00	1.67	2.80	11.90	2.73	2.20	2.00	2.46
1995	–59.29	3.12	0.71	1.00	2.15	2.70	2.50	0.52	1.25	2.18	2.54
1996	–16.24	2.49	0.65	0.20	1.43	1.67	1.54	0.54	2.49	2.52	0.56
1997	–1.03	3.32	0.53	–1.40	0.79	1.30	0.98	0.50	2.83	1.96	1.26
1998	0.81	3.87	1.08	–0.33	1.98	2.51	1.10	0.59	1.16	–0.45	1.32
1999	6.21	3.13	2.88	0.42	1.83	2.89	0.54	0.54	–0.09	–0.45	2.01
2000	4.10	3.06	1.58	0.67	1.50	0.90	0.34	1.40	–0.66	–.45	1.08

Source: Computed from IMF International Financial Statistics Yearbook, 2001.

Table 10.8: Real Rates of Interest on Treasury Bills (1992-2000)

Years	Nig.	USA	UK	Germany	France	Switzerland	Italy	Spain	Belgium
1992	–26.71	0.46	5.24	13.22	8.09	3.41	9.22	6.54	6.90
1993	32.70	0.02	3.65	1.82	6.31	1.45	6.08	6.08	5.72
1994	–44.13	1.67	2.65	2.25	4.09	3.07	5.17	3.41	3.17
1995	–60.30	2.71	2.93	2.70	4.78	0.98	5.65	5.09	3.17
1996	–17.05	2.12	3.37	1.90	1.84	0.92	4.46	3.63	1.09
1997	3.80	2.77	3.38	1.42	2.15	0.95	4.33	3.02	1.78
1998	1.96	3.22	3.42	2.52	2.71	1.22	2.59	1.99	2.51
1999	11.22	2.42	3.44	2.28	2.22	0.47	1.31	0.21	2.62
2000	8.10	2.32	2.50	2.12	2.31	1.21	1.52	0.61	1.52

Source: Computed from IMF International Financial Statistics Yearbook, 2001.

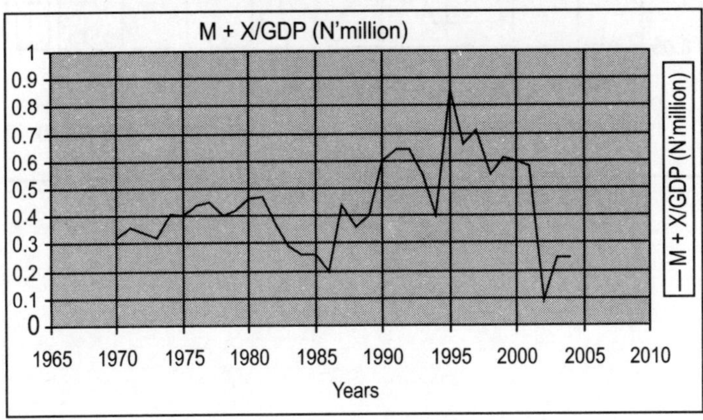

Fig. 1

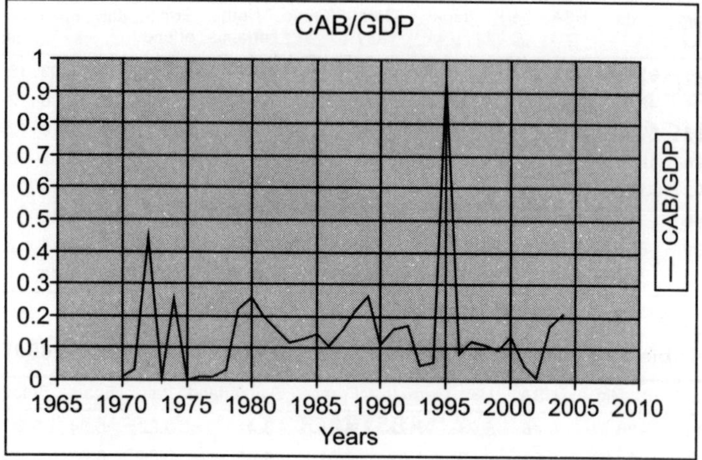
CAB/GDP
1
0.9
0.8
0.7
0.6
0.5
0.4
0.3
0.2
0.1
0
1965 1970 1975 1980 1985 1990 1995 2000 2005 2010
Years
— CAB/GDP

Fig. 2

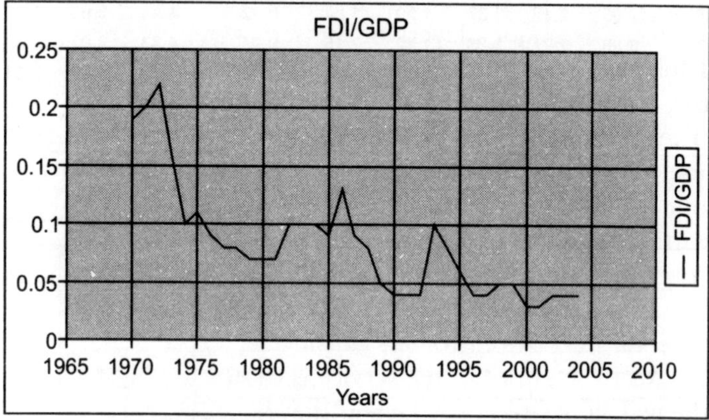
FDI/GDP
0.25
0.2
0.15
0.1
0.05
0
1965 1970 1975 1980 1985 1990 1995 2000 2005 2010
Years
— FDI/GDP

Fig. 3

Customer Service in Service Sector: A Key Differentiator for Success

S.K. Bose

ABSTRACT

The service industry is that section of the economy that supplies the need of the consumer but produces no tangible goods. Service cannot be stored and it makes direct contact to the customer. The major players of the service sector are Banking and Insurance, Hotel and Restaurants, Transport, etc. In any sector, whether it is manufacturing or service, the Customer is the King, especially in today's buyers' market. The father of our nation, Mahatma Gandhi, said, "... We are not doing him a favour by serving him. He is doing us a favour by giving us an opportunity to do so". The success of any business depends on customer satisfaction, the driving force for survival and growth and ultimately to achieve the objective of maximization of profit of the company. The customers consider the services as value for money while the price of the service is of secondary importance to them. It is well-known fact in the globalised fast changing economy that a rich and consistent level of customer service not only projects the quality of the servicing unit but also the overall managerial strength of the company. Customer orientation has become the key differentiator for competitive success of any company in agriculture, trade, industry and service sectors. It is and probably always will competitors offer a service industry producing an intangible product that is hard to differentiate from the products. For example, one bank's deposit, credit card, or loan looks pretty much like another's deposit, credit card, or loan. However, service accuracy, friendliness, quality of service and timely delivery vary from bank to bank and branch to branch in most market areas. This is why now we give more attention to Emotional Quotient (EQ) than Intelligence Quotient (IQ) while we offer services to our valued customers. EQ is a reliable indicator of one's emotional capability while IQ is a reliable indicator of one's mental capability to serve his/her client(s).

INTRODUCTION

The success of any business depends on customer satisfaction, as *Customer is the King*. Mahatma Gandhi, Father of the Indian Nation, said, "Customer is the most important visitor in our premises. He is not dependent on us. We are dependent on him. He is not an interruption on our work. He is the purpose of it. He is not an outsider on our business. He is a part of it. We are not doing him a favour by serving him. He is doing us a favour by giving us an opportunity to do so." This is applicable in both manufacturing as well as in service industry. Any service sector cannot exist without customer, which is a critical factor for survival and growth and thus fulfilling the objective of maximization of profit of the company.

Service Sector

The service industry is that section of the economy that supplies the need of the consumer but produces no tangible goods. The customers use and depend on services in one form or another and generally, the quality of the services given can add much to the quality of life. The major players in service sector are Banking and Insurance, Transport, Health, Education, Hotels and Restaurants, Retail trade, Public utilities, etc. It is interesting to note that the prices charged in service sector is most of the time of secondary importance while the customers consider the services as *value for money*. For example, a customer may prefer a particular bank branch because of the behavior of the manager and staff and the environment of the branch.

Any service industry has certain special features. Some of the important features of Service Industry are as follows:

- Service is invisible and not a physical product

- Service is rendered to the customer and users
- Service makes direct contact to the customers
- Service cannot be stored
- Service is directly beneficial to the users
- Service provided on demand
- Service quality is judged by the client and not by the supplier (like product)

Customer and Customer Service

As the customer is the king of any servicing company, the service should meet the requirements of the customers in terms of cost, consistency, time frame and usefulness for the purpose. The quality of service is judged on the basis of its *fitness for use.* It is stated that the quality of the service is judged by the customer and not by the supplier. So it is more difficult to maintain the customers' satisfaction in the service sector. To achieve this task, the company should generate customer oriented organizational restructuring, staffing, co-ordination, R&D activities, efficient distribution channels, after sales services, legal formalities, etc. to fulfill the needs of their customers. Best way to come up to the customers expectations is to obtain regular feedback from them and filling the gaps, wherever they exist.

The management should review the policies concerning customer service at frequent intervals to fine-tune them in line with customer needs. Complaints redressal mechanism should be quick, responsive and prompt. Additionally, the company should tone up their organizational systems and introduce new management techniques with a view to improving the services offered to the existing customer to retain while it is also important to expand the customer base by inclusion of new potential customer. In modern economy it is important for any company not only to make the customer satisfied but also to fulfill customer delight as the focal point to serve the objective of maximization of profit of the company. So it is now must not only to serve better but also to deliver the service to the doorstep of the customers. The customer in relation to the courtesy extended and the speed and accuracy with which their transactions are completed judge the efficiency of the service unit. It is unfortunate while often we observe that growth of service industry has proceeded with a sacrifice in the quality of customer service. Further, it is sometime noted that this notion is more visible in some of the public sector companies/undertakings in comparison to private sector players.

Poor customer service reflects in a variety of factors. Some of such factors are mentioned below:

- Insufficient managerial attention to service issues;
- Archaic procedures;
- Poor quality of services offered;
- Slow pace of development in improving the quality of the services due to lack of proper R&D work for developing innovative services;
- Poor motivation of the staff, particularly front office staff;
- Overstaffing and shortage of skilled staff;
- Lack of knowledge and inadequate technology;
- Lack of personalized services;
- Inefficiency of the manager to solve any complaints lodged by the customer(s);
- Poor after sales services.

It is well-known fact in the globalised fast changing economy that a rich and consistent level of customer service not only projects the quality of the servicing unit but also the overall managerial strength of the company. Customer orientation has become the key differentiator for competitive success of any company in agriculture, trade, industry and service sectors. Sometime, it is felt that suitable code of conduct should be followed by the servicing employees of the company while offering varied quality of services to the customers and enlightening the customers of their rights and protection.

Banking Industry

In this regard we can refer the recent moves of most important player of the service sector, the banking industry. Banks are financial service firms, producing and selling professional management of the public funds and performing many other roles in economy. We have observed the entire epic changes sweeping through this vital industry, something in banking never seem to change. It is and probably always will competitors offer a service industry producing an intangible product that is hard to differentiate from the products. One bank's deposit, credit card, or loan looks pretty much like another's deposit, credit card, or loan. However, service accuracy, friendliness, and quality of service vary from bank to bank and branch to branch in most market areas. This is why now we give more attention to Emotional Quotient (EQ) than Intelligence Quotient (IQ). EQ is a reliable indicator of one's emotional capability while IQ is a reliable indicator of one's mental capability to serve his/her client(s).

In India; Reserve Bank of India, the Central Bank of India, has drawn up a comprehensive Code of Banking Practice for improved customer service in Indian Banking Sector. The customers are well informed through this code about their right to get the specified services as per the codified norms, failing which they can lodge their complaints to the appropriate authority for redressal.

It is not possible to make an exhaustive list of features of excellent services to be offered by any company in service sector to delight the customer. The service provided to the customers may differ depending on the expectation and need of the prospective customers.

Following are few examples of good quality service to the customers of a commercial bank in the modern Indian banking scenario:

- Courtesy of the banker;
- To set up May I Help You counter and cleanliness of the lounge of the Bank;
- Consistency in humble behavior of the banker;
- Warm response by the receptionist and front office staff of the Bank;

- Time management of the service to deliver in any scheme;
- Personalised service to offer along with technology driven services like ATM, e-banking, etc.;
- Quick settlement of any complaint and to set up Customer Service Committees;
- Competitive price tag of the services;
- Timely sanction and disbursement of Loans and Advances, Bank Guarantee, Letter of Credit, Export Credit, etc.;
- Timely settlement of Compromise settlement of NPA proposal;
- To send bank statement to the customer on regular basis;
- To inform about any change in Interest Rate(s) on Loans and Advances and Deposits;
- To inform about any change(s) in any scheme or about new scheme;
- To render ancillary services like, payment of electricity bill, Income Tax payment and to file IT return, payment of staff salary, etc.;
- To follow Standing Instruction in time;
- To exchange notes for soiled/torn notes without any charges;
- To pay cash after normal banking hour but within working hour;
- Issuance and payment of Demand Draft at the earliest;
- Payment of interest for delayed credit in the account;
- To set up Service branch and other functional branches like, Personal Banking Branch, SSI branch, Commercial branch, Corporate Accounts Group branch, etc.;
- To give advices in financial matters like Pension plan, investment opportunities, etc.;
- To offer factoring services to manage bill business;
- To offer merchant banking facilities like project counseling, project syndication, consulting services, etc.;

- To offer investment-banking services like underwriting of issue to established company as well as the new company;
- To offer net banking, e-cheque, e-transfer of fund, ATM facilities, Credit and Debit card, etc.;
- To offer value added services like, Multi Option Deposit (MOD), Working Capital Term Loan (WCTL), Current-Plus, etc.;

There are certain other services of the banks like, locker facilities, safe custody facilities, executer's services, etc. that may also be included in the list.

Customer Delightness

It is a never-ending exercise to improve the quality of services to offer in today's fast changing environment of banking. So there should be continuous attempt to improve the level of customers' satisfaction by offering new creation of unique services, which will not only be offered for customers' satisfaction but also for "Customer Delight". Following are some of the important points to consider developing Excellency in the services:

- Extended range of innovative products and services;
- Improve efficiency of internal operation;
- Customer centric approach for product and services development;
- Global presence—Net work;
- To retain flexibility, integration and simplicity in business pyramid;
- To offer something larger—'focused attention on clients'
- To find niche in business world;
- To work hard to earn and maintain the trust of the customers;
- To have positive impact on people i.e. customers-centered not self-centered;
- To apply LIFE (Labour, Influence, Finance/Resources and Expertise) and its impact on the customers;

- To exchange of accurate and timely information, the key to providing good customer service;
- Thorough knowledge of products and services to be delivered;
- Helping the customers succeed is not only more fulfilling to reach their potentials, it is best way to won company's success;
- Ethical is the work that comes in mind, which makes feel good about the services offered to the customers for their best interest.

CONCLUSION

In conclusion it can be stated that there should be continual improvement in quality of services offered to the customers for survival and growth of any company working in service sector because of the following important issues:

- Barrierless open and fast changing economy and the life of any service and product is short;
- Increasing need and expectations of the customers in the buyers' market;
- Delivery of the services in time;
- Agility in delivery of the services to respond quickly to changes in demand;
- To encourage strong R&D activity to improve the quality of the services and to offer innovative services to customers.

REFERENCES

Churchill and Surprenant. "An Investigation into the Determinants of Customer Satisfaction", *Journal of Marketing Research*, Vol. XIX (Nov) 1982.

Kotlar, Philip. *Marketing Management*, Prentice-Hall of India Pvt. Ltd., New Delhi

Mowen, Jolm C. *Consumer Behavior*, Macmillan Publishing Co., New York

Xavier, M.J. *Marketing in The New Millennium*, Vikash Publishing House, New Delhi.

Adoption, Opportunities and Challenges of e-Banking Services in Sultanate of Oman

Abdul Quddus Mohammed

ABSTRACT

Digital revolution transforming and redefining the way business is done. Banking sector is no exception. Several banks are venturing into Electronic banking in an attempt to cut costs retain old customers, attract new customers and importantly for gaining competitive advantage. The Internet is transforming the banking in terms of the nature of core products and services and the way these are packaged, proposed, delivered and consumed. Consumer Adoption of Electronic Banking (EB) as new way of doing banking and e-Banking Security has received significant attention of several research practitioners. This paper, first evaluates the Banking websites in Sultanate of Oman using Diniz (1998) model, Secondly it focuses on e-Banking adaptation including drivers and inhibitions of e-banking customers in Oman, and finally it discusses e-banking challenges.

INTRODUCTION

It has always been a chicken-and-egg dilemma in business. Either firms wait for the market to mature until customers are ready for the products and services. Or, firms can go ahead and offer the products and services, hoping that their customers will catch on soon. The same is true for new products and services that have emerged — and continue to emerge — in the world of electronic banking (e-banking).

What is e-banking: "Banks using Internet as a channel for receiving instructions and delivering their products and services to their customers". This form of banking is generally referred to as Electronic Banking[5] E-Banking offers a new dimension for banks to reach greater heights in customer service banking services, convenience to the customer and employees, etc.

E-banking is changing the banking industry and is increasingly becoming a "need to have" rather than a "nice to have" service. From all new banking technologies, the net banking has the highest customer acceptance and offers the best way to improve customer service and at the same time reduce operational cost.

The introduction of new technologies has radically transformed banking transactions. In the past, customers had to come physically into the bank branch to do banking transactions. Then Automatic Teller Machines (ATMs) were introduced which allowed people to do their banking on their own, practically anytime and anywhere. The Internet then bought e-Banking which allowed customers to do financial transactions from their PCs at home via Internet. Now, with the emergence of M-Banking (Mobile Banking) using Wireless Application Protocol (WAP) technology, banks can use the infrastructure and applications developed for the Internet and move it to mobile phones. Now people no longer have to be tied to a desktop PC to do their banking. The WAP interface is much faster and convenient than the Internet, allowing customers to see account details, transaction details, make bill payments, and even check credit card balance.

E-banking can be offered in two main ways. First, an existing bank with physical offices can also establish an online site and offer e-banking services to its customers Secondly there are several e-banks that exist only on the Internet, allowing users to work with a "virtual" bank. For Example, NetBank, Smile Bank (www.smile.co.uk)

Some of the distinctive opportunities of e-Banking are:

1. **It removes the traditional geographical barriers** as it could reach out to customers of different countries/ legal jurisdiction., disseminating information about one's business at a relatively cost effective manner is tremendous.

2. **Convenience:** Many customers now prefer to do their financial operations from home and office Easy access and very low cost of transaction.
3. **Low cost of e-banking transaction:** The average cost of a direct banking transaction via web is $ 0.010. In comparison an ATM transaction costs $ 0.27, phone transaction $ 0.54, and a physical branch transaction $ 1.07 [1].
4. **New products and services can be offered:** New financial products cropping up almost everyday, such as credit cards, telephone banking, self-service banking, mobile phone banking and TV-banking, and e-money and e-wallet have also come true, Mobile phone recharge, Payment of bills.
5. **Banking services quality can be improved** by replying to customers' queries through e-mail, setting up (Frequently Asked Questions) FAQ pages for anticipated queries, offering interactive help line, accepting customers' complaints online 24 hours a day and attending to the same, etc.
6. **Efficiency and profitability:** Investing in Internet banking will reduce banking costs and raise profitability.
7. **Competitive advantage:** Using e-banking give advantage to bank against those banks which are not offering e-banking services. It poses a strategic risk of loss of business to those banks who do not respond in time, to this new technology, being the efficient and cost effective delivery mechanism of banking services.

This study will (1) Evaluate bank websites in Oman using Dinaz Model[6]; (2) Identify e-banking service usage among e-banking users and finding what Drives them in using e-banking services and also finding inhibitors of e-banking in non users of e-banking; (3) challenges of e-banking.

REVIEW OF LITERATURE

Not many studies have been conducted on current status of e-banking in Sultanate of Oman. Thus, almost no literature is available on this subject in Oman. Therefore, this paper is an attempt to reflect current status of e-banking websites and consumer adoption of e-banking in Oman. There are numerous papers on e-banking internationally for instance, Sathye (1997) surveyed Australian banks and it was found that 52 banks started e-banking services, however there was lot room for internet banking to expand Australia.

Dinaz [6] reported a survey of websites of banks in USA. It was found that most of bank websites were basic and intermediate level. No website was found to be advanced level.

Al-Sabbagh[9] reported a survey on Adoption of internet banking in Oman and it was found that Internet banking is only recent phenomenon in Oman and only two omani banks offer internet services and other three omani banks only maintain informational websites and consumers are concerned about security and privacy.

Jasimuddin (2001) found that within one year of introduction of internet service in KSA (Kingdom of Saudi Arabia) 73 per cent of Saudi banks has informational websites and only 25 per cent of banks offer full services over internet [10]. Internet banking is particularly widespread in Austria, Korea, the Scandinavian countries, Singapore, Spain, and Switzerland, where more than 75 per cent of all banks offer such service and with up to one-third of bank customers in Finland and Sweden use Internet Banking. 60 per cent of e-business in the UK was concentrated in the financial services sector, and with the expected 15-fold increase of the British e-business market by 2006. In USA in mid-2001, 44 per cent of national banks maintained transactional websites, almost double the number in the third quarter of 1999. While most U.S. consumers have accounts with banks that offer Internet services, only about 6 per cent of them use these services [12]. In India, approximately one per cent of high and middle-income group banking customers conducted banking on the Internet in 2000 compared to 5 to 6 per cent in Singapore and South Korea. In US, according to UNCTAD, online banking is growing at an annual rate of 60 per cent and the number of online accounts are expected to reach 25 million by 2007. The

United States has about 30 virtual banks; Asia has 2, launched in 2000 and 2001 [12]. The Gulf States have responded better to the challenges of e-banking than many other Arab countries. Three GCC countries—Bahrain, Kuwait and the UAE—boast adoption rates equal to or higher than those in the US; 29 per cent in Kuwait, 21 per cent in the UAE, and 17 per cent in Bahrain [12].

Banking in Oman: Banks in Oman are generally in good financial shape because of close regulation by the Central Bank of Oman. In 2002, there were fiteen local and foreign commercial banks and four specialized banks which provide housing and industrial loans to Omani citizens at favorable terms. The Economist Intelligence Unit reports that five of these Fourteen banks are domestic and that nine are foreign branches. According to the U.S. Department of Commerce, the largest local bank is Bank Muscat, followed in size by the National Bank of Oman, Oman International Bank, Oman Arab Bank, and Bank Dhofar.

Banks in Oman

In Oman all 5 local banks, Two specialized and Seven foreign banks and 1 central bank (Central Bank of Oman) have websites.

Local Banks (Omani)		Specialized Banks (Omani)		International Banks (Foreign)	
**Bank Muscat		**Oman Development Bank		**Bank Melli Iran	
**Bank Dhofar		Oman Housing Bank		**Bank of Baroda	
**National Bank of Oman		**Alliance Housing Bank		Bank Saderat Iran	
**Oman Arab Bank		Industrial Bank of Oman		**Banque Banorabe	
**Oman International Bank				**HSBC Bank Middle East	
				**Citibank N.A	
				Habib Bank Ltd.	
				**Standard Charted Bank	
				National Bank of Abu Dhabi	
				**SBI (State Bank of India)	
Total	5	Total	4	Total	10

Source: Central Bank Of Oman.

** Banks with website

National Bank of Oman (NBO) pioneered the Sultanate's first Internet banking service in February 2002. Bank Muscat (BM) followed suit by launching online service in June 2002. As of September 2003, these two banks are the only banks providing IB services in Oman. However, other banks such as Oman International Bank, Oman Arab Bank, and Central Bank of Oman maintain an informational Website with basic interactive capability [7].

Brighter future for e-banking in Oman: According to the internet World statistics (2005), the Oman internet penetration rate is more with 10.1 per cent compared to Middle East region average 9.6. There has been 172.2 per cent growth in internet uage from 2000 (90, 000) to 2006 (245, 000), these statistics are positive sign for the future success of e-banking in Sultanate.

With government initiatives for digital Oman and e-governance the day is not far when you see 100 per cent e-banking. Oman is all set to clinch its quantum of business benefits out of this new technology moves in e-Banking.

METHODOLOGY

This exploratory study has three folds,

Section one: 5 local Omani e-banking websites were chosen for evaluation using Dinaz model [6] which was used for evaluating e-banking websites in USA, this evaluation consisted of elements shown in Table 12.1. The evaluator recorded the absence or presence of each element.

Section two: This second part of study explored the factors that affect Omani consumers' adoption and use of e-banking. Data collected from 500 Customers of two banks (Bank Muscat and NBO), two questionnaires were prepared.

The questionnaire included questions based on studies of Chang (2004), Shih and Fang (2004), Al Sabbagh and Molla (2004) and Singh and Malhotra (2004) about the type of banking products and services that they currently use, what drives using internet banking (users of e-banking) and what are inhibitions in the minds of non-e-banking users in Sultanate of Oman. This survey administered in Sultanate of Oman during January-April, 2006 with Arabic and English versions of questionnaire We followed convenience sampling 500 bank customers (200 users and 300 Non-users of e-banking) were approached in Bank branches, Muscat festival ATM's and Lulu centers of Muscat and Salalah, Muscat festival and Khareef exhibition.

Section three: Deals with e-banking challenges.

Dinaz Model Framework for e-banking website evaluation:

Table 12.1: Framework for Websites Classification

Information delivery		
Basic Interactivity Level	Intermediary Level of Interactivity	Advanced Interactivity Level
Electronic brochure	Report downloads	Use customising resources
Promotional information	Recruitment forms	Some subscription option
Contact and location details	Hot links to other sites	Advertisement
Special offer announcements		Discussion groups
Banks use the Web to improve relationship with customers		
Basic Interactivity Level	Intermediary Interactivity Level	The Advanced Level of Interactivity
e-mail and forms are the ways a client has to make suggestions and complaints	advising tools (calculators, for example)	More advanced technologies, such as video conferencing
The Web is a vehicle for the most common transactions		
Lowest Level of Interactivity	Intermediary Interactivity Level	Advanced Level of Interactivity
Opening accounts	Clients can access their account details and statements online	Promoting e-cash as a way to develop Web-based transactions
Requesting products and services	Fund transfer	
Card requests	Bill payments	
Investment and credit applications	Client has to have some access to the bank's database	

Source: adapted from Diniz (1988).

Section one: Evaluation and Findings of Bank websites in Oman

The results of evaluation are discussed in detail in following paragraphs. The presence and absence of each Dinaz Model element was checked against information published on bank websites. The FAQ on internet banking/Demo options are useful for evaluation. As this paper is meant only for evaluation of website, no contact is made with bank for any additional information which we are planning to do next. So we can say that our observation is from the point of view of a user who is looking for a bank to do business with. The score for each bank website was calculated in percentage by dividing total number of elements present by maximum score of 48 (Dinaz Model, 1998), some new elements added to old Dinaz Model elements so that it suit modern requirements for evaluation. The scores provide indication of performance differences that exist among the 5 banks and also denote e-banking capabilities/offerings of each bank (Table 12.2).

The following codes are used in evaluation table (Table 12.2) against bank websites:

BM for Bank Muscat (www.bankmuscat.com), NBO for National Bank of Oman (www.nbo.co.com), OAB for Oman Arab Bank (www.omanab.com), BD for Bank Dofar (www.bdof.org), OIB for Oman International Bank (www.oiboman.com)

Inference: After evaluation of banking websites in Oman, my findings reveal that Bank Muscat, NBO are the only 2 banks in Oman who are providing e-banking services in Oman, and these banks satisfy 79 per cent (BM), 69 per cent (NBO) content requirements proposed by Dinaz Model [6]. However, other banks like Bank Dofar, Oman Arab Bank and Oman International Banks are maintaining informational websites without any transactional capabilities. There is much need to improve advanced transactional services and advanced Customer relation services with customization features in all banks in Oman.

Table 12.2: Evaluation of Bank websites with Dinaz Model Elements

	Banks Use Internet for Information Delivery Services					
	Information Services Contents	BM	NBO	OAB	BD	OIB
Basic	Bank Products and Services Information	1	1	1	1	1
	Promotional Information	1	1	1	1	1
	Branch Address	1	1	1	1	1
	Branch map	1	1	1	0	0
	Addresses of ATM	1	1	1	1	1
	Top management Information (Board of Directors)	1	1	0	1	1

(*Contd...*)

	Information Services Contents	BM	NBO	OAB	BD	OIB
	Electronic brochures	1	1	1	1	1
	Easy cash deposit locator	1	0	0	0	0
	FAQ	1	1	0	1	0
	Demo of internet banking services	1	1	0	0	0
	Help function	1	1	1	1	1
	Branch Timings	1	0	0	0	0
Intermediate	Site Search	1	1	0	1	0
	Form downloads	1	1	0	0	0
	Stock Information of Muscat Securities Market	1	1	1	0	1
	Career/Job openings	1	1	1	0	0
	Deposit Interest rates	1	1	0	1	1
	Headlines & News	1	1	1	1	1
	E-Security Help	1	1	0	1	0
	Forex (Foreign Exchange) rates	1	1	1	1	1
Advanced	Customization Personal settings	1	1	0	0	0
	Online chat with customer care	0	0	0	0	0
	Discussion Groups	0	0	0	0	0
	Banks Using Internet for Performing Transactional Services					
	Transactional Service Contents	BM	NBO	OAB	BD	OIB
Basic	Online account opening forms	0	0	0	1	1
	Online Demand Draft Request	1	1	0	0	0
	Online Check Book & Card lost request	1	0	0	0	0
Intermediate	Access to accounts through statements	1	1	0	0	0
	Utility bill payment	1	1	0	0	0
	Online Electronic Fund Transfer	1	1	0	0	0
	Applying Online loans	0	0	0	0	0
	Online Mobile recharge	1	0	0	0	0
	Online trade finance	1	0	0	0	0
	Web shopping	1	1	0	0	0
	Online Fixed deposit account	1	1	0	0	0
	Change of password	1	1	0	0	0
Advance	Online Personnel Investment guidance	0	0	0	0	0
	SMS Banking (Mobile E-Banking)	1	1	0	1	0
	Virtual banking with e-check-cash and Digital signatures	0	0	0	0	0
	Using Internet Banking for Improving Relationship with Customers					
	Customer Relationship Service Contents	BM	NBO	OAB	BD	OIB
Basic	Contact and Email	1	1	1	1	1
	Suggestions and Complaint forms	1	1	0	0	0
	Currency converter tools	1	1	0	1	0
	Loan calculators tools	1	1	0	0	0
Intermediate	Savings Calculators tools	1	1	0	0	0

(Contd...)

	Customer Relationship Service Contents	BM	NBO	OAB	BD	OIB
	Financial decision making tools	0	0	0	0	0
	What-If Analysis	0	0	0	0	0
Advanced	Video conferencing	0	0	0	0	0
	Online Marketing research of Bank	0	0	0	0	0
	Call Center (Toll Free Number)	1	1	0	1	0
	Total Number of presence	38	33	12	18	13
	Score for each bank in percentage	79%	69%	25%	37.5%	27%

Section two: Study of customer adoption of e-banking services in Oman

From the study of section one it's very clear that Bank Muscat and National Bank of Oman are pioneers of e-banking services in Oman, This second part of my study explores the factors that affect Omani consumers' adoption and use of e-banking.

For this purpose, a survey was conducted during January-July'2006 with Arabic and English versions of questionnaire. 500 customers of National Bank of Oman (NBO) and Bank Musact (BM) were contacted using convenience sampling at Muscat Festival ATM' and Khareef festival Bank Branches and Lulu centers in Salalalh and Muscat. It was found that 200 customers use internet banking service and 300 were non-users of internet banking in spite of these services were offered in their banks. Data collected in Sultanate of Oman two separate questionnaires were prepared for users (sample size 200) and non-users of internet banking (sample size 300). The questionnaire given to e-banking users included questions about the type of banking products and services that they currently use, what drives them to use internet banking. The questionnaire given to non-users of internet banking include questions about inhibitions customers to adopt e-banking in Sultanate of Oman.

Inference: Tables 12.3 shows demographic and adoption profile of e-banking customers who are mainly male young, educated Omani, Arab, Indian populations with average income between 200-1000, mostly managers and administrative staff who do e-banking from office and home whenever required.

Table 12.3: E-Banking Customers Demographics and Adoption Profile

Profile	Category	Frequency	Percentage
Gender	Male	150	75
	Female	50	25
Age	<25 Years old	60	30
	26-30 Years old	80	40
	31-40 Years old	40	20
	41-50 Years old	15	7.5
	>50 Years old	05	2.5
Ethnic groups	Omani	80	40
	Arabs	30	15
	Indians	50	25
	Pakistani	05	2.5
	Others (British, US, EU)	15	7.5
Education	Doctorates	30	15
	Masters	30	15
	Bachelors	86	43
	Diploma	34	17
	Secondary/Primary	20	10
Monthly Income in OMR	<200	10	5
	201-400	50	25
	401-600	70	35
	600-1000	40%	20
	1000-2000	25%	12.5
	>2000	5%	2.5
Job Level	Managerial	80	40
	Administrative	65	32.5
	Non-Managerial	55	27.5
Access	Home	76	38
	Office	80	40
	Internet Café	10	5
	Others	34	17
Frequency of Internet Banking			
	Every Day	23	11.5
	Once in a Week	22	11
	Once in a Month	31	15.5
	Whenever, necessary	124	62

E-Banking usage in Oman: Out of 200 customers of NBO, BM who went e-banking 95 per cent used e-banking for account statement enquiry, 60 per cent used for Speed International Fund Transfer, The next most popular items were Fund transfer to other bank account (56%) followed by Utility bill payment (45%), Credit and Debit card applications (40%) and Loan applications (30%) and Mobile phone recharge (30%) (Table 12.4).

Table 12.4: E-Banking Product/Service Adaptation

Products/Services	Used		Not Used	
	Number	Percentage	Number	Percentage
Saving account	164	82	36	18
Current account	64	32	136	68
Fixed deposit	40	20	160	80
Utility bill payment	90	45	110	55
Credit and Debit card applications	80	40	120	60
Account statement enquiry	190	95	10	05
Check book order	108	54	96	48
Card lost information	50	25	150	75
Mobile phone recharge	60	30	140	70
Speed International Fund transfer	120	60	80	40
Fund transfer to local account	112	56	88	44

What are drivers of Internet Banking in Oman: We asked 200 respondents who adopted E-Banking services in BM, NBO banks about what factors that motivated their decision to do online banking on Five point, 10 items on likert scale, the results of survey is shown in Table 12.5.

Table 12.5: Drivers for e-banking

Factor for using e-banking (Drivers of adoption)	Adopters Mean Score
Convenience of services (Anytime Any place banking)	4.05
Internet banking is easy to use	4.10
It's convenient for me to manage my finances	3.8
Saves my cost and Time	3.7
I want to experiment new technology	3.4
Social recognition as modern person	2.5
My friends, colleagues and family members use Internet Banking	2.4
Financial incentives from bank	0.0
Suitable to my life style	4.30
I don't like to stand in queue at my bank service	3.4

Scale: 5=Extremely important, 4=Very important, 3=Important, 2=Less important, 1=Not important

Inference: The most important drivers for using internet banking is suitability to life style of people, Convenience and Easiness to use e-banking services are important ones, however, factors such as saving time, cost and experimentation with new technology and consumers unwillingness to stand in queue in bank are also important factors for e-banking adopters.

What are Inhibitors for Performing Internet Banking in Oman?

To study this, 300 respondents who are not using Internet banking services of NBO and BM are surveyed about what is stopping them to do e-banking on 5 point 10 items likert scale.The results are shown in Table 12.6.

Table 12.6: Inhibitors for e-banking

Factors for not using e-banking (Inhibitors of adoption)	Non-Adopters Mean Score
I don't know how to use Internet banking	4.8
I don't have Computer at Home or Office	3.9
I believe in Face to Face Personal traditional banking	3.6
I am concerned with security of E-Banking services	4.9
I used Internet Banking but not happy	3.8
I don't trust Internet banking	3.9
I am concerned about privacy of my information	4.2
No financial benefit of using Internet banking	3.7
I don't take any risk with my finances (I don't believe new technology)	3.8
I can't understand English Language website	4.7

Scale: 5=strongly agree, 4=Agree, 3=Neutral, 2=Disagree,1=Strongly Disagree

Inference: Among the inhibitors of e-banking services the security, inability to use, privacy, Trust and non-belief of technology and most important English Language websites are major factors. Hence, banks in Oman must concentrate on Arabic language websites with User friendliness and Security and privacy of user in e-banking.

Section Three: Challenges of E-Banking Services in Sultanate of Oman

The information technology in itself is not a panacea and it has to be effectively utilized. The most important requirement for the successful working of Internet banking is the adoption of the best security methods. This presupposes the existence of a uniform and the best available technological devices and methods to protect electronic banking transactions. Some challenges for successful implementation of e-banking include: Social challenges, Technology challenges, Security challenges, Legal challenges, Operational challenges, Reputational challenges and other challenges. These challenges are general in nature applicable for all banks in the world including sultanate of Oman.

Social Challenges

- Digital Divide (within the country itself most of the times).
- Language Barrier (Arabic contents and Arabic Domain Names).
- Literacy rates.
- Awareness.
- National vision and planning: Still need more commitment, collaboration and awareness.
- Resistance to change and Internet usage.

Technology Challenges

To remain competitive, banks will have to renew their commitment to investing in new technology strategically—to reduce costs, improve efficiencies, and boost revenue-generating initiatives

(i) Need for standardization of hardware, operating systems, system software, application software to facilitate interconnectivity of systems across branches.

(ii) Hardware and software prices.

(iii) Limited connectivity.

(iv) Telecommunications infrastructure high levels of security.

(v) Technology planning with periodical up gradation.

The biggest challenge is to understand and manage the complexity of technology risks like defensive mechanisms such as virus detection, intrusion management and authentication tools.

Security Challenges

One of the biggest attractions of Internet as an electronic medium is its openness and freedom that is creating security concerns. It's very clear from section two of my study that consumers are interested to do e-banking but they are hesitant about the security aspect of e-banking which is major inhibitor for e-banking. Security issues are a major source of concern for everyone both inside and outside the banking industry. E-banking increases security risks, potentially exposing hitherto isolated systems to open and risky environments increased cross-border transactions resulting from drastically lower transaction costs and the greater ease of banking activities, and from the reliance on technology to provide banking services with the necessary security.

Some more avenues for frauds in this emerging e-banking scenario

- **Mail Spoofing—E-Mail Forgery:** sending wrong information to bank customers as if its from authentic bank sources.
- **Web Spoofing—Website Forgery:** Diverting the customers of a bank to an exactly duplicated forged website and impersonating those customers on real bank site.
- **Attacking the User Computer:** To take control of that machine.
- **Attacking a Bank's Server:** To take control of that machine.
- **Media Tapping**—recording the whole transactions of a bank, or customer, etc. and replaying the same for their advantage.
- **Denying Service:** Though the server is available, making it not able to render service, by poisoning the Network Infrastructure.
- **Bogus Attack:** Hacking the servers run by ISP of Bank.
- **Phishing Attacks.**

Security Solutions for Successful E-Banking Implementation (Secure Horizons)

A close observation reveals that all frauds happen due to impersonation, sniffing information on its travel and hacking into the computer. The impersonation can be for an individual, a website, a computer, a router, etc. The frauds due to impersonation, sniffing can be minimized by adopting PKI—Public Key Infrastructure. Frauds due to hacking and not able to deploy PKI, etc. can be minimized by firewalls, IDS—Intrusion Detection System [1], Password smearing, Log file modifications, Smart cards, Hardware tokens, Spy ware, Browser tools such as SpoofStick or ScamBlocker. etc.

E-Banking security should consider following aspects in designing security system

(i) **Authentication:** Assurance of identity of the person in a deal,

(ii) **Authorization:** A party doing a transaction is authorized to do so,

(iii) **Privacy or Confidentiality of data, information** relating to any deal,

(iv) **Data integrity:** Assurance that the data has not been altered, and

(v) **Non- repudiation**, a party to the deal cannot deny that it originated the communication or data.

Legal Challenges

Because the Internet allows services to be provided from anywhere in the world, there is a danger that banks will try to avoid regulation and supervision relating to the jurisdiction of law, validity of electronic contract including the question of repudiation, gaps in the legal/regulatory environment for electronic commerce. On the question of jurisdiction the issue is whether to apply the law of the area where access to Internet has been made or where the transaction has to be taken. Allied to this is the question where the income has been generated and who should tax such income. There are still no definite answers to these issues. There is need of more effective comprehensive IT ACT and Internet security act for Oman.

For banks it's more difficult to stay abreast of regulatory changes. As a consequence, virtual banks could unknowingly violate customer protection laws, including on data collection and privacy, and regulations on soliciting. In doing so, they expose themselves to losses through lawsuits or crimes that are not prosecuted because of jurisdictional disputes.

Challenges Related to Online Money Laundering Through Bank

Money laundering includes move illegally acquired cash through financial systems so that it appears to be legally acquired. It is an age-old criminal activity that has been greatly facilitated by electronic banking because of the anonymity it affords. Once a customer opens an account, it is impossible for banks to identify whether the nominal account holder is conducting a transaction or even where the transaction is taking place. To combat money laundering, many countries have issued specific guidelines on identifying customers. They typically comprise recommendations for verifying an individual's identity and address before a customer account is opened and for monitoring online transactions, which requires great vigilance.

Bank Operational Challenges

The reliance on new technology to provide services makes security and system availability the central operational risk of electronic banking. Security threats can come from inside or outside the system, so banking regulators and supervisors must ensure that banks have appropriate practices in place to guarantee the confidentiality of data, as well as the integrity of the system and the data. Banks' security practices should be regularly tested and reviewed by outside experts to analyze network vulnerabilities and recovery preparedness. Capacity planning to address increasing transaction volumes and new technological developments should take account of the budgetary impact of new investments, the ability to attract staff with the necessary expertise, and potential dependence on external service providers.

Challenges Related to Managing Reputation of Bank

Breaches of security and disruptions to the system's availability can damage a bank's reputation. The more a bank relies on electronic delivery channels, the greater the potential for reputational risks. If one electronic bank encounters problems that cause customers to lose confidence in electronic delivery channels as a whole or to view bank failures as system wide supervisory deficiencies, these problems can potentially affect other providers of electronic banking services. Reputational risks also stem from customer misuse of security precautions or ignorance about the need for such precautions. Security risks can be amplified and may result in a loss of confidence in electronic delivery channels. The solution is consumer education—a process in which regulators and supervisors can assist. For example, some bank supervisors provide links on their websites allowing customers to identify online banks with legitimate charters and deposit insurance. They also issue tips on Internet banking, offer consumer help lines, and issue warnings about specific entities that may be conducting unauthorized banking operations in the country.

Other Challenges

- It is the challenge for the bank to increase the awareness and usefulness of the e-banking, beside the traditional-based banking services.
- Encourage more of the Internet using population to bank online and to develop more profitable relationships with existing online bankers.
- The technology of e-Commerce determines what can be offered to customers, but only customers determine which of those technologies will be accepted. The key to success for e-Commerce lies in knowing customer.

Four Ley Tools to Address the New Challenges Posed by the Arrival of e-banking

For successful implementation of e-banking in Oman, Banks can concentrate on following tools[14]:

Adaptation of Technology: To review the key aspects of the security control process, which should include measures to authenticate the identity and authorization of customers, promote nonrepudiation of transactions, protect data integrity, and ensure segregation of duties within e-banking systems, databases, and applications. Banks must also ensure that their staffs have the relevant technological expertise to assess potential changes in risks, which may require significant investment in training and in hardware and software. Expansion of electronic money is also important.

Legalization: New methods for conducting transactions, new instruments, and new service providers will require legal definition, recognition, and permission. For example, it will be essential to define an electronic signature and give it the same legal status as the handwritten signature. Existing legal definitions and permissions—such as the legal definition of a bank and the concept of a national border—will also need to be rethought.

Harmonization: International harmonization of electronic banking regulation must be a top priority. This means intensifying cross-border cooperation between supervisors and coordinating laws and regulatory practices internationally and domestically across different regulatory agencies. The problem of jurisdiction that arises from "borderless" transactions is, as of this writing, in limbo. For now, each country must decide who has jurisdiction over electronic banking involving its citizens. The task of international harmonization and cooperation can be viewed as the most daunting in addressing the challenges of electronic banking.

Integration: This is the process of including information technology issues and their accompanying operational risks in bank supervisors' safety and soundness evaluations. In addition to the issues of privacy and security, for example, bank examiners will want to know how well the bank's management has elaborated its business plan for electronic banking. A special challenge for regulators will be supervising the functions that are outsourced to third-party vendors.

CONCLUSION

From the evaluation of e-banking websites it is concluded that e-banking is at inception stage and only 4 years old most importantly. Bank Muscat and National Bank of Oman are only two banks which are successful in e-banking and the day is not far when these two banks offer secured virtual bank services. The adoption trends show that consumers perceive e-banking to be easy and convenient way to conduct traditional banking transactions. Most users studies claimed that it fits in with their lifestyles and among the inhibitors the privacy and security are major area of concerns for adopting e-banking. In security, the latest Phishing attacks are major areas of concern but by implementing PKI, Password smearing, Log file modification and spy ware it can be minimized. Some e-banking challenges include Social challenges, Technology challenges, Security challenges, Legal challenges, Operational challenges, Reputational challenges and other challenges. The ideas of developing Arabic version of website, customer awareness, incentives to e-banking customers and offering training to customer groups can make e-banking popular in Oman. However, an e-banking system itself does not give competitive advantage and competitive advantage comes from how the bank interface that e-banking system with it's customers and how making customers perceive.

Findings of section two can't be generalized to general population as convenient sample was used and most of the respondents were specific educated group. Nevertheless, the results provide fair indication of what e-banking services users find useful and what are motivations and inhibitions of e-banking in Oman. Hence, findings can be considered preliminary and "Inshallah" would be explored further with more rigorous comparative study on local and foreign banks websites with interviews with banks officials, customers and on latest challenges for e-banking in Oman.

However, it is unrealistic to expect huge profits through overnight e-banking and the value of developing e-banking lies in the long-term.

"Technology is dominated by two types of people: those who understand what they do not manage and those who manage what they do not understand".

REFERENCES

Kurtas, A. (2000). "Analytical study of investment opportunities in direct and internet banking" (Translated). *Arab Banks Union Magazine.* June, p. 35.

Menezes, A.J., P.C. van Oorschot and S.A. Vanstone. *Handbook of Applied Cryptography*, CRC Press, 1996.

Soroor Javad. "Implementation of a Secure Internet/Mobile Banking System in Iran", *Journal of Internet Banking and Commerce*, December 2005, Vol. 10, No. 3.

Kumar Abhishek. "Phishing the new age attack", www.paladion.net

Singh, Balwinder, Malhotra, Pooja. "Adoption of Internet Banking: An Empirical Invisugation of Indian Banking Sector" p. 3.

Diniz, Eduardo (1998). "Web Banking in USA" *Journal of Internet Banking and Commerce*, Vol. 3, No, 2, June 1998.

Guru B., Shanmugham, B., Alam, N. and Parera, C., (2003). "Evaluation of Internet Banking sites in Islamic Countries", *Journal of Internet Banking and Commerce*, Vol. 8, No. 2, November.

Shih, Y. and Fung, K. (2004). "The use of decomposed theory of planned behavior to study Internet Banking in Taiwan", *Internet Research*, 14, 3, 213-23.

Al-Sabbagh Imtiyaz and Alemayehu Molla. "Adoption and Use of Internet Banking in Sultanate of Oman", *Journal of Internet Banking.*

Schaechter Andrea and Saleh M. Nsouli. "Challenges of E-Banking Revolution", IMF, www.imf.org

Radha, V. and Gulati, V.P. "Preventing Technology based Frauds", *Journal of Internet Banking.*

www.researchandmarkets.com

www.internetworldstats.com

Saleh M. Nsouli and Andrea Schaechter. "Challenges of the "E-Banking Revolution" *Finance and Development* A Quarterly Magazine of IMF, September 2002, Volume 39, Number 3.

Organizational Culture and Service Delivery: A Cross-Cultural Study of Banks in Sultanate of Oman and India

13

Mohammed Naved Khan,
Feza Tabassum Azmi and *Mahfoodh Al Sabbagh*

ABSTRACT

The paradigm shift from business focus to customer focus has resulted in customer-orientation being on the corporate radar screens across all major industries, and most visibly in service industry. This necessitates establishing an organizational culture that facilitates customer-orientation and effective delivery of the service. In fact, competitive companies are already undertaking the introspective soul-searching necessary to set up such a culture.

The single most important difference between products and services is the characteristic of intangibility. This characteristic has a profound effect on the success of service organizations. Peculiar issues arise due to intangibility which requires subtle modifications in the service delivery process. The organizational culture plays a pivotal role in facilitating the seamless execution of service delivery, communicating service quality attributes and creating the desired service experience. Organizations that take a strategic approach to culture issues tend to create innovative solutions centring on customers and the employees. For them corporate culture is an overarching management perspective tethered in the belief of long-term success over myopic profit-driven transactions.

Several factors play a key role in creating and shaping corporate culture. Primarily, national and regional differences have a strong bearing on corporate dynamics. Such cross-cultural differences between nations get reflected in corporate functioning. It was with this perspective that the present study was undertaken to analyze differences between organizational cultures existing in the service industry of two countries i.e. Sultanate of Oman and India. The study is based on the concept of OCTAPACE culture; an acronym for openness, confrontation, trust, authenticity, proaction, autonomy, collaboration and experimentation. The objectives of the study were to generate and compare the OCTAPACE profile of two largest banks of Sultanate of Oman and India.

INTRODUCTION

The fluid and hyper competitive global economy of today has created a new competitive landscape. The world is witnessing the collapse of archaic systems, methods, processes and techniques. Business organizations under such bizarre settings are unlearning traditional ways of working. Organizational boundaries have become less confining, allowing dramatic changes in the workplace. It requires companies to transform from the traditional industrial enterprises of yesteryears into the modern post-industrial ones-open, flexible and innovative (Khan and Azmi, 2005).

In this context, organizational culture assumes immense significance as a vital tool for attaining sustainable competitive advantage. Organizational culture is hypothesized as playing a critical role in the development of corporate identity. This in turn provides organizations with the opportunity of leveraging their identity for achieving strategic leadership. Cultural influences have a strong bearing on the character and persona of an organization. Peters and Waterman (1982) have opined that excellent companies are people oriented and focus on corporate culture.

Organization Culture and Service Industry

Schein (1990) described culture as a set of shared assumptions, values; beliefs and norms about expected behaviour. Schwartz and Davis (1981) see culture as a pattern of beliefs and expectations shared by organization members. Organizations can have a dominant culture and numerous subcultures (Robbins, 1988). Deal and Kennedy (1982) defined organizational culture as the way things get done around here. Handy (1985) linked organization structure to organizational culture. Ouchi (1981) puts it as a set of symbols, ceremonies and myths that communicate the underlying values and beliefs of an organization.

With regard to the service industry, the customer's total experience with the organization is instrumental in customer satisfaction and transforming them into lifetime organizational assets. The paradigm shift from business focus to customer focus has resulted in customer-orientation being on the corporate radar screens across all major industries, and most visibly in service industry.

The single most important difference between products and services is the characteristic of intangibility. This characteristic has a profound effect on the success of service organizations. Peculiar issues arise due to intangibility which requires subtle modifications in the service delivery process.

This necessitates establishing an organizational culture that facilitates customer-orientation and effective delivery of the service. In fact, competitive companies are already undertaking the introspective soul-searching necessary to weave such a culture.

Review of Literature

Pareek (2002) discussed the concept of ethos, as the underlying spirit of character or group and is the root of culture. He defined organizational ethos as eight values relevant to institution building. These eight cultural values are also called as OCTAPACE. In addition to being an acronym for the eight values, OCTAPACE symbolizes *octa* or eight and *pace* or steps to create functional ethos. Pareek (2002) describes OCTAPACE as:

- **Openness:** Sharing of feelings and thoughts without defensiveness.
- **Confrontation:** Facing challenges rather than shying away from problems.

- **Trust:** Maintaining the confidentiality of information shared by others.
- **Authenticity:** Congruence between what one feels, says and does.
- **Proaction:** Taking initiative, preplanning and taking preventive action.
- **Autonomy:** Using and giving freedom to plan and act in one's own sphere.
- **Collaboration:** Willingness to work as a team through mutual help.
- **Experimenting:** Encouraging innovative ways to solve problems and thinking out of the box.

Except for a few studies on OCTAPACE (e.g. Srivastav, 1995; Erakovich et. al., 2002; Srivastava and Srivastava, 2004; Niranjana and Pattanayak, 2005), empirical evidences of studies using the concept of OCTAPACE are few and far between. Most studies have been conducted in the Indian context. The researchers have not come across any cross-cultural study using the concept of OCTAPACE.

Objectives of the Study

Of late, Indian companies have started making their presence felt in Oman. The Government of Oman too, has adopted a no-holds-barred policy *vis-à-vis* investment by Indian companies. Gestures such as these are indicative of a burgeoning economic and commercial relationship between India and Oman. These developments warrant a meticulous examination of the organizational cultures prevailing in the two countries to grasp the subtleties of their respective corporate lifestyles.

It is a globally accepted fact that systems and cultures cannot be built overnight. They evolve gradually, taking roots, over time. Several factors play a key role in creating organizational culture. National and regional differences have a strong bearing on corporate dynamics. Hofstede (1980) demonstrated that there are national and regional cultural groupings that affect the culture of organizations. Organizations symbolize the inherent character of the society and cross-cultural differences between nations get reflected in corporate functioning.

It is, therefore, crucial to investigate the cross-cultural differences in business organizations. It was with this perspective in mind that the present study was undertaken. The need for such a study was felt to understand how organizations differ on various dimensions of corporate culture across countries. The present study undertakes an analysis of cross-cultural differences between banks operating in India and Oman.

In the light of the above, the objectives of the present research were:

1. To analyse the culture of the two largest banks of Oman and India denoted by Bank A (Bank from Oman) and Bank B (Bank from India) on each dimension of OCTAPACE i.e. openness, confrontation, trust, authenticity, proaction, autonomy, collaboration and experimentation.
2. To generate OCTAPACE profile of the two banks.
3. To compare the OCTAPACE profile of Bank A and Bank B.

METHODOLOGY

Research Design

Methodological issues in cross-cultural research have been the subject of inquiry by many scholars (e.g., Davis et al., 1981; Sekaran, 1983; Parameswaran and Yaprak, 1987; Douglas and Craig, 1992; Samiee and Jeoung, 1994; Cavusgil and Das, 1997). In conducting the present study, researchers have been careful to avoid such problems. For the study, the researchers have used OCTAPACE scale which is a reliable and validated instrument developed by Pareek (2002).

Review of cross-cultural research shows that researchers prefer collecting data using quantitative methods and survey is the most frequently used method (Salciuviene et al., 2005). This study too bases itself on survey method. One statistical technique used commonly in cross-cultural research is frequency tables

(Liefeld et al., 1999) which has also been deployed for the present study to calculate mean values of scores.

It has been widely argued that one of the most important issues in conducting cross-cultural research is that of translation equivalence (Samiee and Jeoung, 1994; Sin et al., 1999; Craig and Douglas, 2000; Yaprak, 2003). The researchers took great care to avoid this problem too. Keeping in mind the fact that the original questionnaire which was in English may have posed problems for some respondents, it was also translated into Arabic for respondents from Bank A and into Hindi for employees of Bank B. The respondents had the option of responding to either the English or the translated versions. To avoid discrepancies, back translation method suggested by Green and White (1976) was used.

Van de Vijver et al. (1997) point out that response bias occurs when answers tend to cluster around some point in the scale. To avoid the above problem, a pilot study was conducted to see if responses are normally distributed or skewed in one direction. The distribution of responses obtained was such that it was suitable for further analysis.

Sampling

When conducting cross-cultural research, it is crucial to establish equivalence not only in research instrument, but also in sampling procedure (Green and White, 1976; Samiee and Jeoung, 1994; Malhotra et al., 1996; Sin et al., 1999; Reynolds et al., 2003). Van de Vijver and Leung (1997) suggest a possible sampling method for comparative studies, viz., matched sampling. Hofstede (1991) renders that in matched samples, respondents are functionally equivalent.

This aspect has been taken care of by researchers by focusing on respondents who are "functionally equivalent". In this study the unit of analysis were the two largest banks of Oman and India. Further, both these banks are one of the largest employers in the banking industry of the two countries. Both the banks have a vast network of branches.

The respondents were managerial and officer level employees posted in branches of Bank A and Bank B in the capital cities (i.e.

Muscat and New Delhi respectively) of both the countries. Due to non-availability of suitable sample frame, feedback was obtained from a convenience sample of 160 respondents (Bank A = 40 and Bank B = 120). The staff at the managerial and officer level was included in the study as it was felt that they would be in a better position to respond to items related to corporate culture.

The Instrument

For the purpose of collecting data on the OCTAPACE profile, a questionnaire developed by Pareek (2002) was used. The questionnaire contained 40 items representing five statements for each of the eight values of OCTAPACE and the respondent was required to check (on a four-point scale) how much each item is valued and shared in the organization. For each item, scores from 1-4 were allotted to the four-point scale. In order to avoid biases in responses, certain statements were negatively worded and their scores were reversed so that all items became unidirectional. After evaluating the total scores of all respondents, for each aspect of the OCTAPACE, the mean scores were calculated.

Analysis of Data

The analysis of data from the two banks reveals that although on several items within each of the eight dimensions, Bank A scores more than Bank B but the latter has a higher overall score than the former on openness, confrontation, trust, proaction and collaboration. Bank A has a higher overall score on authenticity, autonomy and experimentation. The mean scores of the two banks on all the eight dimensions are presented in Tables 13.1 through 13.8.

The calculated means of Bank A and Bank B have been compared with low and high norms for OCTAPACE suggested by Pareek (2002) and they are presented in Table 13.9.

Based on the above analysis, a comparative OCTAPACE profile of the two banks is depicted in Table 13.10.

Table 13.1: Mean Scores on Openness

Item No.	Bank A Mean Scores	Bank B Mean Scores
01	3.20	3.73
09	3.05	3.13
17	3.08	3.00
25	1.83	1.53
33	3.28	3.53
Total	14.44	14.92

Table 13.2: Mean Scores on Confrontation

Item No.	Bank A Mean Scores	Bank B Mean Scores
02	3.55	3.67
10	3.18	2.67
18	3.40	3.20
26	1.83	2.60
34	3.33	3.27
Total	15.29	15.41

Table 13.3: Mean Scores on Trust

Item No.	Bank A Mean Scores	Bank B Mean Scores
03	3.28	3.20
11	3.23	2.67
19	3.20	3.20
27	3.33	3.27
35	1.80	2.67
Total	14.84	15.01

Table 13.4: Mean Scores on Authenticity

Item No.	Bank A Mean Scores	Bank B Mean Scores
04	2.98	2.73
12	1.85	2.47
20	2.85	2.87
28	2.10	2.27
36	3.00	2.53
Total	12.78	12.87

Table 13.5: Mean Scores on Proaction

Item No.	Bank A Mean Scores	Bank B Mean Scores
05	2.98	3.40
13	3.28	3.40
21	3.08	3.00
29	3.25	3.53
37	3.23	2.93
Total	15.82	16.26

Table 13.6: Mean Scores on Autonomy

Item No.	Bank A Mean Scores	Bank B Mean Scores
06	2.95	2.40
14	2.10	2.00
22	1.98	1.80
30	2.00	1.93
38	3.00	3.13
Total	12.03	11.26

Table 13.7: Mean Scores on Collaboration

Item No.	Bank A Mean Scores	Bank B Mean Scores
07	3.30	3.47
15	3.13	3.47
23	1.85	2.33
31	2.38	2.27
39	3.28	2.93
Total	13.94	14.47

Table 13.8: Mean Scores on Experimentation

Item No.	Bank A Mean Scores	Bank B Mean Scores
08	3.35	3.13
16	3.40	3.40
24	3.15	3.27
32	3.25	3.00
40	2.30	2.13
Total	15.45	14.93

Table 13.9: Comparison of Mean Scores and Suggested Norms

Values	Norms Low	Bank A	Bank B	Norms High
Openness	13	14.44	14.92	17
Confrontation	13	15.29	15.41	17
Trust	13	14.84	15.01	17
Authenticity	10	12.78	12.87	14
Proaction	13	15.82	16.26	17
Autonomy	11	12.03	11.26	16
Collaboration	13	13.94	14.47	17
Experimentation	11	15.45	14.93	16

Table 13.10: Comparative OCTAPACE Profiles of Bank A and Bank B

Values	Descriptors	Bank A	Bank B
Openness	Free interaction among employees.	↓	↑
	Genuine sharing of information in meetings.	↓	↑
	Free discussion between seniors and juniors.	↑	↓
	Effective managers do not conceal their feelings.	↑	↓
	Free and frank communication.	↓	↑
Confrontation	Facing and not shying away from problems.	↓	↑
	Going deeper to solve interpersonal problems.	↑	↓
	Facing challenges inherent in the work situation.	↑	↓
	Do not pass the buck when there is a problem.	↓	↑
	Solving and not just surfacing problems.	↑	↓
Trust	Offering support and help to colleagues in a crisis.	↑	↓
	Confiding in seniors without fear.	↑	↓
	Interpersonal contact and support among people.	↔	↔
	Trust begets trust.	↑	↓
	People can rely on others in times of crisis.	↓	↑
Authenticity	People do what they say.	↑	↓
	Manipulation is considered wrong.	↓	↑
	Owning up to mistakes.	↓	↑
	Telling truth even if unpleasant.	↓	↑
	People generally are what they appear to be.	↑	↓
Proaction	Preventive action is taken on most matters.	↓	↑
	Encouraging juniors about their development.	↓	↑
	Considering pros and cons before taking action.	↑	↓
	Prevention is better than cure.	↓	↑
	A timely action avoids complications.	↑	↓

(Contd....)

Values	Descriptors	Bank A	Bank B
Autonomy	People take independent actions.	↑	↓
	Close supervision of employees is avoided.	↑	↓
	Independent decision-making.	↑	↓
	Freedom to employees.	↑	↓
	A good way to motivate employees is autonomy.	↓	↑
Collaboration	Team work and team spirit is encouraged.	↓	↑
	Accepting and appreciating help offered by others.	↓	↑
	More concern about large organization goals.	↓	↑
	Emphasis on team work.	↑	↓
	Participative goal-setting.	↑	↓
Experimentation	Trying out innovative ways of solving problems.	↑	↓
	Taking a fresh look at doing things.	↔	↔
	Genuine attempts to change.	↓	↑
	Thinking and doing new things.	↑	↓
	Experimentation is an imperative.	↑	↓

Note:

↑ arrow indicates higher value than the other organization.

↓ arrow indicates lower value than the other organization.

↔ arrow indicates both organizations have equal value.

CONCLUSION

The results suggest that Bank B scores considerably better as compared to Bank A on most dimensions of OCTAPACE. Findings suggest that the culture of Bank B is more open. Also there is focus on confronting problems and facing challenges. Trust seems to be a vital issue with people confiding and relying on each other. There is strong evidence of a team-based and collaborative work environment. Proactive decision making is encouraged. However, it is apparent that organizational members are not granted complete freedom in decision-making. There is close supervision and monitoring by seniors which may have a stifling affect on organizational creativity in the long-run.

Organizational members at Bank A are encouraged to experiment with new solutions to unique problems and have more autonomy as compared to Bank B. However, Bank A scores well below Bank B on most dimensions implying that OCTAPACE values have still not crystallized in Bank A. But, the

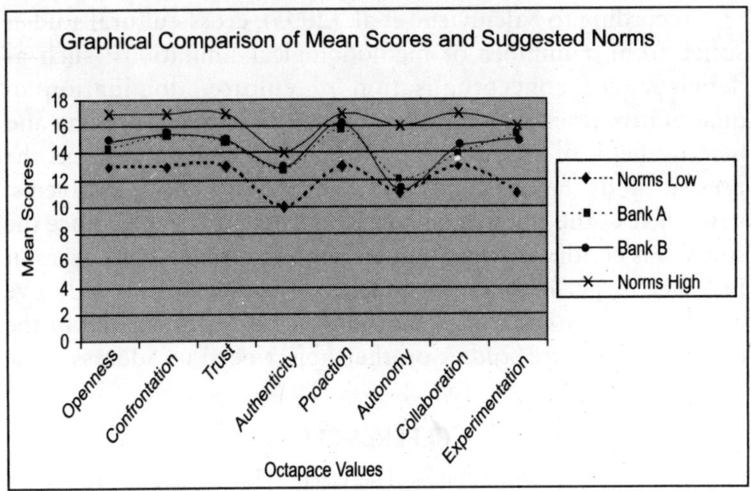

scores of the two banks suggest that both fall roughly in between the tentative norms suggested by Pareek (2002).

The low scores of Bank A on most OCTAPACE dimensions as compared to Bank B may be attributed partially to the fact that Oman has not yet fully metamorphosed into a mature business hub. Since companies in India are more exposed to the blitz of global competition, it seems to have a bearing on the fast paced changes in organizational cultures. Sun (2002) opines that organisational culture cannot exist in a vacuum. It is always embedded into the regional and national culture. The main dimensions of national culture manifest themselves in and through organisational culture. This is clearly reflected in the OCTAPACE profile of the two banks.

For organizations in the service industry, such as banks, it is crucial to investigate the nature of organizational culture since it has a direct bearing on their performance. The organizational culture plays a pivotal role in facilitating the seamless execution of service delivery, communicating service quality attributes and creating the desired service experience. Needless to point out that organizations that have higher scores on the OCTAPACE dimensions will be better positioned to deliver enhanced service quality.

According to Salciuviene et al. (2005), cross-cultural studies suffer from a number of methodological limitations; such as deficiency of conceptualisation of culture, domination of quantitative research methods, non-equivalence in sampling and heterogeneity of cultures, etc. Although the researchers in the present study have taken care to avoid the above problems, nevertheless, the results may not be fully generalizable. Since the study was conducted on a limited number of bank employees, it may not be perfecrly representative. However, it may still give an idea of the nature of organization cultures prevailing in the two banks. Future studies on the subject need to address these issues.

REFERENCES

Alexander, G.S. (2006). "Follow The Client" *The Economic Times*. 17 May. p. 5.

Cavusgil, S.T. and Das, A. (1997). "Methodological Issues in Empirical Cross-Cultural Research: A Survey of the Management Literature and a Framework" *Management International Review*, 37, 71-96.

Craig, S.C. and Douglas, S.P. (2000). *International Marketing Research*. West Sussex: John Wiley & Sons.

Davis, H.L., Douglas, S.P. and Silk, A.J. (1981). "Measure Unreliability: A Hidden Threat to Cross National Marketing Research?" *Journal of Marketing*. 45, 98-108.

Deal, T.E. and Kennedy, A.A. (1982). *Corporate Cultures: The Rites and Rituals of Corporate Life*. Harmondsworth: Penguin Books.

Douglas, S.P. and Craig, C.S. (1992). "Advances in International Marketing." *International Journal of Research in Marketing*. 9, 291-318.

Erakovich, R., Bruce, R. and Wyman, S. (2002). "A Study of the Relationship of Ethical Work Climate and Organizational Culture in Public Organizations." Paper Presented at the American Society for Public Administration National Conference. Phoenix, Arizona. March 23-26. www.aspaonline.org/ethicscommunity/documents/

Ganapathy, N. (2006). "African Safari: Indian Companies Land in LoC Vehicle." *The Economic Times*. 17 May, p. 19.

Green, R.T. and White, P.D. (1976). "Methodological Considerations in Cross National Consumer Research." *Journal of International Business Studies*. 7, 15-23.

Handy, C.B. (1985). *Understanding Organizations*. Harmondsworth: Penguin Books.

Hofstede G. (1991). "Cultures and Organizations. Software of the Mind." *Intercultural Cooperation and Its Importance for Survival*. London: Harper Collins Publishers.

———, (1980) *Culture's Consequences: International Differences in Work Related Values*, Beverley Hills, CA, Sage Publications.

Khan, M.N. and Azmi, F.T. (2005). "Reinventing Business Organizations: The Information Culture Framework". *Singapore Management Review*. 27 (2), 26-37.

Malhotra, N.K., Agarwal, J. and Peterson, M. (1996). "Methodological Issues in Cross Cultural Marketing Research: A State-of-the-Art Review". *International Marketing Review*. 13, 7-43.

Niranjana, P. and Pattanayak, B. (2005). "Influence of Learned Optimism and Organisational Ethos on Organisational Citizenship Behaviour: A Study on Indian Corporations". *International Journal of Human Resources Development and Management*. 5 (1), 85-98.

Ouchi, W.G. (1981). *Theory Z: How American Business Can Meet the Japanese Challenge*. Addison Wessley: Reading, Mass.

Parameswaran, R. and Yaprak, A. (1987). "A Cross-National Comparison of Consumer Research Measures". *Journal of International Business Studies*. 18, 35-49.

Parbat, K. (2006). "Indian Investment on the Rise in Egypt." *The Economic Times*. 17 May, p. 28.

Pareek, U. (2002). *Training Instruments in HRD and OD*. New Delhi: Tata McGraw Hill.

Peters, T.J. and Waterman, R.H. (1982). *In Search of Excellence: Lessons from Americas Best Run Companies*. New York: Harper & Row.

Reynolds, N.L., Simintiras, A.C. and Diamantopoulos, A. (2003). "Theoretical Justification of Sampling Choices in International Marketing Research; Key Issues and Guidelines for Researchers". *Journal of International Marketing Research*. 34, 80-89.

Robbins, S.P. (1988). *Essentials of Organizational Behavior*. Englewood, New Jersey: Prentice Hall.

Salciuviene, L., Auruskeviciene, V. and Lydeka, Z. (2005). "An Assessment of Various Approaches for Cross-Cultural Consumer Research." *Problems and Perspectives in Management*. 3, 147-59.

Samiee, S. and Jeoung, I. (1994). "Cross-Cultural Research in Advertising: An Assessment of Methodologies." *Journal of the Academy of Marketing Science*. 22, 205-17.

Schein, E.H. (1990). "Organisational Culture". *American Psychologist*, 43 (2), 109-119.

Schwartz, H. and Davis, S.M. (1981). "Matching Corporate Culture and Business Strategy". *Organizational Dynamics*, Summer. 15-41.

Sekaran, U. (1983). "Methodological and Theoretical Issues and Advancements in Cross-Cultural Research". *Journal of International Business Studies*. 14, 61-73.

Sin, L.Y.M., Cheung, G.W.H. and Lee, R. (1999). "Methodology in Cross-Cultural Consumer Research: A Review and Critical Assessment." *Journal of International Consumer Marketing*. 11, 75-96.

Srivastav, A.K. (1995). "Teamworking Through ISO 9000-A Reality". Proceedings—Annual Quality Congress, Cincinnati OH. 49, 762-769.

Srivastava, S.K. and Srivastava, P. (2004). "Performance Enhancement through Continuous Improvement". Paper presented at Second World Conference on POM and 15th Annual POM Conference, Cancun, Mexico. April 30-May 3.

Sun, H. (2002). "The Relationship between Organisational Culture and its National Culture: A Case Study". *International Journal of Human Resources Development and Management*. 2 (1/2), 78-96.

Van de Vijver, V. and Leung, K. (1997). *Methods and Data Analysis for Cross-Cultural Research*. London: Sage.

Yaprak, A. (2003). "Measurement Problems in Cross-National Consumer Research: The Sate-of-the-Art and Future Research Directions". *Handbook of Research in International Marketing*. (Ed. Jain, S.C.) USA: University of Connecticut.

Emerging Trends in the Service Industry

R. Vaidyanathan

ABSTRACT

This paper deals with the emerging trends in the service Industry with a particular focus on the financial services. The three things that are impacting the service industry namely Globalization, IT/Telecommunications and Convergence [as in Banking/insurance/investment/retail] are elaborated. Globalization is facilitating trans-border transactions in services. The share of service sector in economies like India is substantial—nearly 60 per cent and the growth rate of service activities are higher than the overall GDP growth rate. In other words, service sector is the engine of economic growth. Due to the impact of IT and Telecommunications, the outsourcing activity is increasing. The paper points out that the software content is increasing in "White-Collar" services. It also discusses the demographic trends in Europe/USA and other emerging markets and concludes that the aging countries of the West will increasingly resort to outsourcing of services particularly financial services whose software content is increasing. The convergence between Banking, Stock Markets and Insurance in the financial services industry has created entities, which are challenges to the traditional regulatory framework. This requires new risk management paradigm and the need to evolve a Global Regulatory framework to deal with cross-border and cross-industry issues.

INTRODUCTION

Services industry has become important in the modern society; they are multidimensional, and they play a crucial role in economic development, and they are the engines of growth in many a developing country. As an economy progresses and grows, the service sector gains precedence over the manufacturing and the agricultural sectors.

Services encompass many different economic activities. Services are very different from goods; they are intangible, though often incorporated in tangible products; they are non-storable; meaning the consumption of a service and the production of a service is simultaneous. They can be defined as activities that add value either directly or indirectly to an individual or to a product. Unlike goods production, ownership of a service is not transferred during the process of service provision. Thus, services cannot be stored; rather, the service supplier stores instead the capacity to provide the service at the point in time where he/she will have access to a service demander.

This has ramifications for the export of services. If a service is to be produced in one country and consumed in another, it means perforce that there is some interaction to conduct the exchange simultaneously. Services have, in fact, often been characterized as "non-tradable" in the sense that provision of services to foreign markets often necessitates the movement of capital (economic activities set up through foreign direct investment) or labor (personnel to manage such activities or to provide different types of expertise, including basic labor).

In the case of services, the few that cross-borders do so incorporated into products, as computer programs in diskettes, or air transport through aircraft, or films in videotapes. Or they may be transmitted via the telecommunications networks. Most services, however, are supplied directly by their providers in a foreign market, and for this reason cannot be dissociated from international movement of capital or labor, as well as accompanying knowledge and technology.

International transactions in services, as agreed upon by the participants of the Uruguay Round of the General Agreement on Trade in Services, is as follows:

- Through cross-border flows in which neither the supplier nor the producer move physically but instead rely upon an intermediate service such as a telecommunications network;
- Through the movement of a consumer to a supplier's country (such as through tourism);
- Through the movement of a commercial organization to the consumer's country, which equates with foreign direct investment; and
- Through the movement of an individual service supplier to the consumer's country.

Major Trends

In the last decade there have been three major trends in the global service industries, which are of utmost importance to all the constituents. One is the Globalization of the service activities, which also brings into focus the inadequacies of the existing national regulatory policies. The second is the significant increase in the role of telecommunications and information technology particularly Internet in these activities, which provide clues to the extinction of large number of traditional intermediation. This is observed more in the financial services sector. Due to this we find the "death" of many intermediaries like arbitrageurs, out–cry specialists, odd lot dealers; paper-based transactions, etc. Even standardized insurance products are sold through Internet making traditional insurance agent an endangered species. Similarly, mobile phones have made substantial changes in the delivery mechanism of many personal business services like plumbing, carpentry, priest, etc. Tele communication industry has increased market efficiency through enhanced price discovery and informational efficiency.

The third is the convergence between different financial services wherein the banking sector, securities industry and insurance business are getting integrated along with retail trade. Individual entities have banking, insurance, Demat, MF, credit card, retail loan, etc. activities and thus the traditional bank is becoming extinct. Currently, the role of Regulator in the financial system is organized geographically and business-wise. For instance, each country has its own set of financial regulations dealing with each business separately i.e. separate regulations for the banking sector, the insurance business, etc. The challenge for regulator to prevent "silos" being created is higher. Hence Globalization, Information Technology/Telecommunication and Convergence are the three major forces, which are shaping the nature of the service industry.

The share of service sector is normally very significant in developed economies followed by manufacturing and agriculture. Interestingly in developing economies like India, share of service sector has increased phenomenally—to as high as nearly 60 per cent—and this has given rise to issues whether emerging markets can side step the traditional developmental model of manufacturing growth followed by service boom.

CONSTITUENTS

The service industry contains several separate and sometimes disparate activities under its banner. For instance, the Standard International Classification would be as given in Table 14.1. The role of non-corporate sector is very significant in seven of the activities, listed in Table 14.1 namely (1) construction, (2) trade, (3) hotels and restaurant, (4) non-railway transport, (5) storage, (6) real estate ownership of dwellings and business services, and (7) other services. Although the service sector has such a pivotal role in the Indian economy, the database of this sector is highly disorganized. There is no well-organized mechanism for maintaining a regular and proper database for this sector.

Table 14.1: Activities Comprising the Services Sector

(1) Construction.

(2) Trade.

(3) Hotels and Restaurants.

(4) Transport including tourist assistance activities as well as activities of travel agencies and tour operators.

(5) Storage and communication.

(Contd...)

(6) Banking and Insurance.

(7) Real estate and ownership of dwellings.

(8) Business services including accounting; software development; data processing services; business and management consultancy; architectural, engineering and other technical consultancy; advertisement and other business services.

(9) Public administration and defense.

(10) Other services including education, medical and health, religious and other community services, legal services, recreation and entertainment services.

(11) Personal services and activities of extra-territorial organizations and bodies.

Note: We have considered "Construction" as a part of service sector in our discussion even though sometimes it is considered as a part of the "Secondary sector".

Source: "Report of the National Statistical Commission" [NSC] pp. 186, Vol II August 2001; Ministry of Statistics and Programme Implementation; New Delhi.

Share and Growth Rate

We have provided in Table 14.2 the share of service activities and the growth rate in a large emerging Economy like India and it suggests that the major share of the national income is from the service sector.

Table 14.2: Share of National Income and Growth Rates [Rs. crore and %]

Category	Sector Share	Sector Share	Growth Rate [at 1993-94 prices]
	1993-94	2003-04	1993-94 to 2003-04
Agriculture and forestry, fishing	229829 [32.9]	293033 [23.0]	2.46
Mining, Manufacturing Electricity	127490 [18.3]	232040 [18.2]	6.17
Services	340673 [48.8]	749001 [58.9]	8.20
Total	100	100	

Note: We have included construction as a part of services. The NDP figures are at 1993-94 prices and the growth rate is the geometric average growth rate at constant 1993-94 prices during the period. It is computed from the NAS 2005.

Source: Computed from data in National Accounts Statistics [NAS]—2005, Central Statistical Organization [CSO], G.O.I. New Delhi.

Between 1950-51 and 1990-91, the share of Services sector in GDP rose by only 13.07 percentage points, which is an increase of about 0.33 percentage points per annum. However, between 1993-94 and 2003-04, the share had increased by 10 percentage points, which is an increase of 0.96 percentage points per annum. Clearly the growth rate at more than 8 per cent is very significant in the last decade.

Whenever, the term Service sector is mentioned, many think of IT companies like Infosys. Factually, all software related activities come under business services, which itself is less than 2 per cent of our national Income. As already mentioned, Service sector covers much larger canvas and this sector is the fastest growing sector in our economy with a large employment. We have provided in Table 14.3 the annual growth rates of some important service activities and find that Trade/Hotels/Restaurant as well as Financial services have shown significant growth and thus acting as engines of economic growth. We find that each year the growth rate of these service activities are above that of the national income growth rate thus proving that they are the major reasons for the growth in the economy.

Table 14.3: Annual Growth Rates of Real GDP at Factor Cost by Industry of Origin [%]

Activities	2000-01	2001-02	2002-03	2003-04	2004-05
Trade, hotels, restaurant & communications	7.1	9.2	9.1	12.0	10.6
Financing insurance, real estate and business services	4.1	7.3	8.0	4.5	9.2
Total GDP	4.4	5.8	3.8	8.5	7.5

Note: At 1999-2000 prices. The last two years are Provisional and Quick estimates.
Source: Table-1.6 page S-10, Economic Survey 2005-06–MoF, GoI.

We have also provided the compounded annual growth rate [CAGR] at constant prices; during the decade 1993-94 to 2003-04 in Table 14.4 and find that major service activities like trade and hotels and restaurant; road transport; finance services have all grown above 8 per cent and thus contributing significantly to the growth in the economy.

Table 14.4: NDP and Growth Rate in Different Service Activities 1993-94 to 2003-04 [Rs. crore and %]

Category	1993-94	2003-04	Growth Rate
Construction	38749	70962	6.24
Trade Hotels and Restaurant	96627	218985	8.53
Of which			
Trade	91324	204438	8.39
Hotels and Restaurant	5303	14547	10.62
Non-Railway Transport	22888	50090	8.15
Real Estate, Ownership of dwellings and Business Services	40431	72001	5.94
Other Services	48275	102156	7.78
Total NDP [including other Activities]	697992	1274074	6.20

Note: The NDP figures are at 1993-94 prices and the growth rate is the geometric average growth rate at constant 1993-94 prices during the period.

Source: National Accounts Statistics [NAS] 2005,Central Statistical Organization [CSO], GOI, New Delhi.

Outsourcing and Service Sector

The outsourcing activities by global majors has also substantially increased in the service activities and in sectors like banking as high as sixty per cent of the cost is associated with software and communication which makes it increasingly easier to out-source. We feel that large number of services is getting more "software oriented" rather than "hardware oriented". As the software content in services increases the possibility of outsourcing becomes more since it becomes non-location specific.

The declining fertility rate in Europe and the associated issues of slow growth of working population combined with reluctance to allow large scale migration from developing countries—makes the process of outsourcing white-collar service task to emerging markets all the more inevitable. The age bomb is ticking in the west. It will significantly affect their "white-collar work force". In the next few decades there is going to be a huge explosion in "outsourcing" or "offshore" work, since onshore work creates what is politely called "social costs"—meaning—brown/black sweat in the midst of white scent, which is increasingly considered not very feasible.

Let us look at the possible demographic profile of Europe and US in the next few decades taken from UN population projections. The average total fertility rates in the year 2000 in developed countries was 1.57, and in developing countries it was 3.05. The rate for Europe is 1.4 and Japan is 1.3. USA is just 2.1, India at 3.1 and China at 1.72. It is felt a rate of 2.1 is an appropriate replacement rate, including some death of infants etc. Over the next few decades, the situation could worsen. Estimates suggest that in the next 50 years USA will grow by 100 million numbers and Europe will be less by 100 million numbers. For instance, in another forty years the German population would be lesser by nearly 30 per cent. One third of the population will be more than 65 and they will outnumber children by two to one. Italy's rate is 1.2, and in that Catholic country in another forty years more than 40 per cent will be above 65 years. In Russia, two out of three pregnancies are terminated before birth, and Russian women average 2.5 to four abortions each, and their death rate is, believe me, 70 per cent more than the birth rate. Putin warns that in 15 years there will be 22 million less Russians, that is, seventh of its current population. Japan is already facing the age crisis. Of course, the Whites in England are not having enough children, with London readying to have "ethnic majority" in a decade. One can go on. The aging of the developed countries coupled with a desire of the labor class, including white-collar workers, to work for lesser hours are creating a catastrophe.

The declining fertility rate in Europe and the associated issues of slow growth of working population combined with reluctance to allow large-scale migration from developing countries makes the process of outsourcing white-collar service task to emerging markets all the more inevitable.

For instance, the United States is in the midst of a nursing shortage that is expected to intensify as baby boomers age and the need for health care grows. According to a study published in the *Journal of the American Medical Association* the U.S. will experience a 20 per cent shortage in the number of nurses needed by the year 2020. This translates into a shortage of more than 400,000 Registered nurses. There is a mass exodus of qualified nurses from India into the USA to meet this shortage. Europe and the Middle East have also rolled out the red carpet for nursing staff from India.

Similarly, as school populations grow nationwide, school districts in US urban areas, are struggling to find ways to attract new teachers and keep them there. The bulk of the nation's teaching force is nearing retirement age, with most teachers in their mid-40s to early 50s. Nursing and teaching correspond to the Mode IV of the GATS typology (movement of natural persons). Also outsourced are testing services, grading of online tests, tutorials for college students over video chat, foreign language assistance and translation services, the list is endless.

The services which are "Brown Collar" type—low skill, heavy labor, like garbage clearance or restaurant cleaning or retail sales persons or window cleaning or car washing, etc. needs huge amount of labor in both American and European markets in the coming decades.

We have provided in Exhibit 1, a diagrammatic representation of the age structure—that is, number of people in different age group between developed and developing countries.

The developed countries with a hexagonal age structure are slowly moving into trapezoid or inverted pyramid-shaped structures. In the case of developing countries, they will move from a pyramid age structure to perhaps the hexagonal structure.

This is the nature of the crisis. The labor force will be extremely scarce and expensive in the developed world. The elderly will also demand better protection, and the State will spend all its money to become the caring "mother" for these old people.

Since societal norms [in terms of caring for the elderly by the offsprings, etc.] have gone for the sixes, the aged are the responsibility of the state, and this implies more taxes and a lesser amount available for other activities of the state. Hence, there is a massive crisis in "Social Security" funds in Europe and US.

Exhibit 1

Changing Age structure

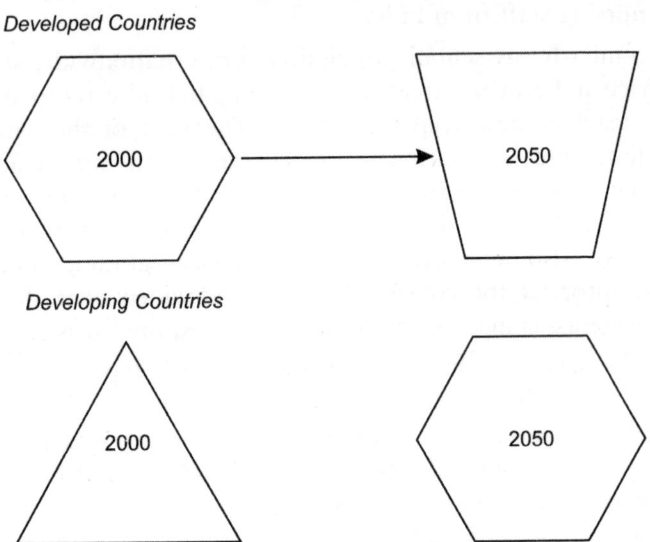

We have provided in Table 14.5 the global population share of different regions and it indicates the impact of the demographic structure on the future of service industry and the increasing aspects of out-sourcing. It shows the differential impact of demographic shifts with Europe affected the most.

Table 14.5: Global Population—Share of Regions

Year	Africa	Asia	Europe	N. America	L. America +Caribbean	Oceania
1900	8.1	57.4	24.7	5.0	4.5	0.4
1950	8.8	55.5	21.7	6.8	6.6	0.5
2000	13.1	60.6	12.0	5.2	8.6	0.5
2050	20.2	58.6	7.1	5.0	8.6	0.5
2100	24.9	55.4	5.9	5.2	8.1	0.5

Source: United Nations Dept of Economic and Social Affairs—Population Division: Quoted in "Key Issues in Insurance," —David M. Holland, F.S.A, President & CEO, Munich American Reassurance Company. —World Risk and Insurance Economics Congress, August 8, 2005, Salt Lake City, Utah, USA.

It is the Pool and not the Rate

It is not only an issue of low wages; it is the pool of talent which is available in a country like India or China The role of this demographic pattern has some interesting results [Exhibit 2]. Again, there are several layers of this pool and so no worry of it over pricing itself. Indian youngsters in this IT world are enthusiastic and willing to put in 70 to 80 hours including Saturdays and Sundays. That is a story, which is yet to be written. The story of sacrifice, the story of work culture and simply "enthu" to get things done.

A survey by the Earth Institute at Columbia University shows that it is both cost cutting as well as the non-availability of skills at home that drive outsourcing. The Ford group, which set up an off shoring/outsourcing center for claims reconciliation at Chennai, India, claims that 'nowhere else in the world is it possible to find thousands of talented, highly qualified accountants in one single place, and at a fraction of the cost as elsewhere' as in India.

Another issue is related to the increasing content of the "outsource able" portion in many activities. As earlier indicated in service sectors like Banking it is more than sixty per cent, including software/voice/audio, etc. In some of the manufacturing activities, the software content is more than thirty per cent. This would induce large firms to go in for more and more outsourcing.

Exhibit 2

Wealth and Labor Force

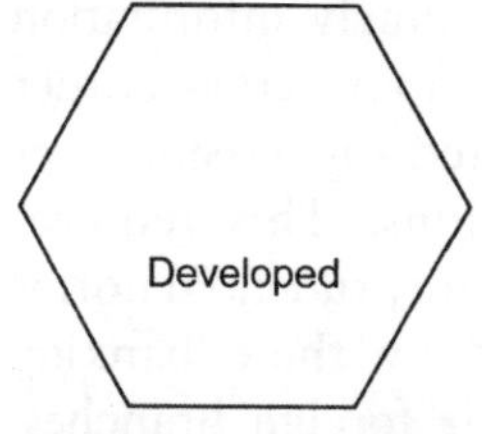

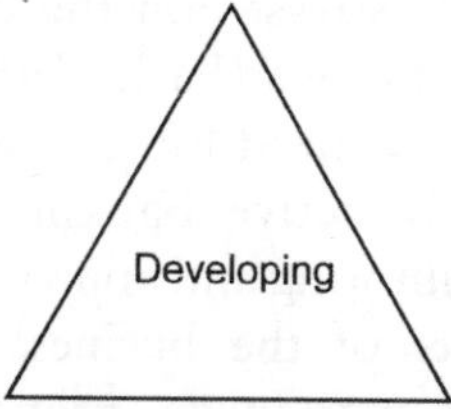

— Wealth: 80% of World's GDP
— Controlled by mature adults & looking for higher returns

— Labor Force: 80% of world's work force
— Dominated by young adults willing to work for low pay

Already we find that the remittances by the labor of developing countries at more than 70 billion USD is higher than the net private capital flows from developing to developed countries at around 65 billion. This is primarily flow, from blue collar workers from the Middle East, USA, and Europe, etc. to other parts of the world. This will undergo an interesting shift since by the process of outsourcing, the labor will not move, only the work will move. It can be medical transcription, record keeping of social security, call centres, back office work for banks, insurance companies, mutual funds, pension funds or maintenance of IT infrastructure and the possibilities are infinite. Most human endeavors can be "off-shored". The services which are "Brown Collar" type like garbage clearance or restaurant cleaning or retail sales persons or window cleaning or car washing, etc. needs huge amount of labor in both American and European markets in the coming decades. As of now, only the "brown collar" service work, like that of garbage removal, road cleaning or grape picking cannot be moved "off shore".

Regulatory Issues in Financial Services

The emerging trends in service industry including increased outsourcing imply that there is a need to evolve appropriate Risk Containment measures to protect against "Contagion" as well as "Regulatory or Tax arbitrage" situations.

The Basle Committee on Banking supervision, with the endorsement of the Central Bank Governors of the group of ten countries, released Basle core principles of effective banking supervision as early as 1997. This lists 25 principles for effective supervision. It stresses on the quality and timely information from the institutions (Basle, 1997). It talks about cross-border banking and the need for global consolidated supervision over internationally active banking organizations. This requires adequate monitoring and applying appropriate prudential norms to all aspects of the business conducted by these banking organizations worldwide, primarily at their foreign branches, joint ventures and subsidiaries.

It also suggests that a key component of consolidated supervision is establishing contact and information exchange with the various other supervisors involved, primarily host country supervisory authorities. In that context it expects banking supervisors to require that the local operations of foreign banks be conducted to the same high standards, which are required of domestic institutions. They must have powers to share information needed by the home country supervisors of those banks for the purpose of carrying out consolidated supervision.

As is rightly pointed out by Rt. Hon. Eddie George, Governor of the Bank of England, to the Euromoney International Bond Congress "adapt and survive" will be the possible motto for the central bankers with a positive rider "those who survive will thrive" (George Eddie, 2000).

He further adds that the role of authorities is simply "to provide as best an economic and regulatory environment in which financial markets can do their job—of allocating capital where it can be most productively deployed—more effectively. On the economic front that means steady growth with low inflation. On the regulatory front, it means the framework of rules that provide for transparency that is essential for the proper assessment and the management of risk and sets clear behavioral standards which do not unnecessarily distort business decisions, but provide clear guidance to market participants—whether they are end-users or intermediaries—as to what is expected of them and what they can reasonably expect of others?"

It is also to be noted that the productivity gains made due to the information technology has also given rise to a set of potential challenges. It has increased long-term profit expectations and facilitated a huge gain in equity prices. As it has been pointed out by Mr. Alan Greenspan, the then Chairman of the US Federal Reserve, "we are seeing the gradual breaking down of competition-inhibiting institutions from the keiretsu and chaebol of East Asia, to the dirigisme of some of Continental Europe. The increasingly evident advantage of applying newer technologies is undermining much of the old political wisdom of protected stability. The clash between the unfettered competitive technological advance and protectionism, both domestic and international, will doubtless engage our attention for many years into this new century" (Greenspan Allen, 2000).

Direct and indirect costs of regulation are not similar in different countries belonging to the developed economies. For instance, it is (Franks et al., 1997) suggested that as far as direct costs are concerned, the cost of regulation for securities and derivatives trading and broking sector are substantially lower for the UK than for the US and France. In contrast, they find that for investment management and unit trust industry, UK costs are significantly higher than those of the other two countries. For the life insurance industry, UK costs are similar to those in France but markedly lower than those for the US. This brings us to the issue of direct and indirect cost of regulation for major sectors of the financial services industry. This also provides us a clue regarding the effect of regulation on the competitive position of the different segments of the financial services industry. And also between emerging and developed markets.

The announcements regarding new regulatory regime by the Australian Federal Government has taken into consideration, the emerging scenario. The new regulatory regime has covered the establishment of the new agency for the supervision deposit taking institutions, life and general insurance company and superannuation funds, the Australian Prudential Regulation Authority (APRA) and the new market regulator and consumer protection body, the Australian Securities and Investments Commission (ASIC). Also there is a financial sector council (FSAC), which will report directly to the Treasurer on regulatory and other changes required (Matthey Peter, 1998).

In UK also, "The report to the chancellor on the reform of the financial regulatory system" (The Report) which has been prepared by the nine regulatory bodies whose functions will be brought together under a single umbrella. In particular, it confirms that the new financial regulatory authority will not only be in charge of banks and investment firms, but also deal with insurance companies and building societies. Such a regulatory body in a sense encompasses all financial activity and provides answers to the issues of convergence taking place in insurance business, securities industry and banking sector. As observed by Philipp Hartman that such an approach will be embracing the whole financial services industry and it is expected to simplify the access for consumer inquiries and complaints (Hartmann, Philipp, 1997).

New Financial Architecture

It is mentioned in the financial world that the markets are two steps ahead of the regulator. So far the attempts have been to create a conglomerate regulator within a country (Australia, U.K.) or to have a cross-country collaboration between G-7 countries on specific aspects like anti-trust regulation. Also, there are some attempts in banking regulation on a European scale. These efforts undertaken so far do not consider and include the big emerging markets like India, China, and Brazil, etc.

The emergence of financial conglomerates, providing a range of financial services like banking, securities, derivatives, asset management, insurance, etc. is of recent origin, which requires understanding. In 1993 a tripartite group of banking, securities and insurance regulators was set up by the Bank for International Settlements (BIS) to consider ways to improve the supervision of financial conglomerates. Financial conglomerates are defined as a group of companies under common control whose exclusive or predominant activities consist of providing significant services in at least two different financial sectors namely banking, securities, insurance.

The second type of development is pertaining to the slow extinction of the intermediaries like brokers in stock markets and agents in insurance business. Even intermediaries like Stock Exchanges and traditional banks fear extinction in the Internet Financial World (IFW) of the e-Globe (e-G).

The other major development is in terms of breaking down of the national barriers in transactions in the financial sectors. Even without Capital Account Convertibility (CAC) countries like India have ADR's listed on the NASDAQ and GDR's quoted on the London Exchange.

In the light of above developments we think the time has come to consider a global financial regulator which takes into account the requirements of big emerging markets like India,

China, Brazil, etc. This is particularly important for emerging markets in the context of issues of credit risk, market risk, forex risk, contagion effect and transaction costs of the small investors.

We feel that the reworking of the global financial regulatory architecture is going to be the most challenging task for the financial services sector in the first decade of the century. There is a need to look at the necessity of having a global regulator or a conglomerate cross-border regulator. This alone would facilitate the pricing of assets in different parts (shall we say Time zones) of the world based on the risk perceptions and risk sharing mechanisms.

The efforts in this direction can be undertaken within the UN protocols or by creating a new international financial regulator wherein the emerging markets have adequate representation. This would also entail the inclusion of major global Internet service providers in the financial field under the ambit of the regulatory mechanism. The regulatory mechanism need take into account the following:

- The growth of conglomerate financial institutions. (Encompassing banking/security/Insurance)
- The breaking down of national borders in the Internet Financial World.
- The extinction of intermediaries like Brokers, Bankers, and even stock exchanges.
- The development of Internet based financial transactions.

In that context, one needs to stress the role of emerging markets in the new scheme. Unless the global financial regulatory mechanism moves in tandem to the global financial service architecture the success of the later is doubtful. The constituents of the new financial architecture need to feel part of the regulatory structure to be enthusiastic about the emerging scenario.

REFERENCES

Basle core Principles for Effective Banking Supervision 1997. — bis.org/publ.

Basle Committee on Banking Supervision "Risk Management for Electronic Banking and Electronic Money Activities" Basle March 1998.

Bennett, John T. "Increasing Financial Transparency in a Global Economy" *Economic Perspectives*, Sept 1998.

Economic Survey 2005-06, Ministry of Finance; Government of India.

Franks, Julian R. Schaefer and Stephen M. Staunton. "The direct and compliance costs of financial regulation", *Journal of Banking and Finance*, Amsterdam, December 1997.

George, Eddie. Speech by the Governor of the Bank of England to the Euro Money International Bond Congress at London on 16/02/2000. Published in *BIS Review* 15/2000.

Greenspan, Alan. Remarks of the Chairman of the US Federal Reserve System before the Economic Club of New York, New York on 13th January 2000. Published in *BIS Review* 3/2000.

Hartmann Philipp."Super-regulator ("NewRO") outlined"; *Financial Regulation Report*, London, Aug/Sep 1997.

InterSec Research Corp. Quoted in the "Development of Global Securities Market", Bernard Asher in "The Future for the Global Securities Market"*Legal and Regulatory Aspects*; Edited by Fidelis Oditah, Clarenden Press, Oxford 1996. Macmillan 1998 (2nd edition).

Jean Crooks Gora. "Bancassurance: Positioning for Affiliations—Lessons from Europe, Canada, and the United States". LOMA 1997.

Matthey, Peter. "Australia: Recent Financial System Reforms", *Financial Regulation Report*; London; May 1998.

National Statistical Commission 2001—Report; [NSC] pp. 186, Vol. II August 2001; Ministry of Statistics and Programme Implementation; New Delhi.

National Accounts Statistics [NAS]—2005,Central Statistical Organization [CSO], G.O.I. New Delhi.

OECD, Fin. Stats: Quoted in the "Development of Global Securities Market", Bernard Asher in "The Future for the Global Securities Market", *Legal and Regulatory Aspects*; Edited by Fidelis Oditah, Clarenden Press Oxford 1996.

Sigma, "Bancassurance: A Survey of Competition between Banking and Insurance" Economic Studies section, Swiss Reinsurance Company. Zurich, 1992.

Tritell, Randolph. "The Application of US Antitrust Law to Foreign Conduct: Recent Developments", Federal Trade Commission, 1999.

Insurance in Developing World

15

Deepak Godbole

ABSTRACT

Uncertainty, Risk and Insurance: Whenever there is uncertainty, there is involvement of risk. The instinct for security is one of the basic motivating factors determining human attitudes. As a sequel to this quest for security, insurance technique must have evolved. The urge to provide protection against loss of life and property prompts people to make some sacrifice willingly in order to achieve security through collective co-operation, the backbone of insurance service.

Service sector developments: From an economic development perspective, there are many compelling reasons for emerging economies to develop their services sector. Expanding this sector helps create national wealth. A positive correlation exists between high GDP per capita and the intensity of service activity in the economy. Services are typically skill oriented and not investment intensive. They are ideal sources of growth for countries with scarce capital and a large, qualified workforce. However, because of weak infrastructures and limited access to technology and distribution network channels, many developing countries do not yet have the capacity to compete effectively in the world market for services.

Financial services liberalisation: If geographical location, size and population determined the availability of financial services in general and insurance in particular, then Asia and Africa would top the charts. However, there are many other socio-economic factors that determine the penetration of insurance services. The world economic scenario has undergone considerable changes as compared to a few decades ago. The use of 'market' as the main form of co-ordinating the activities of the participants in production is a notable feature of the model of the "new economic system". Some of the changes that are being witnessed are deregulation of the banking and insurance industry, development of financial markets, transition into floating rate of exchanges, increasing role of capital markets and global competition, etc. Progressive liberalisation of trade in services is meant to benefit economic development. Exports of labour-intensive services have been an important source of income in many developing countries and have contributed to the upgrading of qualifications in these countries. A country that aspires to achieve rapid growth and join the global knowledge economy ought to encourage the development of its services sector. Service sector has been the engine of growth and employment in developed economies.

Insurance liberalization in India: Insurance business in India is about 200 years old. Insurance industry has seen competition among Indian and foreign players, state monopoly after nationalization in two phases and liberalization after 2000. When market monopolies are broken the share of market is bound to go down. However, the question is how much and how fast would the private eat into their share. Today, after Five years of liberalization, there are totally Thirty players in Indian market.

It would be interesting to take a stock of happenings, analyse the performance of the industry, individual players and their unique strategies, role and effectiveness of regulatory authority, various guidelines ensuring smooth business conduct, protection of policyholders interest, level of insurance penetration and density, changes in distribution, insurance awareness and education, professionalisation of operations, back office support to European insurers and such other things.

Economic Development

1. Economic growth is primarily based on three main factors: (1) the accumulation of the factors of production, including both human and physical capital; (2) the

efficient allocation of resources within the economy; and (3) the improvements in technology over time. Economic development means economic growth accompanied by some other factors that ensure sustainability of the growth and enhance the level of overall economic welfare resulting from the growth. Country's Gross Domestic Product, or GDP, is one of the measures of the size of its economy. The GDP of a country is defined as the market value of all final goods and services produced within a country in a given period of time.

2 The use of market as the main form of co-ordinating the activities of different participants is a notable feature of the model of the current global economic system. Market is a mechanism by which buyers and sellers interact to determine the price and quality. Trade and investment induced market integration has led to deeper forms of economic interdependence among nations, as a growing number of developing and former centrally planned economies have become more closely linked to the global economy. Markets act as reliable pointers of consumer preferences and of social cost of production. Economic development boosts industry as also leads to growth of service sector activities such as hotels and restaurants, storage transport and communication, finance, banking, insurance and other financial services, real estate and other business and community services.

Services

1. Services, unlike products are intangible and involve a performance or an effort. The word service conveys different meanings such as 'work done by somebody for someone else'; 'the system or operation by which people are provided with something they need'; 'to provide a community or organizations with something'. Some of the noteworthy commercial services would be in the form of Computer services, Construction and Engineering services, Distribution services, Educational

services, Financial services, Legal services, Accounting and Auditing services, Transport services, Medical services and Telecommunication services.

2. Services are typically skill oriented and are not necessarily investment intensive. They are ideal sources of growth for countries with scarce capital and large number of qualified human resources. A country that aspires to achieve rapid growth and secure high rank in the global economy require development of a strong services sector. This sector has been the engine of growth and employment in developed economies. However, because of inadequate infrastructure development and limited access to technology, many developing countries have yet to develop the capacity to compete effectively in the world market for services.

Financial Services

1. To many, the term financial service is synonymous to banking. But financial services include a lot more. Development and creative application of financial technology to solve economic problems through exploitation of financial opportunities is the crux of financial engineering resulting into creation and development of effective financial services.
2. There are two types of relationships between the financial services and economic growth. The first is a supply-leading relationship where economic growth can be induced through the supply of financial services. The second is a demand-following relationship where the demand for financial services can induce growth of financial institutions and services. In the early stages of development, economies usually adopt supply-leading patterns of development and create state-owned monopolies as an essential element of economic development.

Insurance

1. Whenever there is uncertainty, there is involvement of risk. The instinct for security is one of the basic

motivating factors determining human attitudes. As a sequel to this quest for security, insurance technique must have evolved. The urge to provide protection against loss of life and property prompts people to make some sacrifice willingly in order to achieve security through collective co-operation, the backbone of insurance service. The insurance contract is an agreement where the policyholder knows that the insurer will pay claims for damages or injury sustained in some future event that may or may not occur. The policyholder obtains peace of mind and financial security against this uncertainty, knowing that any future covered unfortunate events that may arise will be taken care by the insurer.

2. Insurance is an important element of financial services and is complimentary to direct financing. Insurance industry is a key component of the economy by virtue of the amount of premiums it collects, the scale of its investments and the essential socio-economic role it plays in covering personal and business risks. Insurance services not only mobilize and channelize savings but also support trade, commerce and entrepreneurial activities in other sectors. Insurance services are therefore, of major significance in relation to trade and development. UNCTAD has formally recognised it by noting that "a sound national insurance and reinsurance market is an essential characteristic of economic growth".
3. Insurance services include the following activities:
   (i) Direct insurance
   (ii) Reinsurance and retrocession
   (iii) Insurance intermediation (such as brokerage and agency)
   (iv) Services auxiliary to insurance (such as consultancy, actuarial, risk assessment and claim settlement services)
4. Reinsurance is a mechanism which insurance companies use to spread the risks assumed. Without reinsurance or through inadequate reinsurance support, unexpected

catastrophes, unanticipated liabilities or a series of large losses could push an insurer into insolvency. Without reinsurance, most insurers would be able to cover only the safest of ventures, leaving many moderately risky but worthwhile ventures without a cover.

5. Insurance is a reflection of income and wealth. However, savings; price levels; number, size and complexity of risks; risk perception; social and political scenario also have a bearing on insurance penetration. On the basis of premium written and market development, world is clearly divided into 'developed' and 'developing' markets. Barring certain exceptions, insurance markets in developing countries have a number of particular features. These include their small size, undercapitalization, insufficient experience and knowhow.
6. The world insurance premium for 2005, stood at US $ 3426 bn, (US $ 1974 bn [58%] in life & US $ 1452 bn [42%] in non-life insurance) (Table 15.1). Total premium volume grew by 2.5 per cent in real terms (life by 3.9% and non-life by 0.6%). Although nearly 75 per cent of the world's population is to be found in developing countries, the global insurance market is dominated by industrialized developed economies, which account for 88 per cent of the global life insurance market and 90% of the global non-life insurance market (Tables 15.2 and 15.3). However, developing economies are experiencing a rapid overall growth rate of about 7.0 per cent as opposed to 1.9 per cent for developed countries.

Table 15.1: World Insurance Premium—2005 (3426 US $ mn.)

	Premium US$ mn.		Premium as % of GDP		Premium Per capita USD	
	Life	Non-life	Life	Non-life	Life	Non-life
Emerging Markets	256325	170694	2.15	1.42	46.1	30.5
Developed Economies	1717378	1281316	5.15	3.82	1887	1399.8

Table 15.2: Insurance Penetration by Region (%): 2002—2005,

Zone	2002			2003			2004			2005		
	Total	Non-Life	Life	Total	Non-Life	Life	Total	Non-Life	Life	Total	Non-Life	Life
North America	9.39	4.90	4.48	9.4	5.15	4.25	9.17	5.05	4.12	8.97	4.92	4.05
Latin America	2.39	1.47	0.92	2.45	1.51	0.94	2.47	1.46	1.01	2.35	1.42	0.93
Europe	8.06	3.22	4.83	7.98	3.35	4.64	7.89	3.20	4.68	7.78	3.10	4.69
Asia	7.61	1.80	5.81	7.51	1.77	5.74	7.37	1.79	5.58	6.83	1.67	5.16
Africa	4.45	1.17	3.28	4.09	1.16	2.93	4.89	1.48	3.41	4.80	1.47	3.33
Oceania	8.05	3.57	4.48	7.70	3.71	3.99	7.65	3.90	3.75	6.38	3.22	3.16

Table 15.3: Share of World Market-Premium (%) 2002—2005

Zone	2002			2003			2004			2005		
	Total	Non-Life	Life	Total	Non-Life	Life	Total	Non-Life	Life	Total	Non-Life	Life
North America	39.95	50.27	32.62	37.9	48.17	30.12	35.99	46.10	28.36	35.66	46.15	27.94
Latin America	1.52	2.25	1.0	1.42	2.03	0.96	1.52	2.09	1.05	1.71	2.43	1.18
Europe	32.43	31.72	32.93	34.76	34.5	34.96	36.94	36.10	37.57	37.6	35.71	38.98
Asia	23.76	13.65	30.93	23.32	12.89	31.23	22.69	12.88	30.09	22.18	12.85	29.09
Africa	0.92	0.58	1.16	1.05	0.69	1.33	1.16	0.81	1.42	1.17	0.84	1.41
Oceania	1.43	1.52	1.36	1.54	1.72	1.4	1.7	2.02	1.46	1.69	2.01	1.45

Economic Reforms and Convergence

1. Economic reform is the term given to attempts to improve the economic mechanism in a system. In recent years, rapid and significant changes have occurred in the structure of financial services industries around the world. Instigated by liberalization and deregulation, financial services have started converging, may be to enable one-stop shopping convenience for the consumers of banking, insurance, securities, asset management and other financial services. Banking and insurance has been converging in developing economies as well. Non-traditional, non-industry players like travel agents, credit card companies are also getting ready to invade insurance. Integrated financial services are set to replace

traditionally demarcated banking, insurance and other activities.

Some of the Issues Related with Insurance Confronting Developing Countries

1. Insurance consciousness is quite low in the developing countries. There is an urgent need to create a deeper understanding and awareness of what the insurance can do to improve the well-being and quality of life.
2. Insurance distribution is undergoing sea change with entry of corporate agents and brokers, direct marketing, internet sales and bank assurance. Distribution of insurance is getting guided by technology as well. Old trusted methods of selling through agents are proving inadequate. Enhancing knowledge levels of agents and bringing in professionalism in them has become need of the hour.
3. With opening up of developing markets to competition, there is a greater impetus to demand growth and volumes would start dictating economic sizes and pricing. This fuels merger and acquisitions and makes survival of small sized firms difficult.
4. With opening up of closed insurance markets to private and foreign competition, state owned companies find it difficult to compete effectively with the lean and thin new private firms having state of art IT support.
5. Consumer expectations of quality, service, price and timing are higher than ever and increasing day by day. At the same time, future consumer preferences are becoming extremely difficult to predict. This puts pressure on insurers to continuously keep designing new cost effective need based products.
6. Demand for trained and qualified manpower in the areas of underwriting, pricing and claims management is growing. Building supply capacities, recruiting and training insurance professionals are major challenges faced today. With new companies entering the markets,

retaining the talent is also becoming a burning issue for existing insurers.

Regulation

1. The insurance sector is closely linked with macroeconomic factors such as inflation, currency controls and the national income of a country. Liberalisation without safeguards would mean excessive gearing. Developing countries, therefore, seek to establish efficient domestic regulatory framework as a prerequisite for insurance liberalization. By making the regulatory environment, effective yet flexible and simplified and by pursuing national policy objectives, governments help maximize the contribution of insurance services to development.
2. Regulators have a primary responsibility to maintain consumer confidence through solvency of financial institutions. Liberalisation and enhanced foreign participation in financial services sector, of which insurance is an essential element, necessitate stringent prudential regulation. Further, the transition towards creating a single global market demands regulatory standardisation. This calls for higher technically qualified staff with both the players as also the regulator, streamlined business procedures, prudential accounting and adequate loss provisioning.

Data Management

1. Data is critical to many business functions within an insurance company such as underwriting, pricing, financial analysis, claims handling, marketing, product development and strategic planning. Data also measures an organization's success or failure and help identify areas requiring attention. Because of this, it is necessary to understand, manage and protect this critical resource. Whenever, insurance premium is collected, claim is paid, expense is incurred or investment is made, the insurer is supposed to capture and compile values and other information.

2. Lack of authentic data, capable of further analysis is a major problem faced by insurers in developing world. Things are, however, improving with the realization of the fact that authentic data is the backbone of insurance. Additionally, as data is useful in rate regulation, market conduct, exposure analysis, consumer protection, solvency, etc., regulatory authorities have also been ensuring effective data management by insurers.

Insurance in India

1. It would be interesting to look at the structure of Indian financial sector. In India, key fiscal, infrastructure and regulatory decisions on economic management remain at the State level. There are different set of players taking care of Development financing, Commercial banking, Insurance, Mutual funds and Non-Banking finance. Currently there are multiple regulators regulating the financial sector, being Reserve Bank of India (RBI) for banks, Securities and Exchanges Board of India (SEBI) for capital markets, Insurance Regulatory and Development Authority (IRDA) for insurance and Pensions Fund Regulatory and Development Authority (PFRDA) for pension business.
2. Financial sector reforms in India in 90s have advanced the objectives of opening the constituent segments to competition and liberalized operations. The thrust of financial reforms was to promote a diversified, efficient and competitive financial system, with the ultimate objective of improving the allocative efficiency of resources through operational flexibility, improved financial viability and institutional strengthening. Increasing integration with global markets then became another catalyst for further reforms. The management of financial sector has been oriented towards gradual rebalancing between efficiency and stability and the changing shares of public and private ownership. Enhanced competition among diverse players has been encouraged. The banking and insurance system has

witnessed greater levels of transparency and standards of disclosure with greater volume of information being disclosed.

3. Indian Insurance Industry is nearly two centuries old. The financial failure of some insurers at a time when the country was progressively moving towards a centrally planned command economy set the stage for nationalisation of the life insurance business in 1956 and non-life business in 1972. Till year 2000, when Indian insurance sector was thrown open to private and foreign participation, the industry comprised of Life Insurance Corporation of India taking care of life insurance needs and four State owned companies under the umbrella of General Insurance Corporation of India (GIC) taking care of non-life business. Today, there are sixteen life insurance companies, fifteen non-life insurance companies and one reinsurance company licensed by IRDA to operate in India. The sector has a blend of State owned companies, companies floated by Indian private business groups and joint ventures of Indian and foreign partners. As of now (July 2006) Non-life sector has one player exclusively in credit insurance business, one specifically incorporated to take care of agricultural insurance and one specializing in health and allied insurance.
4. Insurance penetration in India is low. But, that also means there is huge untapped potential and the business is growing. It would be interesting to look at the penetration percentages given below as regards penetration in Asia and India. (Table 15.4)

To Sum Up

1. Globalisation is seen to be the major driver over the next fifteen years, causing the global economy to grow by about 80 per cent compared with 2000 and raising average income per head worldwide by about 50 per cent over the same period. Economists world over believe that most of this growth will be in emerging economies

Table 15.4

India-Insurance Density (Premium Per Capita US $)				India's share in global market (Premium %)				India-Insurance Penetration		
Life	Non-Life	Total	Year	Life	Non-Life	Total	Year	Life	Non-Life	Total
11.7	3.0	14.7	2002	0.80	0.27	0.59	2002	2.59	0.67	3.26
12.9	3.5	16.4	2003	0.81	0.29	0.59	2003	2.26	0.62	2.88
15.7	4.0	19.7	2004	0.92	0.31	0.66	2004	2.53	0.65	3.17
22.7	4.4	18.3	2005	1.02	0.33	0.73	2005	2.53	0.61	3.14

especially in Asia, Latin America and the CIS. In developing markets, while traditional lines of insurance business are showing growth, pension, health insurance and credit insurance businesses are also picking up. Insurance is customer-driven.

2. With rapid technological changes, the insurance value chain is getting redefined. Technology is both an enabler and an influencer. Insurers in developing world will have to make effective utilization of technology and design their e-business strategies. Some other areas needing immediate attention are introduction of new innovative products, continued experimentation with different channels of distribution and direct sales, steps to enhance levels of client service, development of sophisticated pricing strategies, maximising efficiencies and contain costs. It's also essential to consider diversifying in risk management, consultancy and such other non-traditional services.

REFERENCES

UNCTAD- various issues

Sigma-Swiss Re-various issues

WTO (GATS)

üInsurance Services Office, United States of America

European Commission

Health Insurance in India: Challenges and Opportunities

16

S.C. Bansal and *Alka Harneja*

ABSTRACT

This paper intends to find out the perceptions of individual health insurance policyholders on selected critical issues and challenges faced by companies offering health insurance plans in India. Two pre-structured questionnaires have been used to collect the desired data. 500 individuals in Delhi, Faridabad, Gurgaon, Ghaziabad, Chennai, Kolkata, Mumbai, and Pune have personally been approached for this purpose. However, only 55 of these individuals had health insurance policies; all of them cooperated by supplying the required information. Seventy-five senior executives in the companies offering health insurance plans in the private as well as public sector have also shared their practices and opinions about their policies. The study reveals that there is a tremendous demand for cashless health insurance policies. However, the companies do not offer exclusive schemes for senior citizens. The policyholders have supported reduction in exclusions, cover on existing diseases, lower premium, and higher discounts in claim free years. The customers complain that settlement of claims is time consuming, lengthy and involves significant paper work. On the contrary, the executives think that the health plans are innovative and designed after intensive market research. The executives in private sector think that their plans are different from those sold by public sector insurers. The senior officers in the insurance companies agree that insured face problems at the time of settlement, but these are primarily due to third party administrators. They also think that slow progress in providing cashless products is due to various teething problems. The burgeoning uninsured middle class in India presents vast opportunities for insurance companies to provide need based medical insurance schemes. At the same time, the customers should also make informed decisions about their health insurance needs.

JEL classification: D14, G22, L84

INTRODUCTION

In India, awareness of insurance, among the educated urbanites is very low. Insurance is viewed as a tax shield or a legal requirement as in the case of motor third party liability. Individuals do not insure their assets like houses and household items as a matter of practice unless it is insisted upon by housing finance companies. The penetration of health insurance in India is pathetically low. Younger people are not interested in it because they feel it is early to think of illnesses and diseases at their age. People generally think about purchasing health cover when they are in forties or fifties. This is the age when the fear of becoming ill looms large in their minds but it becomes too late. At this age, the health covers are available at very high premiums and with many restrictions. India spends about 6.5-7 per cent of GDP on health care (official estimate is at 6%). This is far below than 10-12 per cent in developed countries. According to a World Bank study, an ordinary citizen in India spends more than half of his total expenditure on buying healthcare. Over 40 per cent of the hospitalized people borrow money or sell their assets to cover the expenditure and 35 per cent of Indian population fall below poverty line who cannot afford any type of medical treatment. At any given point of time about 50 million of people are on medication for major sickness. About 200 million workdays are lost annually due to sickness. The study also revealed that about 60 per cent people use private health providers for outpatient treatment while 60 per cent use government providers for indoor treatment. The average expenditure for care is 2.5 times more in private sector than in public sector. The low penetration of health insurance among the masses presents tremendous opportunities for insurers.

Health Insurance Schemes

Uninsured people live with a risk of facing huge medical expenditures due to any major life threatening illness or as a result of a major injury. Treatment for major illnesses or accidents can be unaffordable and empty out savings. Specialized care and long hospital stay can ruin any financially sound family. In present time the cost of health care in India is also very high. In order to have some kind of security it is, therefore, necessary to take health insurance. Health insurance means "any form of insurance whose payment is contingent on the insured incurring additional expenses or losing income because of incapacity or loss of good health." (Black and Skipper)

Health insurance will provide the insured with timely and adequate medical care. The insurer foots the huge medical bills. The policy covers hospitalization and domiciliary hospitalization expenses. The policy generally covers boarding, nursing, diagnostic and medicine expenses. Some insurers also cover pre-hospitalization and post-hospitalization expenses. Health insurance policies available in India have a maximum limit of Rs. 5 lakh.

The salient features of the health schemes available to customers in India are as follows:

1. Central and State governments operate Central Government Health Scheme (CGHS) and Employee State Insurance Scheme (ESIS). CGHS covers about nine million employees who can get treatment in nominated hospitals. This scheme is suffering from number of administrative limitations and alternatives are being searched for its effective implementation. ESIS covers industrial workers and their family. They are provided medical care through special Employee State Insurance Hospitals and Dispensaries.
2. Large organisations administer their health schemes. Some of the employers reimburse costs of medical expenses of the employees with or without contributions by the latter. It is estimated that about twenty million employees are covered under this scheme.

3. Public and private sector general insurance companies offer various health plans. (Table 16.1.)

The most comprehensive health insurance scheme available these days is the Mediclaim.

Other health insurance policies offered by the public sector companies include Bhavishya Arogya catering to hospitalisation treatment after retirement; Senior Citizens' UTI- Linked Health Scheme; and Jan Arogya addressed to the lower income group. They also provide specified policies for major illness like cancer, heart disorders, kidney failure and strokes. The private insurers offer health plans like 'Health Guard', 'Health Shield', 'Medishield' and 'Health Insurance'. The plans offered by various companies have similar features with slight variations in their packaging.

4. Health riders from life insurance companies like critical illness rider and dreaded disease covers are provided as add-ons to the life insurance plans.
5. Cooperative societies and non-government organizations (NGOs) like Child in Need Institute (CINI), Self-employed women's Association (SEWA) are some of the important NGOs offering health services in many parts of India, especially in the rural areas.

The paper has been organized into Five sections. Section II reviews some of the existing empirical works. Section III describes the scope and methodology used to collect the data. Section IV presents major findings and discussion. Section Five gives main conclusion and recommendations of the study.

LITERATURE REVIEW

A number of studies have been made on the subject of insurance, however, the existing studies focused on the various aspects of insurance like the consumers' perception of insurance, the investment policies of policyholders' funds by the insurance companies, the provision of health care by the government.

Table 16.1: Salient Features of Some of the Health Insurance Plans Available to Indian Customers

Features	Health shield gold (Royal Sundaram)	Health Insurance (ICICI Lombard)	Mediclaim (Public sector insurers)	Health Guard (Bajaj Allianz)	Medishield (Iffco Tokyo)	Silver Health (Bajaj Allianz)
Age limit	3 months-75 years	3 months-70 years	3 months-80 years	3 months-55 years	3 months-80 years	46 years-70 years
Reimbursement of hospital bills due to illness or injury	Yes	Yes	Yes	Yes	Yes	Yes
Cashless Facility	Yes	Yes	Yes	Yes	No	Yes
Tax exemption u/s 80 D up to Rs. 10,000	Yes	Yes	Yes	Yes	Yes	Yes
Pre and post-hospitalisation charges	Yes Pre-30 days Post-60 days	Yes Pre-30 days Post-60 days	Yes Pre-30 days Post-60 days	Yes Pre-60 days Post-90 days	Yes Pre-30 days Post-60 days	Yes (Up to 3% on actual claim amount)
Maternity benefits	Yes Up to Rs. 20,000	No	No	No	No	No
Cumulative bonus on renewal if no claim	15% per year Max. 60%	5% discount per year in premium amount	5% discount per year Max. 50%	5% discount per year Max. 50%	5% discount per year Max. 50%	5% discount per year Max. 50%
Family discount	10% for 3 or more persons	N/A	10% for 2 or more persons	5% for 2 or more persons	10% for 3 or more persons	5% for 2 or more persons

(Contd...)

Features	Health shield gold (Royal Sundaram)	Health Insurance (ICICI Lombard)	Mediclaim (Public sector insurers)	Health Guard (Bajaj Allianz)	Medishield (Iffco Tokyo)	Silver Health (Bajaj Allianz)
Age limit	3 months-75 years	3 months-70 years	3 months-80 years	3 months-55 years	3 months-80 years	46 years-70 years
Free health check up	No	No	1% of sum insured for 4 claim free years	Up to Rs. 1000 for 4 claim free years	Yes, on 4 claim free years	Yes, on 4 claim free years
Pre existing disease cover	Yes from 6th year onward	Yes from 5th year onward	No	Yes from 5th year onward	No	Yes, 50% from 2nd year &100% from 3rd year
Pre insurance medical test	60 years onwards	45 years onwards	Above 45 years	Above 45 years for SI over 2 lakh	Above 45 years	For every proposal
Sum insured	Min.- Rs. 75,000 Max- Rs. 5 lakh	Min.- Rs. 2 lakh Max- Rs. 3 lakh	Min.- Rs. 15,000 Max- Rs. 5 lakh	Min.- Rs. 1 lakh (Rs. 50,000 if two) Max- Rs. 5 lakh	Min.- Rs. 15,000 Max- Rs. 5 lakh	Min.- Rs. 50,000 Max- Rs. 3 lakh
Day care treatment	Yes	Yes	Yes	No	Yes (Reimbursement)	No
Premium on Rs. 1 lakh sum insured (at age 35 years)	Rs. 1841	(Min SI 2 Lakhs) Rs.2760	Rs.1443	Rs.1335	Rs.1261	N/A
At age 55 years	Rs.2674	N/A	Rs.2247	Rs.2513	Rs.2120	Rs.3742

Indian

The Committee on Reforms in the Insurance Sector (1993) conducted a survey in the pre-liberalised era. It revealed that public awareness of General Insurance Corporation of India (GIC) and its subsidiary companies was low; Two-thirds of non-auto claimants were satisfied with their last claim settlement; auto claimants were moderately satisfied with the time taken to settle a claim.

The General Insurance Corporation of India's (GIC) strategic research (1999) showed that awareness of life insurance is 100 per cent, for motor it is above 95 per cent, for health and home insurance above 70 per cent among users at prompted level. Among non-users awareness of motor is above 80 per cent, personal accident above 60 per cent, for health and home insurance above 50 per cent.

FICCI survey (October 2001) of some of the insurance companies revealed that the middle income group was expected to experience maximum growth in years to come, almost one half of the respondents believed in incentivising customers through tax benefits, creating consumer awareness about general "need to insure", better customer servicing would be one of the key determinants for any company's success in the liberalised era.

Mishra (1987) concentrated on investment and organizational aspect of Life Insurance Corporation during 1956-86. It covered aspects like investment management, personnel management, development program and reorganization of LIC.

Reddy (1994) found that health care expenditure by public and private sector in India is not low in comparison to other comparable countries but the real reason is inefficiency in utilization and misallocation of resources.

Krishnan (1996) proposed a scheme for universal health insurance for the poor to be subsequently adopted for other sections of the society. He also suggested the need for separate health insurance corporation to be run as a not for profit organisation.

Mathews (1997) felt the need for voluntary health insurance along with inclusion of outpatient care to help ease pressures on hospitals. He also suggested that insurance purchasers should be provided with very strong incentives every claim free year.

Randall, Alam and Gupta (2000) have recommended limiting exclusions for pre-existing medical conditions, greater monitoring of fraud and excess fees, reform of the excessively high premium structure and laying down the time frame within which reimbursement will take place.

Bhat, Maheshwari and Saha (2005) found low awareness among policyholders about the existence of TPA; policyholders mostly rely on their insurance agents, have very little knowledge about the empanelled hospitals for cashless hospitalisation services.

International

A study conducted by Roper Starch Worldwide and Commissioned by the Life and Health Insurance Foundation for Education (LIFE) (1999) revealed that more than twenty five million households had no life insurance coverage. Many American households that had coverage appeared to be under insured and they cited the following reasons; 81 per cent thought that it was too expensive, 60 per cent had no knowledge, 50 per cent worried about making a wrong decision, 33 per cent preferred to put their money somewhere else and 22 per cent did not want to think about death.

Thus, a number of studies have been conducted in India and elsewhere on various aspects of insurance. Most of the studies have focused on life insurance issues; works on health insurance are concerned with provision of health covers for the poor. The reforms in the financial sector and the recent changes in the insurance sector, in particular, have resulted in a wide array of research themes. Little work seems to have been done on the health insurance awareness in the liberalized insurance sector in India. The present study tries to fill this research gap by providing an insight into what the policyholders want from their insurers and insurer's preparedness to satisfy these customers.

METHODOLOGY

This study is exploratory in nature. For this purpose 500 individuals falling in different age, income groups, profession and employment status were randomly selected from Delhi, Faridabad, Gurgaon, Ghaziabad, Chennai, Kolkata, Mumbai, and Pune. However, only 55 of these individuals had health insurance policies; all of them cooperated by supplying the required information. Seventy-five senior executives in the companies offering health insurance plans in the private as well as public sector had also shared their practices and opinions about their policies.

Two pre-structured questionnaires, designed specifically for the purpose and containing both open and close-ended questions, was pilot tested with ten individuals and ten company executives. Adjustments were made in these in the light of the observations and suggestions made by them. All the respondents were personally approached at their work places and homes. An interview-based approach was used to gather information about their health insurance needs and other issues related to health insurance.

The individuals who provided the desired information are from diverse background and there is fair representation of different age, qualification, profession, employment and income group (See Figures 16.1-16.5). The executives are from different age groups, levels of management, work experience from both public and private insurers. Such a diversified sample is likely to enrich the understanding of various issues related to health insurance (See Figures 16.6-16.9).

RESULTS AND DISCUSSIONS

This section presents the findings of the discussions with the individual policyholders on their awareness about their health insurance plan, limitations in the existing scheme, their experience in claims servicing and the suggestions to make their policy more extensive. It also presents the executives opinions about a range of issues that will help the customers in satisfying their health insurance needs.

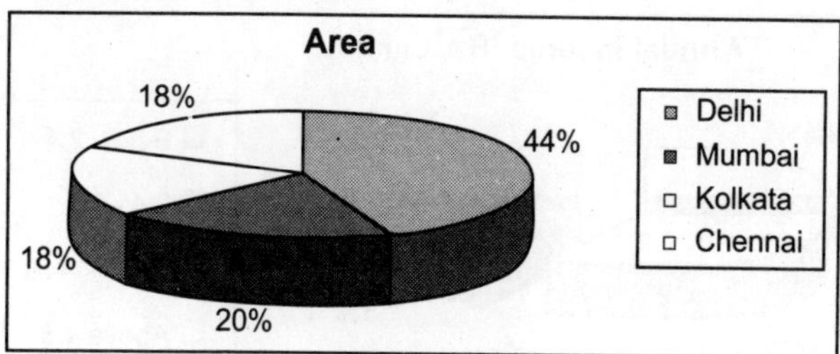

Figure 16.1

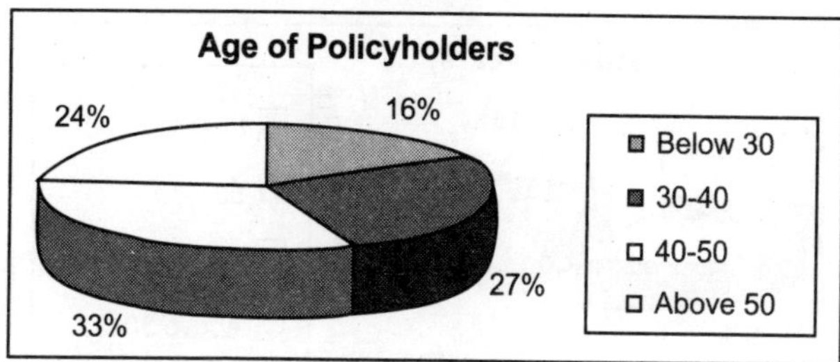

Figure 16.2

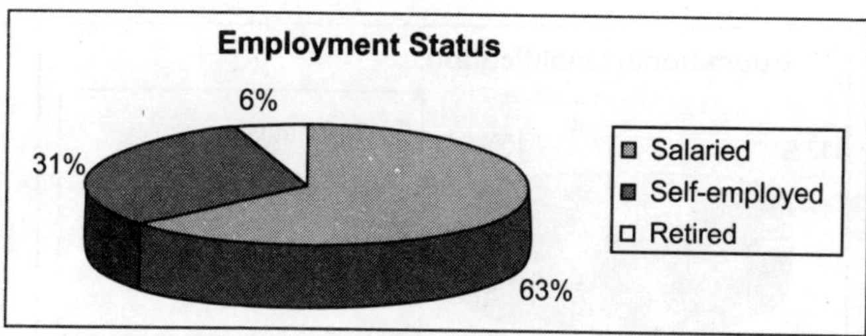

Figure 16.3

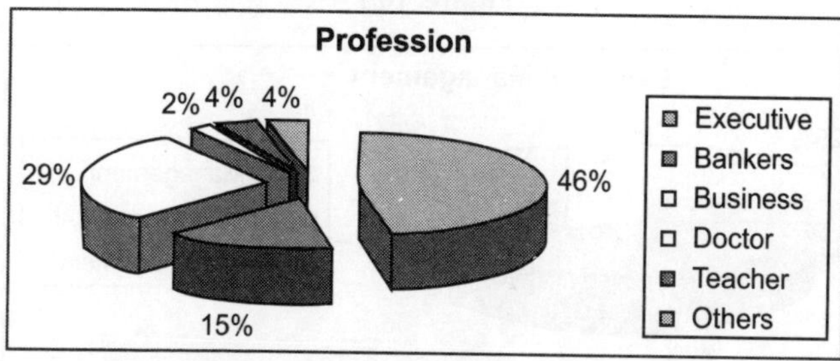

Figure 16.4

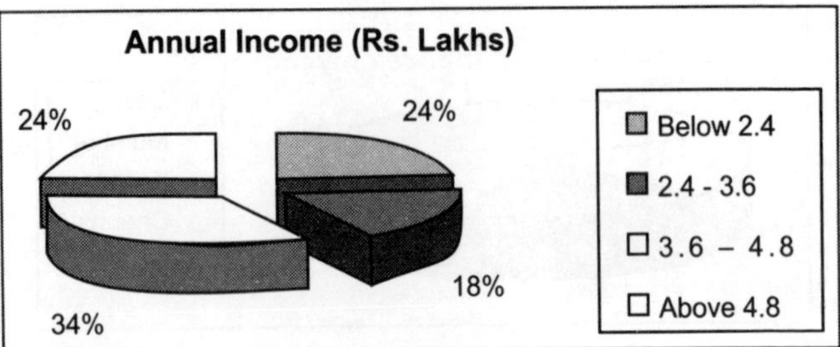

Figure 16.5

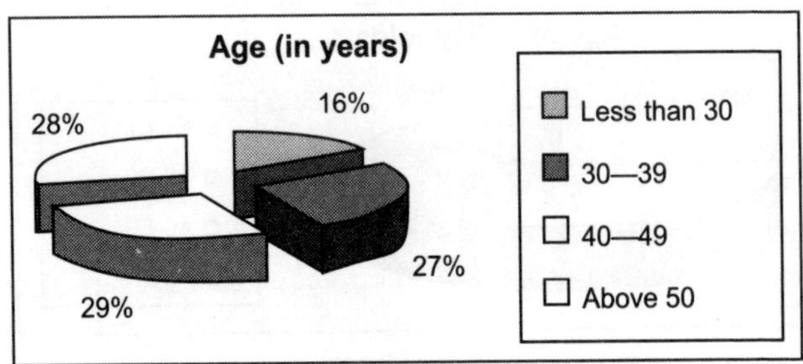

Figure 16.6

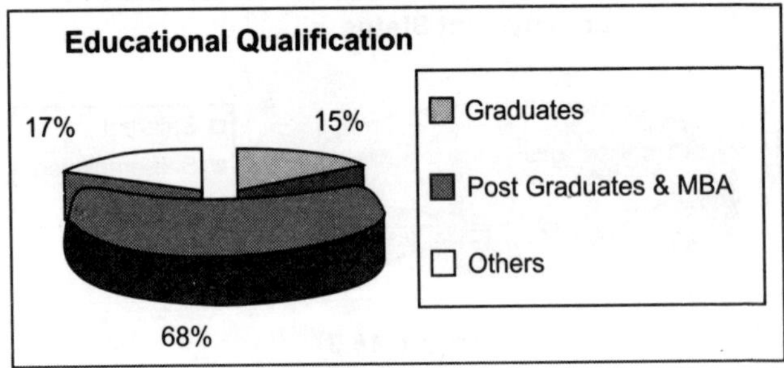

Figure 16.7

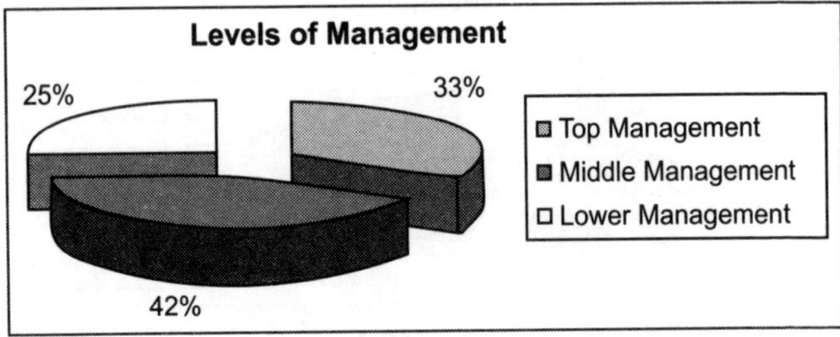

Figure 16.8

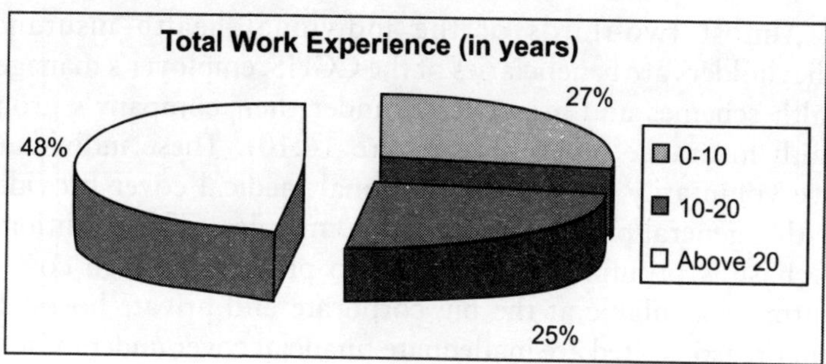

Figure 16.9

The responses of the prospective customer indicate that people are aware of health insurance but are hesitant in its purchase because of associated problems attached with it. These customers are thwarted in their purchase decision by high premiums, non-payment of claims, rejection of claims on flimsy grounds and the fleecing by health service providers. The existing policyholders have shown tremendous response for cashless health insurance and desire hassle-free claim servicing.

The insurers are doing their best in providing need based plans for customers but there are many obstacles that they have to cross before they can have satisfied customer base. The biggest challenge before them is that of the efficiency of Third Party Administrators or the TPAs.

The whole scheme of cashless health insurance revolves around this intermediary. The results indicate that the customers are not being satisfactorily serviced by these very erstwhile and renowned TPAs. This section presents in detail the opinions of the insured and the insurer.

Need for Extra Coverage

In India, only 0.25 per cent of the population is covered under voluntary health insurance scheme. Some form of social or private health insurance covers barely 3 per cent of the population. These schemes are Central Government Health Services Scheme (CGHS), Employees State Insurance Scheme (ESI), Army/Railway, Self-funded and private/voluntary health insurance.

Almost two-thirds of the individual health insurance policyholders are beneficiaries of the CGHS, employer's managed health schemes and are covered under their company's group health insurance policy (See Figure 16.10). These individuals have voluntarily purchased additional medical cover provided by the general/private insurance companies. This additional purchase is prompted by the need to provide for high cost of treatment available at the big corporate and private hospitals. Other reasons cited are inadequate financial cover under existing scheme, difficulty in accessing services of government dispensaries and hospitals. These health service providers are often inadequately staffed, unhygienic and lack of medical supplies and equipments, thus compounding the miseries of the beneficiaries. Deficiencies in the provision of public health services provide huge potential for the insurers to provide quality health plans to such dissatisfied customers. Self-employed individuals and those belonging to the unorganized sectors are at a greater financial risk from severe illnesses and accidents. Such respondents opined that health insurance is a feasible solution for them to protect themselves from such financial risks.

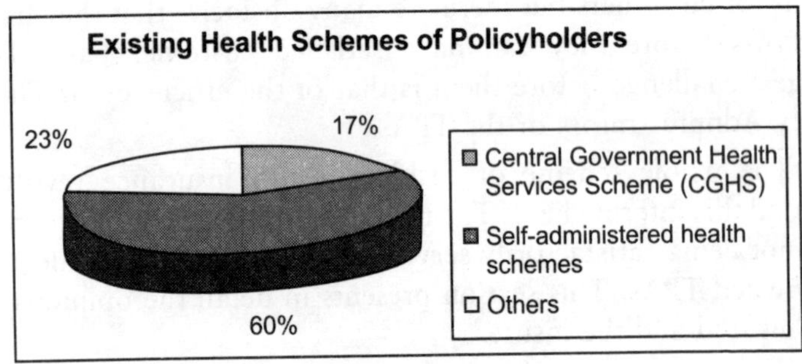

Figure 16.10

Desirable Age to buy Health Insurance

Seeing a greater need for health insurance it is also useful to find out about the most desirable age at which one should purchase it. Majority of respondents are in favour of taking health insurance below the age of 45 years. The reason for this could be that individuals are aware that health insurance, if, purchased at a younger age would cost less. A very few 7 per cent said the suitable age is 46 years and above. This is the age group that requires frequent medical treatment due to age related problems. Seeing a vast potential in this age group, one of the private insurer (Bajaj Allianz non-life insurance company) has launched a health insurance scheme for people in the 46 to 70 years age group. There is a need for such schemes from other insurers also (See Figure 16.11).

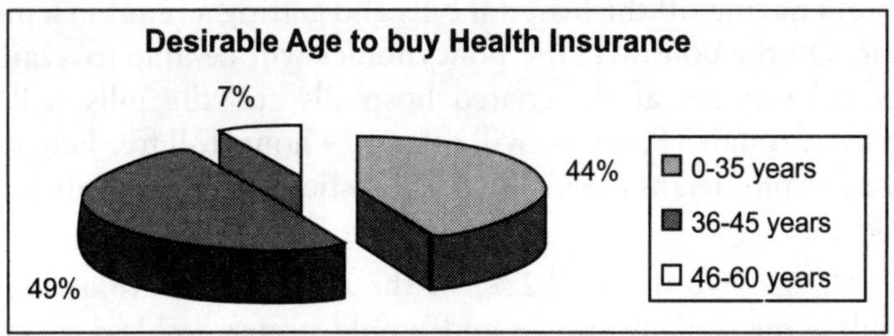

Figure 16.11

Even the executives are of the opinion that health insurance should be purchased when the person is below thirty years of age. A large base of young customers would help in spreading the risks over low, medium and high-risk profile customers. Such a distribution will result in low claims. For this to happen, change in customers' mindset is required. There is also an opportunity for the insurers to provide long-term care benefits for the ageing population.

Thus, it is clear from the above responses that health insurance, at whatever age one buys it, is considered indispensable.

Mediclaim—An Opportunity for Change

A large majority of these individuals are covered by the 'Mediclaim Policy', which is offered by the four public sector insurers and a similar product by other private sector insurers.

More than two-thirds of the insured (69 per cent) said the mediclaim policy in its existing form has many limitations. The inherent drawback of mediclaim policy is that it is a reimbursement policy where the insured pays for his medical treatment first and then files a claim for reimbursement. It is not necessary that the insured will get reimbursement for the full amount.

To overcome this limitation cashless mediclaim scheme was introduced. The insurers got the opportunity, as a result of introduction of Third Party Administrators (TPAs), to offer cashless health schemes to the public. Under Cashless hospitalization, a Mediclaim policyholder will not have to run around paying off the hospital bills and getting a reimbursement later. On the contrary, the policyholder will be able to avail of medical services at designated hospitals and the bills will be settled through TPAs who will offer a 24 hours toll free help line, access to physicians, specialists, diagnostic centers and ambulance services.

Almost two-thirds (62%) of the respondents are aware of cashless medical insurance and would prefer cashless medical insurance to mediclaim policy. A very large majority of respondents (80%) showed preference for direct settlement of hospital bills by the insurer to avoid hassles.

The respondents are well aware that the existing Mediclaim policy is available only in case of hospitalisation and related expenses and not for any outdoor treatment compensation. There are exclusions that limit the scope of coverage. More than half of the respondents said they were aware of the exclusions and want reduction of exclusions.

The executives, however, feel that insurance is unthinkable without exclusions. Exclusions help in restricting the liability of the insurer and also check adverse selection of customers. However, some private sector insurers are covering pre-existing diseases if the policy is in force for more than five years with the same insurer.

It is a challenge for the insurers to provide that what the customers want. The executives, however, think that the present health plans are innovative and designed after intensive market research like the cash less health insurance plans. The executives in private sector think that their plans are different from those sold by public sector insurers. Its seen from the executives' responses that most of the private sector insurers are providing value added benefits which are missing from the mediclaim policy being offered by the public sector insurers. These benefits are the inclusion of preexisting diseases from 5th year onwards; maternity benefits up to Rs. 20,000, some private insurers provide their customers free health check ups on the completion of four claim free years.

Policy Premiums

People have raised concern about steep health insurance premiums. A very large majority of policyholders (87%) said that health insurance premiums should be lower. These respondents (52%) think lower rates would help them buy cover for the entire family. Another 48 per cent mentioned other reasons like affordability that would increase the penetration of health insurance in the country.

For senior executives, pricing of plans is of extreme importance and they believe that by bringing down the claims ratio prices would reduce. However, executives of all the public sector insurance companies have said their prices are at a lower level in comparison with other similar plans. A few of the executives from the private insurers have opined that their company's plans are designed to meet the needs of different income groups. The executives feel the customers now have various options at the most suitable prices. Claiming the no claim bonus can also reduce premiums. Most companies give a discount, to the customer per year for a claim free year. These discounts are an incentive for the customers not to make claims for small medical expenses. Almost all the policyholders agreed that such a discount should be given. Family discounts are also given in case the policy is taken for a family of four members.

Claim Settlement

The customers' experience regarding claims settlement was obtained to find out the improvement as a result of TPAs and the cash less facility. Two-thirds of the policyholders said they had made a claim. Some of the respondents said they were provided the details of the claim procedure while others said no details were given. Respondents covered by cashless facility approached the third party administrators; a little more than one third of the respondents said they got in touch with the agent. While 27 per cent respondents said they approached the company directly. (See Figure 16.12) According to the responses of the policyholders only 42 per cent customers found cashless insurance hassle free. More than half found it time consuming and 55 per cent said there is much paper work involved.

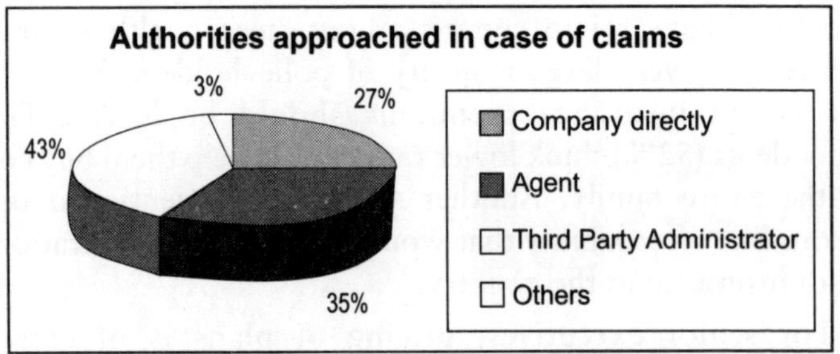

Figure 16.12

These respondents (64%) stated that the time taken to settle the claims ranged between one to three months. Only 2 per cent of the respondents said their claims were rejected on account of incomplete papers and due to pre-existing illnesses. (See Figure 16.13)

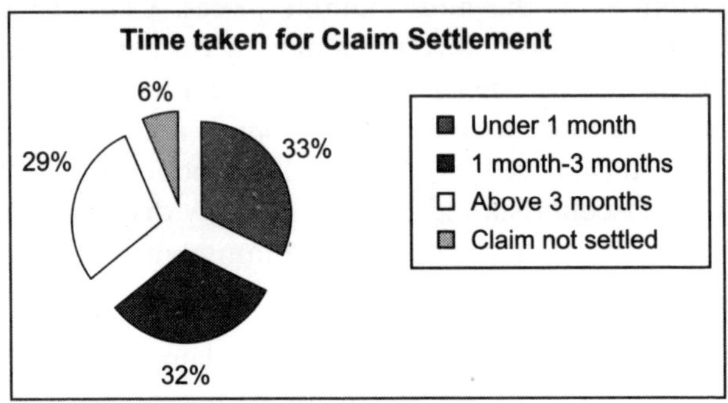

Figure 16.13

According to all the senior executives, the policyholders are provided with details of claim procedure and the concerned authorities they can approach at the time of making claims.

Claim settlement process has been simplified with the use of information technology; the claim forms can be downloaded from the net and filed immediately with the company for processing. Half of the executives said their company is using information technology to help reduce claim settlement time.

The executives said the settlement of claims depended on the completion and submission of necessary papers by the claimant. The executives (43%) said 28-30 days are taken in case of mediclaim, where the insurers inspect all the bills and doctor's prescriptions and then decide on the compensation to be given. The senior officers in the insurance companies agree that insured face problems at the time of settlement, but these are primarily due to third party administrators. They also think that slow progress in providing cashless services is due to various teething problems.

Satisfaction with Mediclaim

The limitations in the existing plan have resulted in dissatisfied customers. Almost three-fourths (74%) of the respondents said they were not satisfied with the mediclaim policy. The respondents gave few suggestions that would improve their current policy. Respondents (82%) want extensive coverage and inclusion of all illnesses. While others said that all treatments whether requiring hospitalisation or not should be covered, removal of exclusions, reduction in premiums and removal of procedural hassles are also desired.

Grievance and Redressal

Not only are the customers dissatisfied with the health insurance policy but also are unhappy with the services of the insurers. More than half of the respondents (58%) said they were dissatisfied with the services of the company. More than one-fifth of the respondents said their claims were either not settled or there were delays in settlement of claims due to interpretation of exclusions. A few respondents said their dissatisfaction was due to lack of trust in the TPA or dispute regarding claim amount. A great majority (87%) of executives agree that maximum complaints relate to interpretation of exclusions in case of health insurance. Thus, leading to dissatisfaction among customers. (See Figure 16.14)

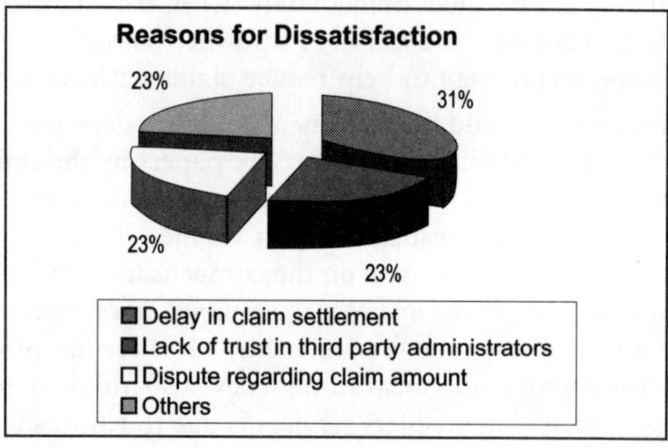

Figure 16.14

The respondents are ignorant about the redressal agencies. About two-thirds of the respondents (66%) had no idea whom to approach for redressal, a few said they had no time and even if they pursued the matter there seemed to be no point in it. This vulnerability of the insured can only be removed if the insurers provide information about the redressal agencies, name and address of the ombudsman and senior officials of their grievance cell.

CONCLUSION

The analysis clearly shows that there is demand for cash less health insurance scheme but the customers want reduction in number of exclusions and inclusion of pre-existing diseases. They want the TPAs to be efficient and perform up to the expectation of the policyholders and insurers. Even though the insurers are providing need based plans but more should be done to meet the needs arising out of changing lifestyles of people. The population of elderly people, in India, is rising and they would require institutional care, which is totally missing. The plans need to include pregnancy related expenses, inclusion of chronic and debilitating diseases, HIV and AIDS. TPAs need to be more efficient in claims processing and providing better networking for the policyholders. These challenges can be overcome by setting up exclusive and stand-alone health insurance companies that are run on non-profit objective. In most of the countries life insurance companies underwrite health insurance. In India, life insurers should be allowed to underwrite health insurance. The tax benefits available at present should be hiked and continued with. The health plans should be wide based in order to include outpatient care along with in-patient treatment. Health savings account needs to be provided to the customers. This service can be provided through bancassurance. There is a need for specific health insurance regulations. Capital requirements for stand-alone health insurers need to be revised. Implementation of some of these suggestions might help increase the penetration of health insurance and also result in satisfied customers and help insurers increase their market share.

REFERENCES

Bhat, Maheshwari and Saha. "Third Party Administrators and Health Insurance in India: Perception of Providers and Policyholders." *Journal of Insurance and Risk Management*, Vol. III, No. 6, (2005) pp. 15-30.

Black (JR.) and Skipper (JR.). *Life and Health Insurance*, Pearson Education, Singapore, 2000, pp. 134.

FICCI, *Survey on Post-Liberalisation Developments in the Indian Insurance Industry*, 2001, pp. 1-3.

Krishnan, T.N. "Hospitalisation Insurance: A Proposal". *Economic and Political Weekly*. February 1996.

Malhotra Committee Report on Insurance Sector Reforms (1994).

Mathews, T. "Medical Insurance for All?" *Economic and Political Weekly*. February 1997.

Mishra. "A Study of Working of LIC of India—Financial and Organizational Aspects", unpublished Doctoral Thesis submitted to the Department of Commerce, Banaras Hindu University, Varanasi, (1987).

Randall, Alam, Gupta. "Health Insurance in India: Prognosis and Prospectus". *Economic and Political Weekly*, January 22, 2000.

Reddy, K.N. "Health Care Expenditure in India: Is It Low?" *Finance India*, Vol. viii, No. 2, June 1994.

Society of Financial Service Professionals. "New Life Study Reveals Crisis of Under Insurance", Society page (1999), Adopted from Rejda, G.E., *Principles of Risk Management and Insurance*. Addison Wesley, 2000, pp. 348.

Srivastava and Srivastava. *Indian Insurance Industry: Transition and Prospects*, New Century Publications, New Delhi, 2001, pp. 188-194.

Surveys conducted by the GIC and National Insurance Academy (1999).

Insurance Industry: Challenges and Opportunities in Oman

17

Damodharan V. S. ACCA and *Jagadish Prasad*

ABSTRACT

Objective: The primary aim of this research is to explore the challenges and opportunities in the Insurance Industry in the Sultanate of Oman with particular emphasis on the Life Insurance Coverage.

Research Design: To address the primary objective, quantitative data is corrected on population, economic growth and the insurance companies in Oman and AGCC countries.

Keywords: Correlation, SWOT Analysis, Time Series, Challenges and Opportunities.

Findings: The results of this research indicate that there are significant gaps between life insurance and other insurance products in the Sultanate of Oman. The findings will also focus on the future potential of insurance products in Oman.

Practical Implications: This research is of practical use to service sector companies attempting to examine how to develop a strategy for life insurance products in Oman. It is of particular use to service buyer operations within the insurance sector i.e. moving from the cash compensation approach to a replacement goods approach.

Originality/Value: Very little has been written about insurance products in Oman in the insurance sector. This paper provides an insight into those issues relating to various new challenges and opportunities within this unique service context.

INTRODUCTION

The concept of risk management can be categorized as under

(1) Identifying and analyzing a risk;

(2) Reducing or removing the said risk; and

(3) Transferring the balance of the risk finally at an "Economic Cost".

However, after identifying and analyzing the risks, there are ways to reduce them and also spread some of these risks. Insurance or Assurance is a common way to reduce personal exposure to loss by guaranteeing a specified sum of money as claim(s) in the event of loss of life, accident, etc.

The insurance industry expands and prospers, based on the assumption that people are generally risk averse. Adequate amount of insurance premium and payment eliminates uncertainty regarding financial loss in the event of adversity. We found out that about 90 per cent of people in Oman do not own any life/health or personal insurance. Perhaps people, in general, simply ignore low probable events (i.e. misfortunes in terms of heavy losses) and believe that such loss could never happen to them at anytime. By way of example, car insurance is mandatory for all car vehicle owners in Oman. Because of this reason, the motor insurance has increased to 200 per cent in the past five years. However, for non-mandatory insurance, such as life insurance, not everybody has insurance protection. The percentage of life insurance has increased only by 40 per cent in the past five years.

One of the interesting facts we came across in our findings showing that out of the total driving licenseholders in Oman on an average works out to 15 per cent of the people who met with accidents and out of which 20 per cent of them on an average succumb. The following issues to be addressed:

(1) Do people prefer risk taking, or do they have difficulty in affording an insurance policy?

(2) What is the reason whether people are not aware of the various life insurance services (or)

(3) The industries are not following a proper strategy in reaching the people?

Whatever, the reasons may be, insurers need to evaluate the market situation and customers' purchasing behavior. Insurers not only face stiff competition from their rivals but also from the fact that their clients do not view them favorably. To build a strong relationship with customers, insurers must improve the quality of their service. There is a need for insurers to undertake a demand audit in order to understand what the policyholder wants and his needs.

The purpose of this study is to assess the insurance industry as a whole in Oman with particular emphasis on the challenges and opportunities in the life insurance sector. The most important issue is to understand the need of the customers and satisfying their requirements. Existing challenges are analyzed and new opportunities are identified in this research with respect to life insurance sector in Oman which will help the insurance industry in developing their services and strategies thereto meet consumers' requirements.

This paper aims to examine in detail the key determinants of the demand for life insurance in Oman. The various analytical tools used in this research are:

(a) Time series Analysis
(b) Correlation Analysis
(c) Percentage Analysis
(d) SWOT Analysis

Insurance Companies in Oman: Present Status

Insurance companies in Oman—both national as well as foreign—are looking forward to stability in the industry. They feel the changes proposed in the insurance law can go a long way in bringing order within the sector. Besides, legislative reforms, the insurance industry is looking forward to some organizational changes within the sector.

In Oman, factors such as a growing middle class which is gradually discovering credit cards and consumer loans, the sultanate's WTO commitment to open its doors by 2005 and finally industry consolidation in the insurance sector to remain competitive are changing the face of the existing sedate insurance business.

Presently, life insurance companies are looking at broadening networks and making services as flexible and accessible as they can. Life insurers are now spreading their wings across the towns and the interior in the search for new pastures. Agents hired on a commission basis are the preferred medium using local talent to connect with the public and also to overcome their reservations with analyzing financial information.

Besides, legislative reforms, the insurance industry is looking forward to some infrastructural changes within the sector. In fact, a move that could rejuvenate the insurance market in Oman is to make medical insurance compulsory for expatriates especially in the wake of the government order that only serious and emergency cases of expatriates could be treated in government hospitals.

Insurance Companies in Oman

Company	Nationality	No. of Branches	Year of Establishment
National Companies		**58**	
1. Al-Ahlia Insurance Co.	Omani	6	1995
2. Oman United Insurance Co.	Omani	11	1996
3. Dhofar Insurance	Omani	29	1989
4. Oman National Life Insurance	Omani	4	1995
5. Muscat Insurance	Omani	4	1995
6. Oman United Insurance Co.	Omani	4	1999
7. Muscat Life Insurance Co.	Omani	6	
Arab Companies		**6**	
1. Arabian Insurance	Lebanese	2	1976
2. Al-Nisr Insurance	Lebanese	1	1976
3. Al -Ittihad Al Watani	Lebanese	3	1977
Foreign Companies		**16**	
1. American Life Insurance	American	5	1971
2. Iran Insurance	Iranian	2	1973
3. New India Assurance	Indian	5	1976
4. Royal Insurance	Indian	1	1977
5. Norwich Winterthur	Indian	3	1967
Total		**80**	

Source: Courtesy - Ministry of National Economy, Oman

Challenges—Insurance Preimum

Total income by way of premium payments to the insurance sector in Oman in 2004 stood at RO 102.828 million, including RO 15.684 million from life insurance and RO 87.144 million from general insurance. The insurance sector is growing day by day because of the increase in the GDP and per capita income, urbanization and education level. The total receipt by way of premium increased to 102.828 million in the year 2004 at a rate of 215 per cent from RO 47.8 million in the year 2000.

Factors that drove the demand growth for Insurance sector are:

1. Privatization of state assets resulting in previously uninsured risks requiring insurance cover for the first time.
2. Favorable demographics.
3. Increase in the per capita income and GDP.
4. Introduction of insurance for medical and third party motor vehicle insurance liability.
5. Takaful products contributing to the growth and helping to overcome social and religious concerns.

The following table shows the growth of insurance premium over a period of five years. The percentage of increase in the way of premium receipts in transport insurance accounted to 310 per cent, and in case of property insurance accounted to 265 per cent and other premium accounted to 182 per cent. The motor insurance premium receipts accounted an increase of 80 per cent over the past five years; the growth by way of life insurance premium is only 42 per cent which is the lowest in the insurance industry. This shows that the insurance companies are not following a proper strategy with respect to life insurance services.

Though the premium growth in Oman was good in the recent past, there has been a perceptible slowdown in 2004 when it grew by about 1 per cent over the previous year to reach RO102.82mn. This is the lowest growth rate in the past five year period. This could be seen as a temporary aberration due to the high base in 2002. Further, the geopolitical conflicts concerning

Iraq had an effect on the pace of acquisition of new business by insurance companies. Slowdown in 2004 has not been a phenomenon across the GCC region and the growth was sustained in Bahrain and UAE markets which grew at 20 per cent and 10 per cent respectively.

Premium Received and Claims Paid by Insurance Companies in Oman

Types of Insurance in R.O.(000)	2000	2001	2002	2003	2004
Life					
Premiums Insurance	10,700	13,626	12,085	13,972	15,684
Claims paid	5,700	10,269	6,220	6,115	11,375
Motor Vehicle					
Direct Premium	23,200	37,472	38,449	39,207	41,711
Claims paid	19,300	23,569	27,119	27,158	28,766
Property					
Direct Premium	4,300	9,106	16,890	16,212	15,699
Claims paid	3,100	2,918	5,013	7,024	4,289
Transport					
Direct Premium	2,100	5,728	6,901	5,215	8,605
Claims paid	500	717	932	41,813	1,003
Others					
Direct Premium	7,500	11,492	20,261	26,622	21,126
Claims paid	2,900	3,101	7,475	8,746	4,065
Total					
Premium	47,800	77,424	94,586	101,228	102,828
Claims paid	31,700	40,574	46,759	90,856	49,498

Source: Courtesy - Ministry of National Economy, Oman.

In the life insurance sector, the share of the national companies was 75.46 per cent and that of foreign companies 24.54 per cent. In the general insurance sector, the share of the national companies was 71.14 per cent and that of foreign companies 28.6 per cent. This shows that Omani firms dominate the total insurance sector as it holds nearly two thirds of the total insurance premium.

Though growth in GCC markets has been erratic, the Oman insurance industry has been successful in maintaining its profitability over the years. Overall loss ratio in the GCC market stood at 57.2 per cent, which can be said to be healthy by the global standards. However, loss ratios across countries varied depending on the composition and nature of the business in each country. The pattern of profitability across insurance classes has been more or less akin to that prevailing globally. Average loss ratio in the last four years has been the lowest for transport sector at 11 per cent and the highest for Motor Vehicles sector at 70 per cent. Insurance companies claim that motor insurance is putting a lot of pressure on them where claims exceed the amount of premium received.

The main reason for increase in claims is due to the increase in the number of accidents. "Motor insurance is a losing business for insurers." The cost of servicing motor claims is increasing, while the rise in premium rates does not commensurate with costs. The reasons for increase are accident claims; labor charges for repair, spare part costs, medical bills, besides court orders to pay hefty compensation are hampering the margins of companies.

The average loss ratio for the entire insurance market in Oman was at 61 per cent during the five year period 2000 to 2004. Though commission levels and claims ratios had an effect on profitability, these were over shadowed by the effect of a booming equity market in GCC in general and Oman in particular. The average return from equity markets in GCC countries was 51.1 per cent in 2003. This has come as a bonanza as the insurance companies here have relatively higher exposure to equity markets than the companies in other markets.

Growth in Insurance Policies

In recent data as published by the Ministry of National Economy, Insurance of Motor Vehicles constituted about 89 per cent of all the insurance policies registered in 2004 whereas, Life Insurance captured merely 3 per cent, which indicates the level of awareness as far as Life Insurance is concerned.

The most interesting thing is that people are giving more importance in insuring the immovable items while life is given less importance. The main area of concern is that the number of accidents is increasing day by day but companies fail to create awareness among the people the need to cover the risk associated with customer's life.

Insurance Policies and its Percentage for the Past Five Years (2000-04)

Types of Insurance	2000		2001		2002		2003		2004	
	No. of Policies	(%)	No. of Policies	(%)	No. of Policies	(%)	No. of Policies	(%)	No. of Policies	(%)
Life	9,376	3	9,203	2	12,987	3	14,140	3	15,996	3
Motor Vehicles	228,148	77	338,526	81	370,155	84	387,125	79	432,066	89
Property	7,625	3	8,194	2	8,510	2	8,889	2	8,264	2
Transport	14,198	5	12,098	3	17,776	4	14,845	3	14,259	3
Others	37,706	13	47,846	12	32,116	7	64,849	13	16,322	3
Total	297,053	100	415,867	100	441,544	100	489,848	100	486,907	100

Opportunity—Accidents and Fatalities

Global statistics show, that deaths from road traffic accidents are currently listed as being the eighth highest cause of all deaths in the world today. These statistics also indicate that by the year 2020, deaths from road traffic accidents would rise to third on that list. Since 1995, road fatalities in Oman have grown by more than 50 per cent. The most pathetic part is that majority of the people do not have life insurance cover.

Graphical Representation of Fatalities From 2001-05

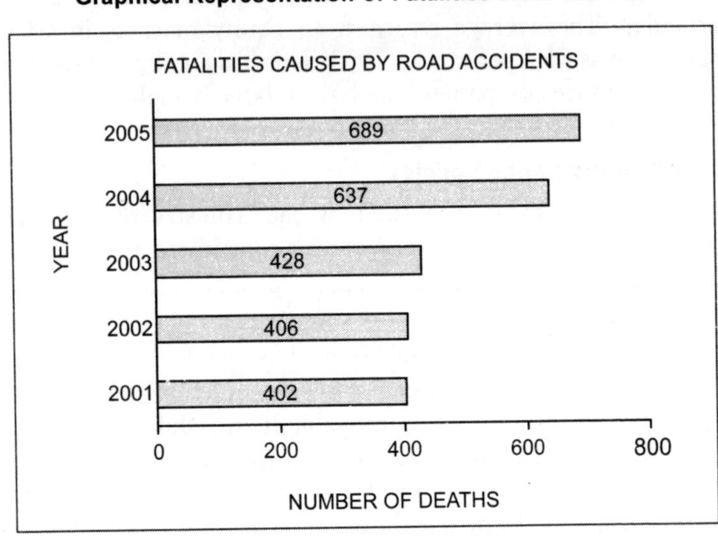

Oman leads with an average of 28 fatalities per 100,000 populations every year, closely followed by Saudi Arabia and the UAE with 21 and 20 respectively. Nearly 700 road accident victims in the year 2006 on Oman's roads out of a total population of approximately 2.6 million is a frightening statistics, urging us to take immediate corrective measures to safeguard this horrific trend. Out of which 42 per cent of the fatalities were young children and youngsters less than 15 years of age and 50 per cent were breadwinners in the family; men aged from 26 to 49 years. Out of the total fatalities Oman accounted for 80 per cent and the remaining 20 per cent of fatalities accounted for the expatriate. Oman's road traffic mortality was 28 per 100,000 populations, far in excess of the global average of 19 per 100,000.

The most tragic aspect is that nearly 95 per cent of the people died in accidents do not have life insurance protection. The emotional trauma and financial cost of road traffic deaths and injuries can impact severely on society, when children and young people are left unsupported and disabled for life. "Road accidents don't just affect the people involved in them. They have an impact on society and the economy."

Research Method

Correlation

There is a significant relative relationship between driving license and number of fatalities. In order to check the result, correlation analysis is carried out with two variable driving license is data x and fatalities is data y.

RESULTS AND ANALYSIS

The results show that the value of r is 0.95 which relates very strong positive significant relationship as between licenses and fatalities, warranting the imperative need for coverage of accidents by suitable/appropriate/adequate insurance policies. Therefore, the more number of licenses without proper insurance coverage will not only result in more number of fatalities but also loss of compensation in such deaths/injuries.

Percentage Analysis

Analyses of road accidents reveal the following facts:

The number of injuries has increased to 70 per cent from 57 per cent while the percentages of death are doubled. Out of the total accidents, the percentage of injury and fatality is 76 per cent in the year 2006 compared to 60 per cent in the year 2001. This shows that more and more people are getting injured because of road accidents.

Percentage of Road Accidents, Injuries and Fatalities

Percentage	2001	2002	2003	2004	2005
Road Accidents/ License	23.73	15.07	15.96	13.82	13.21
Number of Injuries/ Road Accidents	57.25	71.37	66.05	70.15	68.36
Fatalities/Road Accidents	3.07	4.46	4.20	5.18	7.45

SWOT Analysis

SWOT stands for **strengths, weaknesses, opportunities,** and **threats.** SWOT analysis is a tool for auditing an industry and its environment. It is the first stage of planning and helps marketers to focus on key issues.

Strengths

1. As per WTO agreement the Oman government has to open the insurance market for other countries from 2005.
2. The government is giving more importance to insurance industry as it is a tangible source of additional revenue to government.
3. The government will be able to encourage personal investments and savings in order to lessen the state's burden on welfare schemes.
4. The insurance will be encouraging Oman citizens to take greater responsibility for their financial welfare in the long run that will lead to greater levels of social responsibility simultaneously cementing the reform process among the population.

5. The growing Oman car culture is a boost to car insurance premiums.
6. The increase in fatalities and accidents will result in increase in life insurance services.
7. The government's housing reforms have extended home ownership widely in Oman's major cities and have developed a healthy market in property insurance.

Weaknesses

1. Oman's insurance industry in practice remains "an oligopoly" with Omani companies dominating the insurance business.
2. A major weakness for both the domestic and foreign insurers is the lack of trained personnel in Oman, in terms of both sales and back office duties.
3. Despite the introduction of new laws and regulations affecting the industry, the supervisory and regulatory environment requires further relaxation.
4. Poor reputation and inefficient claim settlements are weaknesses within the industry.
5. There is a need for better and broader financial services in the changing country.
6. Insurance operations will be opened to all geographic areas within three years of WTO entry without economic needs, tests or quantitative limits

Opportunities

1. Entry to the World Trade Organization (WTO) could improve the development of the market. It is expected that foreign players would be further encouraged to enter the market.
2. WTO entry would also likely to ease restrictions on areas of insurance currently closed to foreign competitors such as private health insurance and pensions—which accounts for 85 per cent of the total insurance market.
3. The increase in the PCI will increase the receipt insurance of premium quantum.

4. The increase in percentage of injuries in accidents, a finding from this research, will increase the number of people opting for life insurance policies.
5. The increase in fatalities, a finding from this research, will give rise to the demand for life insurance services.

Threats

1. Many of the state-owned insurers believe that market deregulation has happened too fast and that the premature liberalization has adversely affected the development of the domestic industry to the favor of the foreign entrants.
2. Restrictions on the number of licenses issued to foreign-funded insurance companies will need to be further lifted so as to encourage further foreign investment in the sector.
3. The current geographical limits on foreign investment particularly in cities like Muscat and salalah in exclusion of other areas are also a threat to the development of foreign investment in the sector.
4. Currently the insurance laws stipulate that foreign partners in insurance joint ventures may hold no more than 50 per cent stakes and this is limiting foreign investment.
5. Recently established and new entrant insurers undercutting the existing market in order to derive market share will drive down prices and profitability.
6. The constraints imposed by Regulatory Authority on various categories of assets, give us the perception that we are unable to maximize investment returns.

Strategy

Some of the strategies the insurance industry can adopt are discussed below:

Bancassurance

Bancassurance (Bank assurance) represents a strategy whereby banks and insurance companies cooperate in more than one ways to tap the financial markets. The growth and development of banking industry in Oman can help the insurance company to adopt the new method of selling insurance services through banks. The entire bank customers require the insurance services and if both the industry can work together it can tap the opportunities lying in the insurance sector.

Potential of bancassurance lies not only in capturing the market share based on the existing premium turnover but also in increasing the insurance penetration thereby increasing overall premium turnover. The insurance penetration in general and life insurance penetration in particular is abysmally low compared to any other advanced country in the world and herein lies the potential of bancassurance.

Entire untapped market is the potential area which bancassurance can count upon. Compared to average per capita insurance premium of $ 919 in Europe, the average per capita premium in Gulf is $ 155 and in Oman it is only $ 77. The table below shows a comparison of per capita insurance premium of some countries in the Middle East and elsewhere and it also shows greater sales potential in Oman in future as the current per capita premium is par below the average of GCC.

Per Capita Premium in Select Countries

Region/Country	Per Capita Premium
USA	$ 3,266
Europe (Average)	$ 919
Switzerland	$ 4,343
UK	$ 3,394
GCC Countries (Average)	$ 155
UAE	$ 302
Bahrain	$ 220
Kuwait	$ 259
Oman	$ 77

Source: Sigma Report, Swiss Re

E-Business

Insurance companies are right now using the e-commerce technology only for the purpose of operations, educating or for providing information to the customers. The insurance industry can efficiently use the Web as a platform for dealing consumer transactions—specifically, sales. Insurance companies can use e-commerce technology by helping the people in handling the financial transactions in purchasing of insurance, conducting a stock trade, balancing and checking account-online.

The important advantage of selling online is that it can reduce the operating cost. It helps in reducing the number of branches, brokerage commission and other charges for the insurance company which in turn can reduce the premium amount charged to the customers. To be an effective service and distribution channel, it must be integrated with call centers. Some new features of e-commerce can be added including a Web Call-Back Button, which allows a Web user to be called by a customer service representative within fifteen minutes of the request; text-chat connectivity for help online can help in reaching the customer in time.

Customer Relationship Management

As insurance options broaden and services grow more complex, customers seek superior, personalized service more than ever. To maintain competitive edge and viability, insurance companies should focus intently on delivering superior customer service.

A comprehensive customer relationship management (CRM) strategy addresses three imperatives namely:

- providing a unified "Customer View";
- retaining customers with satisfied services; and
- controlling costs in the insurance company.

These three imperatives form a unique interplay that maximizes sales while reducing operational costs—the equation for improved revenue growth and profitability. Insurance companies certainly face a daunting challenge in maintaining and increasing their competitive edge. But by focusing on the above said three key imperatives, insurance companies can turn challenges into strategic/competitive advantage and enhance their long-term viability and profitability.

RECOMMENDATIONS AND CONCLUSION

The study revealed that life insurance is a low priority with most people in Oman. The reason for this is not difficult to guess at. As a concept, it is inextricably connected with problems of accidents and disasters, and not many people want to be linked with those. But the study also shows that there is drastic rise in the number of injuries and fatalities caused by road accidents. The Insurance industry should create awareness among people the necessity of taking life insurance because the worth of life is much more than that of a vehicle.

Insurance firms have to remodel their offerings and services. They have to take into account the population's changing financial concerns by issuing money-back schemes, education and mortgage protection plans and also catering to specific individual motivations.

If the insurance industries can "Create Awareness" in the minds of the people by explaining the following benefits of life insurance services, the current trend can be reversed:

1. Life insurance guarantees to pay a stated sum as per policy of assurance to a family on the death of its income earner(s). In so doing, it affords families a measure of protection against the adverse financial consequences of premature death; gives individuals a greater sense of economic security, and can help to reduce worry and distress and thereby increase initiative. No other privately purchased financial instrument can perform this function.
2. Cash value life insurance can serve as a means through which individuals save. Many persons who might not otherwise save consistently will, nonetheless, regularly pay their life insurance premiums; thus, life insurance might constitute a type of quasi-compulsory savings.
3. Life insurance services, especially annuities, provide a convenient means by which individuals can make financial provisions for retirement.

4. Life insurance can permit more favorable credit terms to borrowers—both individuals and businesses and can decrease the risk of default.

REFERENCES

Beenstock, M., Dickinson, G., and Khajuria, S. (1986). "The Determination of Life Premiums: An International Cross-Section Analysis 1970-1981", *Insurance: Mathematics and Economics*, 5, pp. 261-70.

Browne, M.J. and Kim, K. (1993). "An International Analysis of Life Insurance Demand", *Journal of Risk and Insurance*, 60, pp. 616-34.

Christensen, C.M. (1997). *The Innovator's Dilemma*, Harvard Business School Press, Boston.

Donnelly, J.H., Berry, L.L. and Thompson, T.W. (1985). *Marketing Financial Services*, Dow Jones- Irwin, Homewood, IL.

Gibbs, P.T. (1993). "Customer Care and Service: A Case for Business Ethics", *International Journal of Bank Marketing*, Vol. 11, No. 1, pp. 26-33.

Hammond, J.D., Houston, D.B. and Melander, E.R. (1967). "Determinants of Household Life Insurance Premium Expenditures: An Empirical Investigation", *Journal of Risk and Insurance*, 34, pp. 397-408.

Headen, R.S. and Finley, L.J. (1974). "Life Insurance Demand and Household Portfolio Behaviour", *Journal of Risk and Insurance*, 41, pp. 685-98.

Johne, F.A. and Pavlidis, P. (1996). "How Banks apply Marketing Expertise to Develop New Derivatives", *Journal of Product Innovation Management,* Vol. 13, pp. 440-52.

Sasser, W.E. (1976). "Match Supply and Demand in Service Industries", *Harvard Business Review*, November/December.

Semenik, R.J. and Bamossy, G.J. (1993). *Principles of Marketing: A Global Perspective*, South-Western Publishing Co., Cincinnati.

Websites:

http://www.emeraldinsight.com

http://www.msm.gov.com

http://www.oman.org

http://db.eiu.com

http://www.internationalinsurance.org

http://www.insurancetech.com

The Czech Insurance Market: Running Out of Breath?

18

Drahomira Dubska

ABSTRACT

Later this decade the insurance industry in the Czech Republic seems not to behave in accordance with "classical" way especially from point of view of the consumer demand in this part of the financial market. While in 2005, the Czech household´s gross disposable income was by two thirds higher as against 1995 and their consumption even by more than 70 per cent higher, premiums written also grew otherwise during some periods of the passed ten years, but nevertheless, recently the significant drop of the dynamics can be observed (especially in 2004 and 2005). Volume of the premiums written to GDP in current prices as a indicator of the intensity of the insurance in the economy even decreased in past two years. It is surprising fact because, generally, the stronger tendency to assure is typical for such phase of the countries´ development when households do not have to meet above all their basic needs and, therefore, the expenditure regarding insurance service can be increased—the CR seems to be undoubtedly in this phase of development. Thus, why people decided to reduce their expenditure on insurance? Why even catastrophic floods in 2002 could not change significantly their thinking?

Households give decreasingly from their budgets for insurance. The reasons can be found not only in increasing price of the insurance. Households objectively save fewer (saving rate decreases) which regards especially life insurance as well as hardly repeatable conditions connected with the trade policy of some big insurance companies. Last but not least, the collapse of dynamics in insurance market has "statistical" explication—the previous extreme growth of life insurance in the country caused by low market saturation and the benefits for clients sequent on the new legislation as well (especially tax breaks). Long-lasting (and neverending) debates about pension reform and the unavoidable need to have own money in an old age may influenced the clients' decisions where to allocate their savings. All of it ended in the extraordinary growth of the single premium throughout 2000-03. Besides in the last decade the insurance companies developed the products the Czech insurance market was not any experience by then. Lately insurance linked to investment fund became very attractive. But its strong growth, much more faster in compare with the total insurance market, is not sufficient impulsion for fast-moving of the market so far.

Nevertheless, the most significant score of the deceleration in insurance market is that the Czech Republic became the "paradise" of the consumption, which is fed on not only incomes from the work and private enterprise, but also, unfortunately, on savings created before.

JEL Classification: *D1, D31, G22, H24, H31*

Growth Rate of The Households' Expenditure on Insurance Diminishes

While the total current receipts of households[1] in the Czech Republic increase since 2000 (average annual growth rate during period 2000-05 was 5.3 per cent oscillating from 4.8 per cent in 2000 to for now the highest 6.0 per cent in 2003), on the contrary, the dynamics of their expenditure for safety through insurance is decreasing. In doing so, not only in non-life insurance the share of these costs on the total current households expenditure[2] has gone down but also—and fair dramatically—the dynamics of money which households send yearly to insurance companies as premiums written in life insurance[3] is decreased, as well. It is possible to see that people do not have wish for significantly more spending for property insurance not even when the catastrophic floods afflicted the Czech Republic in

2002. As well as the life insurance is not perceived as one of the important components of the provision for an old age.

The premiums written in life insurance in 2005 grew against 2004 by only 1.6 per cent when in half of the year even the fall of year-on-year volume was noticed. Disillusion of this development was all the more unwelcome in comparison with how much faster the previous growths were developed.

The Reasons of Previous Extreme Growth

On an average 1994-2005 the total premiums written grew by 14.2 per cent year-on-year, in life insurance even by 16.4 per cent. It is very strong dynamics. The biggest gains were quoted during 2001-03 with +20.2 per cent, respectively +24.2 per cent. Just this acceleration implicated notion that the life insurance in the Czech Republic could rise perhaps over and over again.

Underlying occasions of the exceeding accretions of life insurance were partly low market saturation by these products in the Czech Republic and partly also positive tax influence given by new legislation (tax allowance in case of saved sum during one year and duration length of insurance which are required according to Insurance Law). The massive marketing promotion regarding new legislation in insurance sector which highlighted the tax benefits impressed, as well. Long-lasting (and never-ending) debates about pension reform and unavoidable need to dispose of some own saved money certainly played important role at decisions of insurance companies´ clients where to allocate their savings. It results to enormous growth of money sent as single premiums to their accounts in insurance companies. Due to actual statistical methodology the single premium paid-in for 20 years is embodied in the sum of premiums only in the first year of contract duration but not in the next years. It results that in the future the total premiums in all insurance sector seem to be not so high in spite of fact that the clients are assured and part of their money is in the insurance companies as a saving (technical provisions).

Besides, during last decade the insurance companies implemented new products, which the Czech market had not experience with them yet. Since 2002, it is lately sophisticated insurance linked to investment fund become very attractive. But its strong growth, which is much more faster in comparison with the total insurance market, is not sufficient impulsion for fast-moving of the market so far.

Last Two Years the Czech Insurance Market Rises Slowly than Economy

In 2005, it was confirmed that cutting down of growth rate of the Czech insurance market was not only random fluctuation. However, the fall of the dynamics especially in life insurance does not seem to be fatal—above all previous development was extreme. That is a moot question whether the former growths can be repeatable.

During the most of the last decade, the Czech insurance market grew faster than economy according to gross domestic product (GDP) in current prices. But in 2004 and 2005 the growth of the market was slow, as shown in Figure 18.1. If GDP in current prices expanded by 8.1 per cent yearly in 2004, premium written grew by 6.6 per cent. In 2005, the Czech economy rose by 6.1 per cent and the insurance market according, premium increased by 3.7 per cent in that time. Nevertheless, during period 1993-2003 each of year the pace of the premium's growth was higher than the Czech economy growth rate, as Figure 18.2. Market weakening was caused shown in above all, by the worse performance in the sphere of the life insurance, as, Figure 18.3—the disappointment was significant especially in

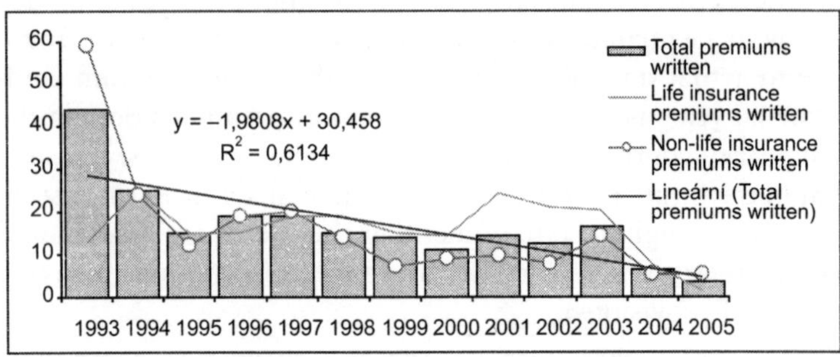

Figure 18.1: Insurance Companies' Premiums Written in the Czech Republic (1993-2005, % changes, y/y)

comparison with situation in 2001 when premium written boomed nearly by fourth part of volume of 2000.

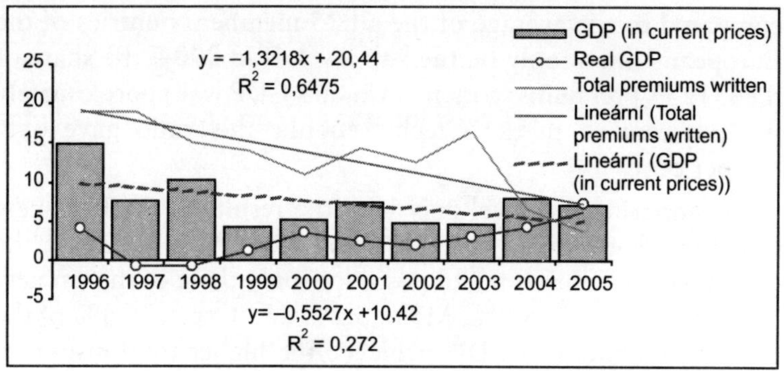

Figure 18.2: GDP and Premiums Written in the Czech Republic (1996-2005, % changes, y/y)

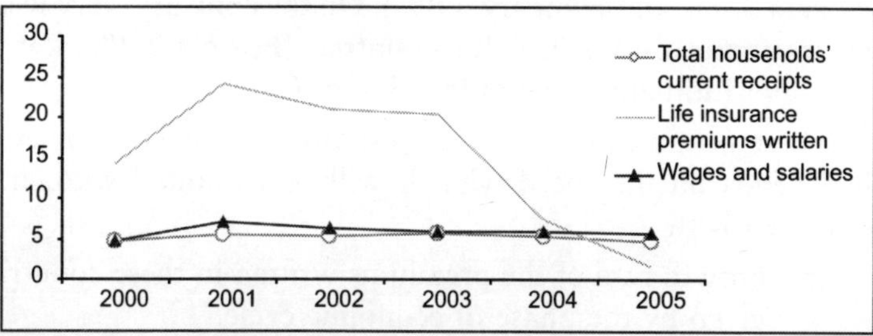

Figure 18.3: Life insurance and households' incomes in the Czech Republic (2000-2005, % changes, y/y)

Total Insurance Penetration Does not Grow on a Large Scale...

The development described above, i.e. the insurance market growth was slower than economic growth, must put on the total insurance penetration, defined as a ratio of premiums written to GDP. This indicator is always very low compared to the European Union 25 (the EU 25) average and the Czech Republic still lags far behind developed countries of the Europe. In addition, the results of 2005 caused that the favourable trend of this ratio observed during the previous years made a stop. The weaker performance of the life insurance market resulted to the decrement of the proportion of the whole sector in so far that relative decline was seen also in ratio of the total premiums to GDP.

... and It is Constantly Lower in European Context

In the Czech Republic the total insurance penetration is, compared to the average of the all 25 member countries of the European Union, only on the half level. If in 2004, the share of the EU 25's premiums written to Union's GDP was approximately 9.0 per cent so in the Czech Republic this ratio gave only 4.5 per cent.[4]

Comparing this level only with the results of the EU's new members that entered there in wave from May of 2004, the Czech Republic has not bad position—only three of the ten new members (Slovenia 5.8%, Malta 5.2% and Cyprus 4.8% of the premiums written to GDP) achieved the higher total insurance penetration. Slightly lower penetration was recorded in neighbouring countries of the Central Europe (Poland 3.6%, Slovakia 3.5% and Hungary 3.0%). On the contrary, very weak penetration is always in Baltic countries (Estonia 2.2%, Latvia 2.1% and Lithuania even only 1.3% of GDP).

These proportions indicate substantial potencial. However, all depends on the speed what it will be exploited with. It is connected with

(a) growth rate of the premiums written in these countries given by the phase of economic cycle,

(b) changes in the households´ behaviour (different accent on the consumption),

(c) range of the competition of the saving products which are offered by the other subject on the financial sector,

(d) progress in the reforms of the pension systems in these countries, etc.

Differences in Dynamics in Comparison with the EU

The view on the recent figures regarding the European insurance market shows the development of the premiums written in the Czech Republic in interesting light. Its dynamics based on the nominal explication (non-adjusted by inflation) was otherwise lower than the growth in the EU 25 in two parameters (total premiums written +6.6% against 7.8% in the EU 25 and also premiums in the life insurance premiums +7.5% against +9.1 %

in the EU 25), but the premiums written in non-life insurance grew in 2004 in the Czech Republic faster than the same indicator in EU 25 (+6.0% against +5.7%).

Different picture is possible to see with the figures considering inflation—due to slow increasing of the consumer prices in the Czech Republic (CPI 2.8% y/y in 2004, 1.9% in 2005) the statistics showed that Czech insurance market expanded faster than insurance market in EU 25 both in the total premiums written and also two branches (in the life insurance and in the non-life insurance, as well). Also in comparison with the figures comprising countries with the euro currency (eurozone) the Czech insurance market came up.

What Underlies Beyond the Weakening Dynamics

Do people really decide to cut their expenditure aimed to insurance? The insurance companies emphasize that so called current paid premiums written (not single premiums) has on the whole relative good dynamics. Its weight on the total premiums in life insurance is approximately two thirds—in 2004 it was 67.3 per cent of total premiums, in 2005 slightly more (72.4%). Single premiums in the Czech Republic achieved EUR 0.44 bil. in 2005, i.e. more than one quarter of the total premiums written in life insurance.

... a Less Money From Families' Budgets?

Households give decreasingly from their budgets for insurance. Share of the expenditure aimed to non-life insurance on the total households' current expenditure went down quickly—from 3.25 per cent in 2003 to 2.75 per cent in 2004 and in 2005 this share was only 2.63 per cent.

... Generally Weaker Savings?

The Czech households objectively save fewer (saving rate decreases) which regards especially life insurance. From macroeconomic point of view if the saving rate (as ratio of the households' gross saving in certain year to their yearly disposable income) was 14.2 per cent in 1995 then in 2005 it fell off to 7.3 per cent which is lower level in European context in spite of fact that the Czechs belonged to the most saving nations in

Europe for many decades ago. Therefore, if the tendency to save weaks now generally in the Czech households we can see this fact as one of the reasons why life insurance products with the saving component are not sold more successfully in this country.

... Non-reccuring Circumstances?

The conditions connected with trade policy of some big insurance companies on the Czech insurance market (which were visible three or five years ago) can be hardly repeatable now. For example, the biggest insurance company in the country, "Ceska pojistovna", had begun from 2001 to 2003 to convert the old insurance contracts with clients to new ones which were more expensive for clients. But this effect does not continue yet. Alike insurance company "Pojistovna CS" which is number three on the insurance market; its mother company is the biggest Czech retail bank with almost five mil. clients (the Czech Republic has ten mil. inhabitants and this fact describes very strong share of the market of this bank). In mentioned period this bank offered on its counters the possibility to convert the clients' money, till then saved as deposits on anonymous saving books, to any other form of deposits (it was enforced by new law). Single premiums seemed to be a good opportunity for it and this circumstance attracted hundreds of thousands of clients to the bank counters in that time. But naturally also this occasion of the massive growth of the premium written which was induced by trade policy of these big financial companies gave out soon afterwards.

Last, but not least, the collapse of dynamics in insurance market has "statistical" explication, i.e. high comparative base of the previous extreme growth in life insurance in the country caused by low market saturation and the benefits for clients sequent on the new legislation, as well (especially tax breaks).

...Competition of Another Financial Product?

In comparison with life insurance the flow of money towards competing financial products is more massive in the Czech Republic. Some insurance products especially in life insurance accentuate often so much the saving component that insurance companies can offer even only saving, without insurance.

Nevertheless, insurance of survival/death or survival, as a "classic" form which is mostly sought after by clients, holds the line very strong on the market.

If the life insurance with its capital component is the certain form of the saving for clients it is naturally exposed to the competition of some financial products, especially of these ones which are provided with the relief from state budget. In the Czech Republic there are:

(a) the pension saving with the 25 per cent state contribution to the monthly client's payment and with the tax allowance as well (in addition the currently imputed yields from side of pension funds, of course)

(b) saving construction which is directed not only for housing but many of clients use it as the "normal" saving because, after keeping necessary duration of the saving money on their saving construction accounts, they can withdraw all the sum and use it without announcement of the purpose (it needs not to be directed only for housing as mentioned above). The state contributes by 25 per cent of the yearly sum which client saves up. Moreover, the interest is attributed from side of the construction saving banks. All these deposits are assured in the Deposits Insurance Fund which was found by banking sector according to law.

Due to state contribution the effective interest rate in case of these two described financial products is more favourable for clients in comparison with life insurance. Therefore, it is handicaped by them. But they exist more than ten years on the market in parallel with the life insurance and only in last years the clients choose massively the pension saving (in 2005 almost one third of all population participates in pension funds). The construction saving was very popular since the beginning of its constitution in 1994 due to perfect balance of the yield and risk. But in the late of last decade the contributions became rather big burden on the expenditure side of the state budget. Therefore, the conditions for obtaining of state contribution for clients had to be tightened up since 2004.

With respect to the changes of the structure in the Czech households' savings the share of life insurance on total savings in 2005 was 8.7 per cent against 8.6 per cent in 2001. Basically, it is only stagnation of this share and in comparison with competing financial products the change of share is inexpressive—on the contrary, construction saving boosts its share on total households' saving in the Czech Republic from 10.6 per cent in 2001 to 20.8 per cent in 2005 and mutual funds from 5.8 per cent to 11.3 per cent. The pension saving has a slight share but it grow up gradually, as well (from 5.4% of the total households' saving in 2001 to 6.9 % in 2005) and it begins to be getting near the share of the life insurance.

Why Does Mortgage Boom not to Help

People borrow money for housing more and more. During 1997-2004 total value of the mortgages jumped almost twenty times and increased from 0.3 per cent of GDP in 1997 to 4.4 per cent in 2004. So including loans provided from construction savings (which are destined to housing, naturally) the total loans for housing amounted 7.4 per cent of GDP in 2004. The dynamics seemed to be fast but this share is always a lot less as compared with the situation in EU old member countries. In 2004, the value of loans for housing in the Czech Republic reached for 72 per cent of the value of the total credits given to the Czech households in that year.

From this point of view the question rises: why enormous interest in mortgages does not result in higher growth of premium written when the banks require the life insurance as a security for a debt? The answer is that the most routine form of credit insurance is only insurance covering the risk of death. The insurance company specify that (in a big average) the price of insurance covering risk of death is approximately only one tenth in comparison with the price of insurance on survival. It means that the saving component amounts 90 per cent in premium written and the risk component only 10 per cent. Or else, metaphorically, if only one capital insurance (with the saving component) should be compensate by risk insurance (with insurance on death), it would be necessary to compensate one "piece" by ten "pieces". And it is not possible to obtain simply.

Therefore, the decreasing of the capital insurance can be only very difficult caught up by the risk insurance. The mortgage market would have to grow up far more faster yet to be able to compensate the losses of the insurance companies which they sufferred in capital insurance.

Expensive Proprietary Insurance

Apparently non-life insurance seems to be expensive for the clients because the proprietary insurance show the increasing of insurance rate by the same way as accross the world taking into account higher price of reinsurance. Just it determines that price of insurance for the clients is higher. It seems to be the main reason why people in the Czech Republic do not learn from catastrophic floods which affected country neither in 1997 and above all in summer of 2002. The damage consequential on floods in 2002 was initially set too high a valuation, i.e. 4.5 per cent of GDP (it regarded not only sector of households but all economy). Lastly, the burden of losses was enumerated as 2.6 per cent of GDP and of all this almost two third paid the insurance companies.

Larger amount of money which clients directed to non-life insurance in 2003 was probably immediate aftermath of the disastrous floods in 2002. Nevertheless, in 2004 the drop could be noticeable and then, in 2005, stagnation of net premium in non-life insurance came on.

As mentioned above, during only two years (from 2003 to 2005) the share of households' expenditure for non-life insurance on their total current expenditure dropped by one fifth (from 3.25% to 2.63%).

Czech Households are not Poor

The empirical evidence confirms theoretical assessment that a lot of money directed to insurance is not spent in such economies where people have low earnings. Generally, that is to say, the insurance is financial product which does not keep forefront in rank of the preferences. Such situation is typical especially until the basic life necessaries are not supplied. This worldwide phenomenon is confirmed not only by ratio "expenditure for insurance/total current expenditure" in sector of households, but also by premiums written per capita and by insurance penetration as a proportion on GDP. In the Czech Republic there was not so deep fall of premiums written as in others the countries in period of transforming to the market economy. In some of these countries this underflow was even deeper than decreasing of their total economic activity (for example, in Balkan countries or in Russia the value of premiums written in 1995 was only 40% of level in 1988).

But the Czechs do not seem to be poor—in 2005 they have total saving (deposit in banks in Czech crowns and foreign currencies, mutual funds, construction savings, pension funds, technical provisions of life insurance, stocks and estimated money kept at home) on the level which was more than half thirds of GDP in current price. And in addition, during some last years they vehemently restructure these savings (due to low interest rates almost half of value of term deposit at the banks was passed to alternatives especially to construction saving), mutual funds (mostly the stock funds profiting from the development on capital markets) and pension funds, as well. Nevertheless, the life insurance stood slightly apart from this movements.

As far as 70 per cent of the Czech inhabitants said in surveys in the first months of 2006 that they create a financial reserves. But only one quarter of this number would by able to keep up these reserves more than at least six months, as said. Life insurance is one of the form of savings for the old age. In the light of the lower increases of insurance market during 2004 and 2005 (when expecially in 2005 the dynamics of the premium written was more than three times smaller than dynamics of the households´ current expenditure) can be observed that the Czech Republic is approching to the financial developed countries only very slowly in this area. For example, in Germany the savings in pension funds and technical provisions in life insurance participate on total households' saving by 29 per cent, in Great Britain this portion is even 57 per cent. The Czech households saved through these two products only 17 per cent of their total savings.

The branch of non-life insurance with the proprietary insurance and damage insurance put down in 2004 and 2005 the lowest dynamics year-on-year within last twenty years in respect of the whole insurance market. In the sector of households only the net premium written[5] showed stagnation in mentioned two years.

CONCLUSION

Insurance companies are not the saving banks. In the securing against risks the insurance company cannot be substituted but in intermediation of the saving it can. Volume of the premium written in life insurance is determined just by development of its saving (capital) component.

Maybe, the segment of life insurance could be strenghtened by higher rate of profit for the clients of insurance companies operating on the Czech market, maybe also more distinct declaration of its role as a way of the security in an old age with accent on its unreplaceable role in insurance against risk of death. In the first case it is possible to get it by higher interest rates or by decision of the insurance companies to pay out higher shares in profit to their clients. In the second mentioned case then it would be necessary to say final word regarding the prospective pension reform in the Czech republic.

NOTES

1. Total households' current receipts include according methodology of European Statistics Accounting (ESA 95) these items: D1 Employee compensation (as wages and salaries including social contribution from employers), D.4 Property income and D.7 Other current transfers (the part of them is also Compensation for non-life insurance). Data revised from 2002.
2. Total households' current expenditures include according methodology of European Statistics Accounting (ESA 95) these items: D.4 Expenditure on property, D.5 Current tax income, D.61 Social contributions, D.7 Other current transfers (inc. D.71 Net premiums in non-life insurance). Data revised from 2002.
3. ESA 95 monitors only item Net share of households on provisions in life insurance. But volume of the technical provisions can have different dynamics in comparison with dynamics of premiums written (differences are caused i.e. costs of insurance companies).
4. Annual Report of the Comité Européen des Assurance (CEA), June 2005.
5. Gross premiums written adjusted the payments for services.

REFERENCES

Annual Report 2004-05, Comité Européen des Assurance (CEA), pp. 5-9. http://www.cea.assur.org/

Annual Report 2004, Czech Insurance Association. Prague, 2005. http://www.cap.cz/english/dokument.aspx?id=21

Dubska, D. (2005). "Net balance of the Czech households´ property income decreases". *Czech Statistical Office: Analyses and Commentaiers*, May 2005. http://www.czso.cz/eng/csu.nsf/informace/akta052405.doc

Dubska, D. (2005). "Zmìny v sektoru domácností – úspory a zadluženost". *Czech Statistical Office: Case Study*. Prague, November 2005. Chap. 4.2. pp. 20-22. (Czech). http://www.czso.cz/csu/edicniplan.nsf/p/1533-05

Dubska, D. (2006). "Pojistný trh rostl loni opìt pomaleji než ekonomika", *Ekonom Weekly*, Prague, April 2006. (Czech). http://ekonom.ihned.cz/index.php?s1=4&s2=0&s3=0&s4=0&s5=0&s6=0&m=d&article[id]=18330390

Dubska, D. (2006). "Tempo výdajù èeských domácností na pojistnou ochranu se snižuje", *Czech Statistical Office: Analyses and Commentaiers*, Prague, June 2006. (Czech). http://www.czso.cz/csu/csu.nsf/informace/tv2006061506.doc

"European Life Insurance Market 2004", Comité Européen des Assurance (CEA), Eco N° 22, March 2006, http://www.cea.assur.org/cea/download/publ/article234.pdf

"The Single EU Insurance Market: How Does It Work? Frequently Asked Questions." (2006) Brussel, January 2006. http://www.cea.assur.org/cea/v1.1/actu/pdf/uk/annexe262.pdf

Multi-Channel Distribution in Life Insurance: Utopia or Reality?

Karunesh Saxena and
Rajendra Prasad Sharma

ABSTRACT

Life insurance industry in India is growing rapidly ever since the sector opened up for the private and foreign players. The industry is in the throes of competitive market forces. The new players have heightened up the competition by adopting and strategic marketing practices for getting a larger share of the market and the opportunity. The backbone of strategic marketing is the capability to have access-based penetration. Distribution channels have changed the way life insurance is being marketed. Apart from using the well-established agency channel, all the major players, particularly the private players have started using alternative channels for promotion and distribution of life insurance products. Some of these are bancasurance i.e. convergence of banking and insurance, e-marketing, etc. The rural areas require a separate dedicated channel for distribution involving tie ups with NGOs, etc.

Though none of the alternative channels as such are in position to replace the personal selling through the agents, the players have been vying with each through a combination of innovative channels in their endeavor to reduce the cost of distribution and satisfying the customers. In a country like India, the alternative channels might take time to prove their worth but they are also a differentiating tool. The present research paper makes an attempt to understand the practices in the area of distribution management as applicable in life insurance industry in India and explains the relative significance of personal selling based channels, evaluates the efficacy of newly emerging alternative channels, and examines the need for separate rural distribution channels. The paper establishes that every player today requires to design a hybrid multi-channel distribution mechanism for achieving their marketing objectives.

INTRODUCTION

Services sector forming an integral part of India's economy is evident from its more than 50 per cent contribution to the GDP. A vast spectrum of services are emerging and changing the landscape of business and marketing and insurance is one of the major constituents of the sector. The last five years have witnessed intensification of competition and the Indian insurance industry has shown a renewed vibrancy in terms of opportunities and challenges due to its opening up to the private and foreign players.

Innovative products, smart marketing, and aggressive distribution have enabled fledgling private insurance companies to sign up Indian customers faster than anyone expected. The private life insurance companies are making their presence felt through the use of unique and differentiated strategic marketing practices and approaches. One of them is use of innovative channels of distribution.

Against this backdrop, an attempt has been made in the present research paper to:

- (i) explain the role of distribution channels in life insurance marketing,
- (ii) chalk out the relative significance of personal selling based channels,
- (iii) evaluate the efficacy of newly emerging alternative channels,
- (iv) examining the need for rural distribution of insurance products, and
- (v) design the hybrid multi-channel distribution mechanism which is appropriate for the players in Indian life insurance industry.

Role of Distribution Channels in Life Insurance Marketing

The remarkable progress of the private players in the Indian life insurance market since its liberalization is evident from the fact that new players have got approx. 23 per cent of the total new business generated and the distribution channels have played a significantly crucial role in this laudable achievement. It has been established beyond doubt among the players that the distribution needs to be more vigorous as it holds the key for growth. Placement includes the various activities the company undertakes to make the product accessible and available to the target market. Stern et al. (1996) defined marketing channels as sets of interdependent organizations involved in the process of making a product or service available for use or consumption.

Gera (2003) has argued that distribution in the life insurance industry includes the promotion and the personal selling functions. The customer needs to be moved through the stages of awareness, interest, desire, action to generate a sale and then provide after-sale functions, viz. policy delivery, premium payment reminder and claims settlement, etc.

PERSONAL SELLING BASED CHANNELS

It is always to be kept in mind that "life insurance is seldom bought, it is always sold." Jawaharlal and Seethapati (2002) opined that most of the personal selling methods and techniques developed because of the challenges of selling unsought goods. Personal selling in life insurance is done primarily through the agents but of late the organizations have started having their own feet-on-the-street for the same.

(i) Agents

Conventionally, insurance products have been sold through agents, who are not the regular employees of the organization but the organizational success, however, critically depends on the effectiveness of these people (Bhat, 2005). An agent is the public face of an insurance company. Most of the insurance clients never get to see anyone else besides the agent. They are known by a myriad of names like financial advisors, insurance agents, life advisors and certified financial consultants.

Kalyani (2004) shared about the changing profile of an insurance agent in India due to the competition in the industry as well as other substitute investments like mutual funds and housing property to compete for the same rupee. Today, investment is becoming more sophisticated and the customer more demanding. Agents are more of a necessity because of the fact that insurance is primarily a concept that needs to be sold before the product and they play vital role in servicing the customers.

Jawaharlal (2003) too expressed that since insurance companies have realized the importance of prompt customer service in the competitive market, the insurance agents must have to be on their toes catering to the growing customer needs and serving them always. The future referrals can come from satisfied customers. The agents need to carry out jobs like collection of premia, revival of lapsed policies, nomination and assignment, grant of loans, payment of survival benefits, settlement of surrender value, policy alterations and the Settlement of claims.

The role of the agent today is becoming more and more important. The agents are linked to one insurer. They get a commission on the policies sold, which is usually a fixed percentage on the premium. The Indian experience shows that LIC, the monolithic organization has an agency force of more than ten lacs. In case of private players too, around 70 per cent of business is achieved through tied agency force. This necessitates that the agents interests have to be kept in mind while developing products.

(ii) Direct selling

Direct selling is normally done by the company executives. Since the agents in India primarily work on part-time basis, their commitment levels with the insurers is low. To reduce the dependence on the tied agents, companies have started looking at the direct sales channel. This channel is more useful for corporate sales i.e. group insurance business (Jampala, 2005) and even for catering to the High Networth Individuals (HNIs).

Selling insurance at the worksite has been happening for years under such names as: salary savings; payroll deduction; and now worksite marketing. Today, worksite marketing's importance continues to be demonstrated as a growth area. However, there are some challenges like the cost effectiveness, product customization and efficient post-sales servicing, which determine regular business, need to be delved upon.

ALTERNATIVE CHANNELS OF DISTRIBUTION

The life insurance players need to develop alternative distribution channels, as the traditional channels alone are not financially viable. India Infoline article, (August 2004) maintained that though currently, insurance agents are still the main vehicles through which insurance products are sold but in a huge country like India, one can never be too sure about the levels of penetration of a product. Traditionally, insurers in a top-down product development approach create products with features attractive to agents (Verma, 2004). Many new and innovative products conceived and developed by the LIC of India failed to take off because the commission rates offered to the agency force for selling these products and the incentives offered to the development officers were both not very attractive to them.

The commissions they are paid and the international productivity standard of 4-6 sales per month makes this a highly expensive distribution system overtime. It results in low productivity due to the amount of time the agent spends on prospecting or trying to find the right customer. Since they canvass business through the personal contacts, more than half of an agent's time goes towards prospecting, sometimes for deals that may not even fall in place. An illuminating research by Banumathy and Manickam (2004) concluded that agents offer good services before the policy is issued and while it is in operation but don't offer such services at the stage of maturity when a customer approaches them for settlement of claims. It, therefore, makes sense to look at well-balanced, alternative channels of distribution.

Though LIC is well-established and have an extensive reach and presence, the new players find it expensive and time consuming to bring up a distribution network to such standards. Yet, if they want to make the most of India's large population base and reach out to a worthwhile number of customers, making use of other distribution avenues becomes a must. Alternate channels will help to bring down the costs of distribution and thus benefit the customers. Prominent alternate channels in practice are being presented in this section.

(i) Bancassurance

Bancassurance is the convergence of banking and insurance. It involves distribution of insurance products through a bank's branch network. While bancassurance has developed into a tremendous success story in Europe, it is a relatively new concept in Asia, and of course in India. Bancassurance has been developing as an alternative channel of the agents/advisors selling personally. The next section deals with how the synergy between the insurer and the bank is achieved. The Table 19.1 below shares a partial list of insurance companies and their bank tie-ups.

Table 19.1: Insurance Companies and Their Bank Tie-ups

Insurance Company (Life)	Banks
Birla Sun Life Insurance	Bank of Rajasthan, Andhra Bank, Bank of Muscat, Development Credit Bank, Deutsche Bank and Catholic Syrian Bank, Citibank.
Aviva Life Insurance	Canara Bank, Lakshmi Vilas Bank, American Express Bank and ABN-AMRO Bank.
HDFC Standard Life Insurance	Union Bank of India, HDFC Bank, Indian Bank.
ICICI Prudential Life Insurance	Lord Krishna Bank, ICICI Bank, Bank of India, Citicorp, Allahabad Bank, Federal Bank, South Indian Bank, Punjab and Maharashtra Co-Operative Bank.
Life Insurance Corporation of India	Corporation Bank, Indian Overseas Bank, Centurion Bank, Vijay Bank, Oriental Bank of Commerce, Central Bank.

(Contd...)

Insurance Company (Life)	Banks
Met Life India Insurance	Karnataka Bank, Dhanalakshmi Bank and J & K Bank.
SBI Life Insurance	State Bank of India, Rural Banks, State Bank Affiliates.
Tata AIG Life	HSBC, Bank of Rajasthan
Bajaj Allianz Life Insurance	Standard Chartered
ING Vysya Life	ING Vysya Bank
Max New York	Yes Bank, Thane Janta Coop Bank

Source: Chari (2003).

In India, there are around 65000 branches of banks and approximately each branch caters to around 15000 customers. These banks possess inside information about the financial needs and savings preferences of their customers. For insurance companies this becomes an untapped and successful mode of distribution. In India, sales are already underway through insurance staff located in bank branches and also through bank staff directly. Aggarwal (2004) stated that the results from both models have been very encouraging showing that there is no single universal model and what is of supreme importance is the quality of performance.

(ii) Corporate Agents and Brokers

Corporate agents are tie-ups with non-banking finance companies to act as corporate agents. The corporate agency system works a lot like brokers, except for the fact that they are restricted to selling a single insurer's products. There are more than 1000 corporate agents in the country. Brokers are distinct intermediaries in the life insurance distribution system. Contrary to agents and corporate agents, brokers are supposed to be directly looking to the interest of the customers and not the insurance company. The client appoints a broker and he conducts a fact finding on customer's need and his financial position to properly represent his client to the insurers.

Verma (2004) commented that the brokers are specialists and are unlike agents. They facilitate insurance activity on the most basic level, by getting clients the protection they need at the price they can afford and at the time they need it. Agents may not be able to strike best deals, as they do not have access to the entire insurance market but brokers can do wonders for their clients.

(iii) e-channels

Most insurance companies, particularly the traditional ones do not have automated systems for product offerings and quote generation, leave aside the issue to generating policies and accepting transactions online. Some of the insurance companies are reluctant to automate their product offering to the consumer for fear that such complex products cannot sell without a traditional human interface. Figure 19.1 and 19.2 below depict the use of IT in insurance marketing and the multi channel distribution systems the marketers use.

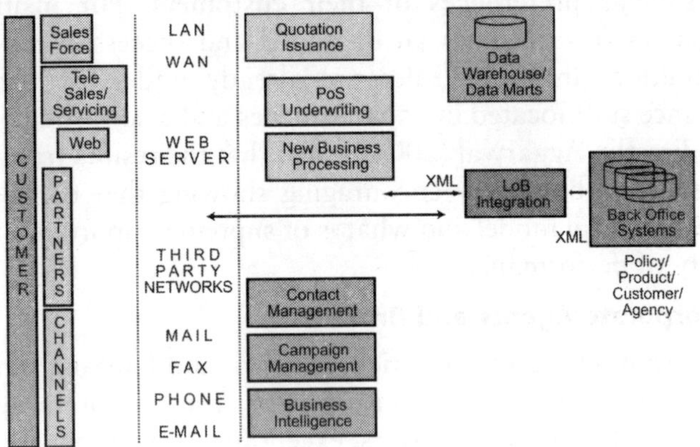

Figure 19.1: Use of IT in Insuarnce Marketing

Source: http://www.wipro.com/pdf_files/Wipro_XML_in_Insurance.pdf, Rai, UK (2005) *Realising XML benefits in Life Insurance*, White Paper, Wipro Technologies

Chandarashekahar and Das (2003) too maintained that the technology not only creates new business opportunities, but also improves the business profitability and efficiency. LIC can have a competitive advantage over private players, as they have a large amount of past data generated over the years though their problem could be that they are data-rich but information-poor.

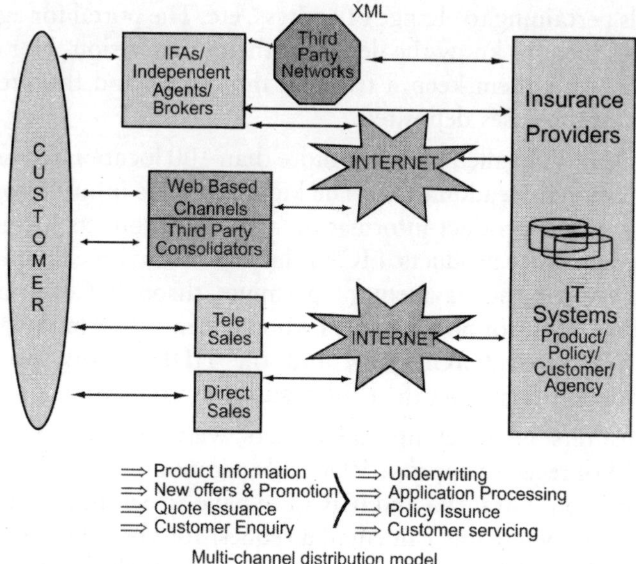

Figure. 19.2: Multi-channel Distribution of Insurance Services

Source: http://www.wipro.com/pdf_files/Wipro_XML_in_Insurance.pdf, Rai, UK (2005) *Realising XML benefits in Life Insurance*, White Paper,Wipro Technologies

E-channel practices of players: Almost all the players have websites. The sites offer a set of services such as a Bonus Calculator, Insurance Advisor, Tax Calculator, etc. LIC has been one of the pioneering organizations in India, which ushered in the use of information technology in their business on a very large scale to deliver more value and satisfaction to the policyholders. Koirivi (2004) shared about the LIC's initiative of a massive data warehousing project to get a holistic picture of customers i.e. to capture, study and analyze their purchase behaviour patterns, their needs and desires.

LIC has launched two portals—One for the customers and the other for agents. The portal meant for customers helps them to view the status of their respective policies. They can also know the amount of loan they can get against their policy. They can download the forms needed to purchase another policy. In addition to this, they can also deposit the premiums and the details pertaining to change of address, etc. The portal for agents enables them to know the details of their commission. Not only this, it helps them keep a track of the claims and the present status of the cases deposited.

LIC has installed kiosks at more than 100 locations covering its Divisional Headquarters. The kiosks provide information on policy status, product information about all products including group insurance products. LIC has launched 'Anytime Premium,' a facility for the payment of premium through Corporation Bank's ATMs, for policyholders who are depositors in the bank. The ATMs of ICICI Bank and the HDFC Bank provide information regarding their life insurance products.

Insurers have set up call centers with toll-free numbers. ICICI Pru receives approx. 5000 calls per month as inquiries for information. Tata AIG and ICICI Pru have an arrangement with rediff.com where one can email a request for visit of company's agent. Tata AIG sends direct mailers to HSBC customers. Premium can be paid thru credit cards or free courier pick ups. Follow-up calls by a pleasant voice are made. Everyone is using push marketing strategy. Even ICICI Pru and HDFC Standard have been using parent company's databases.

(iv) Other Channels

There are other direct marketing practices like marketing through mailers, pamphlets, etc. The products sold through the mailers are customized, simple products. The unavailability of good database in India, and the high expenses to reach the target audience through direct mailers is a cause for concern.

Ramesh (2004) expresses that insurance selling appears to be going the 'home loans' way, where all a player requires is to set up a point-of-sale i.e. a canopy, a desk and a chair. These little 'offices' have sprung up in places least suspected them to be present in and clearly, insurance is going to be pretty much the same. Like the other oil companies, HPCL too is straining its eye on the customer, doing up the retail outlets and throwing in a few extra conveniences. Insurance is one of them. Starting with motor insurance the HPCL outlets are looking at selling all types of insurance. Insurance industry experts are hardly surprised.

Soon, medical shops could be selling medical insurance. Innovation in distribution channels is the order of the day, and perhaps one factor that could make a difference to a company in the competitive market.

Chief Post-Master General of Chennai has mooted the idea of 'retailassurance', where some products, after being cleared by IRDA, could be sold by any retail outlet—such as post offices. There are 1.53 lakh post offices in the country, more than twice the number of bank branches, which can potentially sell some pure vanilla products.

For promoting sales of its Smartkid policy, ICICI Prudential has tied up with Derek O'Brien, the quizmaster of Bournvita quiz contest and Brand equity quiz to facilitate access to parents of children studying in selected schools in 25 cities. This Derek -Knowledge Quiz Advantage offers soft skills training to the students.

AN EVALUATION OF THE ALTERNATIVE CHANNELS

Since there have been many channels in use, it makes sense for the players to understand the efficacy of alternative channels. Shikha Sharma, MD, ICICI Prudential Life Insurance opined that alternate channels now contribute more than 25 per cent of the business. Table 19.2 shows the percentage of business generated by life insurance companies in India using alternative channels.

Table 19.2: Percentage of Business Through Alternative Channels

Company	% of business
Aviva	70
SBI Life	53
Birla Sunlife	35
ICICI Pru	30
Bajaj Allianz	25
Max New York	23
HDFC Standard	22
ING Vysya	17
LIC	0.49

Source: Chari VG (2005) "Insurance: A re-look at the distribution strategy" *Insurance Chronicle*, March 2005, The ICFAI University press pp. 28-36.

Though Aviva and SBI life have been getting reasonable success in the bancassurance channel, still both of them are too keen to expand their distribution channels through agency system. Though the emerging channels of distribution, are relatively cheaper than the traditional agent, their effectiveness as a promotional tool is much less. No player can bank only on any single promotional tool i.e. advertising, promotion, Direct Marketing, PR or personal selling. All of them need to be integrated to deliver the required result from the target segment. Thus, instead of treating the emerging channels only as distribution channel *per se*, there is a need to treat them as promo-cum-distribution channels.

90% of life insurance the world over is sold through agents since it is a complex product. The business generated will continue to be the maximum from the tied agent's route. Selling of life insurance requires personal interface. Selling of life insurance through banks or bancassurance raises a number of issues that needs to be addressed. First of all, selling of life insurance is more difficult and takes more time than persuading people to open fixed deposit accounts.

The products that sell well through bancassurance are commodotised term and annuity products. Also, products that combine insurance and banking needs help to create demand such as loan cover, term assurance and simple products that can be sold over-the-counter at banks. Another advantage is that banks, with their network in rural areas, help to fulfill rural and social obligations stipulated by the Insurance Regulatory and Development Authority (IRDA).

Mishra (2004) tracked the feedback obtained from some existing bancassurance customers and discovered that 13 per cent customers did not know the details of policy they have purchased and its future usage or benefits, 19 per cent customers felt they have not got sufficient cover for insurance needs of their family, 96 per cent of customers rated LIC as the best financially stable insurance company and 17 per cent of customers felt private insurers can better service the claims than PSU insurers but rest 83 per cent considered PSU insures as better in claim paying ability and systems.

Rao (2004) expressed his views that the number of policies sold through bancassurance model is modest as of now. Those in charge of sales should be trained adequately to avoid any miscommunication. Kumar (2000) in the SWOT analysis of the Bancassurance system mentioned about obstacles bancassurance faces in India. Parihar (2004) opined that even in bancassurance where career agents, special advisors or the salaried agents are utilized, personal selling assumes an important role. Insurance products with low complexity can be sold through bancassurance but products with high complexity will have a lot of difficulty in terms of time, effort and cost to train bank employees.

In India, the Internet is yet to take shape as an alternative sales channel since insurance is still a product that is 'sold and not bought'. However, the internet is still a valuable, facilitating medium to conclude actual sales transactions. Call centres are utilised only for generating leads. As the market keeps expanding, call centres have the potential of becoming an important medium for customer relationship management (CRM) and upselling to the customers.

RURAL DISTRIBUTION CHANNELS

There is excellent opportunity in the insurance industry to employ access-based positioning by targeting the rural insurance sector. For rural marketing, the companies are looking forward to the advisors with thorough knowledge of products and local language and who have an ability to work very hard. They also must be well versed in the art of public speaking and having excellent public relations with the local/state government and municipality officials.

The players in rural markets are now exploring new distribution channels like a tie-up with the Micro Finance Institutions (MFIs). The FOTRTE research found out that there is an extensive network built by the rural development agencies, the banks, the cooperative institutions, the NGOs and even some industrial houses in the rural sector. They have advised the insurance players to work out collaborative arrangements with these institutions for a mutual advantage. Moreover, Self-help Groups, youth clubs and co-operative societies can be utilized for the group insurance policies too. Besides this, to extend its services to rural areas, LIC is looking forward to increase its satellite branches, specifically in rural areas. Presently, it has 24 satellite centers nationwide.

The channels for distribution of insurance products in rural areas are the panchayats, district cooperative banks, agriculture and dairy cooperatives, and of course the agents. Since no player is using these channels for effective rural reach, it can well be said that the rural market is not sleeping any longer; the insurance players are. The NGOs based in rural areas and cooperatives are helping the new players get a foothold in the rural market. These channels have the potential to make the difference as they enjoy the trust of the people. ICICI Prudential Insurance and HDFC Standard Life Insurance have partnered with NGOs to sell some low cost insurance in rural areas.

HYBRID MULTI-CHANNEL DISTRIBUTION

Bhat (2005) maintains that keeping in mind of complexities of the industry, multi-product, multi-segment and multi-channel route needs to be followed for growth. Muralidharan (2004) has enlisted the distribution channels being utilized by the life insurance industry. They include tied agents, direct selling, corporate agents, group selling, worksite marketing, brokers and cooperative societies, call centres, marketing through mailers, etc.

The private players are using multi-pronged attack strategy and hybrid Multi-channel distribution is must for fighting the warfare in Indian life insurance market. The experiences of private players proves the point beyond doubt. Sujit Ganguli, head of marketing, ICICI Prudential life opined that their multi-channel distribution model has greatly helped them to quickly ramp up their base and reach out to a diverse customer base. Rohit Mull, Vice-president, Marketing, Tata-AIG Life held that keeping customer convenience in mind, they offer their products closer to doorstep and thus, are able to reach out to a wider base.

To sum up, it is apparent that multiple distribution channels will help an insurance company to offer a range of contact points to the customer, thereby increasing the chances of success.

All the alternative channels discussed in the paper like bancassurance, rural marketing channels like NGO and e-marketing hold lot of potential in the future. However, alongwith these distribution channels comes the challenge of relationship management, and therefore, agents as a distribution channel may not be replaced fully. Complex insurance products need a considerable amount of sales push as one has to find prospects, create need awareness and then provide solutions in the form of advice and access to products.

REFERENCES

Aggarwal, V. (2004). "Bancassurance: Concept, Framework & Implementation" *The Journal of Insurance Institute of India*, Jul-Dec., pp. 34-51.

Bhat (2005). "Insurance Industry in India: Structure, Performance & Future Challenges," *Colloquium,* Vikalpa, IIMA, Vol. 30 No.3, July-Sept. 2005

Banumathy, S. and Manickam, S. (2004). "Customer Services provided by Life Insurance Corporation of India—A Case Study", *The Insurance Times*, June, pp. 30-33.

Chandarashekahar and Das (2003). "Data Warhouse, Datamining & CRM" National Insurance Academy, *Bimaquest*, July.

Chari, V.G. (2003). Bancassurance: A Business Sourcing Model to Indian Banks, *Insurance Chronicle*, Sept. 2003, The ICFAI University Press pp. 32-35.

—— (2005). "Insurance: A re-look at the Distribution Strategy", *Insurance Chronicle*, March 2005, The ICFAI University Press, pp. 28-36.

Gera, R. (2003). "Distribution of life Insurance in India—A Fresh Perspective", *Insurance Watch*, April, pp. 30-32.

Rai, UK (2005). "Realising XML benefits in Life Insurance", White Paper,Wipro Technologies. http://www.wipro.com/pdf_files/Wipro_XML_in_Insurance.pdf.

India Infoline; "Alternative Channels of Insurance Distribution" article (retrieved on 21 August 2004).

Jampala, R.C. (2005). "Insurance Sector: Emerging Distribution Channels", *Indian Journal of Marketing*, July 2005, pp. 24-27.

Jawaharlal, U. and Seethapati, K. (2002). *Life Insurance Vol. II, Insurance series*, ICFAI University, Annexure pp. 33-54.

Jawaharlal, U. (2003). "Customer Service: Challenges Ahead", *Insurance Chronicle*, Sept. ed., The ICFAI University Press, pp. 20-22.

Kalyani, K.N. (2004). *IRDA Journal* Volume III No. 1, Dec. 2004.

Koirivi, S.R. (2004). "Insurance Sector in India—Challenges Ahead", *Insurance Chronicle,* January, pp. 38-40.

Kumar, M. (2000). "Bancassurance: A SWOT Analysis", *Financial Express*, April 11, retrieved from http://www.einsuranceprofessional.com/ inscomp.htm.

Mishra, K.C. (2004). "Bonding Benefits", *Asia Insurance Post*, Nov. pp. 17-18.

Muralidharan, S. (2004). "Distribution Strategies: New Avenues" *Chartered Financial Analyst*, February.

Parihar (2004). "Bancassurance: Challenges and Opportunities in India," *Insurance Chronicle*, July 2004, pp. 51-56, The ICFAI University Press.

Rao, C.S. (2004). "Emergence of Bancassurance in India," Address at the Banking Technology Excellence Awards (2003-04) & Launch of National Financial Switch on 27th August, 2004 at IDRBT.

Stern et al. (1996). *Marketing Channels*, 5th ed., Prentice Hall.

Verma, V. (2004), "Insurance Broking In India: Scope Challenges and Prospects" *The Journal of Insurance Institute of India*, Jul- Dec., pp. 106-116.

Service Sector Marketing in the Global Era: A Case Study

20

Pramod Pathak

ABSTRACT

Globalization has initiated far-reaching changes in Economies across the world. India is no exception. Providers of Financial services are a case in point. There was a time when Indian Corporate Giant Life Insurance Corporation of India had a virtual monopoly in Insurance and there was no need for them to be customer friendly. Once the Indian Markets were opened up, private and government players from India and abroad entered the Indian Insurance Market and the whole complexion of the game changed. Against this backdrop, the present paper is conceived and it takes into account the ground realities that exist today for Life Insurance Corporation of India and what strategies it is adopting to cope with competition, national and international. The leader that Life Insurance Corporation of India was has been forced on the backfoot and is fighting to survive. This study takes into account the various strategic marketing initiatives that the Insurance giant is taking to retain its foothold in the dynamic Life Insurance Market in India.

Services play a key role in Indian economy. Industries that deliver help, utility, experience, information, or other intellectual content have expanded rapidly in recent decades and now account for more than 70 per cent of total value added stream. Market-based services (that is, excluding those typically provided by the public sector, such as education, health care, and government) account for 50 per cent of the total and have become the main driver of productivity and economic growth in India, especially as use of IT services has grown. The growing importance of services in the economy implies that efforts to improve standards of living, boost productivity, and create jobs must focus increasingly on the service sector. Whereas, the service sector has often been characterized as a locus of low wage, unproductive, and un-innovative jobs, recent evidence gained through innovation surveys and better statistical data discredits this view, confirming that services are indeed innovative and, in some areas, more innovative than manufacturing. In fact, knowledge-intensive services, whose value added is intangible rather than incorporated in physical products, play an increasingly dynamic and pivotal role in today's knowledge-based economy, contributing to innovation in all economic sectors.

Marketing of services has always been a difficult task. The main reason has been the abstract nature of services. Insurance giant LIC, a leading service sector organization was till very recently enjoying a monopoly and very little efforts were needed on the part of the company to reach the customers The state owned LIC sold insurance as a tax instrument, not as a product giving protection. Most customers were under-insured with no flexibility or transparency in the products. However, with the opening up of the insurance sector in 1999, and the entry of the powerful private insurers the rules of the game have changed and with the rapid dwindling of its market share, LIC is slowly waking up to the need for marketing. Thus, it is now trying to create a need for insurance, reach the customer, create awareness among masses and maintain a close relationship with the customer. There is a growing emphasis on new innovative products, better distribution channels and better customer service. Instead of plain vanilla insurance, today innovative features like free-look period, automatic cover maintenance, and riders like double sum assured, critical illness are being offered. The power of IT is being harnessed to provide better customer services. The alternative channel of distribution like bancassurance and corporate tie-ups are being explored. The advertising slogans have undergone a sea change from emphasis on providing protection to the family in case of accidental death, to providing a comfortable life in post-retirement phase. Against this backdrop, the case study of LIC has been carried out.

INSURANCE SECTOR—THE PARADIGM SHIFT

Historical Perspective and Evolution

Although the concept of insurance is a development of the recent past, the story of insurance is perhaps as old as mankind itself. Its beginning can be traced back to almost 6000 years with the evolution of village and community life by ARYANS. The term 'Yogakshema', which means 'well-being' is used in the Rig-Veda suggesting that some form of community insurance was practiced by Aryans in India over 3000 years ago. There are references in Kautilya's Arthashastra to some kind of social security system for the welfare of the subjects. Scientific life assurance is a heritage from England, where the first life policy providing temporary cover for a period of twelve months was issued as early as 1583 A.D. The development of mortality table was a landmark in the history of life assurance.

Life Insurance in its modern form came to India from England in the year 1818. Oriental Life Insurance Company started by Europeans in Calcutta was the first life insurance company on Indian Soil. All the insurance companies established during that period were brought up with the purpose of looking after the needs of European community and Indian natives were not being insured by these companies. However, later with the efforts of eminent people like Babu Muttylal Seal, the foreign life insurance companies started insuring Indian lives. But Indian lives were being treated as sub-standard lives and heavy extra premiums were being charged on them. Bombay Mutual Life Assurance Society heralded the birth of first Indian life insurance company in the year 1870, and covered Indian lives at normal rates. Starting as Indian enterprise with highly patriotic motives, insurance companies came into existence to carry the message of insurance and social security through insurance to various sectors of society. Bharat Insurance Company (1896) was also one of such companies inspired by nationalism. The Swadeshi movement of 1905-07 gave rise to more insurance companies. The United India in Madras, National Indian and National Insurance in Calcutta and the Co-operative Assurance at Lahore were established in 1906. In 1907, Hindustan Co-operative Insurance Company took its birth in one of the rooms of the Jorasanko, house of the great poet Rabindranath Tagore, in Calcutta. The Indian Mercantile, General Assurance and Swadeshi Life (later Bombay Life) were some of the companies established during the same period. Prior to 1912 India had no legislation to regulate insurance business. In the year 1912, the Life Insurance Companies Act, and the Provident Fund Act were passed. The Life Insurance Companies Act, 1912 made it necessary that the premium rate tables and periodical valuations of companies should be certified by an actuary.

The first two decades of the twentieth century saw lot of growth in insurance business. From 44 companies with total business-in-force as Rs. 22.44 crore, it rose to 176 companies with total business-in-force as Rs. 298 crore in 1938. During the mushrooming of insurance companies many financially unsound concerns were also floated which failed miserably. The Insurance Act 1938 was the first legislation governing not only life insurance but also non-life insurance to provide strict state control over insurance business. The demand for nationalization of life insurance industry was made repeatedly in the past but it gathered momentum in 1944 when a bill to amend the Life Insurance Act 1938 was introduced in the Legislative Assembly. However, it was much later on the 19th of January 1956 that life insurance in India was nationalized. About 154 Indian insurance companies, 16 non-Indian companies and 75 provident were operating in India at the time of nationalization. Nationalization was accomplished in two stages: initially the management of the companies was taken over by means of an Ordinance, and later, the ownership too by means of a comprehensive bill. The Parliament of India passed the Life Insurance Corporation Act on the 19th of June 1956, and the Life Insurance Corporation of India was created on 1st September, 1956, with the objective of spreading life insurance much more widely and in particular to the rural areas with a view to reach all insurable persons in the country, providing them adequate financial cover at a reasonable cost.

Thus, the LIfe Insurance Corporation of India came into existence on the 1st day of September 1956. To remember this historic event insurance week is celebrated from 1st to 7th of September every year thereafter. The objective of nationalization were defined as conducting the business with utmost economy in true sense trusteeship, to charge premium no higher than narrated by strict actuarial consideration and to invest the fund for obtaining maximum yield consistent with safety of capital and render prompt and efficient services to the policyholders.

LIC had 5 zonal offices, 33 divisional offices and 212 branch offices, apart from its corporate office in the year 1956. In the later years to expand the operations and place a branch office at each district headquarter, re-organization of LIC took place and large numbers of new branch offices were opened. As a result of re-organisation servicing functions were transferred to the branches, and branches were made accounting units. It worked wonders with the performance of the corporation. It may be seen that from about 200.00 crores of New Business in 1957 the corporation crossed 1000.00 crores only in the year 1969-70, and it took another ten years for LIC to cross 2000.00 crore mark of new business. But with re-organisation happening in the early eighties, by 1985-86, LIC had already crossed 7000.00 crore Sum Assured on new policies.

Today, LIC functions with 2048 fully computerized branch offices, 100 divisional offices, 7 zonal offices and the Corporate office. LIC's Wide Area Network covers 100 divisional offices and connects all the branches through a Metro Area Network. LIC has tied up with some Banks and Service providers to offer on-line premium collection facility in selected cities. LIC's ECS and ATM premium payment facility is an addition to customer convenience. Apart from on-line Kiosks and IVRS, Info Centres have been commissioned at Mumbai, Ahmedabad, Bangalore, Chennai, Hyderabad, Kolkata, New Delhi, Pune and many other cities. With a vision of providing easy access to its policyholders, LIC has launched its Satellite Sampark offices. The satellite offices are smaller, leaner and closer to the customer.

The digitalized records of the satellite offices will facilitate anywhere servicing and many other conveniences in the future.

LIC continues to be the dominant life insurer even in the liberalized scenario of Indian insurance and is moving fast on a new growth trajectory surpassing its own past records. LIC has issued over one crore policies during the current year. It has crossed the milestone of issuing 1,01,32,955 new policies by 15th Oct 2005, posting a healthy growth rate of 16.67 per cent over the corresponding period of the previous year.

LIBERALIZATION AND TRANSFORMATION OF THE INSURANCE SECTOR

The first step towards liberalization can be said to have been initiated in 1993 when the then Government headed by P.V. Narasimha Rao set up the Malhotra Committee under the chairmanship of insurance secretary and RBI governor R.N. Malhotra. The frame of reference of this committee was to evaluate the Indian insurance industry and recommend its future direction. The committee submitted its report in 1994 and recommended structural and regulatory changes to suit a newly liberalized regime. One recommendation was to bring down the stakes in the insurance companies to 50 per cent and private companies with a minimum capital of Rs. 100 crore to be allowed entry in the industry. The most significant recommendation was opening the industry to foreign players in collaboration with domestic companies.

The Insurance Regulatory and Development Authority (IRDA) act was passed and IRDA was formed in the year 2000. The authority promulgated regulations covering various activities of the insurance companies, both in public and private sectors. The idea was to regulate the conduct of insurance business in the best interest of various stakeholders. For regulating the insurance sector, the Authority has been issuing regulations covering almost the entire segment of the insurance industry, namely, regulation on insurance agents, solvency margain, re-insurance, registration of insurers, accounting procedures, etc.

The insurance industry in India is now open and the new entrants have already started capturing the market share of LIC.

With the liberalization of insurance industry and its deregulation the strong private players from India and abroad with strong financial muscle have entered the market and are forging formidable collaborations with each other. There are fifteen players in the life insurance sector till date, which are competing with each other to garner a substantial pie of the entire life insurance business in India. The monopoly status of LIC is now being threatened and it is slowly losing market share to other entrants. One estimate is that LIC has lost some 15 per cent already and the contenders are adopting aggressive marketing strategy such as adoption of bancassurance by Aviva that the private players may soon give LIC a run for their money. With government no longer sympathetic to the state owned corporation and FDI in the insurance sector to be increased from 26 per cent to 49 per cent, LIC has to fend for itself. To borrow the catchphrase from their competitor AVIVA they need to think about exercising **Kal Par Control** (Control on future) as they are slowly losing market share to other entrants. LIC has realized this and is gearing to take up the challenge by devising effective marketing strategies.

LIFE INSURANCE PRODUCTS

Life insurance products usually veer around two basic elements—**Risk cover** (benefit payable in the event of death) and **Savings** (benefit payable in the event of survival). However, in India life insurance policies have often been viewed as a means of tax saving, particularly for the salaried class. Thus, we can say that plans of life insurance are combinations of all three elements—risk cover, savings and tax incentives.

Generally, the following types of plans are available:

Term Life—Here, the sum assured is payable in the event of death during the term, e.g. LIC's Term Policy.

Whole life Insurance—Here, the risk is covered for the entire life of the policyholder and the policy money plus the bonus are payable to the nominee or the beneficiary only on the death of the policyholder, e.g. LIC's Whole Life with Profits, LIC's Convertible Whole Life Policy.

Endowment Type Plans—These policies cover risks for a specified period at the end of which the sum assured is paid back to the policyholder along with bonuses, e.g. LIC's New JanaRaksha Policy, LIC's Bhavishya Jeevan Sp. Endowment Policy, LIC's Jeevan Saral, LIC's Jeevan Samridhi.

Money Back Policy—It is actually a variation of the endowment policy. It is intended to provide protection and a periodic benefit to meet certain unplanned expenses, e.g. LIC's Jeevan Surabhi, LIC's Jeevan Rekha.

Combination of Whole Life and Endowment Type Plans—e.g. LIC's Jeevan Anand.

Children Assurance Plans—These are deffered assurance plans providing risk cover on the life of child after it has attained 18 years of age, e.g. LIC's Jeevan Kishore, LIC's Komal Jeevan.

Annuity and Pension Plans—In these plans when a person purchases a life insurance contract, he agrees to make a series of payments (premiums) to the insurer and in return the insurer agrees to pay a specified sum to the beneficiaries, e.g. LIC's Jeevan Dhara, LIC's Jeevan Akshay.

Unit Linked Insurance Plans (ULIPS)—It is a hybrid product, which offers a combination of market-linked returns beside insurance cover, e.g. LIC's Bima Plus.

CHALLENGES AND OPPURTUNITIES OF LIBERALISATION

In the present scenario after liberalization, even though fifteen players are operating in the insurance market and the share of LIC has steadily eroded it is still on a strong footing *vis-à-vis* its competitor. According to data compiled by IRDA, in April-May 2006, fifteen life insurance players collected 119 per cent more premium at Rs. 5,869 crore compared to Rs. 2,678 crore a year ago. LIC registered an increase in premium income by a whopping 106 per cent to collect Rs. 4,183 crore by selling 20 lakh policies to garner 71.27 per cent of the market pie. The other fourteen players (OM Kotak, Allianz Bajaj, ING Vysya, AMP Sanmar, SBI Life Insurance, Tata-AIG, HDFC Standard, ICICI-Prudential, Birla Sunlife, Aviva, Max New York Life, Met Life, Sahara India and Shriram Life Insurance) expanded the premium collection by 159 per cent to Rs. 1,686 crore and have increased their market pie to 28.73 per cent. The insurance consciousness is creating the market and according to analysts with 49 per ent increase in the foreign direct investment, the Indian insurance industry is sure to take a jumbo leap by the year 2010. An exponential growth of 500 per cent is projected in the insurance industry in India within the next four years. With rural and semi-urban consumers contributing about $36 billion, out of which $24 billion will come through life insurance while the rest will be derived from non-life insurance sector, the industry will observe an exceptional spurt in the next four years. The shoot in the industry will make the insurance industry in India a $60 billion business by the year 2010.

The new entrants with their aggressive penetration strategies have been notching impressive growth and are slicing a huge chunk of LIC's market pie as LIC has already lost 15 per cent of their market to the new players. The monopoly of LIC is over, as new players are emerging everyday. The Indian insurance sector provides huge opportunity as there is tremendous growth and India is utterly underinsured. The scenario is that only 20 per cent of the population has any insurance cover worth its name. Moreover, such a cover meets only 25 per cent of their needed and affordable insurance cover. As a percentage of GDP life insurance premium in India is 1.8 per cent, whereas, it is 5.2 per cent in the US and 10.1 per cent in Japan. Nearly 80 per cent of Indian population is without life insurance cover while health insurance and non-life insurance continues to be below international standards. And this part of the population is also subject to weak social security and pension systems with hardly any old age income security. This is an indicator that growth potential for the insurance sector is immense.

The Indian economy, predominantly an agrarian economy, offers enormous growth opportunities for the insurance sector. As per experts, rural sector can become a prominent contributor in the overall growth of the insurance industry in India, provided the needs and occupational structure of people living in villages is understood. For instance, various crops that are comparatively expensive need to be covered under crop insurance schemes.

Also, there are various other requirements of the farmers that need to be looked after by the insurance companies. With an annual growth rate of 15-20 per cent and the largest number of life insurance policies in force anywhere in the world, the potential of the Indian insurance industry is huge. The total value of the Indian insurance market (2004-05) is estimated at Rs. 450 billion (US $10 billion). According to government sources, the insurance and banking services' contribution to the country's gross domestic product (GDP) is 7 per cent out of which the gross premium collection forms a significant part (nearly 2 per cent of GDP). The funds available with the state-owned Life Insurance Corporation (LIC) for investments are 8 per cent of GDP. The obvious conclusion is that 'Sky is the limit'. LIC needs to take guard and prepare for strike.

STRATEGIC INITIATIVES BY LIC

That LIC is a market leader is an irrefutable position and will continue to be so in the years to come. LIC with its wide reach and deep penetration has to concentrate on utilizing its wide reach and brand equity. The greatest strength is the immense faith that people of India have on LIC. Despite stiff competition from new entrants in the market, LIC's market share of 75 per cent in new business premium and 87 per cent in new policies in a competitive environment is testimony to the faith reposed by customers in the public sector insurance player. With over 2000 branches and 10 lakh agents LIC have a huge advantage over its competitors. LIC's premium income grew by 48 per cent to Rs. 18,085 crore in 2005-06. The company has reported a profit of Rs. 5,800 crore for the period. LIC's focus is on building assets through long-term investment in stock markets. LIC, which is celebrating its golden jubilee year, has introduced new products in life insurance, pension and annuity. It is planning to introduce a micro insurance product for the rural poor. LIC is targeting a 30-35 per cent year-on-year growth by selling more policies and introducing innovative products in the market. Life Insurance Corporation of India has embarked on a nationwide voyage on rails to reach out to people to spread awareness. It has initiated LIC Zindagi Express, an exhibition on wheels to mark

LIC's Golden Jubilee Year celebrations. The following strategic dimensions can reap great rewards for LIC:

Creating New Markets

Given the brand equity, visibility, creditability and wide reach the LIC enjoys, tapping unexplored markets will not be difficult. The vast and under explored rural market is a case in point. LIC can tap the rural markets efficiently by using its huge sales force. According to Sections 32B and 32C of the IRDA act it has been made obligatory for life and non-life insurers to undertake a certain percentage of the business in the rural market. Today, every marketer wants to get a sizeable chunk of the untapped rural market. The Indian economy, predominantly an agrarian economy, offers enormous growth opportunities for the insurance sector. As per experts, rural sector can become a prominent contributor in the overall growth of the insurance industry in India, provided the needs and occupational structure of people living in villages is understood. For instance, various crops that are comparatively expensive need to be covered under crop insurance schemes. Also, there are various other requirements of the farmers that need to be looked after by the insurance companies. This is one area in which LIC can take a big lead over its competitors. LIC is contemplating to enter into separate tie-ups with National Insurance Company, Oriental Insurance, United India Insurance and New India Assurance for selling composite micro-insurance policies to the rural masses. It is planning to use the network of rural players like ITC e-choupal in remote villages in states like UP, MP, Karnataka and AP to sell its products besides focusing on high income Northern India villages.

LIC is also contemplating to spread its wings outside India and tap the offshore market in Asia, US and Europe. In an effort to attract investments from the over 1.3 million-strong non-resident Indian (NRI) community in the UK, the Life Insurance Corporation of India has launched three new products and services. The three new products launched were 'Bonusbuilder Savings Plan,' 'Guaranteed Lifetime Protection Plan' and 'The Capital With Profits Bond'. Chinese and South-East Asian insurance markets are growing at an exponential rate and can be tapped to reap extraordinary results. Even in the urban markets of India niches such as those for children, students, women and aged can be carved out with innovative products such as unit linked insurance plan, annuity and pension plans, children plans. Today, a sizeable chunk of womenfolk form the workforce—both in white collar and otherwise. Even the housewives can be targeted and the idea of insurance as a vital part of their lives has to be packaged and sold. Targeting them with specially designed tailor-made products can be highly beneficial.

Innovative Product Line

The customer of today is having more to choose in terms of policy instruments as new players have come up with innovative product line. LIC need to be seen in this light and suitable steps taken to customize the products. It needs to change its product mix to suit customer needs. Further, it can carve a niche for itself with the help of these innovative product lines. Infact, LIC has already started launching these products with a view to targeting new markets Aiming for 35 per cent compound growth in business this year, the Life Insurance Corporation of India (LIC) is planning to create a subsidiary for foraying into health insurance, while focusing on attracting the youth segment with new products. LIC has launched "Bima Bachat", a single premium money-back policy to cater to the demands of the market. It is targeting five per cent of its policies through the new product while planning to tap the $7 billion SBI's India Millennium Bond, which got redeemed in 2005. As part of its aggressive drive to expand business, Life Insurance Corporation (LIC) has launched two new products in 2006—Jeevan Tarang and Jeevan Akshay-4. The wholelife policy 'Jeevan Tarang' is open to persons aged up to 60 years and provides risk cover up to 100 years. The plan gives tax benefits under Section 80C and 10(10D); a guaranteed annual survival benefit at 5.5 per cent of sum assured throughout life after premium paying term. The annuity plan 'Jeevan Akshay-4' provides for payment of pension immediately on purchase of the policy.

Life Insurance Corporation, country's largest life insurer, which launched a souvenir scheme Bima Gold in September 2005 to mark its Golden Jubilee celebrations, has been a resounding success. Life Insurance Corporation of India (LIC) has launched its unit linked pension plan—Market Plus. The new product combines investment and pension benefit with option of insurance cover during the term of the policy. It is planning to introduce a micro insurance product for the rural poor. The life insurer has sought the Insurance Regulatory and Development Authority's approval for the micro-insurance product. With such innovative products in its arsenal, LIC can borrow ICICI Prudential's catchphrase **We cover you. At every step of life.**

Technological Initiatives for Better Customer Service

LIC has introduced a Metropolitan Area Network (MAN) system in Ahmedabad, Pune, Hyderabad, and Calcutta. A policy holder will no longer need to visit the branch office and run from pillar to post, to check the status of a policy for he will soon be able to do this online. MAN will enable customers to pay premiums and get status reports from any of the branches in that city. MAN already exists in Mumbai, Delhi, and Bangalore. They will eventually connect up to 27 cities in their Wide Area Network (WAN). Out of the 2050-odd branches that LIC has, over 1940 has managed to implement the front-end applications. The company has also started the Interactive Voice Response System, which helps the customer to get to know the details of his/her policy over the telephone. The company is also looking at selling its products via the Internet. With a vision of providing easy access to its policyholders, LIC has also launched its Satellite Sampark offices. The satellite offices are smaller, leaner and closer to the customer. The digitalized records of the satellite offices will facilitate anywhere servicing and many other conveniences in the future. With these initiatives in customer service arena, LIC can safely proclaim HDFC Standard Life catchphrase **Service that makes you smile.**

Improved Distribution Channels

As the agent network was not found good enough to retain its market in the competitive scenario, LIC must now stress on alternative distribution channels to increase its penetration. The cost effectiveness of agent network channel of distribution has suffered with LIC paying bonuses and commissions twice to agents and Development Officers—for every new policy and subsequent renewal of premiums. LIC needs to spread its wings through bancassurance and corporate agency tie-ups. Rural and semi-urban sectors are the ones that could be serviced by bancassurance model.

Other approaches such as call-center, direct marketing and Internet will grow dramatically over the next several years. LIC needs to utilize the multiple channel delivery networks that must be integrated tightly to deliver on the promise of quality service anywhere and improve customer relationship.

Creating Awareness for Insurance

Initially, all advertising by private insurers ended up reinforcing the LIC brand image as the PSU was still synonymous with life insurance. The break with tradition came when ICICI Prudential arguably became the first private insurance company to recognise and harness the power of TV advertising, with its 'Sindoor' campaign in 2001. Then came its retirement solutions campaign with the tagline **Retire from work, not life.**

CHINTAMANI, the mascot of the middle class, has become a household name. Thanks to him, ICICI Prudential now enjoys a brand recall of 92 per cent next to LIC's 97 per cent, according to AC Nielsen's Brandtrack 7 study out last year. Most private players have 50-70 per cent of their ad spend skewed in favor of television. Marketing budgets have been soaring for the past three years. Reportedly, on a budget of Rs. 5.8 crore for February 2005 alone, ICICI Prudential's 'Retirement solutions campaign' was the highest spending brand, pipping several HLL brands to the post. The various campaigns have also tapped several ideas associated with insurance, an alternative to LIC, which harped on the idea of protecting your family against the wage earner's death. HDFC Standard Life, for instance, uses the idea of 'self-respect' as its platform. Tata AIG's boy planting a sapling that grows into a 'tree' works on the idea of planning ahead.

In wake of this advertising onslaught from private players last year, LIC's Rs. 125 crore budget was divided with 20 per cent going to TV, 25-30 per cent for print and 35 per cent for outdoor. Throughout last year, LIC had ads across all products being beamed on TV. The insurance major also undertook scientific studies to look at its target audience. The company, which spent Rs. 2 crore on the Internet advertising, has been successful in reaching the urban middle and upper class. With the private players flexing their muscles, the LIC pie has hit a down curve—down from 83 per cent in 2004 to 78 per cent in 2005. Many private insurance companies are estimated to increase their marketing expenditure by 30-40 per cent this year. The emphasis will be on creatives and the accent on awareness. And it is TV that is proving to be new vehicle to carry the insurance business. In this new dynamic environment, LIC always had a very effective punchline 'We know India better' but in the given circumstances and in the changed scenario of globalization it has to change it to 'We know insurance better'. LIC should borrow the idea of coke 'Thanda Matlab Coca-Cola', and position itself in the minds of the customers in such a way that for them insurance should mean LIC. It must go for aggressive and innovative marketing. Customer is the king and customization holds the key.

CONCLUSION

The insurance industry in India has witnessed a sea-change ever since it was opened up to private players in 1999. The liberalization transformed the industry's outlook towards the huge Indian market. The sudden rise in the number of players has brought about innovation in product development, customer service and distribution channels. The Indian customer, thus, has a whole new range of insurance products to choose from. There is a choice for every societal segment.

Competition is an essential ingredient of open markets, which benefits both the customer and society at large. It is obvious that with the customer having a wide menu to choose from, customer service benchmarks are improving. The reason is very simple—if you don't hold the customer tight he will slip away to some other suitor. Insurers are now forced to recognize customers' needs, exploit new opportunities and risk in venturing into newer market areas. With the advent of new distribution channels and payment mechanisms, customer awareness is expected to improve further forcing the industry to become more customer friendly. The industry has now to deal with customers who know what they want and are more demanding in terms of better service and speedier responses. The dynamic interaction is certainly leading to a win-win for both parties.

LIC needs to welcome competition with open arms and treat it as an opportunity rather than a threat. With the entry of the private players the insurance consciousness of the country have increased and the industry is witnessing a tremendous growth. The ultimate objective of reforms is to increase insurance-density and insurance penetration levels by designing more tailor made products for customers, for both urban and rural segment, individuals and institutions. LIC now needs to use its reach, visibility and brand strength to penetrate deeper into Indian markets. The challenge for the LIC is three-fold creating the need where it is not there, changing the need into their want and turning the want to demand, which they must be able to satisfy. LIC should adopt a new catchphrase **Our motto- to cover every Indian in a better way.**

The following steps can transform LIC into a world-class competitor:

Disseminating insurance information and knowledge towards untapped market.

Customization of various insurance products to satisfy every class of customer in the market.

Targeting the low premium-paying segment of the market by taking advantage of its wide reach.

Continuous product innovation to meet the demands of dynamic environment.

Application of IT and other technological tools for better customer service.

Differentiated focus on diverse market segment.

Efficient and cost-effective channel and distribution network.

Managing the funds for optimum return at minimum risk.

Proper investment in training and quality research for better customer satisfaction.

Proper utilization of its strong brand equity and public trust to create new markets.

Sound corporate governance mechanism to manage the conflict between various stakeholders.

REFERENCES

Pathak, Pramod and Singh, Saumya. "LIC—The Leader on the Backfoot," *Insurance Theory and Practice*, Prentice Hall of India, New Delhi, 2005, pp. 38-49.

——. "Increasing Competitiveness through Marketing—A Case Study of LIC," *The Alternative*, Vol. 2, No. 1, pp. 32-38, (October 2002-March 2003).

Report Card: Life, *IRDA Journal*, Vol. 4, No. 8, pp. 26-34, (July, 2006).

Report Card: Life, *IRDA Journal,* Vol. 3, No. 6, pp. 23-34, (December 2005).

The Insurance Times, VOL. XXXII, No. 8, pp. 36-48, (October 2005).

The Protagonist *vs.* Antagonists, *Insurance Plus*, pp.4-12. (May 2004).

Market Intelligence, *Yogakshema*, Vol. 48, No. 5. pp. 51-53, (October 2003).

Stuart, Purdy. 'A Challenge for Players', *The Hindu Survey of Indian Industry*, pp. 71-73, (2005).

Parihar, Rachana. "Bancassurance: Challenges and Opportunities in India", *Insurance Chronicle*, December 2004, pp. 51-56.

SEBI, Annual Report, (2005-06).

Life Insurance in India: Challenges and Opportunities in the Post-Liberalised Era

S.C. Bansal, Y.P. Singh and *Sneh Lohia*

ABSTRACT

The objective of this paper is to identify the challenges and opportunities in the life insurance sector in India after liberalization of the economy. It fills a research gap: many studies based on secondary data and examining the investment systems, operations, principles and practices of Life Insurance Corporation of India (LIC) have been reported; the works exploring the impact of liberalization on the quality of plans and services offered, and opportunities for growth in this area are limited in number. The data were gathered with the help of a detailed questionnaire from 560 individuals belonging to Delhi, Noida, Gurgaon, Faridabad, Mumbai, Pune, Surat, Kolkata, Chennai, Bangalore, Varanasi, Gorakhpur and other cities in India. It has been observed that the companies have added new features in the life insurance products to meet the challenges of the post-liberalized era. Entry of many new players within a short span of time has made the insurance market more challenging. The companies offer policies through various distribution channels and adopt new ways to penetrate deeply into new geographical areas. Tremendous improvement in the quality of services offered by the LIC has been observed after the entry of new companies in the industry. A large number of individuals are in favour of flexibility in type, premium and sum assured in the plans. They also support lower premium for both females and non-smokers. In the new environment, the companies should incorporate various features in their products commonly practiced in developed markets. They should face the challenge by offering specific plans for customers according to their needs with toppings of attractive riders and after sale service. The life insurance companies should be rated by an independent body on the basis of their management, investment policy, safety and products offered by them.

JEL classification: D14, G22, L8

INTRODUCTION

After the opening up of Insurance Sector in 2000, many new players have entered into the market, totally changing the face of life insurance in India. Competition among them has increased manifold since six years of liberalization and each one is coming with innovative insurance plans through new channels of distribution to meet the need of each and every customer.

Life insurance was earlier bought for saving income tax rather than a risk coverage tool. However, with the entry of new players, the insurance market has dramatically changed. The advisors now, try to sell insurance according to the need of the individual after a detailed financial analysis and study of future requirements of the potential buyer. In other words, life insurance is sold keeping in mind the basic purpose of the insurance cover, not as a tax saving tool. The new players are exploring various distribution channels instead of concentrating on individual agents only. There is a huge untapped insurance potential in India. Changes in the Indian life insurance industry have come with a host of challenges. However, opportunities in the future are unlimited. Along with the tremendous opportunities there exist tremendous challenges.. the insurance companies by creating competitive advantage with a clear vision can convert the challenges into the opportunities.

This paper identifies the challenges and opportunities in the life insurance sector in India after liberalization of the economy and tries to explore the improvements which can be made in the life insurance policies and services to meet the expectations of the policyholders. It is hoped that the work would be beneficial to the operators, insured, regulators, prospective policy purchasers, insurance agents and other stakeholders in the sector.

REVIEW OF LITERATURE

A large number of studies have been made on life insurance sector. But, most of the existing literature on life insurance is based on the secondary data. Some of the studies have attempted to examine the impact of investment and mobilization of savings by Life Insurance Corporation of India (LIC) on economic development (Chaudhury and Kulkarni, 1991; Mishra, 1987). Performance of the life insurance companies on parameters like operations, renewal expense ratio, post sale service (Rao, 1976; Ray, 1981) profitability, and market share (San, et al., 1996) have also been covered by the researchers. Other aspects related to life insurance sector like specific legal rules on insurance contracts in UK, US, Germany, Switzerland, Sweden, and France (Insinger and Pauly, 1986); specific policies of the insurance companies (Banerjee, 1983); managerial discretion and voluntary disclosure (Adams and Mahmud, 1998); economies of scale (Kellner and Mathewson, 1983); relationship between life styles and sources of customer value (Tang, 2001); costs of direct and independent distribution (Ward, 2002) and determinants of life insurance consumption (Hwang and Greenford, 2005); have been surveyed in various countries.

However, these studies have covered different aspects that are not directly related to quality of life insurance plans and services in the post-liberalised life insurance sector.

National Council of Applied Economic Research (1979) conducted a survey of attitudes of households towards life insurance cover. 5125 households supplied the desired information for the study. About 80 per cent of the respondents had opted for insurance to cover the risk. One-fifth of them had inspirations of building up estates for the family, whereas, about 10 per cent intended to get some tax relief. The relative importance of factors prompting policyholders to take up the plans remained unchanged between the urban and rural areas.

Doss (1995) conducted a study examining the distribution system in LIC covering 100 agents in two branch offices of LIC. The study found that 91 per cent of the agents thought that training was a necessity for improving their efficiency. One-half of the agents found that office support was satisfactory in policy servicing. The study also surveyed the policyholders' perceptions of the services by the agents.

Business India (2001) conducted a survey about the new players in life insurance sector after privatization. The views of the Managing Directors in the new insurance companies were taken on various issues. It was found that the new players were planning to offer more value added products focused on customers' needs. The Insurance Regulatory and Development Authority (IRDA) had specified a training of 100 hours to the agents, but most of the companies were going beyond the stipulated period.

In Japan (Jiji Press, 2003), 89.6 per cent of 6500 households surveyed had one or more life insurance policies. This proportion had dropped below 90 per cent for the first time in the past 27 years, highlighting a growing shift away from life insurance. Furthermore, 51.7 per cent of households regarded their insurance coverage as sufficient, while only 35.7 per cent of them were satisfied with their coverage.

Insurance Marketplace Standards Association (Chordas, 2003) found that 79 per cent of the 1009 respondents in the USA did not go online to research life insurance in spite of widespread use of internet for searching and purchasing other goods and services. A large majority (88 per cent) did not buy life insurance over the internet. Agent's reputation for honesty and integrity, benefits of the policy, price of the plan and company's financial rating also affected the decisions of consumers while buying the life insurance products.

Chandhok (2004) examined the distribution channels of life insurance products in India in the post-liberalized period. New York Life had made training an ongoing process to make the quality of the agents its mains differentiating factor, HDFC Standard Life decided to rely on individual consultants and corporate agents for distributing its products.

Saunders and Lu (2004) studied the China's Insurance potential. They suggested that insurer could select a different operating area, distribution method or product offering. They expected that with the country's huge captive work forces, an insurer tailoring worksite marketing expertise, would be desirable.

Thomas (2005) reported a study conducted by AIG American General about the life insurance practices of 337 individuals in the mass affluent market in the USA. It was found that about one-third of the policyholders in the mass affluent market preferred term insurance to protect their families and assets. Only one-fourth of the insured had whole life policies of less than $ 5,00,000.

Limra International (Chu, 2005) found that about one-half of the households in the US believed that they needed more life insurance in 2005. As compared to it, only about 34 per cent of them felt that they needed more insurance in 1998. The main reason for this trend was that many people were concerned about their financial prospects and maintaining a guaranteed, continued income.

Thus, though many studies covering various aspects of life insurance have been conducted, only a few of these works have concentrated on examining the scope for further improvement in life insurance sector on the basis of a survey of the prime stakeholder, i.e., policyholder. The present study attempts to bridge this gap. In particular, it covers the opinions of the insured on some important issues of life insurance like objective, planning and selecting the life insurance policy keeping in view the various relevant issues and needs; improvement in the quality of life insurance plans and servicing and various innovative aspects of life insurance like alterable policies, one policy for the whole family and rating of life insurance companies.

RESEARCH METHODOLOGY

The study is exploratory in nature and identifies the scope for further improvement in life insurance plans and services offered in India to take competitive advantage. The research is based on the primary data collected with the help of a detailed questionnaire. A draft questionnaire was canvassed among fifty individuals to seek their opinions about the comprehensiveness and understandability of the questions. It was adjusted in the light of the suggestions given by the respondents.

The adjusted questionnaire was distributed to 800 individuals belonging to Delhi, Noida, Gurgaon, Faridabad, Mumbai, Pune, Surat, Kolkota, Chennai, Bangalore, Varanasi, Gorakhpur and other cities in India. All of these individuals were personally approached for seeking clarification and discussing the selected issues in detail. 560 of them completed the questionnaire for the work giving a response rate of seventy per cent. The time taken to answer the questions contained in it ranged from 90 to 120 minutes.

The reliability of an empirical work depends on the quality of information obtained for it. Authenticity of information collected can be judged by scanning the experience, age, qualification, income, and occupation of the respondents. Respondents in the study include policyholders of all the age groups; individuals of various educational background like graduates, postgraduates and professionals; and persons of various occupation and income groups. The collected information has been processed on SPSS (version 12.5).

FINDINGS AND DISCUSSIONS

1. Objective of Buying Life Insurance

There can be many objectives of buying insurance policies, like life cover, saving and tax benefits. Analysis as shown in Figure 21.1 exhibits that 'covering risk of life' is the primary objective of purchasing a policy. 'Tax benefit' has come out as the next most preferred objective of buying the life insurance policy. 'Other objectives' of buying insurance includes 'good rate of return' and 'education and marriage expenses of children.'

2. Lives Covered in the Insurance Policy

This is general trend in our society that insurance is bought only by the head of the family and no insurance cover is taken for the spouse or children. Figure 21.2 tries to find out the lives covered by an insurance policy in the respondent's family. A large majority (97.3%) of the individuals have taken insurance

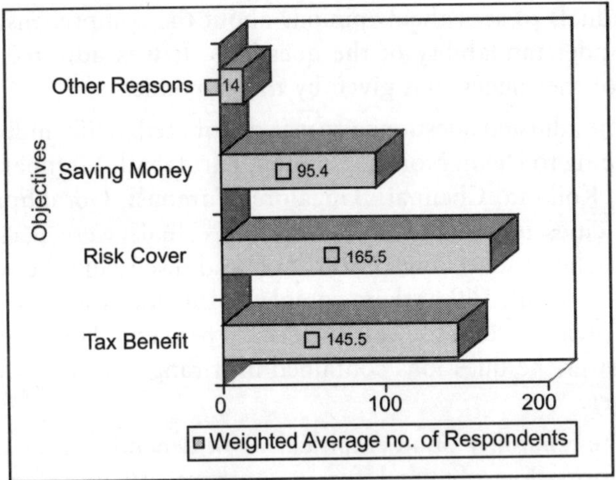

Figure 21.1: Objective of Buying Life Insurance

for their life. Life of the spouse is covered by approximately three- fourths (74.1%) of the respondents.

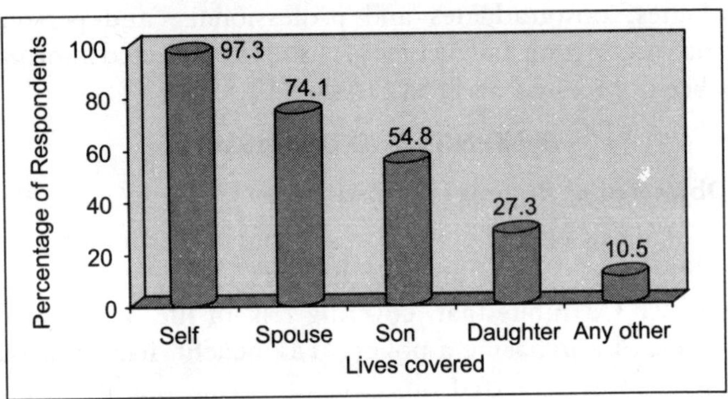

Figure 21.2: Lives Covered in the Policy

3. Name of the Insurer Company

In the post-liberalised era, many new players have entered into the Indian life insurance industry. Figure 21.3 shows that approximately all respondents (96 per cent) have taken their policies from the LIC. ICICI Pru, Tata-AIG and Bajaj Allianz are the other companies preferred by the insured. Since a large no. of policies were purchased in the pre-liberalised era, they had no

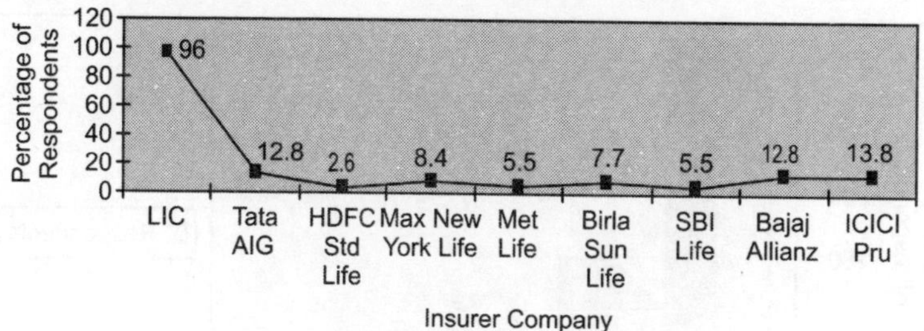

Figure 21.3: Name of the Insurer

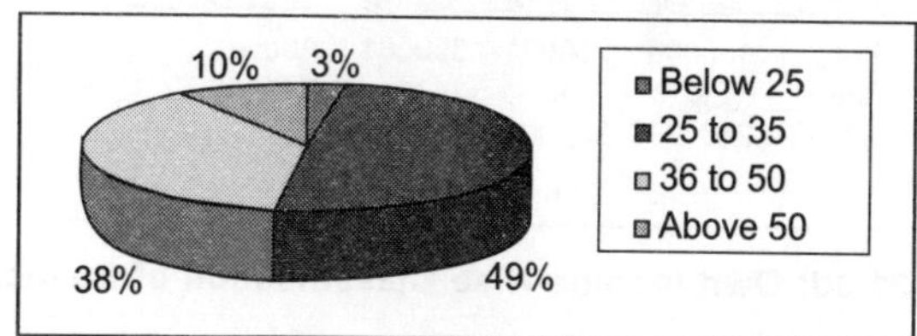

Figure 21.3a: Age-wise Classification of Respondents

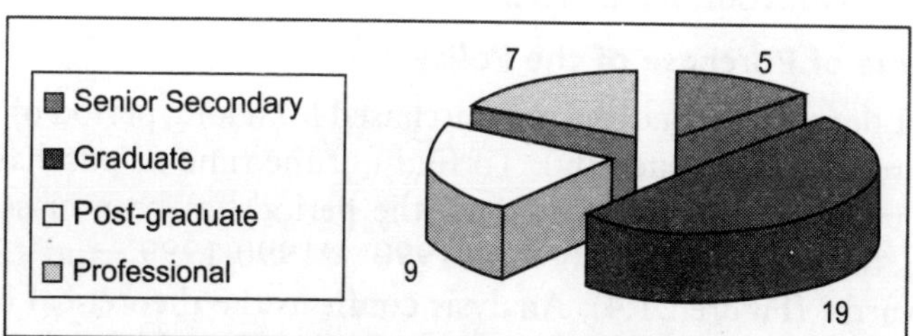

Figure 21.3b: Qualification-wise Classification of Respondents

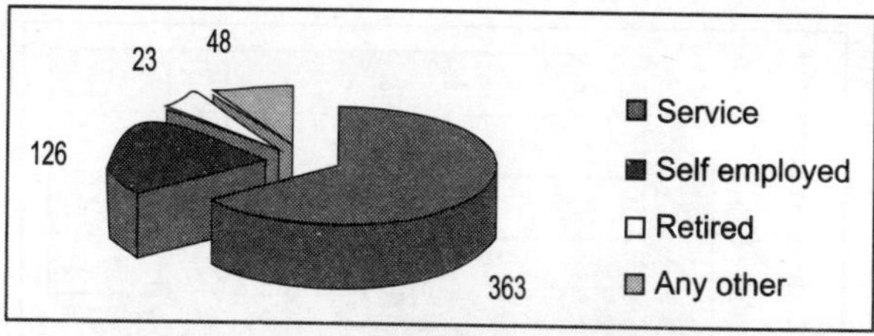

Figure 21.3c: Occupation-wise Classification of Respondents

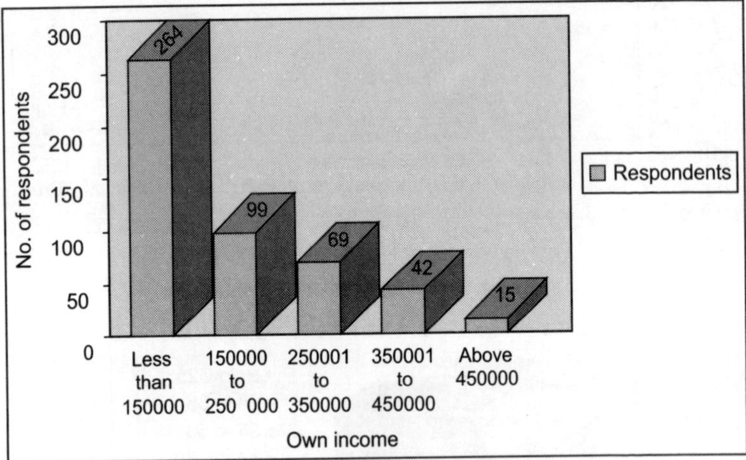

Figure 21.3d: Own Income-wise Classification of Respondents

other choice except LIC. Another reason for the popularity of LIC is its favourable image.

4 Time of Purchase of the Policy

Life insurance covers are purchased for a long period of time (10 to 25 years generally). To find out the time of purchase of the policy by the policyholders, the period has been classified into three categories 'before 1990', '1990-1999' and '2000 onwards' (Figure 21.4). Analysis confirms the theoretical belief that liberalization will improve the knowledge of life insurance among people and per capita premium will increase as maximum

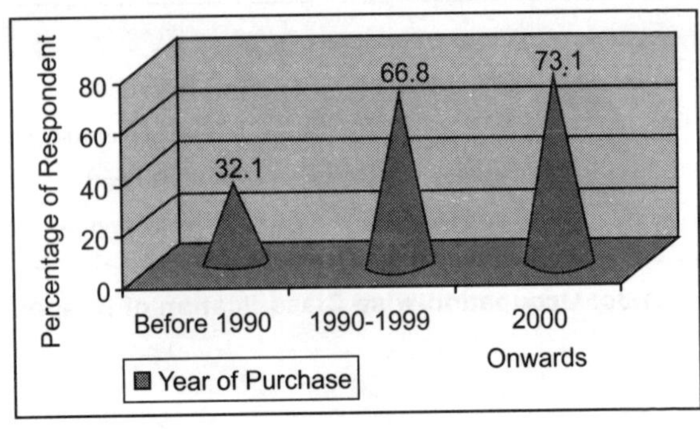

Figure 21.4: Year of Purchase of the Policy

number of respondents have purchased policies in the period '2000 onwards'.

5 Type of the Policy Purchased

Life insurance companies offer various types of life insurance policies. Some are investment oriented while other emphasis on risk-coverage only. Approximately three-fourths of individuals (71.9%) have purchased money-back plan. The reason of popularity of these plans being dual advantage of periodical return along with risk coverage. Endowment plan is the next most preferred policy because it provides a good lump sum return on maturity along with risk cover of life. Unit linked, though a new product, is popular among the individuals because of good return in the recent past.

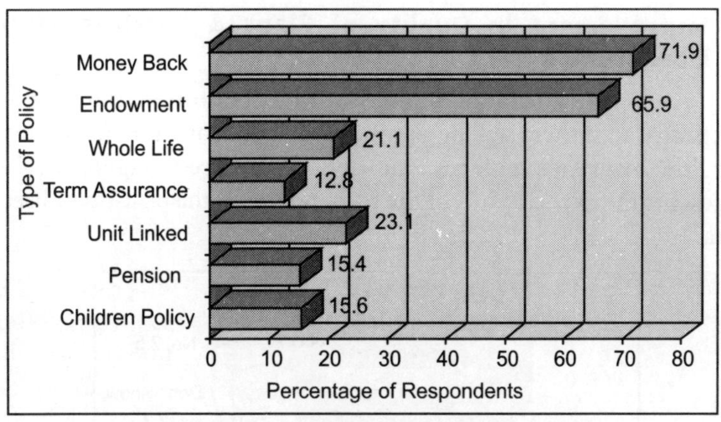

Figure 21.5: Type of the Policy Purchased

6. Important Issues Before Buying an Insurance Policy

Insurance policy is a complicated plan and consists of various terms and concepts. Before buying an insurance policy, one should keep in mind these factors and then only select the most suitable insurance policy. Various issues to be kept in mind include (as exhibited in Figure 21.6) 'premium to be paid', 'guaranteed return', 'bonus paid by the company', 'reliability of the company' and 'availability of rider options.' Majority of the individuals (68.8%) consider 'reliability of the company' because in the liberalised era many private companies are in competition and their solvency is an important issue. More than one-half of respondents (55%) have considered 'bonus' and 'guaranteed return' being a major part of maturity amount of the policy.

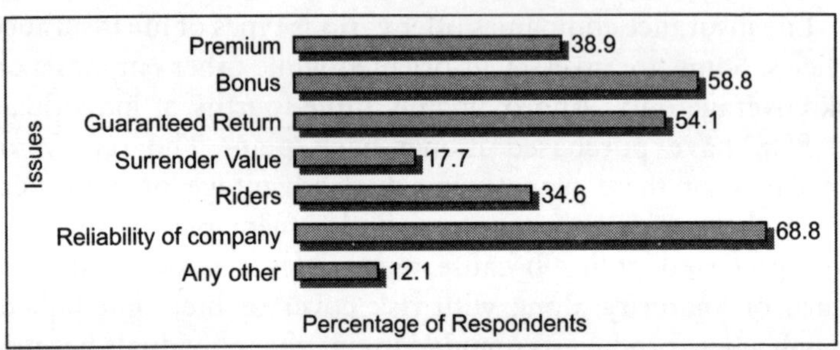

Figure 21.6: Important Issues Before Buying an Insurance Policy

7. Improvement in Quality of Plans & Services After Liberalization

After liberalization of the insurance sector in India, it is expected that there will be significant improvement in the quality of life insurance policies and services offered. Figure 21.7a presents the expectations of the respondents in the post-liberalised era.

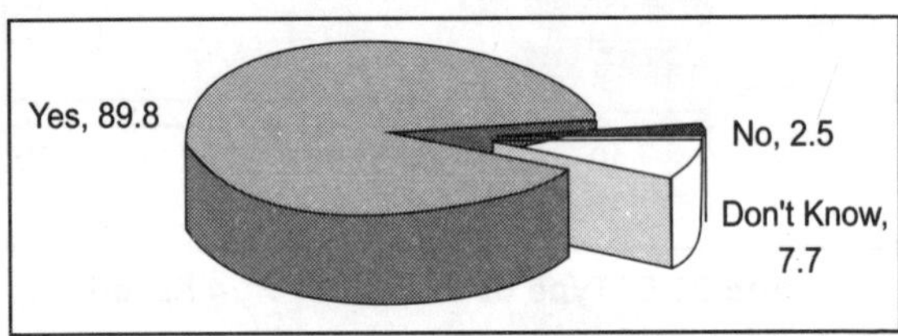

Figure 21.7a: Improvement in Quality of Policy and Service after Liberalisation

A large majority (77.1%) of the individuals expect wide range of policies after liberalization. (Figure 21.7b) Approximately two-fifths of persons think that liberalization will result in 'lower premium', 'new channels of distribution' and 'increased working hours'. Around three-fifths of respondents opine that 'customized policies' 'will be offered and life insurance companies will be more 'customer friendly' in the post-liberalised era. Most of these expectations of the policy owners are based on the experience of other countries after opening up of the insurance sector as well as the practices seen in the post-liberalised era.

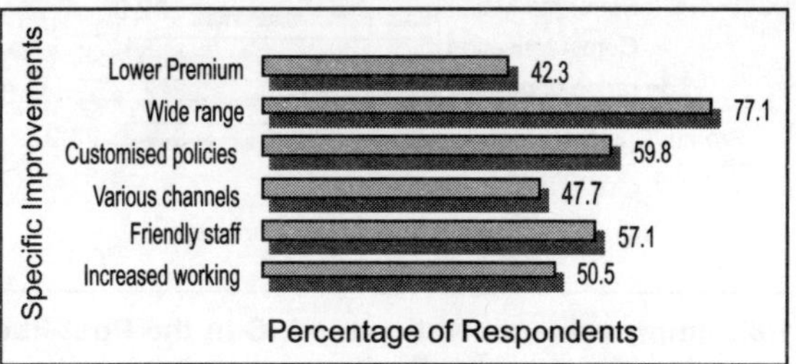

Figure 21.7b: Improvement Expected in the Post-liberalised Era

8. Change in the Service of LIC after Liberalization

Life Insurance Corporation of India was established in 1956. Since then, it was the only life insurance company until the insurance sector was opened up for private players. In the opinion of three-fourths of the respondents, the services of LIC have improved in the past few years (Figure 21.8a).

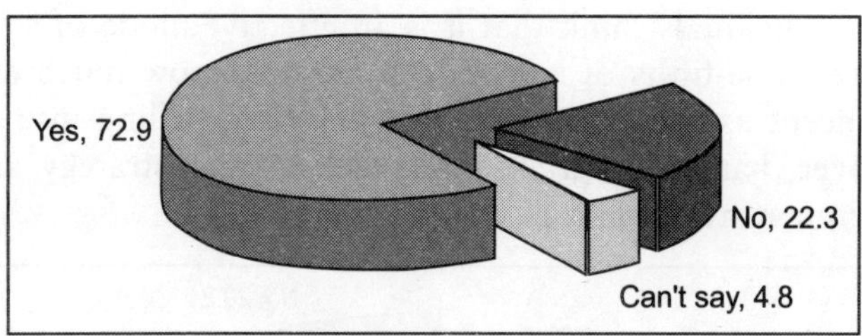

Figure 21.8a: Change in the Service of LIC

They have acknowledged various improvements, as shown in Figure 21.8b, namely, timely payment of survival/maturity benefits, regular premium reminders, better marketing practices, computerization, prompt and friendly staff, and facility of making payment of premium at any branch of the company.

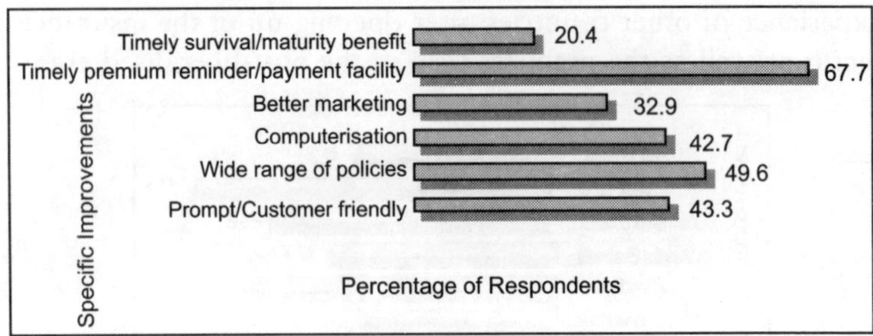

Figure 21.8b: Improvements Noticed in LIC in the Post-liberalised Era

9. Selling Insurance Through Bancassurance

After liberalization of insurance a new concept of selling insurance has come into existence in India—Bancassurance. In bancassurance insurance is sold through a bank's established distribution channels. An attempt was made to find out whether selling insurance through bancassurance would be beneficial to the policyholders. As presented in Figure 21.9, more than one-half of individuals think that it is an effective mode of selling. However, one-fifths of respondents do not know much about the concept as they have not seen any bank selling insurance Moreover, bank's programs also 'lack a clear strategy and a commitment from the top' (Thomas, 2003).

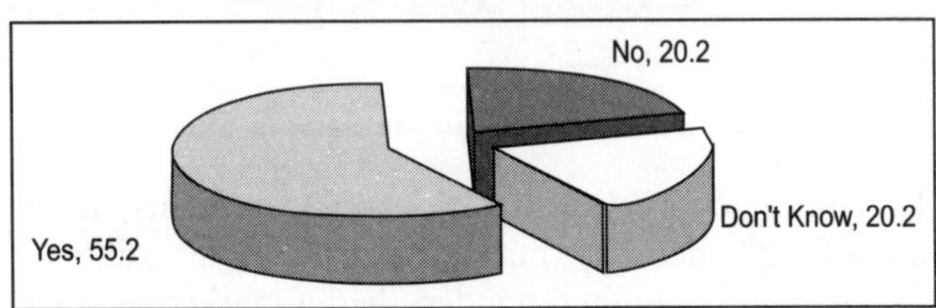

Figure 21.9: Selling Insurance through Bancassurance

10. Riders in the Life Insurance Policy

In the liberalized era, riders have become one important characteristic of life insurance plans. Riders are add-on benefits attached to policies in case of eventualities. Approximately, three-fourths of the persons think that riders are one of the best things to happen to insurance sector post-liberalization (Figure

21.10). They have made the plans more customized according to the specific requirement of the policyholder.

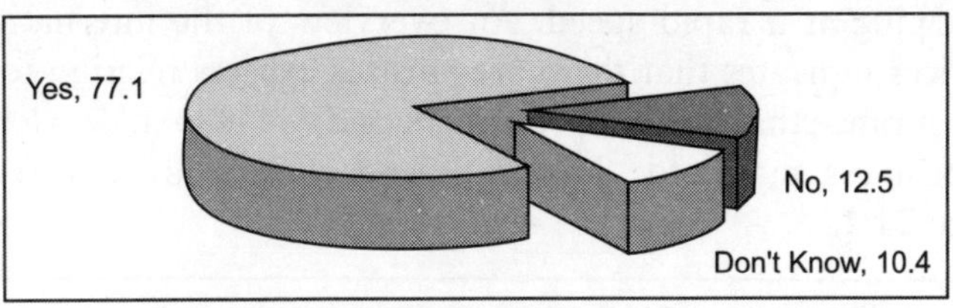

Figure 21.10: Riders in the Insurance Policy

11. Alterable Life Insurance Policies

Alterable life insurance policies are the plans with flexible terms like flexibility in type, premium amount, sum assured, and other associated aspects. A large majority (89.6%) of the persons think that type of insurance policy should be alterable, as it will provide opportunity to change the policy with change in circumstances in life (Figure 21.11). More than three-fourths of the individuals favor flexible premium installments.. Most of them (89.8%t) are of the opinion that policies should also offer flexibility in the total sum assured. Most of the insured support flexibility because it takes care of the change in requirements with time span and helps facing uncertainties. However, some of the respondents are of the view that alterable terms might create confusions.

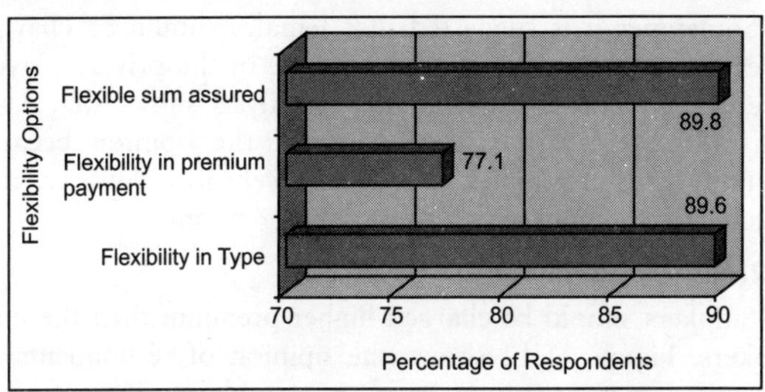

Figure 21.11: Alterable Life Insurance Policies

12. Other Aspects Related to Life Insurance Policies

Life insurance industry has been recently liberalized and is developing at a rapid speed. An overview of the international practices indicates that there are various aspects relating to the life insurance that need improvement and can help in developing the business manifold. Some of these aspects are covered in Figure 21.12.

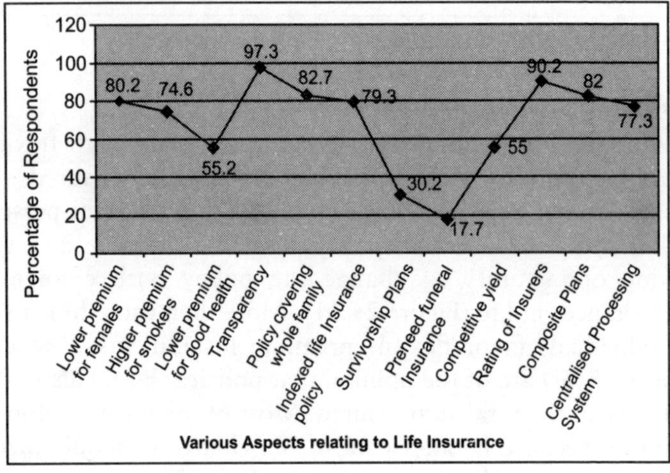

Figure 21.12: Various Aspects Relating to Life Insurance

12.1. Lower premium for females

Sometimes it is suggested that females should be charged lower premium for life insurance. Some of the private players have already started this practice. Analysis shows that four-fifths (80.2%) of individuals support the opinion because mortality rate of females is comparatively low. Further, it is difficult for the housewives to pay the premium.

12.2. Higher premium for smokers

Smokers should be charged higher premium than the non-smokers. Figure 21.12 shows the opinion of respondents on charging lower premiums from non-smokers. Three-fourths (74.6%) of them support the opinion because non-smokers are exposed to less risk of life as against smokers.

12.3. Lower premium for good health and better life-style

Persons with good health and better life style may be charged lesser premium than others. Figure 21.12 exhibits that the view is supported by approximately one-half (55.2%) of individuals as good health and better life style reduces chances of risk. However, those who are against the suggestion, think that life style can change with time and it is very difficult to predict such elements.

12.4. Transparency

To survive in the competitive environment, transparency is a pre-requirement. Life insurance policies should be transparent i.e. the insured should be informed about disposal of policy fund—premium, death benefit, bonus credited, expenses incurred and surrender value through annual statements. Approximately all the respondents (97.3%) support the view because insured should also know about utilization of their funds (Figure 21.12).

12.5. Whole life policies

Life insurance companies should issue a policy that would cover risk of life of whole family. For instance, a whole life policy purchased by a person with a premium based on his age can also provide term insurance to spouse and children. Analysis shows (Figure 21.12) that a vast majority of the individuals (82.7%) are in favor of policies covering risk of whole family. Main reasons in support of the policy are 'covers risk of entire family', 'gives advantage of many policies' and 'encourage insurance of all the family members'.

12.6. Indexed life insurance policies

In some of the developed economies, the companies offer life insurance plans whose face value increases with increase in the inflation as per measure of some national price index. An attempt was made as exhibited in Figure 21.12 to find out the view of the respondents on such policies. A large majority (79.3%) of individuals think that these policies will help in meeting the cost of inflation and maintain the purchasing power of money.

12.7. Survivorship life insurance (Second-to-die life insurance)

In Survivorship Life Insurance policy, the insurance cover is given for two lives and claim is paid only on the death of the second (or last) insured. Only one-third respondents (Figure 21.12) favor such kind of policies. Most of the individuals think that such policies are not much suited in India because its basic concept have arisen in the countries where families are nuclear and both the parents are working.

12.8. Preneed funeral insurance

Sometimes, it is suggested that there should be life insurance cover specifically intended to 'prefund future funeral expenses'. Only few respondents (17.7%) think that this type of policy is required in India. Majority of individuals opined that this is not needed in India because of its human and social values.

12.9. Competitive yield on life insurance policies

Often, it is suggested that life insurance policy's yield may be competitive with returns on other investments. (Figure 21.12) More than one-half of the respondents (55%) are in favor of competitive yield of life insurance policies because it would motivate people to go for more life insurance and promote healthy competition. Now, with the advent of Unit-Linked plans, the companies are offering competitive yield on life insurance policies.

12.10. Rating of insurance companies

Existence of many companies in any industry give rise to the need of their rating by an independent and reputed authority. It is suggested that their rating will help the prospective policyholders in selecting a better company. This section, as reflected in Figure 21.12 presents the view of respondents on rating of life insurance companies. It shows that rating of life insurance companies is supported by a large majority of the individuals (90.2%). They think that rating of insurance companies will facilitate selection of appropriate insurance company. It will also promote healthy competition among insurance companies to obtain the higher ratings.

12.11. Composite insurance

The companies may cover the life of the policyholders as well as provide insurance for the health, car and home (General Insurance) under a single contract. Most of the individuals (82%) support the thinking because it would provide all type of insurance covers under one roof.

12.12. Centralised processing system

In some of the countries, a centralized payment processing system (CPPS) is followed. In this arrangement the insured sends the documents by post, which are processed at a centralized place. Approximately three-fourths of respondents favor centralised processing system. (Figure 21.12) They hope that that it will make the policy servicing more quick and hassle free.

Thus, innovative opinions on various aspects of life insurance have been supported by the respondents as these make insurance policies more flexible, customer oriented and competitive.

13. Necessity of Regulations in Insurance Industry

Indian life insurance industry is subject to government regulation. After liberalization regulations in India has been tightened and a new regulatory authority is being appointed. A large majority (92.1%) of the respondents are in favor of insurance regulations because in today's liberalised and competitive environment regulation is a necessity (Figure 21.13). Only few respondent think that there should be free competition and regulation is not required.

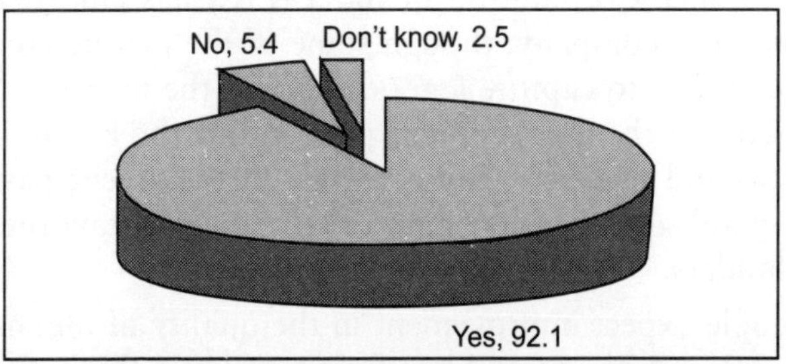

Figure 21.13: Necessity of Regulations

14 Rationale for Regulation of Insurance Industry

There can be many rationales for regulating a sector, including life insurance like 'protecting fair terms and pricing', 'ensuring solvency of insurer', 'controlling fraudulent activities and misappropriations' and 'ensuring orderly growth of insurance.' Figure 21.14 presents preference of respondents for various rationales for regulation of insurance industry. It shows that maximum number of the individuals prefer 'Protecting fair terms and pricing' as their objective because it is necessary to safeguard the interest of the insured. 'Ensuring solvency of insurer' and 'controlling fraudulent activities and misappropriations' are the next most preferred rationale of regulations.

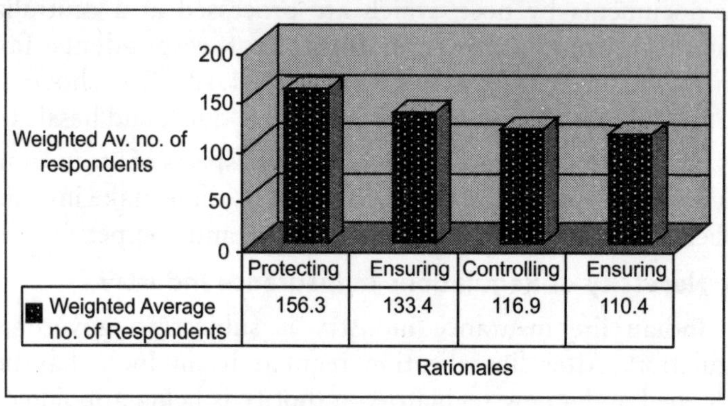

	Protecting	Ensuring	Controlling	Ensuring
Weighted Average no. of Respondents	156.3	133.4	116.9	110.4

Figure 21.14: Rationale for Insurance Industry

CONCLUSION

Life insurance is mainly bought for the twin objectives of 'risk coverage' and 'tax benefit'. Even in the post-liberalised era, Life Insurance Corporation of India (LIC) has emerged as the most popular company, though some of the private companies have been able to capture a good share of the market. 'Money-back' remains the most popular plan among the Indian insured, giving second place to 'Endowment'. In the recent past, 'Unit linked plan' and 'Pension plan' also remained favorite of the policyholders.

People expect improvement in the quality of life insurance plans and services after liberalization. They think that wide range of customized policies will be offered through new innovative and friendly staff of the insurance companies. They opine that the insurance companies will offer the best from their side to win the confidence of the insured/potential insured in the existing cut-throat competition. Most of the policyholders have noticed improvements in the services offered by LIC and think that the company is working hard to maintain its image and share in the liberalised era.

The policyholders appreciated adding new features in the plans like flexibility in type, premium and sum assured; lower premium for females and non-smokers, indexed life insurance policies, policy covering life of the whole family and transparency in operation. The insured assert the necessity of the regulatory mechanism and think that effective regulation of insurance sector in India is required to protect fair terms and pricing, ensure solvency of the insurer, and control fraudulent activities and misappropriations.

In the new competitive environment, the individuals have a wide choice. To have better plans and services, the policyholders should properly plan their insurance needs and conduct a detailed cost-benefit analysis of the options keeping in mind the related issues before short listing a particular product. The individuals should try to keep themselves abreast with the changes in the life insurance industry, as it will help them in selecting better products.

The life insurance companies should try to improve their plans and services by developing the products having features practiced in international companies like flexible premium, flexible sum assured and one policy for the whole family. They should add more favourable riders to their plans as these would make them more customized and valuable.

The life insurance industry is full of challenges. However, Indian Insurance Industry has a huge potential and opportunities are also unlimited. The companies can follow efficient benchmarks (turned around time) and provide more customer satisfaction through better servicing.

It is hoped that these suggestions would help the companies in facing the challenges in the life insurance sector. These ideas would help them in meeting the expectations of the policyholders and also raise the confidence of the present and potential policy-holders in the companies.

REFERENCES

Adams, Mike and Hossain, Mahmud, (1998). "Managerial Discretion and Voluntary Disclosure: Empirical Evidence from the New Zealand Life Insurance Industry". *Journal of Accounting and Public Policy*, 17(3), 245-281.

Banerjee, Bhaskar (1983). "Life Insurance as an Investment: A Critical Study". *Decision*, July, 169-175.

Bhakti, Chuangee (2001). "A Survey of Life Insurance Industry". *Business India* February 5-18,126-137.

Chandhok, Anil (2004). "Emerging Issues in the Distribution of Life Insurance Products". *Insurance Chronicle*, December, 2004, 28-32.

Chaudhury, S.K. and Kulkarni, K G (1991). *Role of Life Insurance Corporation in Economic Development of India*. Mumbai: Himalaya Publishing House.

Chordas, Lori (2003). Survey: Most Americans don't Use Web to Research, Buy Life Insurance. *Best's Review*, 104(6), 116.

Chu, Kathy (2005). Survey Finds Rise in Demand for Life Insurance, *Wall Street Journal* (Eastern ed.), April 12, 2005, D.3.

Doss, G. Steward (1995). "Distribution System in LIC," *Dnyanajyoti*, Vol. 12, No. 2 December 1995, 5-17.

Hwang, Tienyu and Greenford, Brian (2005). "A Cross-section Analysis of the Determinants of Life Insurance Consumption in Mainland China, Hong Kong, and Taiwan." *Risk Management and Insurance Review*, 8(1), 103-25.

Jorg, Insigner and Pauly, Mark V. (1986). *A Cross National Study—Economics of Insurance Regulation* London : The Macmillan Press Ltd.

Kellner, S. and Frank, Mathewson G. (1983). "Entry, Size Distribution, Scale, and Scope Economies in the Life Insurance Industry." *The Journal of Business*, 56(1), 25-44.

Mirmirani, Sam, Li, H.C., and Zhou, Qi (1996). "Profit-market Share Relationship: An Empirical Study of the Life Insurance Industry". *American Business Review*, 14(1), 54-59.

Mishra, M.N. (1987). *A Study of Working of LIC of India: Financial and Organisational Aspects*. Jaipur : RBSA Publishers.

More Japanese Moving Away from Life Insurance : Survey, 2003. Tokyo : Jiji Press English News Service.

National Council of Applied Economic Research (1979). *Survey of Attitude towards Life Insurance Cover*. New Delhi: Cambridge Press.

Rao, B.S.R. (1976). *Functionong of LIC—An Appraisal*. Madras: Lalita Publication Press.

Ray, R.M. (1981), *Life Insurance in India—Perspective in Social Security*. New Delhi: Times Press.

Saunders, Mark V.T. and Lu Eric (2004). "China's Insurance Market—The Giant Awakens", *Insurance Chronicle*, October, 2004, 60-65.

Tang, Buck Peng (2001). The Relationship Between Lifestyles and Sources of Customer Value: An Empirical Study of the Life Insurance Industry in Singapore." *Services Marketing Quarterly*, 23(1), 39.

Thomas, Trevor (2003). "Bank Life Insurance Sales Programs Often Lack Clear Strategy". *National Underwriter, Life & Health*, 107(6), 36, 38.

Thomas, Trevor (2005). Study Finds Mass Affluent Need More Life Insurance. *National Underwriter, Life & Health*, 109(2), 10, 41.

Ward, Damian (2002). "The Costs of Distribution in the UK Life Insurance Market". *Applied Economics*, 34, 1959-1968.

A Critical Analysis of Accounting Services in India

22

Shurveer S. Bhanawat

ABSTRACT

The changing and vibrant environment is signaling a rapid adjustment. The professional journey is never ending. There are a lot of challenges from international accounting firms that have already established their global brands. The challenges for the profession as a whole, and for the different stakeholder groups within profession, is to adopt a structure and mindset that can rapidly adopt to change in the profession and business community. In order to make small Indian accounting firms fit in a liberalization scenario, there is an urgent need to re-engineering their functioning. This article examines current scenario of accounting profession in India and how smaller firms have to meet out challenges. These small firms have to tie up with the firms with the expert knowledge in various accounting field. The size of accounting firms has been also explained through data. There are only 0.12 per cent accounting firms having more than ten chartered accountants in 2001 and in 2004 this ratio is slightly increased by 0.38 per cent. There is on an average only two chartered accountants in India. Survival of some firms depends on their ability to re-engineer themselves. Merger of smaller firms appears to be the best solution. The institute has to play an important role in re-engineer of small chartered accountant firms. It should amend regulation, if required, to facilitate mergers, to relax restriction on advertising and to allow networking with other professionals. The recent trend shows that the maximum newly qualified chartered accountants in India are absorbed by service sector like banking, BPO, insurance, etc. Approximately 63.62 per cent of total placements are absorbed by service sector in campus interview held by ICAI in February-March 2006. In order to maintain in the line of global practices some suggestions have been incorporated in this article.

INTRODUCTION

'Service' is a product of human activity. It satisfies various needs of society. Services are intangible and perishable in nature. Services also include 'Accounting Services'. These services can be obtained from skilled accounting professional, technical and managerial personnel. Service sector has been the fastest growing component of international trade during the past decade. But India's trade in accounting services is at present virtually negligible. However, due to deregulation of the economy there is considerable scope for increased trade of accountancy services in the future[1]. The accountancy sector in India already enjoys considerable advantages both in mode one and mode four (GATS has identified four modes of supply of services, viz., cross-boarder supply, consumption abroad, commercial presence and movement of natural persons). In mode one, India has clear advantage with regard to offshoring of accounting services with its high quality manpower and world class IT and telecommunication infrastructure. In mode four, the sector has advantage in view of huge pool of trained and skilled accountants, auditors and other related professionals with good command over English and with established reputation amongst foreign companies. The preset article critically analyzes accounting services in India.

What is Accounting Services

As per the WTO's service sectoral classification list (W/120)[2] Accounting Services refers to accounting, auditing and book keeping services. It includes wide range of additional services also like insolvency services, taxation services, investment services and management consulting. Demand of accounting services result from both mandatory legal requirement as well as client's seeking advice on various issues. In India, there is another category of services Company Secretoryship—which is also relevant for the functions of a company like accountancy. However, it does not include in the classification list of WTO.

The Current Scenario

The birth of accounting services in India can coincide with the formation of Institute of Chartered Accountants of India (ICAI) in 1949. Accounting services in India are regulated through a combination of legal and professional bodies like ICAI, the Institute of Cost and Work Accountants of India (ICWAI) and Institute of Companies Secretaries of India (ICSI) as well as through specific provision in companies act, Income Tax Act, etc. Most of accounting firms in India are of small size. The accounting professionals are only allowed to operate either as partnership firm or as a sole proprietorship firm. Since the Partnership Act of India permits only 20 or less professional under one firm. So, the number of partners in Indian accounting firm is limited to 20 or less. Further the numbers of statutory audits of companies per partner are restricted to 20. Indian regulations also prescribe inter-disciplinary professional models, i.e. Accounting firms are not allowed to hire management professionals to perform consulting and management services.

Accounting Professionals in Service Sectors

There are about 1,30,000 members of ICAI,[3] every year nearly 6,000 members are added to the existing accounting professional force. As far as gender data are concerned in accounting professional, are not available because these are not disclosed in any annual reports. Women have shown keen interest in pursuing the Chartered Accountants (CA) course is very likely that they are nearly 5 per cent of total members of Institute of Chartered Accountants of India. A review of the membership data reveals that new members are absorbed largely by the services sector like banking, insurance, telecom, finance, security market, etc.

In campus placement programme conducted by ICAI during February–March 2006 the maximum jobs are offered by "Business Process Outsourcing" to newly qualified Chartered Accountants. The sector-wise absorption of newly qualified Chartered Accountants in February–March 2006 campus interviews held by ICAI are as follows:

Table 22.1: Sector-wise Absorption of Chartered Accountants Through Campus Placement

S. No.	Industry	No. of Companies No.	No. of Companies %	Job Offered No.	Job Offered %
1.	Business Process Outsourcing (BPO)	4	3.92	334	29.19
2.	Information Technology	10	9.81	125	10.93
3.	Chartered Accountancy Firm	8	7.84	116	10.14
4.	Insurance	2	1.96	61	5.33
5.	Banking	8	7.84	53	4.63
6.	Business Consultancy	1	0.98	21	1.83
7.	Financial Services	5	4.90	18	1.57
8.	Others	64	62.75	416	36.38
	Total	102	100.00	1144	100.00

Source: The Chartered Accountants CA, Volume 54, No. 11, May 2006, page No. 1668

On examining the above Table 22.1 it is revealed that service sector like BPO, Business Consultancy, Insurance Companies, Banking; IT and other financial services have emerged as the important destination for the new members of the Institute. With as many as 728 jobs offered by service sector out of 1144, reflecting about 63.62 per cent. An inference can be drawn that the entities engaged in BPO stands in the top in terms of number of jobs offered to recruit newly qualified chartered accountants.

Size Distribution of Accountancy Firms

Out of 1685 registered/approved CAs in 1949 only 1100 were in practice most of them were having proprietary concerns. As at April 1, 2001 there were 42,339 CA firms. The average size of those firms in terms of number of partners was 1.53 partners. There are 43,000 audit firms, with an average of two chartered accountants per firm in 2004.

Table 22.2: Size Distribution of CA Firms as at April 2001

No. of Partners	1	2	3	4	5	6	7	8	9	10	>10	Total
Total Firms	31144	7161	2104	796	375	305	206	101	61	34	52	42339
%	73.56	16.91	4.97	1.88	0.89	0.72	0.49	0.24	0.14	0.08	0.12	100

Source: The Chartered Accountant, Volume 50, No. 7, January 2002, page No. 827.

The above Table 22.2 clearly indicates that 73.56 per cent accounting firms are in nature of sole proprietorship. Approximately 90 per cent firms have less than three partners. only 0.12 per cent firms having more than 10 partners. At present as per WTO this is only 0.5 per cent. There is a marginal improvement of 0.38 per cent in 2004 as compared to 2001. The scenario is not very encouraging. Analysis of the distribution of income according to firm size would have provided a better insight into the dynamic of the profession. In the absence of data we could not analyze the income distribution among firms. The situation will change with the change in the environment. In order to survive, small firms need to re-engineer themselves.

Challenges Facing the Accounting Profession

The Indian accounting firms are facing the challenges from international firms, which have already established their global brands. FDI is not allowed in this sector and Foreign Service providers are also not allowed to undertake statutory audit of companies as per the provisions of the Institute of Chartered Accountants of India. Further, there are restrictions on advertising and the use of international brand names is not allowed. Nevertheless, the 'Big Four' accounting firms (Deloitte & Touché, Price Water House Coopers, Ernst & Young and KPMA) have set up offices in India as management/consulting firms and it is alleged that they are actually providing accounting services by partnering with domestic accounting firms. Since there is no statutory limit on the number of professionals hired by consulting firms, the Big Four have more accountants on their rolls than the domestic firms. Multinational enterprises, which have set up their business in India, either as a Joint Venture partners or otherwise prefer to have service from international CA firms. It is only natural. Trust is the only thing of relationship between an audit firms and its clients. This trust comes from 'brand', the firm's name, and not just from the quality of individuals who provide the services. Usually multinational enterprises appoint the same firms that provide them service at home.

Information Technology has become an integral part of the business, and its use for audit is increasing rapidly. Therefore, investment in information technology by accounting firms has become a hygiene factor, and does not provide any competitive advantage. Thus, in the new environment, accounting firms' investment in technology and training is much higher than that in the past.

New opportunities for the profession will pose challenges to both individual Chartered Accountants and to their professional body. The challenges for the profession as a whole, and for the different stakeholder groups within profession, is to adopt a structure and mindset that can be rapidly adapt to change in the profession and business community. A core skill will be change management with willingness to abandon the old and more toward the new.

Suggestions

India, with reservoir of professionals, should upgrade the infrastructure and harmonize its policies in the line of global practices. The following suggestions can be made in this connection:

- In India professional services are generally rendered by partnership firm and cannot be registered as companies. In contrast, professional and consulting firms like bearing point (formerly KPMG Consulting), Navigant Consulting, FTI Consulting, Hewitt, etc. are corporate entities and listed on international stock exchanges. In India too, formation of accounting services companies and their listing on stock exchange should be allowed.
- Survival of small firms depend on their ability to re-engineer themselves. A merger of small firms appears to be the best solution. Accounting firms must focus on all the five determinants of quality of services. These determinants are—Reliability, Responsiveness, Assurance, Empathy and Tangibles. This will require significant investment in technology, people and tangible assets.
- In India, Chartered Accountants should be allowed to advertise and solicit business in lines with international practices.

- The bank credit to service sector should be increased to 50 per cent from present level of about 36 per cent of total bank credit in line with other countries like 48 per cent in UK, 63.8 per cent in Thailand and 66.4 per cent in Philippines.[5]
- In order to survive in this fast changing world, there is urgent need for re-engineering of small accounting firms. In this scenario one who innovates, creates, thinks big, acts faster, will survive.
- According to Allvin Toffler "One who adapts to change will survive and other will die." Accounting firms must be willing to change from traditional folio of accounting audit and taxes, and provide new services. They should always explore new opportunities. Firms should be specialized in specific area and build brand name in market.
- The accounting firms have to professionally tie up, not only with expert small Chartered Accountants firms who possess the expert knowledge in Direct/Indirect Taxation/Audit/Financial Consultancy/Information Technology but also can think of providing allied services under one roof with proper tie up with Company Secretaries, Cost Accountants, Lawyers and Other Professionals. Then only the client will get attracted and will stay on with the smaller firms.
- The developed countries should grant recognition of educational and professional qualifications and simplify rules of registration and practices of professionals from developing countries.

CONCLUSION

India has a strong base of accounting services. Most of accounting professionals are absorbed by service sector. In India almost 74 per cent accounting firms are in nature of sole proprietorship less than 1 per cent firms having more than 10 partners. Survival of small firms depends on their ability to re-engineer themselves. There is a challenge from international accounting firms also. The increase in the number of multinational enterprises in India has increased the demand for service from international firms or their representatives in India. In order to make these small firms fit in a liberalized scenario, there is an urgent need to re-engineer their functioning. Small firms can be merged to form a mammoth accounting firm, e.g. wiped with new generation leaders who specialize in various field and are capable of meeting the challenges of new work environments.

NOTES

1. Chanda R., *Globalization of Services – India's Opportunities and Constraints*, Oxford University Press, New Delhi.
2. "WTO Services Sectoral Classification List", Council for Trade in Service, MTN. GNS/W/120, 10 July 1991.
3. *The Chartered Accountants*, CA, Vol. 54, No. 11, May 2006, ICAI New Delhi, page No. 1562.
4. "Sustaining India's Service Revolution Access to Foreign Markets, Domestic Reforms and Iinternational Negotiations", *The World Bank* 2004.
5. *The Chartered Secretary* Vol. XXXV, No. 8, August 2005, ICSI, New Delhi, page 1129.

ABBREVIATIONS

BPO	Business Process Outsourcing
CA	Chartered Accountant
GATS	General Agreement on Trade in Services
ICAI	Institute of Chartered Accountants of India
ICSI	Institute of Company Secretaries of India
ICWAI	Institute of Cost & Works Accountants of India
WTO	World Trade Organization

A Comparative Study on the Sectoral Performance of MSM 30 Applying Financial Ratios and Multivariate Analysis

M. Selvam, Rengasamy Elango and
Mohammed Ibrahim Hussein

ABSTRACT

Successful investing is a long-range endeavor and knowing where to invest requires well-informed in-depth research. An investor who expects immediate return on his investment is considered unsuitable to long-term investments. This is particularly true if one wishes to make investments in stock markets that are quite often compared to gambling activities. Even before choosing the scrip or company for investment purposes, an investor has to decide on the sector in which he should invest his funds. In this regard, it should be mentioned that although there are innumerable techniques available to choose the right stock, hardly any research studies have been conducted to identify the right sector as a guidance for investing especially in the Middle East markets. To serve this end, we have chosen Muscat Securities Market (MSM) for this study on sectoral performance.

The main objective of the present study is to compare the sector-wise performance of the MSM companies. This paper further aims at determining the ability of a set of selected financial ratios, more specifically, the widely applied price-earning ratio for choosing the best sector as a guide to investment decisions. Apart from normality test, a set of appropriate non-parametric multivariate statistical tests were also applied on the three sectors in the MSM 30 index companies.

Our results indicate that the mean price-earning ratios were 10.85, 14.62, 10.59 for Banking and Investment, Industry and Services and Insurance respectively which indicate a mild difference in performance. The results of Kruskal-Wallis test applied on five variables/ratios *vs*. Price Earning ratio to test the significance of difference among the three sectors revealed a mild statistical significance in respect of only two variables, i.e., Total Assets and Share Price. This proves the poor ability of the Price Earning ratio to capture the differences in the performance of the sectors analyzed.

INTRODUCTION

Multitude of investment alternatives in the capital market makes investment choice perplexing in a global market plane. In this context, the use of Ratio Analysis, particularly, Price-Earnings ratio in conjunction with other accounting ratios could be of good use in selecting the right investment. This paper relates to decision-making with respect to the choice investment sector.

Sector Analysis

After deciding the economy where one wants to invest, one has to decide the economic sector or sectors in which one should deploy one's funds, as sectors are becoming more and more relevant to the asset allocation and portfolio management process as a whole. This becomes more relevant, due to the political and economic developments since early 1990s that resulted in integration of the world markets, with varied implications for varied sectors of world economies. Having narrowed down to a particular sector or sectors, one should choose the industry or industries within a sector or sectors and then the company or companies within an industry or industries. At every stage, one should select the best investment alternative. Readers will appreciate that the Sector Analysis could be schemed into fundamental analysis after Economy Analysis, but before Industry Analysis, followed by Company Analysis.

Review of Literature

Not many research studies have been carried out to identify the right investment sector or sectors, especially in the Middle East markets. The present study is a pertinent attempt to fill the gap. To serve this purpose, the researchers thought it fit to choose an emerging market and obviously, Muscat Securities

Market (MSM) stands atop in our choice, not only because of its proximity with the researchers, but also in terms of credible strides it has made amply qualifying for research studies of this kind.

Ordinary investors do not have access to detailed and in-depth information about even individual companies, not to speak of information on economic sectors. Perhaps fund managers and equity analysts have access. Owing to the dearth of information, the ultimate tool that is available to ordinary investors is the widely used ratio analysis to compare and differentiate between sectors. Price-Earning Multiple, Return on Investment and Equity Multiple (a surrogate for leverage) could be used in this regard. Several past studies have applied financial ratios and more particularly price-earnings ratio to analyze the performance of companies. A succinct review of the previous research works reveals mixed opinions with regard to usage of ratios. The authors indicate that due care and caution needs to be exercised while applying financial ratios as criteria for selection of investment avenues.

Ben Amoko-Ado[1] and Brian Smith (2002) have analyzed the causal links between interest rates and the Price Earning ratio of the Toronto Stock Exchange 300 Index (TSE 300) and of seven major Canadian industries 1965-97. The results revealed that there was a negative correlation between Price-Earning ratio and Treasury Bill rates, differing between industries. They have noticed that the Treasury Bill rates explained 95 per cent of Price-Earning ratio variation for the TSE 300, although it was not significant for the gold and silver industry. Another interesting finding was that dividend payout ratios and lower investor risk aversion are positively correlated to Price-Earning ratio but that the growth rate had a more variable influence.

Ting-Ya Hseieh[2], Morris H.L.Wang (2001) examined the relevance of ratio analysis in looking into a firm's financial status. The authors have concluded that the ratio analysis would serve as an excellent way of looking into a firm's financial status. However, they have cautioned that in performing ratio analysis, due caution should be exercised in the selection of ratios for use. They have further cautioned that in a multi-criteria decision-making framework, poor quality of criteria selection i.e. financial ratio will consequently undermine the quality of evaluation. The study aimed at establishing a systematic approach for finding critical financial ratios to assist in financial analysis.

Kathleen A Kaminski[3], T. Sterling Wetzel, Liming Guan (2004) made an attempt to analyze whether financial ratios could detect fraudulent financial reporting. The study was exploratory in nature to determine whether financial ratios of fraudulent companies differ from those of non-fraudulent companies. Fraudulent firms were identified by examining the SEC's Accounting and Auditing Enforcement Releases issued between 1982 and 1999. The authors have matched fraudulent firms (n = 79) with non-fraudulent firms on the basis of time period and industry. Using the matched-pair design, ratio analysis for a seven years period, was conducted on 21 ratios. The analysis resulted in interesting conclusions. Overall, 16 ratios were found to be significant. Of these only three ratios were significant for three time periods. Of the 16 statistically significant ratios, only five were significant during the period prior to the fraud year. Finally, the authors have applied discriminant analysis to classify the firms and the misclassifications for fraud firms ranged from 58 per cent to 98 per cent. These results provide empirical evidence of the limited ability of financial ratios to detect and/or predict fraudulent financial reporting.

Yoram C. Peles[4] and Meir I. Schneller (1982) in their article titled, "Financial ratios and the analysis of marketing policy" made an attempt to demonstrate how financial ratios can be used in order to analyze certain aspects of a firm's marketing policy. They have stated that accounting ratios were affected by the firm's marketing management philosophy. With the financial data for a set of UK companies, they examined the impact of their marketing policy on the behavior of financial ratios applying a cross-section analysis over-time. They have concluded that high levels of marketing policies are associated with higher levels of operating profitability.

Mohammed Amidu[5], **Joshua Abor** in their article titled, "Determinants of dividend payout ratios in Ghana" examined the determinants of dividend payout ratios of listed companies in Ghana. The analyses were performed using data derived from the financial statements of firms listed on the Ghana Stock Exchange during a six year period. Ordinary Least Square Model has been used to estimate the regression equation. Institutional holding was used as a proxy for agency cost. Growth in sales and market—to book value are also used as proxies for investment opportunities. The results showed positive relationships between dividend payout ratios and profitability, cash flow and tax. The results also show negative associations between dividend payout and risk, institutional holding, growth and market to book value. The significant variables in the results that influence dividend payout ratios are profitability, cash flow, sales growth and market to book value.

Selvam, M.[6] (1994) in his paper 'Interpreting High P-E Ratio', has observed that P-E ratio is a marriage between Technical and Fundamental Analyses as Price data, the preserve of the chartists and earnings data, the preserve of fundamental analysts, are combined in P-E. High P-E ratios during boom, normal and depression market conditions mean different things.

Research Questions

The research questions of the present study emerge as follows:

(i) How do the three different sectors of MSM 30 perform? Is there any significant difference in performance amongst the sectors?

(ii) Does Price-Earning ratio ably capture the differences in sector performance to be employed as a guide to investment decisions?

Objectives and Description of the Study

As stated in the research question, the main focus of the present research is to investigate the sector-wise performance of the MSM 30 companies. As a sub-objective, the paper further aims at determining the ability of a set of selected financial ratios, more specifically, the widely applied price-earning ratio for choosing the best sector as a guide to investment decisions.

Test of Hypotheses

The present study has the following null and alternate hypotheses.

The *Null Hypotheses* of the study are:

(i) There is no statistically significant difference among Price-Earning ratio of the three sectors in MSM 30 companies.

$$H_o: PE_{BKI} = PE_{IND} = PE_{SERIN}$$

(ii) There is no statistically significant difference among Return on Investment of the three sectors in MSM 30 companies.

$$H_o: ROI_{BKI} = ROI_{IND} = ROI_{SERIN}$$

(iii) There is no statistically significant difference among Equity Multiples of the three sectors in MSM 30 companies.

$$H_o: EM_{BKI} = EM_{IND} = EM_{SERIN}$$

(iv) There is no statistically significant difference among Total Assets of the three sectors in MSM 30 companies.

$$H_o: TA_{BKI} = TA_{IND} = TA_{SERIN}$$

Alternative Hypothesis H_a: There is statistically significant difference among three sectors on the above respective performance factors.

Data and Sample

The sample for the purpose of the study consisted of the three sectors of the MSM 30 (Muscat Securities Market 30 Index companies). The three sectors are as follows:

1. Banking and Investment (BKI)
2. Industry(IND)
3. Services and Insurance(SERINS)

- The sample consists of 29 companies out of the MSM 30 Index. No data were available for Renaissance Services, a company in Services and Insurance Sector; hence excluded from the purview of analysis. (List of companies, given in Appendix 1)

- The data were sourced from Muscat Securities Market's Annual Statistical Bulletin 2005.
- The data were annualized and standardized applying suitable techniques.

Limitations of the Study

The sectoral mean ratios are simple arithmetic means of ratios of companies in respective sectors. Ideally, weighted means should have been used. The period covered is brief. But we feel the methodology right.

Analytical Tools

Financial Ratios/Variables used in the study are:

(i) **Price-Earning Ratio (Multiple) = Market price at any point of time/Earnings Per Share.**

Earnings Per Share = Net Income After Taxes/No. of Shares Outstanding. Price-Earning Ratio is used to measure how cheap or expensive the share prices are, relative to EPS. The price per share (numerator) is the market price of a single share of the stock of a company at any point of time. The earnings per share (denominator) is the net income of the company for the most recent 12 month period (past earnings), or the next 12 months (projected earnings) divided by a number of outstanding shares of the company. The Price-Earnings ratio of a stock describes the price of a share relative to its earnings.

(ii) **Return on Investment (ROI) (%) = (Net Income after taxes/Total Assets) × 100.** Return on Investment is a performance measure used to evaluate the efficiency of an investment or to compare the efficiency of a number of different investments. The numerator is the net income after taxes and the denominator is the total assets of the company. Clearly higher ROI indicates better performance and *vice versa*.

(iii) **Equity Multiple = Total Assets/Shareholders Equity.** Equity Multiple is the ratio of Total Assets to

Shareholders' Equity. This ratio is a surrogate of leverage. A higher ratio means higher leverage and *vice versa*.

(iv) **Total Assets:** Total Assets of Companies is a factor considered for associative analysis. Total Assets, despite the level efficiency of assets, proportionately affects earnings, for all positive ROI. So, more total assets mean more earnings.

Analytical Results I: Descriptive Performance Analysis of Different Sectors

The summary results on the performance of the three sectors are as follows in Table 23.1(a).

Table 23.1(a): Sector-wise Analysis: Ratios & Total Assets: Descriptive Data

Details	Sector	Mean	Std.Dev
P-E Ratio	BKI	10.85	6.78
	IND	14.62	6.82
	SERINS	10.59	7.92
ROI	BKI	9.07	9.57
	IND	13.73	6.46
	SERINS	9.77	5.65
Equity Multiple	BKI	11.53	17.59
	IND	2.38	0.98
	SERINS	5.03	5.38
TOTASS	BKI	562.40	770.99
(in RO)	IND	45.87	41.72
	SERINS	97.19	85.16

(i) The analytical results indicate that the mean P-E ratio is the highest in the case of Industry Sector (IND) with 14.62 times with a standard deviation of 6.82. This would mean that an investor intending to invest in Industry sector of the MSM have to pay RO 14.62 for every RO 1 of earnings of the Industry Sector on an average. This would further mean that either the stock is (a) relatively over priced or the current earnings are less or (b) the potentials of the sector are higher. Banking and Investment and Services and Insurance sectors fare with lower P-E multiples. They have almost equal P-E, but relatively more standard deviation. So the companies in these sectors have more volatile P-E. Should an investor prefer a lower P-E Banking and Investment and Services and Insurance sectors or the higher P-E Industry sector?

(ii) A cursory look at the ROI figures indicates that the Industry sector has out-performed the other sectors. The higher ROI of the industry sector would have resulted in higher earnings per share, given the debt-equity ratio. And with higher EPS, P-E ought to have been lower. But the same is higher. And that shows the market values the stock for its potentials as well. This leads us to opine that P-E ratio is indeed a true indicator of the performance of a company/industry/sector.

(iii) An analysis of the Equity multiple has revealed that the Industry sector has the lowest value. That is leverage is lower compared to other sectors. With lower leverage EPS gets reduced, hiking P-E ratio. Industry sector's higher P-E ratio is explained by the lower equity multiple perhaps. Traditionally, the banking sector is known for its high equity multiple, that is raising more assets with less equity, but with more debt funds. This leads to trading on equity effect, which could reduce P-E ratio. That is a kind of efficiency.

(iv) Mean total assets of companies in the Industry sector is the lowest (45.87) of all the three sectors. Mean amount of total assets of companies in the Banking and Investment sector is the highest.

Test of hypotheses for equality of chosen factors across the different sectors made using non-parametric Kruskal-Wallis Test, as the data set failed normality test. The data are given in Table 23.1(b). The sectors differed only with respect to total assets as revealed by Table 23.1(b).

Analytical Results II

Does P/E ratio ably capture the differences in sector performance to be employed as a guide to investment decisions?

Table 23.1(b): Sector-wise Analysis: Ratios & Total Assets : Kruskal-Wallis Test

Details	Sector	Mean Rank	Chi-Square	P-Value
P/E	BKI	13.70		
	IND	18.30	2.348	0.309
	SERINS	12.78		
ROI	BKI	12.30		
	IND	18.80	3.183	0.204
	SERINS	13.78		
Equity Multiple	BKI	17.05		
	IND	14.75	1.085	0.581
	SERINS	13.00		
TOTASS	BKI	20.50		
	IND	9.25	8.749	0.013*
	SERINS	15.28		

* Significant (S) at 0.05 level

The lower the PE, the less one has to pay for the stock, relative to what one can expect to earn from it. Higher the PE, the more over-valued the stock is. But a lower PE need not mean less price and higher PE need not mean high price, as well, when expectancy factor as to future prospects is also taken into account. So does the PE ratio tell past performance only or reflect the future as well? A low PE could mean worthlessness of the stock with feeble potentials to perform and high PE could mean great potentials of the stock concerned. Given the PE, does that indicate apt valuation of the stock or not? This could be known, by reading how the PE goes with or correlates with other important parameters such as ROI, Total Assets and Equity Multiple. This will help us in deciding to rely or not or how much to rely on PE as a guide to making investment decisions. Table 23.2 gives the relevant data.

It is good in the context, to associate ROI with PE multiple. In PE multiple, the 'earnings' is the denominator, while in the ROI the 'earnings' is the numerator. So, PE and ROI could normally be found to have negative correlation. For all the three sectors, it is found that the correlation coefficients are negative and significant too for two sectors. For Banking and Investment sector the correlation coefficient is highly significant and for Industry sector it is significant. So PE could serve an investment decision criterion along with ROI. As the association is highly significant for Banking and Investment Sector, that sector emerges as the first choice.

Table 23.2: Spearman's Rho - Correlation Analysis

Correlated Factor Pairs	Sector	Correlation Value	P-Value	Result
ROI & PE	BKI	–0.782	0.008***	HS
	IND	–0.588	0.074*	MS
	SERINS	–0.350	0.356	
TOTASS & PE	BKI	0.612	0.060*	MS
	IND	0.515	0.128	
	SERINS	–0.250	0.516	
Equity Multiple & PE	BKI	0.588	0.074*	MS
	IND	0.515	0.128	
	SERINS	–0.633	0.067*	MS

* Mildly Significant (MS) at 0.10 level

** Significant (S) at 0.05 level

*** Highly Significant (HS) at 0.01 level.

Return on Equity (ROE), given the ROI is influenced directly by the equity multiple. Note that ROE = ROI x Equity Multiple. So, ROE and Equity Multiple are directly associated. As in ROE, the earnings figure is factored, while in PE the earnings figure is the factor, Equity Multiple and PE tend to be negatively correlated. In our study, we find a significant negative correlation in the case of Services and Insurance sector only. So this could be our second choice sector for investment.

More total assets, for all positive rate of return, mean more earnings. More earnings mean, reduced PE. Thus between total assets and PE, negative correlation could be expected. In our study, we find an insignificant negative correlation in the case of Services and Insurance sector only.

SUMMARY OF FINDINGS AND CONCLUSION

The study analyzed the sector performance of the three sectors in MSM 30 index and found that the sectors differed only with respect to total assets. The study tested whether P/E could serve as a reliable tool in sector selection. A set of three ratios/variables were associated with P-E. It emerged that P-E ratio could be used as a tool to select the right sector provided the intrinsic performance of the company supports the market price. P-E and ROI could be correlated to spot the right sector. The first choice sector happens to be the Banking and Investment sector, followed by Insurance and Services sector. And both the sectors had lower P-E ratios compared to the Industry sector. It is summed up that lower P-E is a definite guide to investment choice making. Smart investors pick up securities with unbelievably lower P-E ratios.

APPENDIX 1

MSM 30 Index Companies

Sl. No.	Banking and Investment Sector	Industry Sector	Services & Insurance Sector
1.	National Bank of Oman	Oman Chromite	Dhofar Insurance
2.	Dhofar International Dev. & Investment Holding	Oman Textile Mills Holding	Port Ser. Corporation
3.	Oman International Bank	Dhofar Cattle Feed	Oman Fisheries
4.	Oman Investment & Finance	Oman Flour Mills	United Power
5.	Ominvest	Raysut Cement	Al Jazeira Services
6.	Oman & Emirates Inv.(OM)	Oman Cement	Shell Oman Marketing
7.	Alliance Housing Bank	Al Anwar Holding	Salalah Portr Services
8.	Al Sharqia Inv.Holding	Al Khaleej Polypro	Al Maha Petroleum
9.	ONIC Holding	Al Jazeera Tube Mills	AES Barka
10.	Bank Muscat	Oman Chlorine	Renaissance Services

REFERENCES

(a) Research Papers

1. Ben Amoako-Adu, Brian Smith. *Analysis of P/E Ratios and Interest Rates, Managerial Finance*, April 2002, Volume: 28, Issue: 4, pp. 48-59.
2. Ting-Ya Hsieh, Morris H.L.Wang. "Finding Critical Financial Ratios for Taiwan's Property Development Firms in Recession", *Logistics Information Management*, January 2001, Volume; 14, Issue: 5/6, pp. 401-13.

3. Kathleen A. Kaminski, T.Sterling Wetzel, Liming Guan. "Can Financial Ratios Detect Fraudulent Financial Reporting", *Managerial Auditing Journal*, January 2004, Volume:19, Issue1, pp. 15-28.
4. Yoram C. Peles, Meir I. Schneller. "Financial Ratios and the Analysis of Marketing", *European Journal of Marketing*, Year 1982, Volume 16, Number 5.
5. Mohammed Amidu, Joshua Abor. "Determinants of Dividend Payout Ratios in Ghana", *The Journal of Risk Finance*, Year 2006, Volume: 7, Issue: 2, pp. 136-45.
6. Selvam, M. "Interpreting High P-E Ratio", *Fortune India*, Year 1994, Vol. XII-22, p. 32.

(b) Reports

Muscat Securities Market, Annual Statistical Bulletin 2005.

Real Estate Financing in India: Challenges and Opportunities

24

S.C. Bansal and *Kaveri Bansal*

ABSTRACT

The real estate sector plays a catalytic role in ensuring prolific and sustainable growth of an economy. The nature of the industry requires significant investment at various stages of construction and development. The gap between the desired and the available funds can be bridged by procuring loans from banks, housing finance companies (HFCs) and other financial institutions. This paper examines the problems faced by the realtors in arranging funds for projects from these institutions in India. It also identifies the challenges faced by the financiers while extending loans to the developers. The necessary information has been obtained with the help of two structured questionnaires prepared to find out the systems and opinions of providers and takers of real estate loans. After conducting a pilot study, the final questionnaires were canvassed among 20 real estate companies and 15 housing finance institutions having their registered offices at Ahmedabad, Delhi, Haryana and U.P. However, only two-thirds of the housing finance institutions and three-fourths of the real estate companies provided the desired information. The sample size has been deliberately limited to a small number to have a deep insight into the practices of real estate developers and financers. The study reveals that Indian reality market is witnessing a frenzied activity. Financial institutions have laid down overall ceilings for real estate advances. Banks and HFCs grant loan for acquisition of land as well as construction of building. The amount of loan is determined by cost of project, contribution by the developer, and amount of booking advance. The application for a large loan is sent to the head office along with necessary documents for approval. The loan proposals are appraised from four angles, namely, organizational, financial, technical and legal. Real estate loan is normally provided on the basis of first equitable mortgage on the property and personal guarantee. Loans are usually disbursed in installments. A separate escrow account is maintained for each project by the realtor for payment of interest and principal. It has been suggested that, in wake of increasing competition, financial institutions and real estate companies should position themselves effectively. Quality lending should become an order of the day and developers should ensure timely completion at the least possible cost. It is hoped that the study would be useful to diverse stakeholders of realty financing.

INTRODUCTION

In the present age, economic progress of a country depends, to a large extent, upon the quality and quantum of infrastructure development. Real estate is a part and parcel of these facilities. Broadly speaking, real estate refers to 'land, including the air above and the ground below it, and any buildings or structures on it'. It includes all activities involving ownership, development, purchase, sale, financing, and leasing of land, residential accommodation and commercial buildings. The main players in this industry are landlords, builders, developers (realtors), investors, real estate agents, tenants, financial institutions and buyers. Also known as *realty* or *real property*, it is a capital-intensive industry. A large volume of funds is required to convert vacant tracts of land into housing or commercial edifices. A realtor may not have enough funds to meet such requirements. The gap between desired and available funds can be bridged by raising funds from banks, housing finance companies (HFCs) and other financial institutions.

The real estate sector in India is on upturn. According to Economic Times, (April 23, 2006), the real estate sector has grown into a $ 20 billion industry in India. It contributes to 6 per cent of GDP and 29 per cent of organized employment. It is expected to grow from the current USD 20 billion to USD 102 billion in the next ten years. The main growth thrust in this sector is likely to be experienced due to favorable demographics, increasing purchasing power, existence of customer-friendly financial institutions and reforms initiated by the government to attract domestic as well as global investors.

The present study intends to find out the practices of the providers and borrowers of real estate funds, particularly, banks, HFCs, builders and developers. It also examines the challenges faced by bankers and realtors in providing and availing loans respectively. Section II reviews some of the existing empirical works. Section III describes the methodology used to collect data. Section IV presents major findings. Finally, Section V gives the conclusion.

LITERATURE REVIEW

No study seems to have been reported on real estate financing in India. However, this Section reviews some of the works which may be helpful in analyzing the broad observations of the present study.

Carter (2003) conducted a study on the credit supply effect on commercial real estate loans by commercial banks. It focused on the relationship between non-performing commercial banks and variables such as loan volume, credit spread, average vacancy rate and unemployment. It revealed that the credit supply effect existed in commercial real estate lending.

Hegstad (2003) emphasized on land registration and the need for efficient management of title and other property information, with focus on the Norwegian system.

Holsonback made a study in 2003 on Initial Public Offerings (IPOs) and Real Estate Investment Trusts (REITs). It compared the IPOs of four industries: retail, manufacturers of communication equipment, software development and REITs. It was observed that due to tight credit in real estate markets, private real estate companies often formed as REITs in order to raise capital. Iwatsubo (2003) reported bank lending and bank firm relationships in Japan. It investigated the shift in the loan portfolios of Japanese bank towards real estate in the 1990s.

Bakimow (2004) identified the financial performance of banks and their lending responses to monetary policy changes. He suggested that financially weak banks reported more to monetary policy changes than otherwise financially sound banks. Furthermore, the observation pattern appeared to be driven by the behavior of a bank's real estate loan portfolio.

Kunzel (2004) highlighted inefficiencies in the real estate market. He suggested that special institutional characteristics of the real estate market produced inefficiencies that contributed to price volatility.

Thus, it can be said that many issues associated to real estate have been covered but areas related to real estate financing such as different means of funding available to realtors, procedural aspects involved in procuring term loans from financial institutions, documentation and risk involved have not been covered. The present study, therefore, is likely to bridge an important research gap.

METHODOLOGY

The study is exploratory in nature. Initially, a list of various real estate companies and housing finance institutions was compiled from the commercials given by them in various newspapers, as no authenticated data was available. In-depth discussions were held with two bankers and two developers about the varied aspects of financing real estate projects.

Two structured questionnaires, containing both open- and close-ended questions, were pilot tested on two financial institutions and two real estate companies. Adjustments were made therein in the light of observations and suggestions given by their senior executives. The final questionnaires were personally canvassed among 20 real estate companies and 15 housing finance institutions having their regional and registered offices at Ahmedabad, Delhi, Haryana and U.P. All of these banks and real estate companies were personally visited to elicit the information. The sample size has deliberately been limited to a small number to have a deep insight in their practices.

However, only two-thirds of the housing finance institutions and three-fourths of the real estate companies cooperated by providing the desired information. The time spent in interviewing the executives ranged from two to eight hours. Most of the selected organizations have recorded outstanding performance in their segments. The executives, mainly head of the finance department (credit wing), are contacted for information. Majority of the responding executives are 'more than 40 years' in age. A large proportion of them have a total work experience of 11-15 years (Figure 24.1) in their respective fields. Figures 24.2 and 24.3 depict that most of the executives have academic as well as professional qualifications.

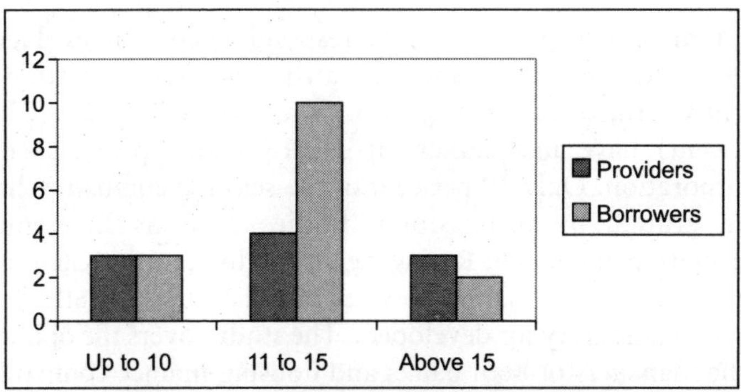

Figure 24.1: Total Work Experience (years)

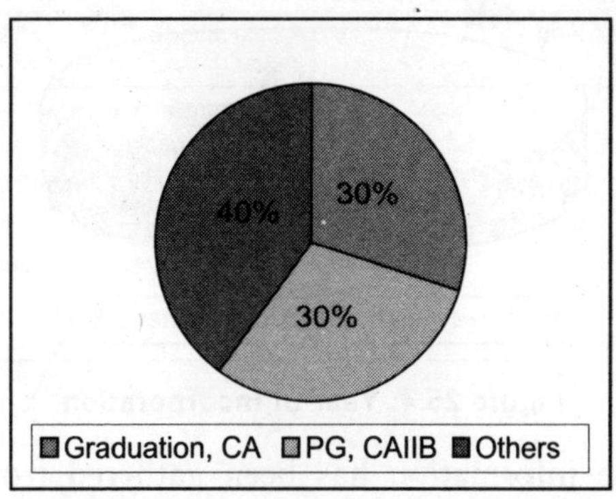

Figure 24.2: Qualification (Providers)

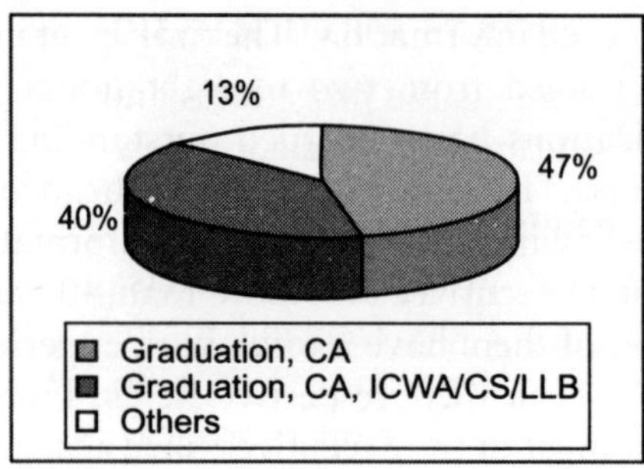

Figure 24.3: Qualification (Borrowers)

Year of incorporation of the responding companies (Figure 24.4) shows that the study has fairly good representation of recently formed real estate groups. Majority of the firms (73.33 per cent) have undertaken up to 15 major projects since incorporation. Only 20 per cent of the selected companies have been graded by professional bodies such as Investment Information and Credit Rating Agency of India Ltd. (ICRA) and Credit Rating Information Services of India Ltd. (CRISIL) since it is not mandatory for developers. The study covers the opinions of the managers of both banks and housing finance companies.

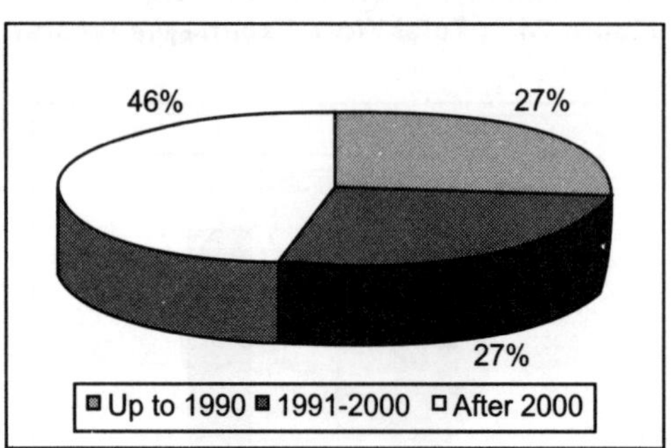

Figure 25.4: Year of Incorporation

Thus, the information has been gathered from matured, knowledgeable and highly experienced senior executives in various housing finance institutions and real estate companies that have entered in the arena.

RESULTS AND DISCUSSION

This Section presents the procedures and practices followed by real estate practitioners in India.

1 Provision for Loan

The Indian real property sector has undergone radical transformation since 2000. Demand for residential as well as commercial space has stepped up. In order to match this growing demand, more and more developers are gearing up in the market by acquiring land and announcing new projects. Real estate is an expensive activity. However, funds are not a problem nowadays. A large number of banks and HFCs have entered the arena to augment their bottom lines.

2 Purpose(s) of Assistance

Banks and HFCs provide loans to builders and developers for various purposes. Figure 24.5 indicates that all the lending institutions grant funds for purchase of land and construction of housing/commercial units. Finance is also provided for mere construction activity. However, loan for acquisition of plots is normally not entertained by financial institutions, since it may be utilized for speculative activity. The figure also shows that majority (9 out of 15) of the real estate companies avail

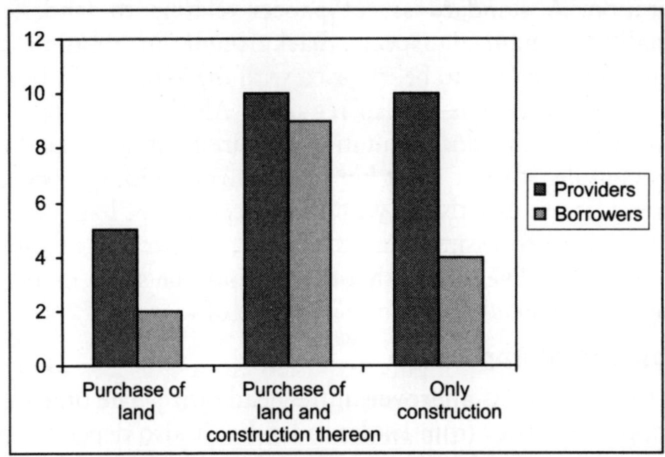

Figure 24.5: Purpose(s) of Assistance

construction finance for payment for land and construction of units on it. Different banks and HFCs also allow the facility of refinance or takeover of existing project loan.

3 Quantum of Finance

The quantum of finance that any realtor is eligible for depends upon certain factors such as project cost, margin money and sales advances. Financial institutions, usually grant a maximum of 50 per cent of the total estimated cost of proposal as construction loan to builders. The estimated cost of the project is calculated on the basis of land price, development cost, construction expense, architect and consultant fees, marketing, advertisement and administrative overheads, finance charges and contingencies. The amount of margin money is negotiable depending upon the profile of the developer as well as proposed project. Realtors, usually provide a discount of 10-15 per cent to the buyers of property in case of lump sum payment. As a result of which 70 per cent of the project cost is generally financed through advance bookings of units. The remaining is funded through own funds and loans from banks/HFCs.

4 Application for Loan

Any proposal for construction finance has to be submitted in a prescribed format to the concerned official of the financial institution. A standard set of papers relating to land, legal formalities, financial aspects, background information and proposed project are to be enclosed with the loan application. A processing fee cheque is also required. All the developers are satisfied with the documentation required for availing loan. They consider it to be strict but fair. However, 33.3 per cent of the realtors are unsatisfied with the percentage of loan amount being paid as processing charges (usually, 1-2 per cent of applied loan amount). They think that there should be some monetary limits for it depending upon the volume of loan.

5 Approval of Application

The proposal is approved at the head office. The time taken for approval varies from lender to lender. It also depends upon the profile of the developer and project under consideration.

Real estate groups are satisfied with the time taken by lending institutions for sanctioning any proposal for construction finance.

6 Appraisal of the Proposal

In order to ensure timely repayment of loan along with interest, every bank/HFC carries out an appraisal exercise to ascertain the viability of the project. Every proposal is evaluated from four angles—organizational, financial, technical and legal (Figure 24.6). On the basis of these parameters, a score is given to each developer, which determines the amount of loan and rate of interest. Each of these aspects is equally critical for assessing any project. However, some of the organizational parameters such as number of years in business, future projects in hand and credit rating by professional agencies is considered unnecessary by realtors.

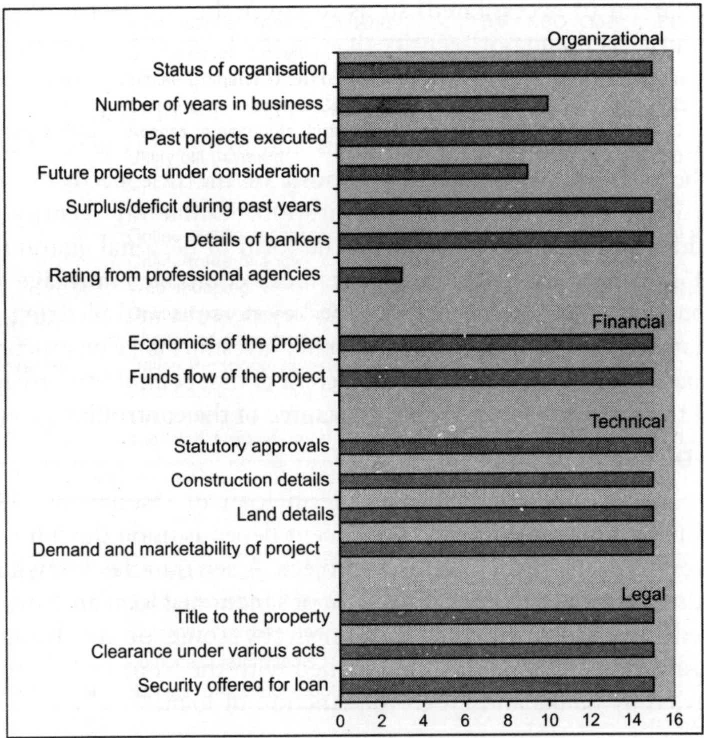

Figure 24.6: Appraisal of proposal

7 Rate of Interest

Every bank/HFC has its own Benchmark Prime Lending Rate (BPLR) which is based on its cost of funds, risk cost, transaction cost, capital cost and profit. Depending upon the profile of the real estate group as well as the project, the financial institution adds a percentage to its BPLR to calculate the rate of interest to be paid by the developer. Generally, construction finance is available at BPLR + 3-4%. Developers are however not satisfied with the rates of interest being charged by banks and HFCs. They are of the opinion that since realtors are the major providers of construction services in the country, therefore, they should be charged the minimum rates.

8 Security for Loan

Any real estate loan is backed by security—prime and collateral (if necessitated) so as to cover the risk factor. Prime security is the major security. It is in the form of first equitable mortgage of the land over which the building is proposed to be built along with the superstructure. The value of security covers the loan amount, interest charges and margin (as prescribed). The mortgage is created by deposit of the title deeds of the property with the lending institution. Collateral security is additional security. It can be in the form of personal guarantee of key persons, corporate guarantee, equitable mortgage of some other properties held by the key persons and pledging of marketable securities (shares and other investments). Construction finance is normally provided on behalf of first equitable mortgage of the property and personal guarantee of the controlling group.

9 Disbursal of Loan

Banks and HFCs disburse term loan in instalments. The number and value of each instalment depends upon the funding requirements of the proposed project. A separate fee known as administrative fees (usually 1-2 % of sanctioned loan amount) is deducted from the first instalment by some of the lending institutions. Developers are satisfied with the front-end charges levied by banks and HFCs for sanction of loan.

10 Repayment of Loan

The period within which entire loan has to be repaid by the borrowing agency is called the tenure of loan. Lenders are free to decide the period of repayment of loan depending upon their policy guidelines. The repayment of construction loan is divided into two parts—repayment of interest and repayment of principal. Interest is normally paid on quarterly basis, including the project implementation period, as and when levied. Repayment of principal is generally made in equal quarterly /half-yearly instalments after the end of moratorium period. The moratorium period depends upon the project completion date. The due dates for payment of interest and principal are worked out in advance and are mentioned in the loan agreement. The borrower to the lender gives Post Dated Cheques (PDCs) for both interest and principal in advance. The lender debits the current account and credits the escrow account on due date and gets the payment. However, all lending institutions charge penalty in case of deferment of repayment schedule. Developers, generally strictly adhere to the agreed schedule of dates.

11 Risk Involved in Construction Finance

Banks and HFCs consider dealing in real estate to be a risky business. Various kinds of risks involved in this are credit, operational and concentration risk. In order to mitigate with such possibilities, all lending institutions have developed their own in-house solutions. Financial institutions are very careful in selection of borrowers to avoid cases of default. All the respondents asserted that the major risk involved in providing construction finance is the inability of the borrower to meet commitments on time (credit risk). Risks arising from downturn in the economy, human error, administrative and legal reasons are also taken into consideration (operational risk). Finally, risk may also arise due to confining portfolio to a particular geographic area or a specific class of borrowers (concentration risk). Sending reminders, personally meeting, recovering losses from guarantors, encashing collaterals and initiating legal action are some of the measures taken by financial institutions to ensure a low rate of default.

CONCLUSION

This study has identified the intricacies involved in the process of providing and availing real estate loans. The main objective of banks and HFCs for going into the arena of construction finance is to enhance their bottom lines. Term loans are provided for a variety of purposes. Cost of project, contribution by builder and margin money receipts determine the quantum of loan.

Application for construction finance has to be submitted in the format as prescribed by the financial institution. Real estate projects involve a lot of risk, therefore, all financial institutions insist upon heavy documentation for availing a project loan. Financial institutions levy processing fees to recover the cost of processing the loan application. It is to be paid as a certain percentage of the applied loan amount. Since the workload involved in processing loan of varied amounts is almost the same, banks and HFCs should work out some monetary limits for processing charges according to volume of loan.

Financial institutions appraise the real estate proposals from varied angles—organizational, financial, technical and legal. Four-fifths of the responding real estate companies have not got themselves rated by any professional agency. In the wake of increasing competition, a statutory norm may be implemented so that only graded entities and projects can secure finance.

Determination of rate of interest is case-specific. Depending upon the profile of the developer and the proposed project, banks and HFCs add a percentage (usually three to four per cent) to their Benchmark Prime Lending Rate (BPLR) to calculate the rate of interest. Rates of interest offered to builders should be brought down in line with individual rates, as they are the major providers of construction services in the country. However, builders and developers should develop only good projects (timely completion at least possible costs). It will bring in good return, which will further provide a fillip to the industry as a whole.

Real estate groups provide personal guarantee of key persons along with equitable mortgage of the property for availing loan. Project loans are disbursed in instalments as per the funds flow of the project. Repayment of loan is made through post-dated cheques as per the schedule mentioned in the loan agreement.

Finally, the sector has suddenly become a cash cow for everyone. Developers are acquiring available land to raise projects. Banks and HFCs should, therefore, ensure quality of real estate advances. They should adopt a cautious approach by way of intensive credit appraisal and risk assessment.

It is hoped that the recommendations would help the concerned persons in developing suitable strategies and framing future courses of action.

REFERENCES

"Credit Policy and the Real Estate Sector", *Deccan Herald*, May 05, 2006.

"Funding in India," *Hindustan Times*, May 06, 2006.

Jack Cummings. *Real Estate Finance and Investment Manual* (1997), Prentice Hall, Englewood Cliffs, New Jersey.

Journal of Real Estate Literature, Vol. 13 (2005) No. 3, Vol. 13 (2005) No. 1, Vol. 12 (2004) No. 3.

RBI, *Report on Trend and Progress of Banking* (2002-03)

www.economictimes.com

www.hdfcrealty.com

www.indiaproperties.com

Financing the Service Sector

25

Y. Sree Rama Murthy

ABSTRACT

One of the important issues to tackle in the process of encouraging and developing the services sector in the Oman is to ensure adequate availability of funds for establishment and growth of service oriented businesses. Financing is important for both new service ventures as well as established service organizations.

Entrepreneurial activity in some service sectors is hindered due to lack of financing. Lenders hesitancy in financing such service oriented businesses needs to be overcome by use of innovative procedures and fresh thinking.

This paper analyses the trends in financing the service sector in Oman and the upcoming challenges in this area. It also looks at the need for introduction of new service financing products and the parameters to be used in assessing the service related lending.

One of the important issues to tackle in the process of encouraging and developing the services sector in any country as well as in the Sultanate of Oman, is to ensure adequate availability of funds for the establishment and growth of service oriented businesses. Financing is important for both new service ventures as well as established service organizations.

Unlike other businesses service oriented business organizations typically suffer from financing difficulties.

Financial constraints is a well researched topic. Fazzari, Hubbard and Petersen (1988) published a seminal paper on estimating financing constraints in 1988. Since then a large number of empirical research papers (Ghosh, 2006) have been published on the topic of financing constraints. Kaplan and Zingales (1997) in a study published in 1997 classify firms into discrete categories of financial constraint and relate these classifications to accounting variables. Lamont, Polk and Saa-Requejo (2001) constructed a KZ Index of financial constraint using the accounting variables suggested by Kaplan and Zingales (1997). The KZ Index is an indicator of the level of financial constraint under which a firm is operating, and higher the index the more constrained is the firm financially. Lamont, Polk and Saa-Requejo (2001) use the KZ Index to study the linkage between financial constraints and stock returns. Beck, Demirguc-Kunt, Laeven and Maksimovic (2004) looked at the determinants of financing obstacles in an empirical study spread over 80 countries. One of their conclusions is that institutional development is the most important country characterisitic explaining cross-country variations in financing obstacles. One of the conclusions of the present paper is similar. The present paper argues that service sector businesses face difficulty in obtaining adequate finance because of lack of institutions and/or products specialized in providing finance for service businesses.

Constraints in Service Financing

Difficulties in financing service sector firms arise from a variety of factors which are peculiar to the services industry. One, service oriented businesses are relatively new as compared to manufacturing oriented businesses. The rise of the service sector in terms of contribution to GDP, in terms of percentage of employment and importance to the economy is a relatively new phenomenon both in the developed countries as well as in the developing countries. In the past agriculture and manufacturing were seen to the important economic sectors. But in the last two decades the services sector has over taken both agriculture and manufacturing whether the measure is in terms of output or in terms of employment. However, techniques for providing finance to the service sector are not fine tuned to the same extent as financing methods which are available for agriculture and manufacturing. Bankers and other financiers who typically use centuries old financing methods are more attuned to lending to manufacturing organizations. Security based lending dominates the world of bank credit. Typically, bankers insist on security which may be in the form of fixed assets or in the form of inventory/stocks. Feinburg (1988) commenting on the trends in U.S. says that lending attitudes have been changing in the secondary loan market. Feinburg (1988) in his article titled "Service companies find lenders less wary" says that banks are now viewing service companies as more acceptable credit risks.

The second factor due to which service oriented organizations face difficulties is lack of inventory. Manufacturing organizations which typically have three types of inventory—raw material, semi-finished goods and finished goods—can get finance from banks and other financial institutions for all three types of inventory. However, many service oriented business have little or no inventory. For example, a computer software firms inventory will be the software programs which are not acceptable to a banker as security for providing finance, while the same banker would be willing to finance a good percentage of raw material and finished goods of a manufacturing firm.

Trends in Oman

Table 25.1 shows the trends in GDP from services and commercial bank credit to the service sector. The data is drawn from various annual reports of the Central Bank of Oman.

During the period 2001 to 2004, GDP from service sector grew from 3499 million rials to 4288 million rials. In terms of growth rate, service sector GDP registered a healthy growth of 7 per cent per annum during the period 2001 to 2004. Available data also indicates most of the subsectors within the service sector like wholesale and retail trade, hotels and restaurants, transport and communication, education, health, etc. also registered similar growth rates during this period.

Table 25.1: Trends in Oman

In Millions Rials Omani

Year	GDP from Services	Ratio of Service GDP to Total GDP	Bank Credit to Services	Ratio of Bank Credit to Services to Total Credit	Bank Credit to Services (Enlarged)	Ratio of Bank Credit to Services (Enlarged) to Total Credit	Ratio of Bank Credit to Services (Enlarged) to GDP from Services
2001	3499	46%	232.2	7.16%	478.5	14.7%	13.6%
2002	3675	47%	233.4	7.1%	423.6	12.9%	11.5%
2003	3904	47%	233.0	7.0%	412.7	12.4%	10.5%
2004	4288	45%	225.8	6.4%	416.4	11.8%	9.7%

Source: Central Bank of Oman: Annual Reports.

However, bank credit to services declined from 232.2 million rials in 2001 to 225.8 million rials in 2004. Even if we enlarge the definition of services to include wholesale and retail trade and transport and communication (which are reported separately), there has been a decline in commercial bank credit to 'services (enlarged)' from 478.5 million rials in 2001 to 416.4 million rials in 2004. In contrast to the decline in credit to services, total commercial bank credit to all sectors in Oman grew from 3241 million rials to 3505.7 million rials.

Figures related to 'bank credit to services (enlarged)' as a ratio of 'GDP from services' show that this ratio has decreased from 13.6 per cent to 9.7 per cent during the period 2001 to 2004, indicating that financing support to the service sector has been on the decline. Service sector in Oman experienced excellent positive growth despite financing constraints and declining credit support.

Life Cycle of a Service Business and Financing Requirements

Financing of service oriented businesses has its own peculiarities. Start up firms in service businesses can be classified into two types. One type is those which need to invest in land and machinery at start-up to provide the service. Others are pure service businesses which normally have low initial funding requirements, since there is no need for substantial investment in land and machinery. Commenting on the life cycle of service firms Bianchi and Hise (1994) say "Service companies don't take much money to start, so there's often less capital at risk before your know the outcome." In the initial stages the equity financing brought in by the owners may sufficient to meet the working capital requirements of such pure service firm. However, as the business grows such firms may find need for more and more external/debt/bank finance to take care of rising wage and salary bills, while they wait for cash payments from services provided to flow in.

Borrowing Ability and Availability

Firms operating in the service sector would typically have lower debt ratios (lower debt to total capital or lower debt to equity ratio) given the fact that their ability to borrow is lower, because of lack of physical inventory. A major component of bank credit for service firms is for financing fixed assets such as buildings, furniture, fixtures, etc.

However, their requirements for financing is high because of the nature of their operating cycle. For a pure service firm major items of expenditure in the process of producing the services are wages and salaries. The service produced is intangible and therefore, cannot be stored and has no shelf life. One would expect that wages and salaries are paid in the Gulf region on a monthly basis (and not weekly unlike some other countries). Cash outflow due payment of wages takes place on a monthly basis. For a manufacturing firm raw material costs are the normally the major items of expenditure in producing the goods. Supplier finance is normally available for manufacturing firms, and further banks are willing to provide finance for raw material and finished goods inventory. For a pure service business cash inflows depend on the nature of the service being sold and produced. Typical service firms (such as those involved in tourism, hospitality, logistics, service contracts, construction services, training, software, IT services) receive cash only when receivables are paid for which can be sixty to ninty days after the date of billing (in some cases the collection period is even longer extending to 120 to 180 days). Manufacturing companies like service companies also have average accounts receivable period of sixty to ninty days, but have the advantage of being able to offset debtors against creditors. Financing constraints related to the operating cycle are therefore, theoretically, more likely in pure service oriented businesses.

Bianchi and Hise (1994) using data drawn from a survey conducted by AT&T Capital Corp and the American Institute of Certified Public Accountants say that start up service companies identified inadequate funding as their biggest hurdle. They blamed lenders. According to the survey results, twenty-eight per cent of service startups said that lenders are too conservative, sixteen per cent reported being unable to find investors and twelve per cent said that lack of collateral is the reason for inadequate funding.

Financial Constraints: Company Analysis

As mentioned earlier, macro level data related to GDP from services and bank credit to service sectors in Oman clearly indicates a decline in the amount of bank credit extended to services both in percentage terms and absolute terms. In this section we examine financial statement data relating to 34 service companies whose shares are traded on the Muscat Securities Market (MSM). The purpose of this part of the study is to find out how many of the service companies quoted on MSM can be classified as financially constrained.

Based on methods suggested by Fazzari, Hubbard and Petersen (1988), Kaplan and Zingales (1997), and Lamont, Polk and Saa-Requejo (2001) we classify a firm as financially constrained if it has a positive real sales growth, a high debt ratio and a low dividend payout ratio. Businesses with negative real sales growth may be in financial distress but are not considered financially constrained. A firm with positive real sales growth needs additional funds to finance increasing sales, and if it is already having a high debt ratio, it necessarily has to depend on internally generated finance which would lead to a policy of high level of retained earnings and low dividends by the firms managers.

Table 25.2: Financial Constraints – Company Analysis
35 S.A.O.G companies* classified as service companies by MSM
Year: 2005 - Table shows number of companies in each category

	High Debt and High Dividend Payout	Low Debt and High Dividend Payout	High Debt and Low Dividend Payout	Low Debt and Low Dividend Payout	Total
Negative Real Sales Growth	1	2	4	1	8
Positive Real Sales Growth	7	1	13	4	25
					33

* 2 companies could not be categorised due to incomplete data
Source: MSM

Balance sheet and income statement data for the year 2005 was used to identify firms which can be categorised as financially constrained: positive real sales growth, high debt and low dividend payout. Firms with more than 33 per cent debt to total capital[1] ratio are classified as high debt[2]. Firms with less than 30 per cent dividend payout (dividends to earnings) are classified as low dividend payout[3]. Results are reported in Table 25.2. Of the 35 companies classified by the Muscat Securities Market as service companies, 25 reported positive real sales growth, 8 reported negative real sales growth, and complete data was not available for two companies. Out of 25 companies with positive real sales growth, 13 been categorised as companies with high debt and low dividend payout—as financially constrained. The above analysis shows that more than 50 per cent of the service oriented firms with positive sales growth are financially constrained or are experiencing financing obstacles.

Both the macro level data and micro (company) level analysis shows that there appears to be some constraints in financing service businesses. Lenders hesitancy in financing service oriented businesses needs to be overcome by use of innovative procedures. Feinberg (1988) commenting on developments in service lending in other countries says that financial institutions are establishing "new units (departments) for service companies that cannot meet traditional collateral credit. Credit risk, cash flow analysis and other intangible assets are replacing collateral as the basis for loans. Equity kickers such as warrants and options are allowing lenders to participate in borrower's profit."

Service Development Banks

Experience in different countries in the world has shown that if a country wants rapid development and growth in a particular sector then there is need for specialised institutions focusing on that sector. History has also shown that specialised financial institutions definitely help the growth and development of a particular sector because the specialised institution would focus on developing strategies, products and procedures which are suitable for proving adequate and timely finance for businesses in that sector. Different countries have successfully experimented with industrial development banks, agricultural development banks, export-import banks, etc. Extending the above argument, a country which views service sector as an important engine of economic growth and development with excellent employment potential, should definitely explore the feasibility of establishing a separate "Service Sector Development Bank."

REFERENCES

Beck, T., Demirguc-Kunt A., Laeven L. & Maksimovic V. (2004). "The Determinants of Financing Obstacles." *World Bank Policy Research Working Paper 3204*, pp. 1-29.

Bianchi, A. & Hise P. (1994). "Service-Industry Starts on the Rise". *Inc.* 16:14, pp. 34-35.

Central Bank of Oman. Annual Reports. 2003, 2004, 2005.

Commins, J.A. (1986). "Borrower's Viewpoint....A New Breed of Loan Officer Needed for Small Growing Companies." *The Journal of Commercial Bank Lending*. 69:4, pp. 26-31.

Fazzari, S., Hubbard G. & Petersen B. (1988). "Financing Constraints and Corporate Investments", *Brookings Papers on Economic Activity*. 1, pp. 141-95.

Feinburg, A. (1988). "Service Companies Find Lenders Less Wary." *The Financial Manager*, 1:3, pp. 58-59.

Gosh, S. (2006). "Did Financial Liberalization ease Financing Constraints? Evidence from Indian Firm Level Data." *Emerging Markets Review*. 7:2, pp. 176-90.

Kaplan, S. & Zingales L. (1997). "Do Investment-Cash Flow Sensitivities Provide Useful Measures of Financing Constraints?" *Quarterly Journal of Economics*. 112, pp. 169 -215.

Kaplan, S. & Zingales L. (2000). "Investment-Cash Flow Sensitivities are Not Valid Measures of Financing Constraints?" *Quarterly Journal of Economics*. 115, pp. 707-12.

Lamont, O., Polk C. & Saa-Requejo J. (2001). "Financial Constraints and Stock Returns". *Review of Financial Studies*. 14:2, pp. 529-54, also published as NBER Working Paper No. 6210.

LaPorta, R., Lopez-de-Silanes F., Shleifer A., & Vishny R.W. (2000). "Agency Problems and Dividend Policies around the World". *Journal of Finance*, 55:1, pp. 1-33.

Myers, S. (2001). "Capital Structure". *Journal of Economic Perspectives*. 15:2, pp. 81-102.

Muscat Securities Market, Shareholder's Guide: Data on Companies Listed on Muscat Securities Market, 2006. No.18.

Rajan, R.G. & Zingales L. (1995). "What Do We Know about Capital Structure? Some Evidence from International Data." *Journal of Finance*. 50:5, pp. 1421-60.

Smart, S.B., Megginson W.I. & Gitman L.J. (2004). *Corporate Finance*. Thomson-South Western.

Strischek, D. (1987). "Safe Loans to Small Firms: Compensating for Credit Risk." *Commercial Lending Review*. 2:3, pp. 3-22.

Electronic Broking Services to Bloom in India

26

Madan Lal Bhasin

ABSTRACT

The Internet has played a vital role in transforming business in the new millennium. Recently, more and more organizations are not only using Information and Computer Technologies to improve their internal operations, but are also changing the way they deal with customers and suppliers. Perhaps, nowhere else is the impact of the Internet felt as much as in marketing of services sector. Internet stock trading in India is a recent phenomenon but is set to expand tremendously in years to come in line with advanced countries. This article focuses on financial services with special emphasis on e-broking of stock.

We familiarize the readers' with the basic concepts, distinct phases in the development of e-broking and the mechanism of e-trading in section one. Section two succinctly portrays the benefits for users and brokers, and a few of the problems caused by switching over to an e-broking system. In section three, we discuss three layers in the cycle, key success factors, and various security models that are adopted by the e-broking industry. Last but not least, an attempt is made to give an overview of an e-broking scenario in India. Finally, we conclude by giving SEBI guidelines, followed by the global prospects for an e-broking industry. Despite all the challenges, the e-broking industry seems like a sector set to grow day-by-day.

The business historians will certainly remember the beginning of the second millennium as a time of unprecedented changes in the business world. In the space of a few years entire industries have been radically transformed, hundreds of thousands of new businesses have been spawned and fortunes made and lost by entrepreneurs and investors, all as a result of digital technologies. New technologies, such as, the Internet, digital television, mobile telephones and intelligent home appliances have all reached critical mass at the same time and are poised to revolutionize businesses in a way not seen since the Industrial Revolution. Over the last few centuries, human beings have experienced two major revolutions—the industrial and electronic revolutions. The former transformed our society from being agriculture based to industrial based, whereas, the latter transformed our society from being mechanical based to electronic based. Turban aptly observes, "As we enter the 21st century, we are seeing the beginning of a new revolution, namely, the network revolution. It interconnects different parts of the world, enabling the seamless flow of information. The Internet is the engine of this revolution and electronic commerce (or e-commerce) is its fuel."

With the advent of latest technologies and advanced cryptographic techniques, it is now feasible to implement e-commerce and e-business over the Internet. The reason, e-commerce became so visible in the second-half of the 1990s was the commercial aspect of the Internet. Once the Internet was opened to commercial activity, this worldwide network became the major carrier of business-to-business electronic data interchange. The total value of e-commerce activities within India has exceeded $ 130 million during 2004-05, according to a research conducted by Internet and Online Association of India (IOAI). The report estimates a 300 per cent plus growth rate during the next couple of years and has targeted $ 229 million worth of e-business conducted within the country by the year 2006-07. Thus, in the mid-1990s, the term "Web economy" had not yet been coined; it is now a common phrase in business circles.

In recent years, however, another term called "e-business" has emerged. Some define e-business as the conduct of business on the Internet, not only buying and selling but also servicing customers and collaborating with business partners (Chen, Stephen). Others include businesses using any electronic network to conduct buying and selling as well as other activities. Thus, e-business is the use of electronic communications networks to allow organizations to send and receive information. Note that this transfer of information can be entirely internal, unlike e-commerce, which typically crosses organizational boundaries. Moreover, like e-commerce, e-business does not have to utilize the Internet or Web (Slyke and Belanger). In general, e-business has a wider perspective than e-commerce. It involves using information technologies in all aspects of the business. Hence, e-commerce can be viewed as a subset of e-business.

Internet-based e-business is only beginning in India. As organizations become more adept at e-commerce, and as consumers become more used to conducting commerce over the Internet, e-business will continue to grow rapidly. E-business can help organizations extend their operations and reach markets across the world. There are a number of potential advantages to be gained from global e-business, including access to new markets, improved internal operations, the facilitation of global virtual partnerships, improved innovation, and the enabling of global supply chains. Mahendra Swarup, Vice-Chairman of IOAI, amply observes as: "This business module is cost effective, easily accessible and profitable in many functional areas. Consumers and retailers both desire a safe, simple and comprehensive online shopping experience that will truly realize the range of power of the Internet. From a business perspective, it offers unlimited shelf space, it is not bound by operational timings and geographical boundaries, and an opportunity to cater to country-wide city markets (for consumers and suppliers alike) at a comparative minuscule cost to an audience all set to grow to a 100 million by 2007. From a consumers perspective, it allows greater access (hence, the high response rate by tier 2 cities) to markets and an opportunity to make informed decisions on purchases." However, there are a number of challenges to global e-business, including the complexity of taxation, differences in privacy and product laws, cultural and language differences, and differences in e-business readiness. However, we feel that there are some technologies and e-business applications that are likely to help shape this future. Currently, we are only seeing the tip of the e-business iceberg.

The e-Service (R) Evolution

Perhaps nowhere else is the impact of the Internet felt as much as in the 'services' sector. According to Amor, "The delivery of a service via the Internet to the consumer or other business can be referred to by the generic term of e-services." There are a wide-range of e-services currently offered through the Internet and these include banking, stock trading, jobs and career sites, travel, education, consultancy advice, insurance, real-estate, broker services, online publishing, and online delivery of media contents (such as, videos, computer games, etc.). This list is by no means an exhaustive and it is growing all the time. However, the focus of the present article is on 'financial' services, with special reference to 'e-broking' of stocks (or shares).

The Internet has, in fact, opened new channels for service delivery, shortened turnaround times, and offered unprecedented convenience to consumers. The financial services sector have leveraged the Internet and exploited its many benefits. e-broking is the financial service most amenable to e-enablement. It has already witnessed a meteoric growth in the U.S. and is staging a similar show in other economies. India too, will not remain untouched by these changes. e-broking offers tremendous benefits to the Indian investor and will probably expand the market itself.

What is e-Broking?

An electronic broker is an intermediary who:

- May take an order from a customer and pass it on to a supplier;
- May put a customer with specific requirements in touch with a supplier who can meet those requirements; and
- May provide a service to a customer, such as a comparison between goods, with respect to particular criteria such as price, quality, etc.

Thus, e-brokers provide comparison-shopping, order taking and fulfillment, and services to a customer. That is the reason why they are sometimes referred to as "electronic" intermediaries. Examples of e-brokers (or intermediaries) include priceline.com, mySimon.com, and bestbooksbuy.com. This class of e-retailers is currently an extension of the notion of a broker in the physical to the cyber world.

In fact, "e-trading" in stock/share stands for "trading in the equity or debt instruments on the stock exchanges through an Electronic Communication Network (ECN)." Although on-line trading strictly refers to the electronic execution of trade, an eco-system of e-stock trading has three dimensions:

- Electronic execution of the trade,
- Payment of the transaction through a payment gateway, and
- Transfer of shares in electronic form. Current developments are, essentially, converting off-line practices to an online equivalent.

By examining the major developments in the sphere of Internet-based share dealings in the new global market place, as reported by Peter Temple, we find that there are three distinct phases in the development of e-broking. These are:

Phase 1: The open-outcry system with the transactions taking place manually in the ring.

Phase 2: The electronic system, enabling brokers to place orders online.

Phase 3: The e-broking system, empowering customers to transact online.

The mechanics of the e-trading system begins with the user logging onto the Electronic Communication Network (ECN) through the Internet. The user then accesses his e-trading account with the help of a secure customer password. The user is now connected directly with the exchange and any transactions would be instantaneous and irrevocable. The user also has access to real-time price movements of various stocks/scrips, and other contextual information to assist him in his decision-making. Lee suggests in his book: "An integrated e-broking system consists of not only a transaction enabler but also a payment gateway for funds transfer and a 'demat' account for the transfer of stocks. Such a service enables smooth, convenient and transparent operations."

It is a healthy sign for the service industry that the number of e-trading sites and the usage of them are mushrooming all over the globe. Several companies, such as, E-Trade, Datek.on-line, American Express Financial Services, etc. allow you to trade stocks, bonds, mutual funds, etc. on the Internet. Figures for 2002-03 show 17 million online traders in the US alone, and a rapid growth in the UK since the first site opened at the start of 1998. In the UK, the sites are offered by some of the traditional British stock broking firms, a number of banks, and the few large US companies having set-up in the UK. A point to be noted here is that in no case can an individual investor trade directly with another investor, all orders are routed thru a broker only. In case of ECN, the trades are reported to the exchange concerned.

Benefits and Problems of e-broking

In recent years, the use of the Internet has spread among investors in stocks and shares. The Internet can make up-to-the-minute information available to a large number of investors that until recently had only been available to those working in financial institutions. Komenar concludes as: "the use of online brokerage services automates the process of buying and selling, and hence, allows a reduction of commission charges. Also, the commodity being traded is intangible, the ownership of stocks and shares can be recorded electronically, so there is no requirement for physical delivery." However, it should be noted that the supply chain for online share dealing remains unchanged, use of the Net just speeds up the whole process and that can be vital in some share deals. Switching over to e-broking results in several benefits, both to the user and to the broker, as summarized in Table 26.1.

The major problem with e-stock trading is that it increases the temptation on the part of influential speculators and stockbrokers to indulge in short-term speculation rather than long-term investment. The history of stock markets (both NSE and BSE) in India is replete with at least a dozen cases of scams,

Table 26.1: Benefits of Online Share Dealing or e-Broking

To Users	To Brokers
Convenience	Global reach
Better information	Better customer service
Competitive price	Low capital cost
Customization	Mass customization
Shopping anywhere, anytime	Targeted marketing
Portfolio & advisory services	More value-added services

where stockbrokers and bankers joined hands to squander the savings of millions of small and institutional investors. As Dr. Lucas has rightly pointed out: "Consumer and business concerns about Internet security are well founded. Amid an explosive upsurge in scams, fraudsters continue to take advantage of the Internet's anonymous transaction environment—with everyone from one-time hackers to organized crime testing the market's boundaries." However, the problems are further compounded by the different legislative frameworks, which are prevalent in countries across the globe.

Technology and Security Concerns for e-broking

Some leading technology companies have already developed "online transaction processing" and "straight-through processing" applications that allow real-time transaction execution. Both allow the user to directly interact with the central system of any market place, without any manual intervention. As Professor Whiteley suggests: "Straight-through processing technology permits financial software products to directly interact with the stock exchange system by communicating with the exchange market structures. This is achieved by developing application programming interfaces (APIs) that talk to the exchange server." As such, there is seamless integration among the systems and processes involved with the complete lifecycle of a trade from execution to settlement to transaction reporting. The benefits of STP solutions are shorter cycles, lower costs, lower risk and stronger business growth. One of the leading technology providers for online trading in

India is Financial Technologies (India) Limited (visit www.ftIndia.com).

It would suffice to say that the cycle of e-broking has to pass through three layers: (a) The Client Interface Layer: the front-end, (b) The Middle Layer: risk management systems that access data from banks and depository participants, calculate client exposure at that instant, and give 'Go/No go' advice on the trade, and (c) The End-Layer: the back-end, where the accounting modules, pay in or pay out schedules, etc. operate. From a technical perspective, there are three key success factors for e-broking. They are briefly described below:

- **Scalability and robustness of the trading system:** It becomes imperative for any Net-based application to have a proven capability for scalability and robustness of a trading system that ensures the ability to handle and process requests from multiple users at any given point in time.
- **Bandwidth optimization:** The application software should demonstrate intelligence in optimizing the available bandwidth by deploying advanced technologies like streaming.
- **Integration with third-party systems:** On the Net, with information feeds available from multiple points, it is prudent to deploy applications that are built on open architecture methodology for interfacing with third party systems.

For any e-trading system to be successful, it should provide security, reliability and confidentiality of data (Chan). This can be achieved through the use of 'encryption' technology before the online trading begins. The exchange must ensure that records maintained in electronic form by the broker are not susceptible to manipulation, and adequate back-ups and storage are available. The security features demanded by 'regulatory' authorities include: unique user identification, and passwords that can be renewed from time to time to prevent hacking by outsiders. The major security requirements of e-broking are: (a) trusted means of authentication over open networks, (b) confidentiality of the transaction, (c) means to ensure integrity of data in-transit, and (d) means to ensure non-repudiation of payment or its receipt (visit www.odysseytec.com).

Various security models are adopted to ensure safe and reliable e-broking transactions. The commonly employed security models in e-Broking are: passwords, Secure Sockets Layer (SSL), Kerberos, Pretty Good Privacy (PGP), Public Key Infrastructure (PKI), Custom Implementations, Linux, etc. Linux continues to gain popularity in the US securities industry, with large brokerage firms leading the adoption charge.

E-Broking Scenario in India

Today, online brokers offer their services to investors, who can be physically located anywhere on earth. All that is needed is a computer, modem and an ISD telephone line to connect to an online broker, and one can trade provided one has an account with an online broker, of course. Account opening charges vary from broker to broker, who have significantly different requirements. There are two ways to trade in stocks electronically, namely: (a) Conventional online trading using Internet browser and a Web-based broker, and (b) Direct Access Trading systems using specialized software and a private network. It is important to understand the key features of, and the differences between, these two forms of electronic trading.

Conventional online brokers provide Web-based trading whereby the client logs in through the broker's Website and places orders through his Internet browser. By the time client loads his browser, waits for the broker's Web Page to load, logs in, enters his order, and the broker reviews the order, several minutes may have elapsed. Further, time may elapse before the order is actually executed after being received and reviewed by the online broker because several intermediaries may be involved in handling the order. In this regard, many online brokerage firms do not always themselves execute client orders directly, but rather may send the orders to other market makers for execution. This can indeed result in slow execution of orders at a higher price than the client may have expected. This is bad news for day traders, as execution speed is critical for successful day trading.

By way of contrast, Direct Access Trading (DAT) system allows one to trade instrument directly with a marketmaker or a specialist on the floor of the exchange, using special trading software and high-speed computer linkages to the NASDAQ, NYSE and the various Electronic Communications Networks (ECNs). With a DAT trading platform, a trader may place orders directly into the market in real-time and trade directly with a market maker on NASDAQ, a specialist on the floor of the NYSE, or with an ECN, without any broker participation at all. There are no middlemen involved between the relevant stock exchanges, ECNs, and the individual trader. If there is a sufficient number of a share available at the price specified by the trader, the order is executed in a fraction of a second and a confirmation is instantly displayed on the trader's computer screen. Because no middleman is involved, the trader will save anywhere from a few seconds to several minutes of time to complete a typical trade. Accordingly, the major advantage of a DAT system is that it results in much faster executions than one can normally achieve using a conventional online broker. In summary, as compared with conventional online brokers, day trading firms offer better access to the markets, much faster executions, and greater control in order routing.

Internet stock trading in India is a recent phenomenon and began as recently as January 2000. Although there are some 50 e-brokers, the industry is still in a nascent stage as online trades account for merely Rs. 700 million, which is a very negligible percentage of the total stock trade. It is estimated that the customer-base for all the portals put together is a mere 120,000 compared to 2.5 million customers in Japan and 14.3 million in the U.S. Showing steady growth, the baseline of U.S. Internet users investing online is projected to rise from 14.3 million in 2000 to 32.4 million in 2004, a 126.9 per cent increase over a five-year period. Some of the leading e-brokers in the Indian markets are: Sharekhan.com, ICICIDirect.com, Indiabulls.com, Motilaloswal.com, Kotakstreet.com, 5Paisa.com, Equitymaster.com, etc. Unfortunately, online stock trading stands at barely 2 per cent of the share trading market today. Indeed, a poor scenario, when compared to 8 per cent in China and the rapid growth in Europe. Moreover, the segmentation of the share trading market in India consists largely of traders and dealers, along with a handful of investors. The term 'investor' generally applies to people who trade around 'twenty' times a year. For example, almost 70 per cent of the volumes traded on Sharekhan.com are 'rolling' settlements and are 'squared off' with just 20-30 per cent resulting in actual delivery. This indicates that even out of the minuscule 2 per cent who deal online, a majority are traders.

Low bandwidth can be blamed for the slow growth of online trading. Slow connections result in orders taking too much time to be processed; every single second counts and sometimes, a delay of even a 'half-a-second' in the execution of an order can result in a loss for the trader. Moreover, Internet browsers also add to the problem. "Browsers were meant to display static data and text like news—not streaming data like stock quotes. Therefore, the page has to be refreshed manually over and over to display the latest quotes. It is true that browsers can be set to auto refresh a page every couple of seconds. But doing this over, as low connection does not help much," says Sharekhan's Mr. Jaideep Arora, executive director (online business).

Most Indian investors, in fact, have not really taken to handling investments online without the advice of a broker. Even though lot of financial information is available online, many prefer to get stock 'tips' from their brokers with whom they maintain a good personal relationship. Also, the market 'grapevine' is missing from online trading. This is critical especially for day traders. "Traders usually thrive on gossip, speculation, tips and calls from each other," says Mr. Kishor Binwal, research analyst at Double Dot, a trading ring. Financial information that is available on the Internet is accessible to everyone. But what really drives the market is the 'speculation'. Investors trading on the Internet are isolated from all the action and gossip that they would normally get through their brokers. For this reason, many online traders also keep in touch with 'offline' brokers.

Arora points out that there are chat rooms, phones and even online bulletin boards where investors and traders regularly post stock tips. However, this practice is not very prevalent in India. Mr. Ravi Kumar of Indiabulls.com observes, "Relationship is important to people who trade online. Thirty to forty per cent of our trades take place 'offline' through phones and our relationship managers, who advise investors and traders. Intra day traders are logged on to Yahoo! Messenger for tips and calls." Sites like Yahoo! India offers tips. International boards like Siliconinvestor.com, Yahoo! Finance board, and investor chat rooms are also abuzz with tips. But everything you read online cannot be 'trusted'. Other reasons that keep people away from online trading include 'age'—Most traders are in their 'thirties' and 'forties', whereas a majority of Indian Internet users fall within the 18-24 age group. All these limitations may not make much of a difference to long-term investors, who trade infrequently. But they do deter active traders from going online.

However, some leading e-brokers are aware of this. Hence, the launch of products and services like Sharekhan's "Speedtrade". Speedtrade is an Internet-enabled trading client that you can install on a PC. It streams 'real-time' quotes to your desktop, along with tick-by-tick charts, price and technical alerts, streaming orders and trade confirmations, all on one screen, so that you do not have to open several windows. "It is almost like having a broker terminal at a fraction of the cost. Setting up a broker terminal involves a VSAT connection, which could cost you anything from Rs. 80,000-100,000," says Mr. Jaideep Arora. He sees software-based direct access platforms like Speedtrade leading to a host of products being introduced for the active trader. Investsmart has already made a distinction between investors and traders, giving them separate accounts.

Day trading is now offered by a large number of players like icicitrade.com, indiabulls.com and mychartalert.com. Value-added services like 'SPOT' trading (offered by quite a few big players) and 'Buy Today Sell Tomorrow' (BTST) offered by ICICITrade offer more flexibility to investors, in addition to just delivery. Tie-ups with major banks like ICICI, Citibank and HDFC for online transfer of funds and depository accounts also make it easier for investors, though most online brokerages require you to set up a depository account with them or the banks they have tied up with. For example, ICICI offers investors and traders an 'e-invest' account (a three-in-one account) that brings broking, trading and demat accounts (all to be opened with ICICI) 'under one roof', saving you a lot of paperwork. A large number of online brokerages have backed up their operation with multi-channel deliveries like phone trading for those who cannot access the Web. There is yet another option: Trading rings or café's like the Mumbai-based DoubleDot offer you the convenience of self-trading (only on the BSE) on a broker terminal, along with analyst advice, research and plenty of market buzz.

E-broking is still an evolving industry in India and the survivors are likely to be those brokers who offer integrated/ consolidated services and are financially resilientee. Increased PC penetration and more accessible broadband could increase the number of online investors. Until then, online trading portals are all set to woo active traders in a bid to increase their numbers. The future of the e-broking industry, thus, largely depends on the extent of the penetration of the Internet in the near future. Moreover, the Bombay Stock Exchange (BSE) and the National Stock Exchange (NSE) have recently developed 'proprietary' trading engines called 'Webex' and 'Dotex', respectively. These engines will obviate the need for a broker to develop his own engine, and thus, result in capital investment savings. However, a user can log on to these engines using the website of the broker and trade electronically. These developments are, therefore, expected to give a strong fillip to the e-broking industry in India. Application of superior technology and establishing integrated systems to provide a one-stop solution to clients will be a key determinant of success.

BSEwebX is the Internet-based trading system of the 125-years old Bombay Stock Exchange. Tata Consultancy Services (TCS), which built BSEwebX for BSE, recently added a slick, easy-to-use interface, SpeedX, to the system. SpeedX combines rich content, order entry and order management features. It does this through UniView, which offers a unified, real-time view of the market and provides speed trading. UniView seamlessly integrates important SpeedX features: Market Watch, Scrip Info, Order Entry and Order/Market Watch lets you add and delete scrips up front. The auto-refresh feature fetches the latest snapshots to keep you wired to market. Scrip Info helps you track the latest prices, volumes and depth to make informed decisions. Order Entry executes orders through the compact SpeedX trading screen while you watch the market move. For rapid trading, use the Multiple Order Entry window. Order/Trade List reports your order/trade status instantly. You can also modify and delete your transactions from this window. Now, instead of having to navigate your way from watching market movements to accessing scip information to placing and executing orders to viewing your risk profile, all you need to do is get to the UniView screen—and all this information is yours at a glance—you can make informed decisions at point-and-click.

E-Integrated Brokerage System (e-IBS) is an integrated brokerage solution targeted at brokers catering to retail as well as institutional clients and offers comprehensive and rich business functionality. It helps achieve Straight Through Processing (STP) by seamlessly integrated and back office operations of brokerage houses. STP is the buzzword that is driving every major initiative in the securities market. Brokers across the country like to use the latest systems built on state-of-the-art technology to extend their reach into multiple markets, multiple segments enhanced customer service. This necessitates the need for an integrated system that addresses their front office, middle office and back office requirements. e-IBS from TCS caters to this need of the securities industry broker/dealers by providing an integrated multi-exchange, multi-segment, clearing and settlement solution with an STP-ready architecture.

Hindrances to the growth of e-broking in India can be summed up as: First, the low density of telephones, low Internet penetration, and low installed base of computers are responsible for the poor availability of the Internet. Second, very few online payment gateways are available, hindering the smooth growth of the industry. Integrated service providers (like ICICIDirect.com), which provide combined banking, broking and 'demat' services, have an advantage over other non-integrated service providers, who have to scout for partners for providing gateway services. Third, data privacy can be ensured through server side certification and here the situation appears to be satisfactory. However, most of the sites restrict access through passwords and identification numbers, but these are not considered adequate and foolproof. Fourth, Institutional investors comprise over 80 per cent of the total investors in the country. The remaining 20 per cent of retail investors, the focus segment of e-brokers, do not contribute significantly to the overall stock-turnover of the country. Thus, there is a theoretical limit to the overall penetration of e-broking. Last but not least, the concept of trading on computers through the Internet requires a change in the 'habits' of people; enhancing 'trust' in these techniques may take more time.

SEBI Guidelines

According to the Securities and Exchange Board of India (SEBI) guidelines (www.sebi.gov.in) on "Internet trading," brokers providing e-trading must have a minimum net worth of Rs. 50 lakh, besides obtaining specific permission of the stock exchange concerned. Stock exchanges should ensure that the systems used by the broker provide for security, reliability and confidentiality of data through use of the 'encryption' technology. For signatures, participants should use 'authentication' technologies and 'certification' agencies, as and when notified later.

Stock exchanges should also ensure that brokers maintain adequate back-up systems and adequate data storage capacity. Brokers should have adequate system capacity for handling data transfer and arrange for alternate means of communication, in case of Internet failure. The following security features are mandatory for all Internet-related trading systems: (a) User ID, (b) First-level password, (c) Automatic expiry of password at the end of reasonable duration, (d) All transaction logs with proper audit facilities to be maintained in the system, (e) Secured socket level security server for access through Internet, and (f) Suitable 'firewalls' between trading set up directly connected to an exchange trading system and the Internet trading set up.

SEBI has decided that Internet trading can take place in India within the existing legal framework through the use of "order routing "systems, which will route orders from client to brokers, for trade execution on registered stock exchanges. SEBI has also recommended minimum technical standards for ensuring safety and security of transaction between clients and brokers, which will be enforced by the respective stock exchanges.

Global Prospects for e-broking Industry

Stock exchanges across the globe are exploring an alliance that will create a 24 hours Global Equity Market (GEM). The New York Stock Exchange and exchanges from three main time zones—Australia, Tokyo and Hong Kong in the Asia-Pacific; Sao Paulo, Mexico and Toronto in the Americas; and Euronext, the combined Amsterdam, Brussels and Paris exchanges in Europe—plan to form a trading mechanism that will allow the trading of stocks in the world's global companies. Each of the partnering markets will retain its brand and form a platform to allow companies with worldwide demand to experience 24 hours trading of their shares. This would be an innovative and a bold move and it is expected to lead to a better price discovery on a global basis.

The proposed GEM will link the trading systems of each exchange to provide a global market structure, based on the principles of transparency, self-regulation and agency auction price discovery. This high-tech linkup of auction markets will certainly create a global pool of liquidity, facilitate global price discovery, and provide investors' with better and faster access to global stocks. The GEM, it is hoped, will address investors' appetite for big-capitalized stocks by providing them easier access to stocks not currently available on their local stock exchanges. The market capitalization of the companies listed on the participating exchanges is expected to exceed $ 20 trillion, representing more than 60 per cent of the world's market capitalization. Like the 24 hours Forex market and its electronic network SWIFT, the GEM will have an Electronic Communication Network (ECN), thereby realizing the ultimate potential of e-broking. The Tokyo Stock Exchange, Inc. and the

New York Stock Exchange, Inc. announced, they would sign an agreement to share market surveillance information in their respective markets.

E-commerce is coming of age in India. The rapid development of e-commerce is forcing companies to adopt business strategies revolving around the Internet. Today, the Internet population is over 25 million and is expected to grow at 100 million by 2007. Changing lifestyles and shopping habits, a similar metro/non-metro consumption of media and Internet, and 'multiple Internet access points' will propel e-commerce transactions to Rs. 2,300 crores in 2006-07 from the current Rs. 1,180 crore projections for 2005-06, an over 100 per cent increase.

E-broking is still an evolving industry in India and the survivors are likely to be those brokers who offer integrated/consolidated services and are financially resilience. The future of the e-broking industry, thus, largely depends on the extent of the penetration of the Internet in the near future. Application of superior technology and establishing integrated systems to provide a 'one-stop' solution to clients will be a key determinant of success. Brokers across the country like to use the latest systems built on state-of-the-art technology to extend their reach into multiple markets and multiple segments so as to enhance customer services. e-IBS from the Tata Consultancy Services caters to this need of the securities industry broker/dealers by providing an integrated multi-exchange, multi-segment, clearing and settlement solution with an STP-ready architecture.

Despite the development of Internet, e-commerce and e-business the hype that surrounds it, the amount of online business done, as a proportion of all retail sales remains stubbornly small. There are about 50 online brokerages in India, but online trading stands at barely 2 per cent of the share trading market today. A poor scenario, when compared to 6 per cent in China and the rapid growth in Europe. The segmentation of the share trading market in India, as in most countries worldwide, consists largely of traders and dealers, along with a handful of investors. This indicates that even out of the minuscule 2 per cent who deal online, a majority are traders. However, online trading in other parts of Asia also has hurdles, and growth is stagnating worldwide.

The e-brokerage industry continues to be battered by several complex challenges, such as, collapse in pricing structures, reduced return on IT investments, shaken value propositions, and crisis in consumer confidence. These challenges may change not just the way brokerage firms conduct their day-to-day business, but may begin to re-define the e-broking industry as a whole. They must make tough decisions as to where to deploy their IT dollars, as well as what strategies and what customers to pursue. They must re-invent themselves in a real-life world where 'service' is the 'key' differentiator. There is an urgent need for firms to place a new emphasis on customer-relationships that combines selling with personal financial consultation to meet clients' specific needs. Thus, financial planning, portfolio allocation and advice tailored to each individual's risk tolerance and life stage will become the hallmarks of the new full-service orientation, as firms are both pushed and pulled toward the brave new world of the retailing of brokerage. Despite all the challenges, e-broking industry seems like a sector set to grow day-by-day.

REFERENCES

Amor, D. *The E-Business (R) Evolution*, Prentice-Hall, 1999.

Bhasin, M.L. (2004). "E-Broking as an Innovative Tool for Marketing Financial Services," *EBS Review*, Summer 2004, Estonian Business School, Estonia, pp.56-65.

Chan, H., Lee, R., Dillon, T. and Chang, E. (2001). *E-Commerce: Fundamentals and Applications*, John Wiley & Sons, Ltd. England.

Internet & Online Association of India (29 June, 2005). "B2C e-Commerce in India to Cross Rs. 2,300 Crore," Report available at www.siliconindia.com.

Komenar, M.M. *Electronic Marketing*, Wiley, New York.

Lee B. (1998). *Doing Business Electronically: A Global Perspective of e-Commerce*, Springer, London, pp. 163-73.

Lucas, P. (1999) "Internet Trading and its Threat to the Traditional Stock Broker", BIT World'99, Cape Town, South Africa.

Slyke, C.V. and Belanger, F. (2004). *E-Business Technologies: Supporting the Net-enhanced Organization*, John Wiley & Sons, Inc.

Temple, Peter. *The New Online Investor: The Revolution Continues*, John Wiley & Sons Ltd., 2000.

Tower Group Research, (Jan. 2004). "Tower Group Names Seven Top Business & Technology Drivers Reshaping Retail Brokerage Industry".

Tower Group Research (Nov. 2003). Tower Group Identifies Top Trends that will Drive Global Financial Services in 2004".

Turban, E., Lee, J., King, D., Chang, H.M., and Lee, J.K., (2000). Electronic Commerce—A Managerial Perspective, Prentice-Hall, Upper Saddle River, NJ, 2000.

Whiteley D. (2000). *e-Commerce: Strategy, Technologies and Applications*, McGraw Hill Companies, London.

E-Audit in India: Challenges and Opportunities

S.C. Bansal and *Lata Sharma*

ABSTRACT

E-commerce has tremendously increased the complexity of transactions as most of the business contracts are made between unknown parties. In this environment, reliability of trading partners, financial viability of companies, data security, and dependability on the system has to be ensured. e-system has also changed the manner of audit, and the nature of services required from an auditor. It has become imperative for the auditors to have expertise in the use of IT, apart from proficiency in their domain areas to ensure that the financial statements fairly present financial position, results of operation and cash flow of an entity. Most of the existing studies on e-commerce have examined the extent of its activities in the advanced countries. However, no attempt seems to have been made to examine the auditing aspects of e-commerce. The present work, therefore, bridges a research gap: it identifies some of the problems experienced by the professionals while auditing in the e-environment. It also highlights the new opportunities for auditors in this system. A pre-structured questionnaire has been used to find out the practices and opinions of 75 professional auditors on various aspects related to e-audit. It has been found that, in the opinion of the auditors, manipulation in the information kept in electronic form can be traced comfortably. The absence of vouchers in e-environment does not cause any difficulty in the audit. It is also possible to detect exploitation of anonymity provided by the internet. e-commerce environment has opened up new vistas of opportunities in many areas, e.g., verification of integrity of data; assessment of electronic payment transfers; audit of accounting for virtual assets; security evaluation; and disaster recovery planning. It is hoped that the present work would be useful to the professionals, policymakers, regulators and managers in developing systems for auditing commercial transactions in the e-environment.

1. INTRODUCTION

With electronic commerce becoming a way of life, business has become dependent on computers. This has increased the complexity of transactions as they are being increasingly done among parties who have never met. In such an environment, it is important to have an assurance about the quality and reliability of trading partners, financial viability of companies, data security, reliability of systems and many such issues.

E-environment has, thus, changed the manner of audit, and the nature of services required from an auditor. It has become imperative for the auditors to be multi-skilled in the use of IT, apart from proficiency in their domain areas of expertise. As audits in the future become virtual, auditors will also be able to globalize their operations. Auditors will be able to concentrate on core management issues rather than routine functioning of scrutinizing various financial documents. An attempt has been made in the present study to discuss the views of the auditing professionals on the various issues related to e-audit. Besides, the study also tries to find out the new possible opportunities for auditors in electronic environment. This paper consists of five sections. Section 2 reviews some of the existing empirical works. Section 3 explains methodology used. In Section 4, the opinions of auditors have been analyzed. Section 5 gives the summary.

2. LITERATURE REVIEW

E-commerce is becoming popular among the organizations nowadays across the world. Many surveys have been made to estimate the growth of e-commerce in various countries. Pricewaterhouse Coopers (2001) conducted a study of 78 large manufacturing corporations in the United States. It found that only 40 per cent of large companies could receive orders online and only 28 per cent could accept payments online.

Jupiter (2001) suggests that in 2005, 80 per cent of B2B transactions will be e-commerce transactions, accounting for some US $ 6.3 trillion. Boston Consulting Group (2001) projects a rise from 13 per cent of inter-company gross purchases (US $ 4.8 Trillion) in 2004. While the figures from these two sources differ, it is clear that B2B overwhelmingly dominates e-commerce. In fact, industry analysts argue that soon business will drop the "e" from e-commerce, because transaction will be undertaken no other way.

According to Forrester Research Inc., world B to B and B to C e-commerce will have totalled US $ 657 billion in 2000, surging to US $ 6.8 trillion in 2004. North America's e-commerce is expected to top the list of regions in both 2000 and 2004, registering US $ 509.3 billion and US $ 3.5 trillion, respectively. Asia pacific will be at second place in 2004, and Western Europe in Third place, with electronic transactions amounting to US $ 1.6 trillion and US $ 1.5 trillion respectively. Online retail sales will grow from $ 172 billion in 2005 to $ 329 billion in 2010. E-commerce will represent 13 per cent of total US retail sales in 2010. At the country level, US e-commerce sales will be highest sales in the world all through the period 2000-04. Internet commerce in the US is expected to amount to US $ 488.7 billion and US $ 3.2 trillion in 2000 and 2004 respectively, followed by Japan and Germany. This trend will probably drive the rest of the world into increasing their e-commerce activities.

In India, a study has been made by Mittal, to find out the state of e-commerce. During 1998-99, e-commerce transactions in India were estimated to be Rs. 131 crore. The bulk of it was from B2B transactions; only 12 crore was from B2C. During 1999-2000, it was estimated to be Rs. 450 crore. NASSCOM, (National Association of Software and Service Companies) expected an increase of 500 per cent in the e-commerce transactions in the country with the enactment of Information Technology Act, 2000.According to a study by IMRB (Indian

Market Research Bureau), the market size of B2B e-commerce would touch Rs. 50,000 crore by 2001.

Confederation of Indian Industries and International Trade Centre conducted a survey of 269 small and medium organizations to find out level of e-commerce activity in India in 2005. The study revealed that e-commerce in India is expected to increase to Rs. 25,200 crore in 2005 from Rs. 450 crore in the financial year 2000. B2B e-commerce will increase from Rs. 400 crore in 1999-2000 to Rs. 23,280 crore in 2004-05. The total worth of B2C activities in India is expected to increase from Rs. 50 crore in 2000 to Rs. 1,882 crore in 2005. Internet and Online Association of India (2005) conducted research in association with Cross Tab Marketing Services to track internet user's activity for shopping online. They solicited the views of 3099 respondents. More than one half (55%) of them had shopped online. 85 per cent of online shoppers were male.

Thus, a number of studies have been conducted in India and elsewhere on various aspects of e-commerce. Most of the studies have suggested an increasing use of e-commerce over the years. A review of the studies on e-commerce shows that their primary focus has been on the estimation of the size of e-commerce and the ways and means of exploiting it for corporate gains rather than a serious attempt to raise issues that may engage the attention of the various regulatory bodies. The present study attempts to identify critical issues related to e-auditing that the professional community is presently confronted with. It also highlights the new opportunities for auditors in this system.

3. METHODOLOGY

This section describes the scope and methodology used for analyzing the effect of computerized information systems environment on the audit. The views of auditors have been collected with the help of a questionnaire consisting of both open and close-ended questions. A draft questionnaire was prepared and discussed with five auditors working in e-environment. Their suggestions were incorporated and a final questionnaire was prepared. The questionnaire was, then, mailed to 100 CAs randomly selected from the directory of CAs prepared by ICAI. Some responses were received from Delhi and its adjoining areas. A few responses were received from Mumbai and Chennai as well. However, the response rate was not satisfactory. Then, CAs in Delhi and its adjoining areas were personally contacted. In all, 85 questionnaires were filled, out of which 10 were rejected because of incomplete information. Seventy-five responses have, thus, been used giving a response rate of 75 per cent.

An attempt was made to ensure that questionnaire was filled by auditors having experience of e-audit. Figures 27.1—27.5 present the detailed profile of responding auditors. The sample of the study is fairly diversified in terms of their age and experience. Though all the respondents are CAs, some have additional qualifications as well, performing diverse activities in discharge of their duties. All the professionals have either expert or reasonable knowledge of computers obtained from different sources.

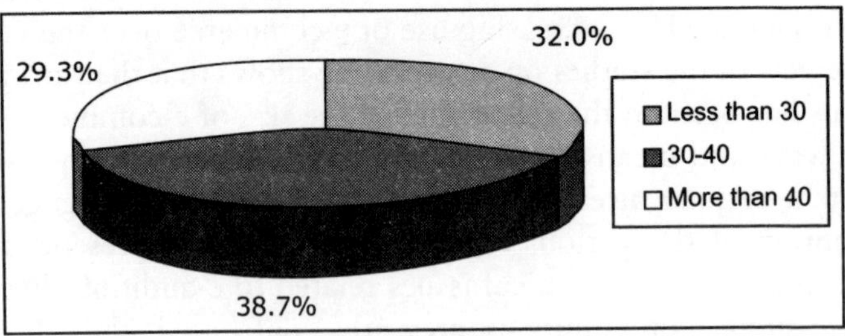

Figure 27.1: Age Groups (Years) of the Auditors

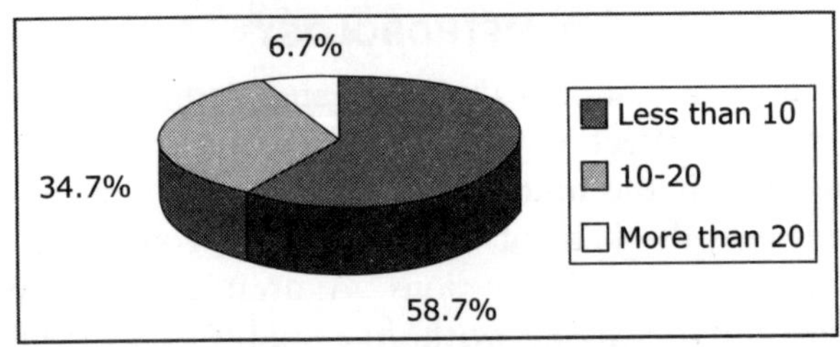

Figure 27.2: Length of Experience (Years) in Their Present Job/ Organisation of the Auditors

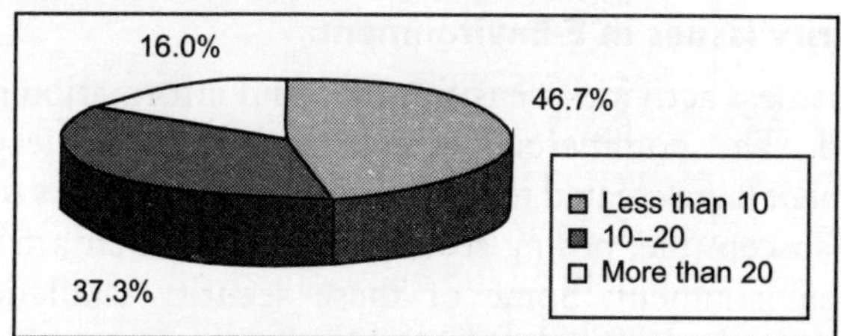

Figure 27.3: Length of Total Experience (Years) of the Auditors

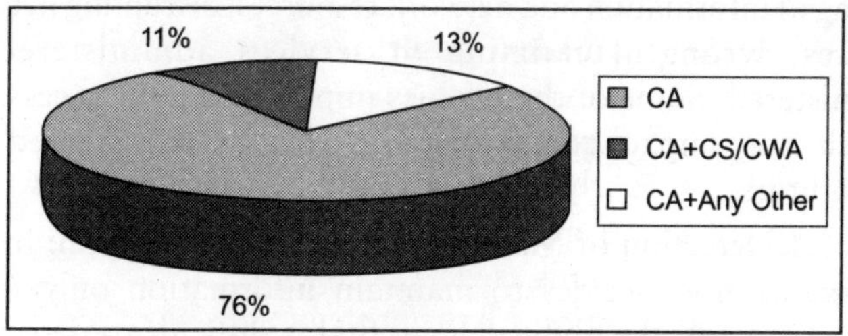

Figure 27.4: Qualifications of the Auditors

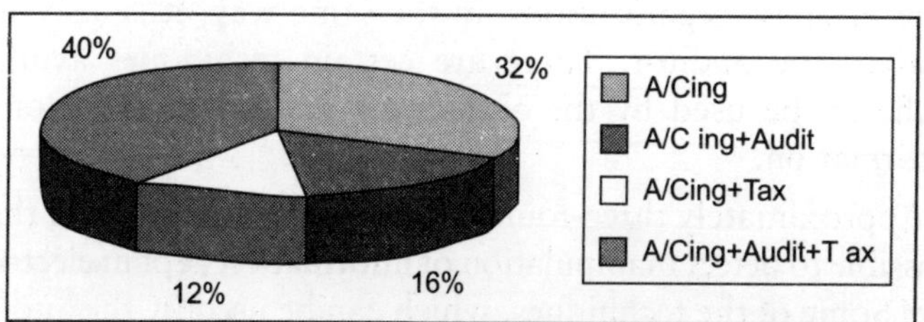

Figure 27.5: Area(s) of Specialization of the Authors

4. AUDIT PROCESS IN E-ENVIRONMENT

This Section presents the findings of the discussions with audit professionals on how, in their view, the audit process is influenced by a company's e-commerce related transactions.

Access to all relevant information and records is critical to forming an audit opinion. Therefore, the auditing professionals were requested to indicate the criticality of this aspect of the audit process. About 90 per cent of the auditors have indicated that the access is an absolute must.

4.1 Security Issues in E-Environment

In business activities, sensitive data and information must be protected. The commercial activities done in a networked environment have created numerous threats and attacks to which they are susceptible, posing security challenges that are specific to this environment. Some of these security challenges are accessing unauthorized network resources, manipulating information, disclosing information to unauthorized people, stealing of information and network resources, disrupting network services, wrongful claiming of services administered/not administered. Some of these issues impinge on their access, and as such, may impact quality of audit. These were discussed with the auditors.

4.1.1 Detection of Manipulations of E-information: In case an organization decides to maintain information only in the electronic form, the auditors may find it difficult to detect any manipulations done in it. But the way technology is being useful to the business organizations, in the same way, it is also being useful to the auditor. There are certain techniques available which can be used by the auditor to detect manipulations in e-information.

Approximately three-fourths of the respondents agree that it is possible to detect manipulation of information kept in electronic form. Some of the techniques, which can be used by the auditors for this purpose are Password to prove the identity; Proper Authorization to control access to particular information once identity has been verified; Audit Trails to trace a transaction sequentially through the system from its source to completion or *vice-versa*; and Computerized Audit Tools (CATs) to gain access and analyze data for a predetermined audit objective and to report audit findings with evidence (Figure 27.6).

Majority (60%) of the auditors are of the view that CATs are quite helpful in detecting manipulations of e-information. Audit Trails may also be used for the purpose. Password and Proper Authorization, though necessary for e-transactions so as to fix the responsibility, are helpful only to some extent. Good internal controls, periodic checks over records maintained, ratio

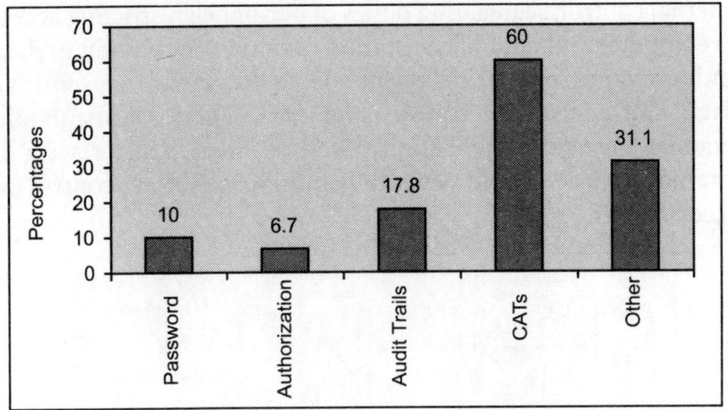

Figure 27.6: Detection of Manipulation of E-information

analysis, exception report, and analysis of major types of expenses are some of the existing techniques which can be equally useful in e-environment as well. Thus, with development in e-commerce, corresponding developments in audit techniques have taken place to help them in conducting proper audit.

4.1.2 Control of Access Rights: To ensure fairness of financial data, the auditor should have control of access rights given to the users of data. This will guard against unauthorized entry into a firm's transaction processing system. Unrestricted access can result in loss of confidentiality, integrity and availability of organizational information. Access control is required to identify the user and to determine and restrict the degree and type of access to resources. A large majority (72.6%) of the responding auditors agree to this view. The auditors should have some control on access rights given to various users of company's computer networks.

The auditors can ensure control of access rights to data users in many ways like audit of access controls themselves, review of password protocol, review of internal controls of the organization and following of the audit trails. In the opinion of large majority (71.7%) of auditors, review of internal controls is the most effective tool in their hands to ensure control of access rights (Figure 27.7). This can be done by developing a strong system of internal control; segregating duties of personnel; restricting access to computer and data files; rotation of duties; encryption of data and program; protecting telephone line; control on sensitive data; and control on laptop computers. The auditors should examine the adequacy of control in these areas. Thus, review of internal controls would be more helpful in exercising control on access rights.

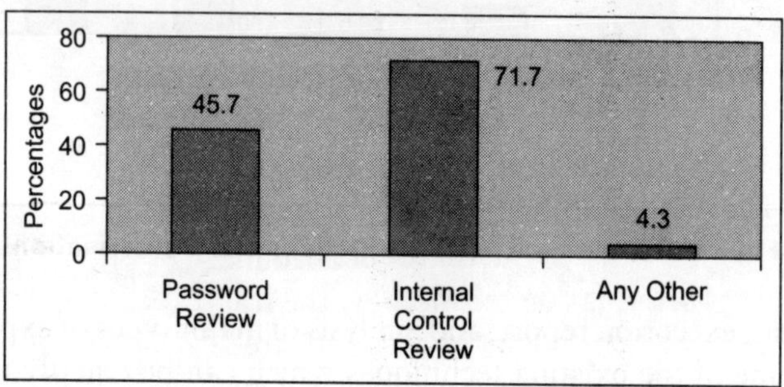

Figure 27.7: Techniques for Control of Access Rights

4.1.3 Monitoring of Access Control: The auditors can further monitor the control on access to computer networks of the organization to improve the effectiveness of the audit process. A majority (65.8%) of the auditors feel that they should do such monitoring.

Here again, internal control review seems to be the best option as suggested by more than two-thirds of the respondents. The auditor can make surprise checking and see whether access to networks is made by authorized persons or not. He should observe the routine followed and verify the adherence to the laid down system. The other important technique, according to one-third of the respondents, is password review. By reviewing the internal controls from time to time, thus, the auditor can easily keep a check on the access to computer networks.

4.1.4 Detection of Exploitation of Anonymity of e-transactions*:* One of the major features of internet is 'anonymity' provided by it. This feature helps in maintaining secrecy. But just as every coin has two sides, the same 'anonymity' can be exploited and misused by the user. In a computerized environment, it becomes very difficult for auditors to detect exploitation provided by the internet. However, more than four-fifths of the auditors opine that, though difficult, it is not impossible to detect and find it out. Some of the methods which can help the auditor in doing so are use of specific softwares developed for this purpose only, use of internal security scanners and physical checks. Thus, with the help of various e-aids, developed specifically for the purpose, auditors can trace the path of e-transactions.

4.2 Verification: Role of Vouchers in E-environment

Traditionally, the auditors verified the financial information given in the books of accounts with the help of vouchers. The vouchers are studied and checked for their correctness and accordingly, the entry in the books of accounts is checked. With the advent of information technology, the transactions are done electronically and the books of accounts are also maintained in e-form. In such a scenario in the absence of vouchers, the auditor may find it difficult to audit the books of accounts.

There are certain techniques, which auditors believe can help them in such an environment. Some of these techniques, as mentioned earlier as well, are CAATs, Audit Trails and Verification of Authority for conducting the transaction and use of data. Most (40%) of the respondents have suggested use of 'Computer Assisted Audit Techniques'. There are a variety of softwares available to auditors to assist in evidence collection. Thus, in the absence of vouchers, auditors use specialized softwares and audit trails to verify the transactions.

4.3 Risk Assessment

In e-environment, new varieties of risks which never existed earlier in traditional environment have developed. In terms of electronic commerce, risk is viewed as the possibility of loss of confidential data or the destruction, generation, or use of data, or programs that physically, mentally, or financially harm another party, as well as the possibility of harm to hardware. The assessment of risk is a key component in the design and evaluation of internal controls. In this regard the auditors may like to refer to SAP-6 wherein it has been clarified that computers can influence the internal controls needed, making traditional internal control techniques ineffective and may even eliminate them.

More than four-fifths of the auditors agree that the assessment of risk for electronic transactions should be done by the auditors, as the possibilities of new uncertainties have developed in e-environment. Review of internal controls from time to time is the most effective technique for assessment of risk, in their opinion. Only a few (5%) are of the opinion that help of IT Department can be taken for the purpose or a comparison can be done with the industrial practice.

4.4 Changing Role of Auditor in E-environment

In a computer information system environment, the nature of activities done by an auditor has also seen a sea change. Almost all (more than 90%) auditors surveyed are of the opinion that an auditor can have a positive contribution with respect to the following aspects of an e-commerce organization:

1. Verification for integrity of data;
2. Assessment of the electronic transfer of payment between and through international banking system;
3. Audit of functional areas like telecommunication, operating system, accounting and business process applications;
4. Verification for source of data;
5. Audit of the accounting for assets which only exist in a virtual state, not a physical one;
6. Verification for completeness of electronic data.

About one-fourth of the respondents suggested that audit-IT interface, should enable the auditors to make significant contributions in the areas of System Analysis—assistance in system conceptualization, designing and implementation; Security Evaluation; Disaster Recovery Planning and Business Continuity Planning; Taxation Audit; and Intellectual Property Rights in Intranet Domain.

4.5 Need for E-knowledge

The main objective of auditing is the evaluation of financial statements to see whether they truly and fairly represent the actual financial position. The auditor also evaluates the relevant systems of the organization to assess the quality of internal evidence. To achieve this objective, it is necessary for the auditor to understand the underlying programs and digital methods that are used to create transactions done electronically. The ICAI Guide on E-audit emphasizes the need for the auditors to have a thorough understanding of the information technology, its key components and how they function. Approximately three-fourths of the auditors are of the opinion that the auditor must have at least reasonable e-knowledge so as to perform his duties efficiently.

4.6 Forensic Accounting

Forensic Accounting is a service provided by accountants that involves investigation of fraud, typically affecting the accounting transaction processing cycles, with a focus on gathering legal evidence to help support the prosecution of the perpetrator. It is a specialized field requiring preservation, identification, extraction, and documentation of computer evidence. An opportunity exists for forensic accountants to engage in investigation on security breaches that involve financial data. Accountants are uniquely positioned to perform this kind of work if they acquire the requisite technological skills. Almost all (89.8%) of the respondents are willing to take up this additional responsibility, as it seems to be quite challenging area of activity and will expand their horizon. This service can be performed better by acquiring the requisite technological skills along with the knowledge of investigative accounting work.

4.7 Liability of Auditors for Use of Pirated Software by Clients

The use of pirated softwares, though a crime, is quite common. The auditors were asked to give their opinion whether they should be held equally liable for certifying the accounts generated from pirated software. Only about one-third (34.3%) of the auditors feel that they should be held equally liable in such a situation. Majority of the auditors regard it as the management's responsibility if they are using pirated software. The auditors' job is to report the matter to the management. Responsibility for piracy rests entirely with the organization committing it. Auditors are responsible only if there is some risk of data or some manipulation is done in the data.

SUMMARY

In this study, an analysis of audit techniques and procedures required in e-environment has been done. The information for the purpose has been collected through questionnaire and personal discussion on critical issues related to e-audit.

The analysis shows that to conduct proper audit in e-environment, auditors must have access to the records maintained in the computer networks of the organization. It is possible to detect manipulation of information kept in electronic form. The absence of vouchers in e-environment does not cause much difficulty in e-audit. There are many techniques available like 'Computerized Audit Assisting Techniques' and Audit Trails to help auditors in verifying the transactions and finding out any manipulations done in them. It is also possible to detect exploitation of anonymity provided by the internet by using specific softwares made for this purpose, internal security scanners and physical checks. This implies that anonymity on the internet cannot be misused any longer.

In electronic environment, there is need for auditor to have control on access rights given to the users of data. They should also monitor the control on access to network. This can be done by reviewing internal control systems and review of passwords. The auditors should also do the risk assessment for electronic transactions. It is now necessary for auditors to understand underlying programs and digital methods used to create e-transactions. They should rely mainly on internal control reviews for e-audit. The auditors do not wish to be held liable for use of pirated softwares used for preparing accounts. Thus, e-commerce environment presents not only challenges before the auditing professionals but also has opened up new vistas of opportunities.

REFERENCES

A & M, 15 January 2001, p.32.

Mittal, D.P. *Law of Information Technology (Cyber Law)*, Taxmann, Delhi, 2000, p.17.

Piturro, Marlene. "Get into E-Commerce without Betting the Store", *Journal of Accountancy, May 1999,* p.56.

"Secrets of Electronics Commerce: A Guide for Small and Medium-sized Exporters," *Confederation of Indian Industries and International Trade Centre,* New Delhi, 2001.

Taylor, David and Tertlune, Alyse D. *Doing e-business-Strategies for thriving in an Electronic Market Place,* John Wiley & Sons, Inc., USA, 2001, pp. 177-78.

United Nations, "Report on Economic and Social Commission on Western Asia", 2001, pp.4-5.

United Nations, "Report on Economic and Social Commission on Western Asia", 2004, pp.4-5.

World Economic Forum Report 2000-01, p. 92.

www.ioaindia.com Internet & Online Association of India, "The Power shoppers IOAI E-commerce Report 2005".

www.forrester.com

Service Quality and Customer Satisfaction of Credit Cardholders—With Special Reference to India

28

J.S. Panwar and *Deepa Kumari*

INTRODUCTION

The Indian payment card industry has immense potential despite a huge unbanked population, a predominant cash culture and propensity to save than to spend. As per the available statistics credit cards issuable population in India stands at 17 million. In the year 2004, 2.4 per cent of the working population in India possessed credit cards. McKinsey predicts that 35 million credit cards would be issued by the year 2010. The prediction is based on a variety of reasons such as a growing middle class that stands at 250-300 million; higher disposable incomes; and exposure to global products and services. If the prediction is right, credit cards would soon become a way of life in India as well.

However, credit card ownership and usage in India are still at a nascent stage when compared to the economies of West Asia and Europe. In India, most of the transactions take place in cash and credit cards are not used very often. Many large value purchases of consumer durables or jewelry, are occasional, and preferred to be paid through cash. For smaller purchases, the retail scenario is a barrier too. Retailers do not promote discounts on the use of credit cards. Cash transactions are generally unrecorded and help retailers in evading taxes. Infrastructural bottlenecks such as absence of card accepting terminals further discourage the use of plastic money.

Many such issues are now being addressed by the banks. Credit cards are being popularized by increasing their acceptance at petrol pumps, restaurants, retail stores and for booking railway and airline tickets. Even smaller towns and cities have been demonstrating encouraging growth results for credit cards. Introduction of newer technologies is helping in bringing out innovative features and targeting newer customer segments and thus giving momentum to the credit card industry in India. As the Indian payment card industry matures, payment products offered to consumers will have to be tailor-made and customized to suit variety of needs and also to offer value added services to its customers. In the wake of globalization of banking and financial services it is imperative on the part of credit card operators to provide better services to their customers and earn profits through customer satisfaction.

OBJECTIVES AND METHODOLOGY

The primary research question being addressed by this paper is to measure various service quality attributes associated with the select credit cards, and consequently to what extent credit cardholders are satisfied with these attributes as well as with the use of their cards.

This paper is based on a descriptive study conducted by one of the authors in the cosmopolitan town of Baroda, in the State of Gujarat, India by personally interviewing the same set of credit cardholders in three different phases during the year 2004-05. It was a sort of tracking study spread over a continuous span of twelve months, involving one complete cycle of service quality experiences of a credit cardholder. The tracking study commenced with the process of acquiring a credit card; records usage experience of the cardholder and concludes with the renewal or non-renewal of the credit card membership. Based on this context the following objectives were framed for the study:

- To measure various service quality attributes associated with the credit card and its' usage.
- To measure the cardholder's satisfaction level over a period of three phases.
- To understand the difference in the perceptions of card-holders regarding various service quality attributes associated with the card and its' usage and the subsequent

satisfaction or dissatisfaction leading to "renewals" or "non-renewals" of credit card membership.

- To identify meaningful clusters (segments) on the basis of credit cardholders' perceptions towards various service quality attributes associated with the cards and their usage.

The study being longitudinal in nature was expected to throw light on the levels of cardholders' satisfaction during the three phases of credit card ownership cycle.

Credit card categories in India are assigned different nomenclatures such as "gold" or "silver" based on the benefits offered by them and their suitability for different socioeconomic classes. The "silver" category of credit cards is ideally suited for the masses and has the maximum customer base in the country. The scope of the study was therefore, deliberately restricted to the "silver" category of credit cards.

A set of three questionnaires was prepared for the purpose of this study. Different questionnaires were employed during the three phases. The questionnaires were framed on the basis of SERVQUAL (Parsuraman et al., 1988) and SERVPERF (Cronin & Taylor, 1992) models developed for the purpose of measuring the service quality and customer satisfaction from the service, with due adaptation of these instruments for specific objectives of the study.

A combination of stratified and judgment sampling plan was employed for the study to give equal representation to all major credit cardholders and also to accommodate only those cardholders, who had a history of using their credit cards at least 8-10 times a year. The credit cardholders of the five prominent banks, both foreign and national were included in the sample. These banks have a fairly large membership base in Baroda. The banks in question are: the Citibank; the Standard Chartered Bank; the ICICI Bank; State Bank of India and Bank of Baroda. A set of the thirty credit cardholders for all five different cards was selected using pre-determined criteria.

The data were collected by personally interviewing the total of 150 respondents spread over three different phases employing pre-tested, non-disguised structured questionnaires. The instruments were pre-tested on a set of fifteen respondents for each phase.

LITERATURE REVIEW

Quality of service has been studied in the area of business management for years because markets are getting increasingly competitive. Over a period of time marketing management has also shifted its focus from internal performance such as production to external interests such as customer satisfaction and perception of service quality (Grönroos, 1992). Yet, even now there has been no agreement on conceptualization of service quality (Cronin & Taylor, 1992; Rust & Oliver, 1994). Different researches have focused on different aspects of service quality. Reeves and Bedner (1994) suggest that, "there is no universal, parsimonious, or all encompassing definition of service quality or model of service quality" (p. 436).

SERVQUAL by Parsuraman et al. (1988), which is based on to the traditional disconfirmatory model, was the first effort to operationalize service quality. It measures service quality as a gap between expectation and perception in a cross-section of service firms. Although SERVQUAL made tremendous contribution to the field of service quality and was very popular among service quality researches in many areas; it is insufficient because of its conceptual weaknesses caused by the disconfirmatory paradigm and its' empirical appropriateness. Later on, several service quality models with more dimensions were developed. Most recent models such as Brady's (1997) hierarchical multi-dimensional model synthesized prior approaches and represented the complexity of the construct of service quality perception.

However, some researchers believed that a direct measure of service quality is more desirable. Cronin & Taylor (1992) developed an instrument called SERVPERF, which is basically a performance based measure of service quality. The SERVPRF instrument uses the attribute approach to customers' experiences of service in question. It used the original SERVQUAL scale and required the customer to rate the service and the service provider's performance on a seven point scale by using a single set of questions. Somehow, this model does not seek to measure expectations. A single measure of service performance may circumvent the issue of changing customer expectations and also the need to administer a two part questionnaire, but on the flip side it would not measure the customer satisfaction.

As indicated earlier, of late marketing management changed its focus to external interests such as customer satisfaction and their perceptions of service quality, therefore it is imperative to consider customer satisfaction in any measurement instrument. Most models of consumer satisfaction and service quality maintain that ex-ante expectations of a product or service are the best measures of satisfaction or perceived quality by the customer (Oliver 1997, 1980; Parsuraman, Zeithmal & Berry, 1985, 1988).

Despite many attempts to measure and explain consumer satisfaction, there still does not appear to be a consensus regarding its definition (Giese & Cote, 2000) or determinants (Spreng, Mackenzie, Olshavsky, 1996). However, most popularly consumer satisfaction is typically defined as being a result of an evaluative process that contrasts pre-purchase expectations with perceptions of performance during and after consumption experience (Oliver 1980, 1981; Rust & Oliver, 1994). Several alternative explanations of consumer satisfaction have been advanced, but the expectation-disconfirmation paradigm has been the most popular of all (Oliver 1980, 1981; Spreng, Mackenzie & Olshavsky 1996; Tse & Wilton, 1988).

This account predicts that expectations and disconfirmation are the two variables that best explain consumer satisfaction. Disconfirmation can be defined as the difference between the expected and perceived product performance, and expectations as predictions of future performance (Oliver, 1980).

The literature on service quality has followed a similar disconfirmation approach with Parsuraman, Zeithmal and Berry's (1985) original "gaps" model. However, there is a debate in marketing regarding the differences and similarities between the consumer satisfaction and service quality constructs (Parsuraman, Zeithmal & Berry 1994; Spreng & Singh 1993; Teas 1993,

1994). Despite many conceptual differences between service quality and customer satisfaction, the way they are measured is quite comparable. This is so because the measured parameters of service quality usually represents customer perceptions rather than objective indicators of quality (Zeithmal 1988, Bitner and Hubbert 1994) and therefore, service quality and customer satisfaction, tend to be highly corelated.

This paper also takes a similar view on service quality attributes and customer satisfaction and treats them interchangeably for the purpose of the study. Credit cardholder's satisfaction, for this paper has been defined as the perception of credit cardholders towards various service quality attributes of credit card usage, experienced by customers at different points of service encounters, spread over a study of three phases. As mentioned beforehand, the secondary research helped in identifying the various service quality attributes that were used in the questionnaires covering the three phases.

FIELDWORK AND DATA ANALYSIS

The foremost objective of the study was to measure the various service quality attributes associated with the credit card and its usage and thereby credit cardholder's satisfaction. In line of the primary objective of the study, credit cardholder satisfaction has been defined in terms of their perceptions towards various service quality attributes associated with the credit card and its' usage. This definition has been framed using the SERVPERF model developed by Cronin and Taylor in 1992. Cronin and Taylor proposed that it is SERVPERF model that best reflects customers' perceptions of service quality. They argued that only performance based measurement is ideal to measure service quality without including expectations in the measurement instrument.

On the basis of literature review, secondary data and interactions with experts, nine major service quality attributes were identified. These service quality attributes were measured in three different phases, spread over a span of twelve months. These nine attributes along with the phases in which they were studied are given in Annexure I.

Annexure-I

SERVICE QUALITY ATTRIBUTES COVERED IN VARIOUS PHASES

Phase-I

- Application form for acquiring the credit card.
- Sales executive of the credit card issuing bank.
- Service manual of the credit card.
- Various fees & interest rates associated with the credit card.

Phase-II

- Benefits associated with the credit card.

Phase-III

- Acceptance of and transactions with the credit card.
- Statements of and payments for the credit card.
- Customer service offered by the credit card issuing banks.
- Schemes offered by the credit card issuing banks.

These nine attributes holistically cover almost all the service experiences of a credit cardholder. They were further divided into various sub-attributes, say in case of application form for the credit card, the sub-attributes were its' length, language and framework. Each of these sub-attributes were measured on a five point Likert Scale and the weighted average scores were computed to define credit cardholders' perceptions towards various service quality elements and thereby credit cardholders' satisfaction. On completion of all the three phases, cardholders were categorized according to their status of membership of their respective cards and were accordingly classified as "renewals" and "non-renewals." Renewals referred to that set of credit cardholders who had renewed their credit cards after the completion of initial membership of one year and the non-renewals referred to those who had not renewed their credit cards after the completion of initial one year membership.

The data collected through fieldwork were analyzed using various statistical tools such as weighted average scores; discriminant analysis and cluster analysis. The weighted average scores helped in measuring credit cardholders' perceptions about various service quality attributes and levels of their satisfaction/ dissatisfaction from the card. The data were further analyzed using discriminant and cluster analyses to understand the difference between two groups of credit cardholders and their profiles on the basis of various benefits they seek from a credit card. The forthcoming sections would discuss these tools and their applications in the context of current study.

1. Perceptions of Credit Cardholders towards Various Service Quality Attributes

The primary purpose of study was to measure various service quality attributes of credit cards and consequently to determine credit cardholders' satisfaction/dissatisfaction from the usage. Nine service quality attributes were identified for measurement in the span of three phases, with the help of pre-tested, non-disguised structured questionnaires. The data were analyzed using the weighted average method. The weighted scores so obtained, are shown in Annexure II.

Annexure-II

Table 28.1: Weighted Average Score for Different Attributes of Various Credit Card and it's Usage

Attributes	Weighted Average Scores				
	Citibank	Standard Chartered Bank	ICICI	SBI	BOB
Application form	4.17	3.97	4.13	4.17	3.97
Sales Executive	3.87	3.53	3.43	3.50	3.67
Service Manual	4.10	3.87	4.17	4.07	3.63
Fee and interest structure	2.23	2.27	2.63	2.77	2.73
Benefits	3.43	3.60	3.33	3.40	3.60
Acceptance & transactions	3.87	3.83	3.77	3.77	3.17
Statements & payments	4.47	4.23	4.27	4.37	4.50
Customer service	3.77	3.23	3.33	3.13	3.33
Schemes	3.40	3.13	2.87	3.33	3.17

Source: Fieldwork.

According to the weighted average scores for *application form for the credit card,* the cardholders of Citibank, the State Bank of India and the ICICI Bank are more satisfied. The Standard Chartered Bank and Bank of Baroda have been perceived as mediocre on this count. Similarly, for the attribute of *interaction with sales executive of the service providing bank*, all five card issuing banks have been perceived as average or below average. For the attribute of *service manual,* ICICI Bank, Citibank and State Bank of India have been rated as satisfactory, while the Standard Chartered Bank and Bank of Baroda have been perceived as mediocre. In case of *fees and interest rates associated with the card,* the customers of all credit card issuing banks are dissatisfied. For other service attributes such as *benefits associated with the credit card; acceptance of card and transactions with the credit card* all credit cards were adjudged at par.

In terms of *statement of accounts and payment procedure* the prevailing practices of all credit card issuing banks have been adjudged as satisfactory. On the basis of *customer service and promotional schemes* all credit cards have been perceived as mediocre or less rewarding. Thus, it is evident from the analysis that on majority of service quality attributes performance of all five credit card issuing banks has been perceived as mediocre or unsatisfactory. They need to do a lot to improve their service ratings.

2. Perception of Service Quality Attributes and Satisfaction of 'Renewals' and 'Non-renewals': An Application of Discriminant Analysis

Customer satisfaction is assumed to be an important antecedent of both, the choice decisions and the likelihood of repeat purchases. The few articles in the marketing literature that explore the relationship between satisfaction and repeat purchase behavior indicate that they are strongly related (Bloemer and Kasper, 1995; Kasper 1988; Labarbera & Mazurusky 1983; Newmen &Werbel, 1973). It is, therefore posited here that the credit cardholders who have renewed their cards after completion of initial membership term of one year, perceive the service quality as satisfactory, than those who have not renewed their credit cards.

The study classified a set of 150 credit cardholders after three phases in the two distinct categories namely "renewals" and "non-renewals." Renewals refer to those cardholders who renewed their cards and non-renewals refer to those who had not. For a sample of 150 credit cardholders, 109 were observed to have renewed their credit cards and 41 had not renewed their card membership.

Discriminant Analysis was used in order to discriminate between the perceptions of two groups towards various service quality attributes of credit cards and eventually to discriminate among the levels of satisfaction of the two groups. In order to conduct discriminant analysis the dependent as well as independent variable/s, both were identified. Perceptions of credit cardholders towards various service quality attributes as discussed in section four of the paper were considered as independent variables and status of membership was treated as dependent variable.

An assessment of the overall fitness of discriminant model helped in understanding whether discriminant function is statistically significant and the classification accuracy is acceptable.

An examination of Table 28.2 indicating a summary of canonical discriminant function (see Annexure III) reveals that discriminant functions are statistically significant as measured by the chi-square statistics. The first function accounting for 100 per cent variance, significant at .000 levels indicates that perceptions towards various service quality attributes of credit cards do discriminate between the renewals and the non-renewals groups. An examination of Table 28.3 of classification results (Annexure IV) reveals the predictive accuracy of the discriminant function, measured by the hit-ratio and its comparison with the maximum chance criterion. Maximum-chance criterion refers to the percentage of items correctly classified, if all the observations were placed in the group with greatest possibility of occurrence. As the hit ratio exceeds the maximum chance criterion, as shown in the Annexure V, the discriminant model for the study may be considered as valid.

Annexure-III

Table 28.2: SUMMARY OF CANONICAL DISCRIMINANT FUNCTION

Eigen Values				
Function	Eigen Value	% of variance	Cumulative %	Canonical correlation
1	0.49	100.00	100.00	0.58

Source: Fieldwork.

First 1 canonical discriminant functions were used in the analysis.

Wilks lambda				
Test of function	Wilks	Chi-Square	df	Significance
1	0.67	57.52	9.00	0.00

Source: Fieldwork.

[a] First 1 canonical discriminant functions were used in the analysis.

[b] Wilks lambda

Annexure-IV

Table 28.3: Classification Results

Status about renewed	Predicted Group Membership		
	Renewed	Not renewed	Total
Original count Renewed (Nos.)	92	17	109
Non- renewed (Nos.)	13	28	41
% Renewed	84.40%	15.60%	100.00%
% Non-renewed	31.71%	68.29%	100.00%
Cross-validated Count Renewed	86	23	109
Non-renewed	14	27	41
% Renewed	78.90%	21.10%	100.00%
% Non-renewed	34.15%	65.85%	100.00%

Source: Fieldwork.

[a.] cross validation is done only for cases in the analysis. In cross validation, each case is classified by the functions derived from all cases other than that case.

[b] 80.0 % of original grouped cases correctly classified.

[c] 75.3 % of cross-validated correctly classified.

An interpretation of the discriminant function would help in understanding the discrimination of two groups on the basis of perception for various service quality attributes of credit cards. The authors have interpreted the discriminant function on the basis of discriminant loadings as they are considered to be more valid than interpreting the discriminating power of independent variables because of their correlational values.

Annexure-V

CALCULATION OF HIT RATIO FOR THE DATA COLLECTED

- Maximum Chance Criterion= (109/150)*100=72.66%.
- Proportional Chance Criterion = $[(109/150)^2 + (41/150)^2]$ =.6025*100=60.25.
- Hit Ratio of both the analysis sample is 80% and the holdout sample is 75.3% thus both the values exceeds the maximum chance criterion of 72.66%.

A further examination of Table 28.4 in Annexure VI gives structure correlations for discriminant functions. It reveals the correlation between the discriminating variables and standardized canonical discriminant functions. It indicates that perceptions towards various service- quality attributes play a role in defining the credit cardholders' satisfaction. It also indicates that credit cardholders who have renewed their card memberships are more satisfied with their credit cards.

Annexure-VI

Table 28.4: Structure Correlations for Discriminant Functions

Independent Variables	Function I
Acceptance of Transactions with the card	0.67
Customer service	0.65
Statements and payments	0.62
Schemes	0.53
Benefits	0.24
Sales Executive	0.21
Application Form	0.21
Service manual	0.19
Fee and interest structure	-0.01

Source: Fieldwork.

The cardholders are more favorably influenced by the various service quality attributes (in descending order) beginning with the acceptance of and transactions with the credit card; customer services offered by the issuing bank; statements of accounts and payment modes; promotional schemes offered; benefits offered by the credit card issuing banks; application form for the credit card; and service manuals. They are least influenced by the fees and interest rates than those who have not renewed their credit cards and are less satisfied with their credit cards.

The output of analysis indicates that credit cardholders who have renewed their cards memberships perceive fees and interest rates to be more important in defining their satisfaction levels. However, if various banks work more on other important service quality attributes such as promotional schemes the negative impact of fees and interest rates could be neutralized to some extent.

In order to survive in a competitive environment credit card issuing banks need to work hard on the existing service quality attributes and find newer attributes to retain their customers and attract new customers.

3. Perception of Service Quality Attributes and Benefit Segmentation: An Application of Cluster Analysis

Since early fifties researchers have been responding to the needs of management by conducting market segmentation studies for various product and service categories. Earlier studies about segmentation were largely based on demographic variables. Later, with the advent of computers more complex psychographic and behavioral constructs came to be used as bases for segmenting the markets, especially for the consumer goods. Marketers have successfully used the 'benefits sought' by the consumers from a product (or service) as basis for segmenting the toothpaste and insurance products markets. Aaker (2001) opined that benefits sought by the consumers from a product or service are the most useful segmentation variables of all, because the selection of benefits can determine the total business strategy.

In order to segment credit cardholders on the basis of benefits sought from the various service quality attributes associated with the credit card and its' usage, cluster analysis was applied. A profile of credit cardholders was developed on the basis of their perceptions towards service quality attributes. It looked at various benefits or a combination of benefits that a credit cardholder seeks from a card to segment them into distinct groups. The service quality attributes were treated as variables for analysis.

For the purpose of this study, an initial clustering solution was obtained using a hierarchical procedure. The number of clusters and cluster centroids that were obtained were further used as inputs to the K-means clustering method. The hierarchical clustering procedure was employed till the choice of cluster solution narrowed down to a two cluster solution. Subsequently, a non-hierarchical procedure was employed using a pre-specification of a two cluster solution for the study.

An examination of final cluster centers (Table 28.5, Annexure VII) revealed two distinct clusters emerging from the statistical procedure. Cluster-I was found to be low on service quality attributes such as fees and interest structure of credit cards and schemes offered by the bank. Cluster-II seems to be high on various service quality attributes such as application form for the credit card; interactions with sales executive of the issuing bank; service manual; statements of accounts and payment procedure; and customer service offered by the card issuing bank.

Annexure-VII

Table 28.5: Quick Cluster

Initial Cluster Centers		
Variables	Cluster	
	1	2
Application form	2	5
Sales Executive	2	5
Service manual	1	5
Fee & interest rates	2	1
Benefits	4	4
Acceptance of transaction with card	2	5
Statements & Payments	4	5
Customer service	2	5
Schemes	1	5

Source: Fieldwork.

Final Cluster Centers

Variables	Cluster	
	1	2
Application form	3.58	4.3
Sales Executive	3.07	3.81
Service manual	3.49	4.17
Fee & interest rates	2.4	2.58
Benefits	3.2	3.59
Acceptance of transaction with card	3.11	3.92
Statements & Payments	4.09	4.49
Customer service	2.67	3.66
Schemes	1.89	3.73

Source: Fieldwork.

Cluster-I, therefore, represents the group of customers seeking mainly the monetary transactions benefit from the credit card, they are not much interested in add on services. This group could be labeled as task oriented or "no frills customers." Cluster-II on the other hand, gives more importance to various service features associated with the credit card and its' usage. They may be termed as more sophisticated or "evolved customers." The banks should study the needs and expectations of the two different groups and evolve service features targeted at them.

CONCLUSION

In the light of these findings, credit card issuing banks must ensure that they understand and serve their credit cardholders the best. Credit card is a relatively newer concept in India and all the more new for the residents of smaller towns and cities of the country. It is, therefore, imperative for the service providers to understand the needs of these customers and retain them for expanding the business faster.

The analysis indicates that services of most credit card issuing banks have been perceived as mediocre or dissatisfactory on various service quality parameters. The Indian credit card industry, therefore, needs to work on the basics to achieve certain minimum standards of service quality. The quality parameters and perceptions of credit cardholders towards these attributes play a vital role in defining the relationship that a credit cardholder would have with the service provider.

The renewal and non-renewal of credit card membership by a customer largely hinges on his perceptions of service quality. The service providers should also explore the benefits a credit cardholder seeks from the card and offer them the basic as well as add on features accordingly. The service providers must understand that unless nuances of customer behavior are well understood and taken care of, India would be far from a popular destination for the card issuing banks.

REFERENCES

Aaker David. (1995). *Strategic Market Management*, New York, John Wiley & Sons.

Bitner, M. J., & Hubbert, A. R. (1994). "Encounter Satisfaction versus Overall Satisfaction versus Quality: The Customer's Voice". In Rust, R.T., & Oliver, R.L. (Eds.). *Service Quality: New Directions in Theory and Practice*. Thousand Oaks, CA: Sage, 72-94.

Bloemer J & Hans, D. Kasper. (1995). "The Complex Relationship between Consumer Satisfaction and Brand Loyalty", *Journal of Economic Psychology*, 16, pp. 311-29.

Brady, M.K. (1997). "Reconceptualizing Perceived Service Quality Hierarchical Model", Unpublished Doctoral Dissertation, The Florida State University.

www.blonnet.com/catalyst/2004/09/23/stories:2004092300801008.htm

www.blonnet.com/catalyst/2004/12/28/stories:2004122802510300.htm

Carman, J. (1990). "Consumer Perception of Services Quality: An Assessment of SERVQUAL Dimensions", *Journal of Retailing*, 66, pp. 33-35.

Cronin Jr. J. J. & Taylor S.A. (1994). SERVPERF versus SERVQUAL: Reconciling Performance Based & Perceptions minus Expectations Measurement of Service Quality", *Journal of Marketing*, 56, pp 56-68.

Deepa Kumari (2005). "Tracking Satisfaction of Credit Cardholders and to study Correlation Between Customer Satisfaction and Renewal of Membership", Ph.D Thesis, G.H. Patel Institute of Business Management, Vallabh Vidyanagar, Anand, Gujarat

www.economictimes.indiatimes.com/articleshow/972396.cms

www.economictimes.indiatimes.com/articleshow/992628.cms

www.ibef.org/attachdisplayaspx?crt_id=84&rt_id=5481

Giese, Joan L. & Joseph. A. Cote. (2000). "Defining Consumer Satisfaction," *Academy of Marketing Science Review* 00(01). Available at http://www.amsreview.org/amsrev/theory/giese00-01htm

Feldman Jack M. and Lynch John G Jr. (1988). "Self-generated Validity Theory and Other Effects on Beliefs, Attitude, Intention and Behavior," *Journal of Applied Psychology*, 73, pp. 421-35.

www.faculty.washington.edu/agg/pdf/spangenberg&havld.JCP.1999.pdf

Grönroos, C. (1992). "Service Management: A Management Focus for Service Competition". In Lovelock, C.H. *Managing Service Marketing, Operations, and Human Resources* Eds. Englewood Cliffs, NJ, Prentice Hall, pp. 9-16.

Hair Joseph F., Ralph. E. Anderson, Ronald. L. Tatham and William. C. Black. (1995). *Multivariate Data Analysis*, New Jersey, Prentice Hall.

Kasper, Hans. (1988). "On Problem Perception, Dissatisfaction and Brand Loyalty", *Journal of Economic Psychology*, 9, pp. 387-97.

Labarbera, Priscillia A. & David Mazurusky. (1983). "A Longitudinal Assessment of Consumer Satisfaction/Dissatisfaction: The Dynamic Aspect of the Cognitive Process", *Journal of Marketing Research*, 20, pp. 393-404.

www.leoline.com/doi/pdf/10.1207/S15327663jcp1401&2_8

Malhotra Naresh. (2004). *Marketing Research: An Applied Orientation*, New Delhi, Pearson Education India.

Newman, Joseph W. & Richard A. Webel. (1973). "Multivariate Analysis of Brand Loyalty for Major Household Appliances", *Journal of Marketing Research*, 10, pp. 404-09.

Oliver, Richard L. (1997). "Effect of Expectation & Disconfirmation on Post-Exposure Product Evaluation: An Alternative Interpretation", *Journal of Applied Psychology* 62 (April), pp. 480-486.

Oliver, Richard L. (1980). "A Cognitive Model of the Antecedents and Consequences of Satisfaction Decisions", *Journal of Marketing Research*, 17, pp. 460-69.

Oliver Richard L. (1981). "Measurement and Evaluation of Satisfaction in Retail Settings", *Journal of Retailing*, 57, pp. 25-48.

Oliver Richard L. (1999). "Whence Consumer Loyalty", *Journal of Marketing*, 63, pp. 33-44.

Parsuraman, Zeithmal and Berry, (1985). "A Conceptual Model of Service Quality and Its' Implications for Future Research", *Journal of Marketing*, 49, pp. 44-50.

Parsuraman, Zeithmal, & Berry, (1988). "SERVQUAL: A Multiple Item Scale for Measuring Consumer Perception of Service Quality." *Journal of Retailing*, 64, pp. 12-37.

Rust, R.T., & Oliver, R.L. (1994). "Service Quality Insights and Managerial Implications from the Frontier" In Rust, R.T. & Oliver R.L. (Eds.) *Service Quality: New Direction in Theory & Practice*, Thousand Oaks, CA; Sage Publications.

Reeves, C.A. & Bedner, D.A, (1994). "Defining Quality: Alternative & Implications", *Academy of Managerial Review*, 19, pp. 419-45.

Spreng, Richard A. & Singh A.K. (1993), "An Empirical Assessment of the SERVQUAL Quality and Satisfaction in Enhancing Knowledge Development in Marketing." (Eds) David Cravens et al. Chicago, *American Marketing Association*, pp. 1-6.

Spreng, Richard A, Scott B. Mackenzie & Richard W. Olshavsky. (1996). "A Re-examination of the Determinants of Consumer Satisfaction", *Journal of Marketing*, 60 (July), pp. 15-32.

Teas R. Kenneth, (1993). "Expectations, Performance Evaluation and Consumers' Perception of Quality", *Journal of Marketing*, 57 (October), 18-34.

Teas, R. Kenneth, (1994). "Expectations as a Comparison Standard in Measuring Service Quality. An Assessment of a Reassessment", *Journal of Marketing*, 58 (January), pp. 132-39.

Tse, David K & Peter. C. Wilton. (1988). "Models of Consumer Satisfaction Formation: An Extension", *Journal of Marketing Research*, 25 (May), pp. 204-12.

"Vadodara to be Visa's Consumer Acceptance Model for Asia Pacific," *Times of India*, 21 June 2001, p. 8.

Service Operating Costs and Efficiency—A Case Study on UAE Banks

29

Srinivas Inguva

ABSTRACT

In today's rapidly moving business environment, agility and responsiveness have become critical factors in the race for survival and growth. Most businesses have some experience in eliminating waste and controlling cost, but there is one area of significant cost that remains a black hole for many organizations to reduce their efficiency. In the present day's economically strapped corporate environment, managers must take much care to eliminate waste and control cost to improve efficiency and to stay themselves afloat. All organizations face pressures to offer cost efficient services in the face of accelerating demands. These pressures have led to many initiatives to improve the management by analyzing efficiency versus cost. Firms must actively manage their cost of services provided to the customers, if they want to prevent competition from other firms and to reduce future risk of reducing demand for their products/services. There are 21 national and 25 foreign banks functioning in the UAE with 344 and 87 branch offices respectively with 16408 numbers of workers. The performance of banks in the UAE has been showing steady growth and despite the size of the market the UAE banking sector is likely to become a top player in the region. All the UAE national banks are positively competing with the international banks in terms of providing services, efficiency in terms of profitability. The purpose of the present paper is to examine some of the available basic service costs of the National Banks of the United Arab Emirates (UAE) and to observe the service cost variations in the national banks and efficiency in terms of profitability. The data for the period 2004/05 have been drawn from the popular web sites related to national banks are considered for the purpose of the study. Data drawn from the secondary sources has been analyzed and interpreted, wherever required. The study is limited to the service costs and efficiency in terms of profitability of national banks of United Arab Emirates only.

RELEVANCE

It's quite obvious that every organization starts expanding their line of business activities in different products/services to grab the new customers. In this process, they start ever new products/ services different product lines to reach nearer to the hearts of the customers and bound to face new operating costs to maintain the operational efficiency and profitability. Although, all the organizations with similar nature of activity offer almost the same type of products/services, but each organizations product/ service costs vary considerably due to that organizations policies and objectives. In this context, a bank with a particularly different operating environment, but managed efficiently, will inevitably face higher costs and *vis-à-vis*. The main objective of the current paper is to observe and analyze the differences and effects of operating costs of various services offered by national banks of the United Arab Emirates and their impact on the efficiency in terms of profitability of the concerned bank. The paper also focuses the variations in the offered services and service operating cost differences among the national banks. It explains the impact of increase in the number of offered services in the national banks in their operating costs and the over all profitability of the bank during 2004/05. This will bring together result from increase in the bank services shell increase in not only the operating costs but also the profitability. A huge number of studies have been conducted in this regard and explained the increase in the services of the bank and their implications on operating costs and overall efficiency and profitability. Due to time and space constraint among many notable studies only a few highly relevant studies are mentioned below.

REVIEW OF LITERATURE

The Efficiency Cost of Market Power in the Banking Industry by Allen N. Berger and Timothy H. Hannan's study focuses on a potentially greater loss from market power—a reduction in cost efficiency brought about by the lack of market discipline in concentrated markets. The study employed data from the commercial banking industry, which produces very homogeneous products in multiple markets with differing degrees of market concentration and find the estimated efficiency cost of concentration to be several times larger than the social loss from mis-pricing as traditionally measured by the welfare triangle.

J. Christina Wang, Merger-related cost savings in the production of bank services utilizes a new flow measure of the true output of bank services to analyze the impact of mergers on the cost and productivity of Bank Holding Companies (BHCs) over the period 1987-99. It shows that there are conceptual problems in the output measures used in previous studies, which may be the reason for their paradoxical findings: Bank mergers are estimated to lead to significant increases in profit, without cost savings or increases in market power. This paper also points out the problematic understanding of diversification in previous studies. To remedy these problems, this paper uses a new measure that accounts coherently for risk in measuring bank service output and recognizes that the funds banks borrow and lend are a special intermediate input. Once one accounts for the better diversification resulting naturally from mergers, the commonly used, book-value-based output measure shows little improvement in cost productivity. In contrast, the new flow measure of bank output shows more improvement, although it is still insignificant-partly because the sample size is relatively small. The gap widens further when one corrects for possible bias in the new output estimate. Thus, the new measure of bank output has the potential to resolve the paradox found in the existing literature, by showing that mergers do lead to cost savings.

A study by Milind Sathye, Adoption of Internet banking by Australian consumers: an empirical investigation, quantifies the factors affecting the adoption of Internet banking by Australian consumers. The sample for this survey was drawn from individual residents and business firms in Australia. It shows that security concerns and lack of awareness about Internet banking and its benefits stand out as being the obstacles to the adoption of Internet banking in Australia. It suggests some of the ways to address these impediments. It further suggests that delivery of financial services over the Internet should be a part of overall customer service and distribution strategy. These measures could help in rapid migration of customers to Internet banking, resulting in considerable savings in operating costs for banks.

BANKING SECTOR IN UAE

In the UAE, a well-structured network of local banks and branches of foreign banks provide a full range of commercial banking services. The UAE Central Bank is the primary regulatory authority. Federal law restricts foreign banks to no more than eight branches each and requires that every commercial bank must have a paid-up capital of at least Dh40 million. There are few investment or merchant banks at present. Under new rules issued in 1996 permission for establishment of representative offices of foreign banks will be granted by the UAE Central Bank provided that the capital of the parent bank is not less than AED 183.7 million (US $ 50 million) and such bank has been in operation in its home country for at least ten years[1]. There are currently 21 national banks and 28 foreign banks carrying out various banking activities in the U.A.E., serving a population of approximately two million people. A well-structured network of local banks and branches of foreign banks provide a full range of commercial banking services in the U.A.E.[2] In the present day competitive world all the national banks are offering different products and services to attract more customers and to suit the needs of customers and their satisfactions. Every bank is trying to capture the customers by applying different marketing techniques to acquire more portion of the total market share in the banking sector. The banking sector in UAE with different categories is presented in the following table:

Banking Sector in UAE

Central bank	1
National banks	21
Foreign banks	28
Specialized banks	2
Investment banks	2
Representative offices	48

The Study

When the time went on it became difficult to engage in trade and other activities with out making use of commercial banks. Banks operating in the UAE had agreed to Charter of EBA with full abidance by and compliance with the provisions thereof which ascertain and denote the internationally recognized banking standard principles in general and those in consistence with local circumstances in particular. There are 21 national banks and 28 foreign banks are functioning in the UAE with 344 and 87 branch offices respectively with 16408 numbers of workers. Although, when compared to foreign banks the national operating banks are low, the number of national bank branches number is high.

According to the Central Bank the list of services offered by the national banks in the UAE are presented at Appendix Table 29.2 respectively. As per the information provided in the table it is clear that, the national bank's services are listed as customer loan services, customer current accounts, services of collection of checks credit card services, ATM card services and bank transfer and daft services. Although all the national banks are providing the same services listed in the appendix table, there is a cost variation in the services provided by the individual banks. This makes the subject-matter of the present study that variation in the service costs of the individual national banks in the UAE and its effect on the efficiency in terms of the profitability of the national banks.

Objective of the Study

The specific objective of the study is to notice the impact of service cost variations on the efficiency in terms of profitability of the national banks functioning in UAE.

Hypothesis

Since all the national banks are functioning in the same operating environment, there is no variation in the cost of services provided and the service cost variation has no impact on efficiency in terms of profitability.

DataBase

The information for the study has been procured from the published annual reports of the Central Bank and the 21 national banks functioning in the UAE during 2004/05. All the National banks carrying various banking activities in the UAE and their service operating costs are considered for the purpose of the study.

Limitations of the Study

The present study is limited to service operating costs of national banks functioning in UAE according to the listed services provided by the central bank of UAE. The study is an analysis of service operating cost of top five profitable and least five profitable national banks of UAE and its impact on the efficiency in terms of profitability only. This study would not reflect any financial implications and investment decisions in the banking sector or any other similar sector.

National banks ranked with the amount of profit before tax during 2004-05 is presented in the Appendix Table 29.1. From the table it is evident that among all the national banks in the UAE, the high profitable bank is National Bank of Abu Dhabi (1163798) followed by Emirates Bank International (1017057), The National Bank of Dubai (927775), Mashreqbank (829454), and Abu Dhabi Commercial Bank (796713). In the order of ranking according to the profitability, the least profitable bank is Dubai bank (4069) followed by Emirates Islamic Bank (16596), National Bank of Sharjah (71316), Commercial International Bank (71735) and Arab Bank for Investment and Foreign Trade (74631). Only top eight national banks are falling above the average profitability (349,801) and the remaining banks (13) are below the average of the total profit. Here the point is that, what is the impact of cost of products/services offered by the national banks? Is high cost of products/services offered by the national banks causing the reduced profitability? The service costs of each product/service offered by the national banks is presented in Appendix Table 29.2.

It is very clear from the Table 29.2 that all the banks provided in the list are offering common and similar type of banking products/services with cost variations from one another. For the purpose of the study analysis, top five high profitable banks and last five low profitable banks are compared with their each product/service cost variations. It is very evident from the available information shown on the table that, in all the top five profitable banks the interest on loans is high except one top bank, and similarly, in the last low profitable banks the interest rate on loans is low except one bank. Although, all the top and least profitable banks are taking management fee for loans, among the top five profitable and among the least profitable banks, only one bank is not taking any management charges for loans.

It's quite general that banks profitability is based on the operating efficiency of the bank and the number of dealing and financial transactions with their customers. Generally, customers start their accounts with the banks where their funds are safe with the minimum required initial balance to open an account. In this regard, the study has observed that the minimum required balances for maintaining an account with the top five profitable banks and least profitable banks. All the top five and least five profitable banks are not charging any amount for maintaining savings bank account. Although, all the banks are charging a minimum of 500 to 5000 AED for all the varieties of customer accounts, among the least profitable banks, two banks are charging low amount for current account maintenance.

A revenue item of the commercial banks is charging fee for collecting customer's cheques. Different banks charge different amount for their services rendered. The present study has observed the differences between the top five profitable and least five profitable national banks in terms of their cheques collection fees. It can be observed from the Table 29.2 that all the top and least profitable banks are not charging any amount as cheques collection fee in case they are drawn on the local banks. Among the top five profitable banks and least profitable bank only one bank is not charging any amount even for the cheques collection outside the city. Among the five least profitable banks the cheques collection fee is varying from 10 to 25 where as the same collection fee for the top five profitable banks is varying from 10 to 50 (excluding postal charges). Among the top five most profitable banks emirates bank International and among the least five profitable banks Dubai bank are not charging any amount as collection fee for the cheques even out side the city limits. Among all the banks, The National Banks of Dubai is not charging any amount even for clearing foreign cheques except the postal charges. The fee for collecting foreign cheques is slightly high in the case of least profitable banks when compared to highly profitable top five banks. Keeping low operating cost and low transaction cost merged with fast service may be one of the reasons for attracting more customers in the top five profitable banks.

Initially, all the banks in the UAE are offering credit cards at free of cost but the credit card annual maintenance fee is different from bank to bank. Among all the banks taken for the study, only one bank is not charging anything for their credit card or ATM card services. For initial ATM cards no bank is charging any thing but for ATM card replacement they are charging only 50 AED per transaction and all together it is varying from 25 to 50 AED only. According to the data provided in the table the banks transfer fee is of three categories. The transfer fee is varying from 25 to 100 among the banks with in the Arab states and South Asian countries; for European countries or Far East countries the transfer fee is ranging from 25 to 150; for the USA or Canada it is 10 to 150 AED in all the top five high profitable and low profitable banks.

SUMMARY

In the UAE, a well-structured network of local banks and branches of foreign banks provide a full range of commercial banking services. All organizations face pressures to offer cost efficient services in the face of accelerating demands. All the

UAE national banks are positively competing with the international banks in terms of providing services, efficient functioning and profitability. The study focuses the light on the variations in the offered services and service operating cost differences among the national banks and its impact on the efficiency in terms of profitability. The national bank's services are listed as customer loan services, customer current accounts, services of collection of checks, credit card services, Among all the national banks in the UAE, the high profitable bank is (amount in AED) National Bank of Abu Dhabi (1163798) followed by Emirates Bank International (1017057), The National Bank of Dubai (927775), Mashreqbank (829454), and Abu Dhabi Commercial Bank (796713). In the order of ranking according to the profitability, the least profitable bank is Dubai Bank (4069) followed by Emirates Islamic Bank (16596), National Bank of Sharjah (71316), and Commercial International Bank (71735) and Arab Bank for Investment and Foreign Trade (74631). All the top five and least five profitable banks are not charging any amount for maintaining savings bank account. Although, all the top and least profitable banks are taking management fee for loans, among the top five profitable and among the least profitable banks, only one bank is not taking any management charges for loans. Among the top five most profitable banks Emirates Bank International and among the least five profitable banks Dubai Bank are not charging any amount as collection fee for the cheques even out side the city limits. The fee for collecting foreign cheques is slightly high in the case of least profitable banks when compared to highly profitable top five banks. Keeping low operating cost and low transaction cost merged with fast service may be one of the reasons for attracting more customers in the top five profitable banks. All the banks in the UAE are offering credit cards at free of cost but the credit card annual maintenance fee is different from bank to bank. For initial ATM cards supply to the customers no bank is charging anything, but for ATM card replacement they are charging only 50 AED per transaction and all together it is varying from AED 25 to 50. The transfer fee is varying from 25 to 100 among the banks if the transfer is within the Arab states and South Asian countries. As the study found that there are no high variations in the cost of services provided by the national banks and the cost of services provided by the individual banks, the set hypothesis of the cost of services have no influence on the efficiency in terms of profitability of the individual bank is accepted. The service operating fee collected by the banks may be one of the reasons for the operating efficiency and profitability of the banks but, it is not the only reason for the high/low profitability of the banks.

REFERENCES

www.uaeinteract.com

www.emirates-banking.com

Allen N. Berger and Timothy H. Hannan. "The Efficiency Cost of Market Power in the Banking Industry", *The Review of Economics and Stasstics*, August 1998, Vol. 80, No. 3, pages 454-65, Posted Online March 13, 2006.

Allen Berger, John Leusner and John Mingo. Paper provided by Wharton School Center for Financial Institutions, University of Pennsylvania in its series Center for Financial Institutions Working Papers with number 94-27

Ann P. Bartel. "Human Resource Management and Performance in the Service Sector: The Case of Bank Branches," National Bureau of Economic Research, Inc in its series NBER Working Papers with number 7467.

www.nbad.com

www.emiratesbank.com

www.nbd.com

www.mashreqbank.com

www.adcb.com

www.alislami.co.ae

www.unb.com

www.dfm.co.ae/dfm/Statments/Profiles/CBD_Profile.htm

www.firstgulfbank.ae

www.invest-bank.com

www.bankofsharjah.com

www.rakbank.ae

www.nbf.co.ae

www.adib.co.ae

www.ameinfo.com

www.uab.ae

www.arbift.com
www.cibeg.com
www.emiratesislamicbank.ae
www.dubaibank.ae
www.cbuae.gov.ae
www.eba-ae.com

Appendix

Table 29.1: 2004/2005 National Banks Ranked with the Amount of Profit Before Tax

(Amount in AED)

1.	National Bank of Abu Dhabi	1,163,798
2.	Emirates Bank International P.J.S.C.	1,017,057
3.	The National Bank of Dubai P.J.S.C.	927,775
4.	Mashreqbank P.S.C.	829,454
5.	Abu Dhabi Commercial Bank	796,713
6.	Dubai Islamic Bank P.J.S.C..	461,033
7.	Union National Bank	452,909
8.	Commercial Bank of Dubai P.S.C.	351,111
9.	First Gulf Bank	244,940
10.	Invest Bank	155,625
11.	Bank of Sharjah	137,049
12.	Rak Bank (The National Bank of Ras-Al Khaimah P.S.C.)	129,228
13.	National Bank of Fujairah P.S.C.	125,483
14.	Abu Dhabi Islamic Bank	122,910
15.	National Bank of Umm-Al Qaiwain P.S.C.	104,017
16.	United Arab Bank P.J.S.C.	88,362
17.	Arab Bank for Investment & Foreign Trade	74,651
18.	Commercial International Bank P.S.C.	71,735
19.	National Bank of Sharjah	71,316
20.	Emarites Islamic Bank	16,596
21.	Dubai Bank	4,069
	Total	7,435,831

Source: courtesy—www.eba-ae.com

Contributors

N.D. Mathur, Professor & Dean, College of Management, Shri Mata Vaishno Devi University, Jammu & Kashmir, India.

M.A. Hashmi, Professor of International Business & Finance, Minnesota State University, Minnesota, USA.

Prasanta Kumar Padhy, Professor in Management, Berhampur University, India.

P. Balaram Babu, Directorate of Health and Family Welfare, Govt. of Orissa.

Satyabrat Dash, Faculty Member, (NIST), Berhampur, Orissa.

R. Dhanuskodi, Lecturer, Dept of Accounting, Jimma University, Ethiopia.

Kambiz Heidarzadeh Hanzaee, Head of Business Management Department, I.A.U. (Science and Research Branch) University, Tehran, Iran. Email: kambizheidarzadeh@yahoo.com; heidarzadeh@sr.iau.ac.ir

Umara Noreen and Pareesa Raza Khan, Islamabad, Pakistan. E-mail: deeya.khan@gmail.com, umaranoreen@yahoo.com

Anil Mehta, Associate Professor, Department of Business Administration, University of Rajasthan, Jaipur-302006 (India).

Shalini Srivastava, Research Scholar, Faculty of Commerce.

C.P. Mall, Reader, Faculty of Commerce, BHU, Varanasi, U.P.

Mohammed Nurul Alam, Assistant Professor, SQU, Muscat. E.mail: nurul@squ.edu.com, man5@rogers.com

I.A.O. Bakare, Department of Economics, Faculty of Social Sciences, Lagos State University, Ojo Campus, Lagos-Nigeria. E-mail: bakgiit@yahoo.com

S.K. Bose, Associate Professor, Department of Management, BIT, Mesra, Ranchi-834215, & Management Consultant, State Bank of India.

Abdul Quddus Mohammed, Salalah College of Technology Post Box: 608, Postal Code: 211, Salalah, Sultanate of Oman. Email: abdulquddus_md@yahoo.co.in, Phone:+968-92303143

Mohammed Naved Khan and Feza Tabassum Azmi, Faculty of Management Studies & Research, A.M.U., Aligarh, India.

Mahfoodh Al Sabbagh, Higher Technical College, Ministry of Man Power, Muscat, Sultanate of Oman.

R. Vaidyanathan, Professor of Finance & Control and UTI Chair Professor in Capital Market Studies, Indian Institute of Management, Bannerghatta Road, Bangalore, India. E-mail: vaidya@iimb.ernet.in

Deepak Godbole, Chief Manager, General Insurance Corporation of India, Mumbai, India.

S.C. Bansal, Associate Professor, Indian Institute of Management, Lucknow (India). E-mail: bansal@iiml.ac.in

Alka Harneja, Senior Lecturer, Lakshmi Bai College, University of Delhi, Delhi (India).

Damodharan V.S. ACCA and Jagadish Prasad, Business Studies Department, Higher College of Technology, Muscat, Sultanate of Oman.

Drahomira Dubska, Czech Statistical Office, Prague, Czech Republic Na padesatem 81, PSC 100 82, Prague 10. E-mail: drahomira.dubska@czso.cz

Karunesh Saxena, Professor & Director, Pacific Institute of Management, Udaipur.

Rajendra Prasad Sharma, Sr. faculty, AES PG Institute of Business Management, Ahmedabad.

Pramod Pathak, Head, Department of Management Studies, Indian School of Mines, Dhanbad (India). E mail: pramod_ism @rediffmail.com

S.C. Bansal, Associate Professor, Indian Institute of Management, Lucknow (India). E-mail: bansal@iiml.ac.in

Y.P. Singh and Sneh Lohia, Delhi School of Economics, University of Delhi, (India). E-mail: ypsing@rediffmail.com, snehlohia@gmail.com

Shurveer S. Bhanawat, Senior Lecturer, Department of Accountancy & Business Statistics, B.N.P.G. College, Udaipur (Rajasthan), India.

M. Selvam, Department of Business Administration, Modern College of Business and Science, E-mail: seldrvam2004@yahoo.co.in

Rengasamy Elango and Mohammed Ibrahim Hussein, Department of Business and Accounting, Majan College(University College). E-mail: drelan63@yahoo.com, sumaybilal@yahoo.com

Kaveri Bansal, Adjunct Faculty, Janki Devi Memorial College, University of Delhi, Delhi. E-mail: kav4@indiatimes.com

Y. Sree Rama Murthy, Assistant Professor, College of Commerce & Economics, Sultan Qaboos University, E-mail: murthy@squ.edu.om

Madan Lal Bhasin, Department of Accounting, Mazoon College, Muscat, Sultanate of Oman. E-mail: madan.bhasin@rediffmail.com

Lata Sharma, Senior Lecturer, Lakshmibai College, University of Delhi, (India).

J.S. Paniwar, Professor & Head MBA Programme, Dean Faculty of Management Studies, Sardar Patel University, Vallabh Vidyanagar-388 120 India, E-mail jspanwar@yahoo.com

Deepa Kumari, Fellow, Institute of Integrated Learning in Management, 3, Lodhi Institutional Area, Lodhi Road, New Delhi-110001 India. E-mail: deepa.kumari@iilm.edu

Srinivas Inguva, Ph.D., Department of Accounting, Faculty of Business Administration, Ajman University of Science and Technology Network, P.O. Box 346, Ajman, United Arab Emirates. E-mail:drsrinivasi@yahoo.com & drsrinivasi@hotmail.com